SAVING THE AMERICAS

SAVING THE AMERICAS

ANDRÉS OPPENHEIMER

RANDOM HOUSE MONDADORI

Published in Mexico by
Random House Mondadori, S. A, de C. V.
Av. Homero No. 544, Col. Chapultepec Morales,
Miguel Hidalgo, C. P. 11570, México, D. F.
www.randomhousemondadori.com.mx

ISBN: 970-030-739-165-0

Printed in Mexico
Distributed by Random House, Inc.

FIRST EDITION

Index

Prologue for the North American Edition

THIS BOOK BEGAN AS A MESSAGE TO LATIN AMERICANS ABOUT THE DECLINE of their region into global irrelevance. But it soon became clear to me that what I was learning was equally important to people in the United States. Though less apparent to most Americans — and less costly — than its blunders elsewhere in the world, the Bush Administration was making major mistakes in Latin America, among other things by declaring the region a major U.S. priority while ignoring it almost entirely, and reflexively pushing free trade as if that alone would ensure hemispheric prosperity.

When it comes to everyday issues that affect most Americans — whether immigration, trade, the environment or, increasingly, energy — no region in the world has a bigger impact on the United States than Latin America. Of the 12 million undocumented workers living in the United States, nearly four out of five are Latin American.[i] Unless Latin American countries can find work for their new generations, mass emigration to the north will continue, no matter how many fences U.S. politicians build across the border. As for trade, the United States exports $225 billion worth of goods annually to Latin America, vastly more than the $55 billion shipped to China or the $10 billion sold to India[ii]. Turmoil in Latin America could harm U.S. consumers in far worse ways than most Americans recognize. The United States imports more crude oil from Mexico than from Saudi Arabia[iii]. A disruption in Mexican supplies could create havoc in the United States, just as an increased supply of oil — and, increasingly, sugarcane-based ethanol — from a stable Latin America could significantly ease U.S. dependence on the Mideast.

And yet, signs that the region is moving in directions favorable to those very substantial U.S. concerns are hard to find. Two recent long-range forecasts from dramatically different sources — the first a CIA think tank, the second a German Socialist who is one of the European Parliament's top Latin America experts — made the few Latin Americans who read them shudder. Both 2005 studies flatly rejected the general view among Western Hemispheric governments that the region was enjoying an unprecedented economic recovery and was heading toward an even more prosperous future. The first was conducted by the National Intelligence Council (NIC), which provides strategic, "over the horizon" research for the U.S. Central Intelligence Agency. The second was written at roughly the same time by German lawmaker Rolf Linkohr in his capacity as chair of the European Parliament's Commission on South American Affairs. Both studies analyzed the future of the region over the next 20 years, and both reached the same conclusion: that in a global context Latin America was irrelevant, and that — if it continued on its current path — it would become even more so.

The Linkohr Report opened by asserting: "Latin America's influence on world affairs is decreasing, not increasing. Its share of world trade is small, and growth in the region cannot be compared to that of Asia."[iv] Having traveled to nearly every country in the region over the past 25 years, Linkohr observed, "It still comes as a surprise that despite all the changes that have occurred [in the world], changes that Latin America too has experienced, little has changed in this rather depressing picture of the continent." Worse yet, he continued, "Although there is relative calm in Latin America at present, the situation could rapidly deteriorate in the future."[v]

The report of the NIC, which is based at CIA headquarters in Langley, Virginia, was a 119-page document containing forecasts from major futurologists from U.S. universities, business, and government about what the world will look like in 2020. And it said practically the same thing Linkohr did, albeit by implication. The NIC's opening paragraph, titled "The Global Landscape in 2020," offered a political-economic map of the world at the end of the second decade of the 21st century in which Latin America was barely mentioned.[vi]

According to the NIC's futurologists, much else will be different in 2020. The United States will continue to be the premier global power, but will not wield the power it does today. Economic globalization will continue, the world economy will expand significantly, and average per capita income worldwide will be 50 percent greater than currently, but the world will be less "Americanized" and more "Asianized." China is likely to become the number two world power by 2020, closely followed by India and Europe, perhaps in that order. Multinational corporations, in their drive to dominate the enormous virgin territories of China and India — whose combined population comprises nearly half of humanity — will have to change their business culture, producing goods aimed at a constantly growing Asian middle class. "By 2020, globalization could be equated in the popular mind with a rising Asia, replacing its current association with Americanization," the study said.[vii] In other words, we will live in a world that is somewhat less Westernized, and somewhat more Orientalized.

The NIC also predicted that global politics will be based less on ideology and more on religious and ethnic affiliations. Islam will continue to expand around the world, perhaps with factions drawn from different countries and cultures combining to create a centralized multinational entity. A new caliphate could emerge, which would span much of Africa, the Middle East, and Central Asia. In Asia, the report speculates, we may see the emergence of a "Chinese model of democracy," which would allow free elections of local officials and a nationwide consultative committee while a single party retains control of the central government.

Where will Latin America fit into this new global context? The NIC devoted only a brief summary to the region nearly at the end of its report. Although the report suggested Brazil would grow in importance in the world arena and saw Chile as a possible oasis of progress, its overall outlook for the region was gloomy. The NIC saw a continent divided between northern countries — Mexico and Central America, economically bound to the United States — and southern ones tied to Asia and Europe. Far from developing successful trade blocs to ensure economic and social progress, the region would be plagued by "internal conflicts," hamstrung by "government ineffectiveness," threatened by criminality, and subject to "an increasing risk of the rise of charismatic, self-styled populist leaders, historically common in the region, who would exploit the popular preoccupation with the gap between rich and poor" to consolidate totalitarian regimes.[viii] Venezuela's radical populist President Hugo Chávez was only a harbinger of things to come, the NIC analysts seemed to be saying.

But the global NIC report barely scratched the surface of what is happening in Latin America. A more focused study by an NIC regional sub-commission, titled "Latin America in 2020," summarized the conclusions of various Latin American and U.S. academics, business executives, and politicians who participated in a meeting to contribute to the global study. The regional conference was held in Santiago, Chile, with the participation of former officials and politicians from various countries, including Chilean-born Arturo Valenzuela, the former senior director of inter-American affairs at the White House during the Clinton administration; Argentina's Rosendo Fraga, head of the Center of Studies for the New Majority; Mexico's Beatriz Paredes, then senator from the Institutional Revolutionary Party and former ambassador to Cuba; former Peruvian president Valentín Paniagua; and former Colombian defense minister Rafael Pardo. The final conference report predicted: "Few countries [in the region] will be able to take advantage of opportunities for development, and Latin America as a region will see the gap separating it from the most advanced nations of the planet grow wider."[ix] It continued: "Economic forecasts indicate that Latin America's share in the world's GDP is poised to decrease as a result of *low growth rates* (as in recent years) and of the *drag* they will cause in productivity and installed capacity."[x] In other words, the region was way behind, and regaining lost ground was going to be difficult.

Moreover, in today's knowledge economy, where services are far more prized than raw materials, "almost none of the Latin American countries will be able to invest their scarce resources in developing large research and development projects," the NIC regional report said. "The gap between the technological capacities of the region and those of advanced countries is set to widen. No broad-based Latin American project of relevant technological adaptations — allowing for creation of an export capacity in line with that of Asian countries, for example — will be developed in the next 15 years," the study said, although it allowed that there might be exceptions, such as Intel's investment in Costa Rica and Brazil's state defense-industry programs.

When I read both studies a few weeks apart, I couldn't help being surprised. Both the NIC study and the Linkohr Report had reached conclusions diametrically opposed to those offered almost daily by Latin American leaders and by institutions such as the United Nations Economic Commission for Latin America and the Caribbean (ECLAC). ECLAC had said recently that for the first time in many years there was a "positive scenario" in the region. After several years of stagnation Latin American countries were once again growing at an annual rate of 4 percent; investments in the region had climbed for the first time in six years and now stood at $56.4 billion dollars.[xi] In South America, presidents had signed a 2004 agreement for creation of a "South American Community," or the "United States of South America," which some leaders claimed would be the first step towards a golden future for the region. Eduardo Duhalde, the former president of Argentina and one of the architects of the South American Community, predicted that the continent's countries would achieve "the dream of those who liberated the Americas: that South America be united," ushering in a peaceful and prosperous future. Mexico's President Vicente Fox was telling his country, "Every day, we are closer to the country we all want: a place where every Mexican man and woman will have a chance for a better life, a Mexico in which we are all ready to do our best for the good of the nation."[xii]

Whose picture was accurate? The NIC and Linkohr Reports, with their dark forebodings? Or the UN's ECLAC and Latin America's heads of state, with their boundless optimism? There were reasons to approach both sides with skepticism. Might not the NIC and Linkohr Reports be biased by the infatuation of wealthy countries with the Asian boom, the Irish miracle, and the reawakening of Central Europe? And on the other side, wasn't there a clear propaganda purpose behind the buoyancy of Latin American leaders, from the messianic Venezuelan president to his more pragmatic counterparts like Fox? Whom should we believe? Who was presenting a realistic picture — who was telling tall tales?

During my research for this book, I interviewed key figures across the political spectrum who wielded major influence over the future of Latin America, including the presidents of Mexico, Argentina, Peru, Colombia, and Chile; U.S. Defense Secretary Donald Rumsfeld and Under-Secretary of State for Western Hemisphere Affairs Roger Noriega; former Bolivian congressman Evo Morales (who would soon become his country's president); former Brazilian President Fernando Henrique Cardoso; and former Spanish President Felipe González. Between 2002 and 2005 I traveled to China, Ireland, Poland, the Czech Republic, Mexico, Venezuela, Brazil, and Argentina to see first-hand what it was that was pushing some nations ahead and holding others back. To expand the work for this North American edition, I went to India in 2007.

The more I traveled and the more people I interviewed, the more convinced I grew that the book needed to awaken Latin Americans to an urgent need: that they learn what other countries have done to achieve 21st-century political and economic success.

I hope to take advantage of my reach among Latin Americans — more than 50 newspapers and magazines publish my column, and more than a dozen television networks in as many countries broadcast my Spanish-language political talk show — to challenge what has become conventional wisdom, that the region's current commodity-driven development strategy is inaugurating a new era of prosperity. This book attempts to put the region's growth in a world context, and shows that its social and economic stagnation is neither normal nor inescapable. The book was published in Spanish in 2005 under the title *Cuentos Chinos* (Tall Tales), a reference to the wrong-headed prescriptions for prosperity offered by leaders in Latin America and Washington. It touched off a fiery debate in the region, and topped best-seller lists in several countries, selling more than 140,000 copies.

Since the book's first edition appeared in Spanish, the re-emergence of radical populism in Latin America continues to accelerate. Awash in oil money, Venezuela's narcissist-Leninist leader Chávez, who a few years ago derided speculation that he would become a radical leftist, was nationalizing electricity and telecommunications companies, denouncing the United States in international forums, and clamping down on his country's independent press. By 2007 Chávez was ending his speeches with the slogan "Socialism or Death," and giving a hero's welcome in Caracas to another disturber of the diplomatic peace, Iranian President Mahmoud Ahmadinejad. Populist leaders close to Chávez had won elections in Bolivia, Ecuador, and Nicaragua, and — with financial help from Venezuela and political advice from Cuba — were attempting to launch a new anti-American regional bloc. Bolivia's Evo Morales, who like Chávez had campaigned as a moderate leftist, was calling capitalism "the worst enemy of humanity."[xiii] U.S. media reports talked of a "Latin American shift to the left," and alarmed U.S. officials were warning about a new cycle of "revolutionary" governments, nationalizations, capital flight, economic slowdown, and greater poverty.

Still, far from seeing these developments as signs of an inexorable trend toward backwardness, or confirmation of the somber long-term predictions of the NIC and Linkohr studies, what I saw in my travels led me to conclude that those dreary projections were far more valid as descriptions of the present than as forecasts of the future. One of the realities that surprised me most was just how rapidly some nations have made the switch from poverty and despair to wealth and economic dynamism. In the pages that follow, I will share with you the things I saw that led me to toward a kind of optimism about the region quite different from the perspective of the NIC and Linkohr forecasts.

A final caution: Some Americans will find that certain points I make — such as the need for Latin America to draw more foreign investment and invest more in education, science, and technology — are self-evident. But those readers should remember that set against the anti-market, anti-globalization dogma that grips much of the region, those ideas are not only politically incorrect, but almost subversive. By the same token, some Latin American readers who read the earlier Spanish-language version of this book found that arguments I made about the need for greater U.S. engagement are obvious, and could have been omitted. But they should consider that these points are far from evident to most Americans — and to most Washington policymakers. Seldom has there been such a disconnect between the northern and southern parts of the Western Hemisphere. If this book can help to debunk stereotypes and persuade skeptics to agree that closer U.S.-Latin American ties — better still, a Community of the Americas — would be in the interests of all, it will have achieved its purpose.

Andrés Oppenheimer

NOTES

[i] Estimate from the Pew Hispanic Center's report "The Size and Characteristics of the Unauthorized Migrant Population Survey," by Jeffrey S. Passel, 2006

[ii] U.S. Bureau of Economic Analysis News, U.S. Census Bureau, Feb. 13, 2007, press release on U.S. trade figures for 2006.

[iii] In 2006, the United States imported 562,211,000 barrels of crude oil from Mexico, and 513,832,000 from Saudi Arabia, according to the U.S. Bureau of Economic Analysis, U.S. Census Bureau, Feb. 13, 2007 press release.

[iv] "Some personal conclusions and recommendations based on my experience in Latin America," Rolf Linkohr, European Parliament Document, October 10, 2004, p. 1, item 1.

[v] Idem.

[vi] *Mapping the Global Future*, Graph "The 2020 Global Landscape," National Intelligence Council, p. 8.

[vii] Idem.

[viii] Idem.

[ix] *Latin America 2020: Discussing Long-term scenarios*, Final report, National Intelligence Council Global Trends 2020 Project, p. 2.

[x] Idem.

[xi] *Boletín de la CEPAL*, March 15, 2005.

[xii] 2005 New Year's Message by President Vicente Fox, Presidency of the Republic, Mexico.

[xiii] The Associated Press, La Paz, Bolivia, May 22, 2007.

CHAPTER 1

The Asian Challenge

Tall tale: "This can be the century of the Americas."
(George W. Bush, Speech in Miami,
Florida, August 25, 2000)

—

BEIJING - BUENOS AIRES - CARACAS - MEXICO CITY - MIAMI - WASHINGTON, D.C. – You need to see China to understand just how far Latin America has fallen behind in the worldwide race for exports, investment, and economic progress. Before arriving in Beijing, I had read a great deal about the spectacular economic growth of the People's Republic and other Asian countries, including Taiwan, Singapore, and South Korea. I was well aware of China's spectacular success in lifting hundreds of millions of people out of poverty since it launched its economic opening more than two decades before. But it wasn't until I actually saw Beijing that I began to grasp how rapidly China and its Asian neighbors are outrunning Latin America.

From the moment I landed on the Chinese capital, I was stunned by the colossal scale of virtually everything. We were still on the plane when I realized, looking through my window, that we were rolling to Gate 305 of the Beijing airport. It was an eye opener even for a frequent flier like myself, accustomed to arriving at Gate B-7 of Miami International Airport, which has 107 gates, or at Gate 28 of the Mexico City airport, with a mere 42. Upon leaving the plane with the rest of the passengers, I found myself in a terminal of an immensity I had never before seen: it looked like a covered football stadium, only five times bigger. With no fewer than 38 million people passing through the Beijing airport every year, it's already in need of expansion, as I later learned. From that point on, the capitalist fever that is raging in China disguised by the regime as an "economic opening" within socialism brought one surprise after another.

As a longtime Latin America correspondent for the *Miami Herald*, I was constantly comparing what I was seeing in China with what I typically see in my travels through Latin America. On the flight to Beijing from Tokyo, I had read in the Asian edition of the *Wall Street Journal* that Venezuela had closed down all 80 of its McDonald's restaurants for three days in connection with an investigation into tax evasion. Venezuela's self-proclaimed revolutionary government said it would no longer tolerate transgressions from multinational companies against its national sovereignty. Officials ordered the franchises closed even before the matter had gone to the courts, and spoke of the action as a proud achievement of the "Bolivarian revolution."

The news itself was no surprise: I'd been in Venezuela a few months earlier and had listened to incendiary speeches by president Hugo Chávez denouncing capitalism and "U.S. imperialism" with his unique blend of narcissism and Lenin. But what struck me was what I read that same day in my hotel room in Beijing. Leafing through recent issues of *China Daily*, the official English-language newspaper of the Chinese Communist Party the *Miami Herald's* Beijing correspondent had left for me, I found a headline that might have been deliberately printed to alert me to the dramatic differences between China and Venezuela. "McDonald's expands in China," the *China Daily* jubilantly announced. The article reported that McDonald's entire board would soon arrive in China, where the directors would be received by top government and Communist Party officials, and where the company would announce plans to expand from its current 600 restaurants in China to more than 1,000 over the next year. "China is our number one growth opportunity in the world," Larry Light, chief of marketing at McDonald's, told *China Daily*.[i] How ironic, I thought to myself: while Communist China rolls out the red carpet to foreign investors, capitalist Venezuela chases them away.

Certainly, the contrast between the words of the Chinese Communists and those of their old-guard ideological cousins in

Latin America is huge. And the differences are not just rhetorical. While the Chinese go out of their way to attract investment, a significant number of top Latin American politicians, academics, and protectionist business leaders delight in scaring investors off. In China, pragmatism and a determination to capture investment to ensure long-term growth have become the new state religion. In Latin America, Chávez tours the region and draws standing ovations for his denunciations of "savage capitalism" and his seizures of key industries. While China privatizes, Venezuela and some of its neighbors take delight in nationalizing. Not surprisingly, Latin America draws an ever-shrinking share of the world's foreign investments. While Latin America and the Caribbean received an average of 51 percent of all foreign investments from the developing world in the 1970s, the region's share had dropped to 27 percent in 2006, according to the United Nations Economic Commission for Latin America and the Caribbean (ECLAC). Meantime, Asia is roaring ahead: its share of foreign investments in the developing world has soared from an annual average of 27 percent in the 1970s to 51 percent in 2006.[ii]

Chinese leaders may continue to use their traditional Marxist-Leninist rhetoric to justify their one-party dictatorship, but in practice they are carrying out what may be the biggest and most ambitious capitalist revolution in human history. Following the 16th Communist Party Congress in 2002, which had agreed to "make economic development the central task of the entire party" and "discard notions that obstruct economic growth," pragmatism has replaced Marxism as China's supreme national value. And, while most of us are appalled by the Chinese dictatorship's human rights abuses and would not like to see China's political model exported to Latin America, it was hard not to be intrigued by China's success in growing at 10 percent a year, and reducing poverty faster than any Latin American country. As we shall see in the next chapter, China's economic progress apparent in the giant construction cranes that dominate the Beijing skyline, the latest models of Mercedes and Audi cars on its streets, and the billboards for haute-couture boutiques such as Hugo Boss and Guy Laroche is enough to leave any newly arrived visitor speechless.

I soon learned that China was even more capitalistic than I thought. In one of my first interviews with officials in Beijing and Shanghai, Zhou Xi-an, deputy director of the National Development and Reform Commission — the powerful department in charge of planning the Chinese economy — told me that 60 percent of the Chinese economy was already in private hands. And, he added, the percentage was increasing daily. Zhou is a man in his early forties with a Ph.D. in economics, who didn't speak English even though he helped run one of the government agencies most closely tied to the West. We spoke at the commission's majestic headquarters on Beijing's Yuetan Street. Curious about how far China had come in its march toward capitalism, I arrived with U.S. newspaper clippings about the wave of privatization that was sweeping the country. Since I was used to Latin American countries where "privatization" is a bad word — in part because of some corrupt deals in the 1990s when state-run monopolies were turned over to government cronies and transformed into private fiefdoms — I suspected some of the coverage overstated China's privatization drive, or that at the very least Chinese officials would not acknowledge the extent of the effort. I was wrong.

"Is it true that you will privatize some 100,000 state-owned companies over the next five years?" I asked Dr. Zhou through my interpreter, with one of the articles on my lap. The official shook his head. "No, that figure is wrong!" he replied, almost angrily. But just as I thought he would start making a speech in defense of socialism, accusing foreign newspapers of exaggerating the privatization story, he added, "Many more! We'll be privatizing many more!" Dr. Zhou proceeded to explain matter-of-factly that the private sector is "the main engine of economic development" in China, and that for China to continue growing at its current rates business initiatives must be granted the greatest possible freedom. Coming from Latin America, I couldn't believe my ears. The world had turned upside down.

My conversations with officials, academics, and business executives in the Chinese capital were packed with similar surprises. In interviews with key Chinese scholars on Latin American affairs, many of them sounded like Republicans from the red-state American heartland, while flanked by red flags and professing full loyalty to the Communist Party. They told me that Latin America needed more capitalist reforms, greater economic openness, more free trade, and fewer pseudo-revolutionary speeches. One of them told me, as I will describe later in greater detail, that one of Latin America's main problems was its continued belief in "dependency theory," the neo-Marxist economic paradigm of the 1960s, according to which poverty in the region is largely the result of exploitation from the United States and Europe. The Chinese Communist Party had abandoned this theory decades ago, declaring instead that China was solely responsible for its own economic performance, the scholar explained. In much of Latin America, the prevailing ideology could be summed up in the words, "We are poor, it's their fault." Blaming others was not only wrong, but counterproductive. It distracted countries from trying to be more competitive, he said. This was the new mantra of the Chinese regime, which overshadowed all others: It's competitiveness, stupid.

Productive investment: The only way out

As I traveled in Europe and Asia gathering ideas about what Latin America should do to break its deepening cycle of inequality, frustration, crime, populism, capital flight, and poverty; I found that whatever their political tilts the countries that were raising living standards and reducing poverty — ranging from Ireland and the Czech Republic to China — had some things in common. For starters, all are investment magnets. This steady influx of capital helps them achieve long-term economic growth, increase employment, and avoid the boom and bust cycles that have plagued Latin America through much of its history. If Latin American countries managed to attract even a fraction of the foreign investments pouring into China's factories, or if they managed to entice their own business people to bring back home a portion of the more than $400 billion that — according to the U.S. investment bank Goldman Sachs — Latin Americans have deposited in offshore accounts; many countries of the region could leap almost instantly to the threshold of the developed world.[iii] If there is one thing that caught my attention in my travels through Latin America, Europe, and Asia, it's how rapidly nations can go from poverty and despair to hope and prosperity, regardless of their professed ideologies. Contrary to the cultural determinism so in vogue in America's academic circles, there are no geographic, cultural, or biological reasons preventing Latin America from transforming itself into an economic development success story almost overnight.

What did the relatively successful countries I visited have in common? On the surface, they are very different from one another. Their populations range from 10 million to more than a billion. Their political systems differ widely: China is a single-party communist dictatorship; Poland and the Czech Republic are former Soviet-bloc countries that have converted into democracies with market economies; Spain and Chile are former right-wing dictatorships that have prospered in recent decades as capitalist democracies governed by socialist parties. Culturally, they couldn't be more diverse: while China can boast of a legendary work ethic, Spain's tradition is of siestas, wine, and nightlife. And yet, despite these huge differences, all these countries share a proven ability to lure vast foreign investments, largely thanks to their capacity to maintain stable economic policies that do not shift with every election, and to their unwavering commitment to educating their populations.

Forget ideologies. In the new global arena there are two kinds of nations: those that attract capital and those that drive it away. Ideology is becoming increasingly irrelevant to the 21st-century map of the world. You have communist, socialist, progressive, capitalist, and super-capitalist countries that are achieving record rates of eco-

nomic growth and reducing poverty as never before; and you can list
a similar array of countries of all ideologies that have failed miserably
in those endeavors. What distinguishes the first group from the second
is their ability to attract investments that generate wealth, jobs, and
— in most cases at least in the West — political freedom.

That may sound pretty basic to most Americans and Europeans,
but it's far from the conventional wisdom in most of Latin America.

The good news in the fight against poverty

Before we go into detail, let's state for the record that contrary to
the apocalyptic view of many critics that globalization has increased
world poverty, the opposite is true. World poverty — while still at
unacceptably high levels — has fallen sharply over the past few years,
nearly everywhere except in Latin America. Globalization, far from
increasing the percentage of poor people in the world, has helped
to reduce it dramatically: Over the last two decades the proportion
of global population that lives in extreme poverty — less than one
dollar per day — declined from 40 percent to 19 percent.[iv] Worldwide
poverty in general — the share of people who live on less than two
dollars per day — has been reduced as well, albeit not as dramatically:
It has dropped from nearly 67 percent of the global population in
1981 to 50 percent in 2002.[v] In other words, the world is becoming a
better place to live, albeit not as quickly as many of us would like.

Unfortunately for Latin Americans, nearly all that poverty reduction is taking place in China, India, Taiwan, Singapore, Vietnam, and
other Asian countries, where most of the world's population live.
You don't have to be a genius, then, to understand why China is
growing so fast. The Chinese are getting an avalanche of foreign
investment, which allows them to open thousands of factories every
year, create new jobs, increase exports, and reduce poverty by leaps
and bounds. Over the past two decades, since China opened up to
the world and joined the global economy, it has managed to lift over
250 million people out of poverty, according to official figures. And

much of the foreign investment has gone to set up export-oriented manufacturing plants. While China increased its exports at average annual rates of 17 percent over the past decade, Latin America did so at a mere 5.6 percent, according to Andean Development Corporation figures. The clock is ticking, and China is making inroads into more markets worldwide, displacing more competitors, growing more formidable. By 2003, China had surpassed Mexico as the second-largest exporter to the United States, after Canada.

What are the Chinese, Irish, Poles, Czechs, and Chileans doing to attract foreign capital? They are looking around them rather than looking inward. Instead of measuring their success against their own situation five or ten years ago, they are constantly assessing their performance against that of competitors around the world. They see the global economy as a train already moving: either climb aboard or be left behind.

Many Latin American nations, on the other hand, suffer from peripheral blindness. Their tunnel vision causes them to measure themselves against their own pasts instead of the contemporary world around them. They are obsessed with then and oblivious to now. In Venezuela, Chávez not only often addresses a picture of 19th-century independence hero Simón Bolívar in his televised speeches, but credits Bolívar as his inspiration for key government decisions. He has even changed the name of the country to the "Bolivarian Republic of Venezuela." Across the continent, Argentina nearly came to a halt during the October 2006 reburial ceremonies of the late president Juan Domingo Perón. Rival Peronist groups clashes and shots were fired, leaving several wounded, during the transfer of Perón's remains from Buenos Aires' Chacarita cemetery to a new $1.1 million mausoleum 30 miles southwest of the city. Virtually all Argentine television networks suspended their regular programming for much of the day to cover the solemn caravan, which included 120 members of the presidential guard on horseback and was cheered by thousands of people on the roadsides chanting "¡Perón vive!" (Perón lives!). Many countries in the region share this longing to dwell on the past. And it's not just their governments or politicians. If you look at the best-selling books in the region, a surprising number are history books or historical novels. At the time of this writing, the region's best-seller was Isabel Allende's *Ines del Alma Mía*, a novel about the wife of Chile's 16th-century conquistador, Pedro de Valdivia.

There is nothing wrong in learning from the past. Trouble is, Bolívar died in 1830, which was 40 years before the telephone and 150 years before the Internet. Perón died in 1974, a decade before the birth of the World Wide Web. Their calls for independence, nationalism, and import substitution may have made sense at their time, but can hardly be taken as policy guidelines today. In a global economy where Wall Street bankers barely out of college move billions of dollars from one country to another with a few computer keystrokes, shouting anti-capitalist slogans or insulting investors can be a dangerous game. At the very least, spending too much energy celebrating — or debating — the past, instead of evaluating the present and charting the future, can be a surefire way to fall ever further behind.

While Latin American politicians cite historical figures to support their arguments against opening up to the world or signing free trade agreements, their discussions about the present often overlook what the Asians understand well, that the key to success in today's world is not just signing free trade agreements, but being competitive. In Latin America there is too much debate about free trade and too little about how to compete — and how to win — once trade barriers are lowered.

"You can still live very well in this country"

When I told various Latin American friends I was writing a book comparing Latin America's development with that of other regions and exploring what Latin America might learn from them, several assured me I was wasting my time. It was an exercise in futility, they said, because it started from the false premise that the region's economic, intellectual, and political elites actually want to change things. Many of Latin American opinion-makers are keenly aware that their economies are stuck in the mud, but they don't have the slightest incentive to change a system that works very well for them, my friends argued. Why would politicians want to create more competitive societies, when they are elected thanks to the very system that trades state subsidies to the poor in exchange for their votes? Why would government cronies in the business world want to change anything, when they receive fabulous contracts from corrupt officials? Why would "progressive" academics and intellectuals who teach at state universities want to make their schools more competitive, when they enjoy the privilege of not being accountable to anybody thanks to the political and professional autonomy of their university systems? Regardless of what they say publicly, none of the groups that make up Latin America's elites wants to risk changes that might harm their pocketbooks, their privileges, or their lifestyles, my friends insisted. My efforts were well intentioned but naïve, and ultimately futile, they said.

I disagree. There's a new factor changing the political equation in Latin America, and that is forcing the region's upper crust to realize their cozy status quo will not endure: an explosion of crime. Poverty in Latin America is no longer a problem exclusively of the poor. Because of rising crime rates, it is now affecting the rich. In the past, poverty levels in the region were extremely high and the distribution of wealth obscenely unequal; but none of this inconvenienced the affluent much. The poor lived on the outskirts of cities and — apart from sporadic outbreaks of political violence — did little to upset the daily life of the upper classes. It's no accident that U.S. and European visitors to Latin American capitals were dazzled by the lifestyle of the well-off. "Latin Americans really know how to live!" the visitors exclaimed. The plush lifestyle of Latin America's upper classes — their four-week vacations, restaurants packed well past midnight, lingering mealtime conversations, Sunday gatherings of extended family, passion for soccer shared with their less privileged countrymen, musical richness, and safe streets to stroll down — was not easy to find elsewhere in the world. Even amid coups and political instability, those with reasonably good incomes would often tell foreign visitors, "Despite everything, you can still live very well in this country." Although Latin America had one of the highest poverty rates in the world and the worst distribution of wealth, its upper classes could afford the luxury of living in denial. True, the poor were always a factor at election time, but they were largely invisible in daily life except as a reliable source of underpaid labor. Poverty was a tragic phenomenon, but one that was hidden behind the walls that line the roadways.

Those days are over. High poverty rates, along with inequality and the communications revolution that brought the lives of the rich and famous to the humblest homes in the region, are creating a crisis of unfulfilled expectations that spills over into frustration, anger, and rising levels of street crime. An undeclared civil war is raging in Latin America, and it has changed the daily lives of rich and poor alike. In the *villas miseria* of Argentina, the *favelas* of Brazil, the *cerros* of Caracas, and the *ciudades perdidas* of Mexico City, legions of the young are growing up, raised outside conventional family structures, on the streets, without hope of decent jobs in the formal economy. What is more, they come of age amid an unparalleled flood of televised messages beckoning them to a world of affluence, at a time in history when — paradoxically — opportunities for those without education or job skills have never been so remote.

The most violent region in the world

The combination of increasing expectations and diminishing opportunities for the least educated is an increasingly volatile mix. It has led growing numbers of marginalized youths to jump the walls of their hidden cities, often armed, often untethered by drugs, and venture into commercial and residential areas, where they mug or kidnap whoever looks well dressed or is carrying something shiny.

As this army of alienated youth advances on the cities, the middle and upper classes retrench even deeper into their walled fortresses. Luxury condominiums in most big Latin American cities are no longer built with just bullet-proof security booths at the entrance, where guards armed with shotguns or assault rifles can check on people wanting to get in. Now these buildings also provide gyms, tennis courts, pools, and restaurants within their walled compounds, so that no one is forced to venture outside. Just as in the Middle Ages, Latin American executives live in fortified castles. They lower their drawbridges — duly manned by private guards — when they leave to work early in the morning, and raise them again at night to keep the enemy out. Today, more than ever, poverty, marginalization, and crime are eroding the quality of life of all Latin Americans, including the rich.

Latin America has an estimated 2.5 million private guards.[vi] São Paulo, Brazil, has 400,000 — three times the number of police officers, according to the daily *Gazeta Mercantil*. Rio de Janeiro is the site of an all-out war: criminals kill some 133 police officers a year — more than two per week — and the police respond with extra-judicial executions of up to 1,000 suspects a year.[vii] Bogotá, Colombia, until recently the world capital of kidnapping, has roughly seven private guards for every police officer. Other security-related businesses are booming too. One of Colombia's security entrepreneurs, Miguel Caballero, told me he's making a fortune designing bulletproof fashion. Now Colombian businessmen and politicians can dress in guayabera shirts, leather jackets, or suits lined with bulletproof material that is largely imperceptible to outsiders. "We've developed a groundbreaking industry," Caballero proudly said. His business sells 22,000 fashionable bulletproof clothing items a year, some of them exported to Iraq and other Middle Eastern countries. "We already have 192 exclusive models. And we're developing a women's line of apparel, with both underwear and outerwear."[viii]

Latin America is the world's most violent region. It has become a running joke at international conferences on crime to say that one is more likely to be attacked walking in downtown Mexico City or

Buenos Aires dressed in business attire than in Baghdad dressed in U.S. military fatigues. According to the Geneva-based World Health Organization, Latin America has an annual homicide rate of 27.5 victims in every 100,000 residents, compared with 22 in Africa, 15 in Eastern Europe, and 1 in industrialized nations. "As a region, Latin America has the highest homicide rate in the world," Etienne Krug, the WHO specialist on violence, told me in a telephone interview from Geneva. "Homicide is the seventh cause of death in Latin America, compared to the 14th cause in Africa, and the 22nd worldwide."[ix] And the likelihood a murderer or thief will go to jail in Latin America is slim: while the prison population in the United States — one of the highest in the world — is 686 people per 100,000 inhabitants, in Argentina it's 107; in Chile, 204; in Colombia, 126; in Mexico, 156; in Peru, 104; and in Venezuela, 62.[x] In other words, criminals in Latin America enjoy an unusual degree of impunity.

"We're facing an epidemic"

Few places anywhere have the quality of life plummeted as sharply as in the great cities of Latin America. Buenos Aires, the majestic Argentine capital that until a few years ago was one of the safest cities in the world, where the locals prided themselves on the fact that women could walk unaccompanied late at night, has become a city terrorized by crime. Even before the economic collapse of 2001, slums had spread deep into the city. The shantytown next to the downtown Retiro train station, for instance, grew from 12,500 inhabitants in 1983 to 72,800 in 1998, and its population has grown far more since then.[xi] Within the walls of these shantytowns, just blocks away from the most elegant areas of the city, are tens of thousands of youths who don't attend school. Many start taking drugs at eight or ten years of age and become criminals soon thereafter. "We're facing an epidemic," I was told by Juan Alberto Yaría, director of the Institute of Drugs at the University del Salvador, and a former top Buenos Aires province drug rehabilitation official. "We are seeing more and more people with their brains so damaged by drugs that they will never be able to lead normal lives. All these kids who don't go to school, never met their fathers, never belonged to a church or a sports club, and who live on the streets and consume drugs, are the criminal working class. And there will be more and more of them because of the growing phenomenon of 'defamilialization' — the number of single mothers in Argentina is skyrocketing — and drug consumption," Yaría said.[xii]

In Central America the *maras*, or street gangs, the region's latest vehicle of organized violence, are spreading from El Salvador, Honduras, Guatemala, and southern Mexico toward the Mexican capital and into Colombia, Brazil, and other South American countries. The *mareros*, marginalized youths who identify themselves by their tattoos and the hand signs they use to communicate with one another, are believed to number more than 100,000 in Central America alone. Nearly half are younger than 15, police estimate.

The *mareros* originated in Los Angeles, California, and spilled into Central America when convicts were shipped back to their homelands by the U.S. government. In Honduras one such gang stopped a busload of passengers who were traveling to their hometowns to celebrate the Christmas holiday in 2004. Gang members murdered 28 men, women, and children in revenge for a police crackdown. For growing numbers of youth, the *maras* are their only chance for social recognition. A *marero* is a neighborhood hero. Youths compete for the chance to take part in an initiation rite — where they may be required to commit a variety of crimes, from selling drugs to killing a police officer — and, if they are captured, they pose triumphantly for the TV cameras. Belonging to the *maras* is a badge of honor.

"The *marero* is the new criminal of the 21st century," Honduran Security Minister Oscar Álvarez told me in an interview. "In the *maras* there are people dedicated to drug trafficking, murder for hire, robbery, kidnapping, dismemberment. In other words, they're killing machines. But unlike other criminals, they don't care about consequences. Unlike a traditional bank robber who wears a mask to hide his face when committing a crime, they don't hide. Instead, they crave the publicity they get from the media, which helps them rise within their group's chain of command."[xiii]

The *Mara Salvatrucha* has more than 50,000 members in El Salvador. They not only steal, mug, and kidnap, but also torture and decapitate their victims as a demonstration of their power. They have become so powerful that growing numbers of Central Americans — especially in the middle and upper classes — are demanding heavy-handed measures, even when they involve things that until recently would have been considered legally or morally indefensible. The expression "mano dura" or "heavy-hand," long discredited because of its association with Latin America's military dictatorships of the 1970s, is increasingly taking on positive connotations.

So much so that Salvadoran President Tony Saca not only won election in 2004 promising to use a "heavy hand" against the maras, but later christened his security program "Super-Heavy Hand." Under his plan, Salvadoran police arrested nearly 5,000 young people suspected of being gang members simply because they wore tattoos. Salvadoran police routinely round up people who look like gang members, demand that they remove their shirts to see if they are concealing any tattoos, then lock them up if they are. Isn't this an infringement on people's freedom of expression? I asked President Saca in an interview. Isn't it a violation of basic civic and human rights, such as the right to carry a drawing on one's body, or walk the streets without state interference? Saca looked at me puzzled, as if I were living in another world. "Why?" he asked. "Their faces or identities should be protected when they are arrested, but they should definitely be put behind bars," Saca said. "A kid might be 15 years old, but if he's a killer, we should enforce the Super-Heavy Hand Plan and send him to jail. In some cases, they're beyond reformation."[xiv] According to Saca and a growing number of Latin Americans, the "heavy hand" is the wave of the future.

The specter of "Africanization"

In Washington, D.C., and major European capitals, there are fears that the crime wave spreading through Latin America may trigger a phenomenon of social disintegration — or "Africanization" — that will further erode governability and create "lawless zones." In other words, U.S. and European officials — especially in law-enforcement circles — fear a proliferation of areas where governments have no authority, and where drug trafficking or terrorist cartels will thrive unmolested. Curiously, while conventional wisdom in most Latin American countries is that poverty spawns crime, and that efforts must therefore be focused on reducing poverty, growing numbers of U.S. experts are saying just the opposite — that crime causes poverty. To them, the region's first priority should be to fight crime. A report by the Council of the Americas — an influential, New York-based group that represents about 170 multinationals with operations in Latin America — concluded that insecurity is one of the main factors holding Latin America back, because it deters investment. After noting that Latin America, with only 8 percent of the global population, accounted for 75 percent of the world's kidnappings in 2003, the Council's study revealed that a poll of multinationals active in Latin America ranked security as "the main threat" to business in the region.[xv] The poll concluded that many multinationals don't invest in Latin America because of the high cost of security: while security-related expenses represent 3 percent of spending for companies in Asia, in Latin America the figure is 7 percent.[xvi]

To my surprise, as I learned in an interview with then U.S. Defense Secretary Donald Rumsfeld, Latin America's crime wave and the inability of governments to control their territories worry the Pentagon even more than the authoritarian excesses of Chávez and his followers. Unlike the fears prevalent during the Cold War, when U.S. presidents fretted that potentially hostile Latin American countries might amass excessive power, today — amid a war on terrorism — the greater U.S. preoccupation is with national governments that are too weak to control what happens within their own borders. When I asked Rumsfeld what his greatest concern was in Latin America, the first thing he mentioned was neither Chávez nor Fidel Castro nor the Colombian guerrillas, nor any other political threat. He talked about crime and the *maras*. Rumsfeld said that "aside from protecting democracy," his main concerns were "the problems of crime, gangs, narcotics, weapons trafficking, and hostage taking; all of these anti-social activities that we see." [xvii]

In the same vein, the former head of the Southern Command of the U.S. Armed Forces, Gen. James Hill, told me in a separate interview that the gang issue "has all the potential in the next five to ten years of becoming the [number one] problem for the region. In Central America, if it continues to grow, it can destabilize the entire region." [xviii] How might that destabilization affect the United States? I asked. Hill indicated that the *maras'* rapings, kidnappings and murders in Latin America are driving up illegal immigration to the United States, and that gangs are spreading their violence into Los Angeles, Miami, and other major U.S. cities. Judging from what Hill said, the U.S. military fears an invasion of Latin American criminals. Hill recounted a conversation he had with former Honduran President Ricardo Maduro. "He told me they were having a negotiation with one gang, and the gang negotiator said, 'I need to clear this talking point with our leadership.' And the gang negotiator called Los Angeles! That ought to make the hair of your back stand up," Hill said. [xix] "It's only a matter of time before the *maras* re-export violence to the United States and start selling their services to organized crime, becoming either drug cartels or terrorist rings," he added. Eventually the gangs will say what the Revolutionary Armed Forces of Colombia (FARC) guerrillas started to say 10 years ago: "Why should I be the middleman, if I can go into business on my own?" Hill said. [xx] The former top U.S. military commander in Latin America concluded by saying that, unless something is done soon, "There will be huge ungoverned slums, lawless areas dedicated to organized crime, with international connections." [xxi]

One of the most visible by-products of Latin America's crime wave at the start of the new millennium was the real-estate boom in Miami. The city, often referred to only half-jokingly as "the capital of Latin America," experienced its biggest construction surge in recent history. Many of the 500 multinationals with Latin American headquarters in Miami — including Hewlett Packard, Sony, FedEx, Caterpillar, Visa, and Microsoft — had moved there in recent years from Latin American countries. In 2005 alone, around 60,000 apartments were under construction in Miami, compared with 7,000 in the previous 10 years.[xxii] And who were buying them? Granted, in many cases, it was U.S. speculators taking advantage of low interest rates and growing numbers of Europeans eager to invest their strong euros in sunny South Florida. But a large number of buyers were Latin American crime victims, or potential victims.

Aside from traditional Latin American investors who want to own real estate abroad to protect themselves from instability at home, large numbers of businessmen were installing their families in Miami to protect them from kidnappings, violent robberies, and murders. Many executives were commuting weekly to Caracas, Bogotá or San Salvador. Colombian businessmen were on the rise in posh Miami enclaves like Key Biscayne. On exclusive Fisher Island there were more and more Mexicans, and in Bal Harbour growing numbers of Argentineans. Many, if not most, had moved because of security concerns. It was a new crowd, different from the Cuban or Central American political refugees of the past, or the working-class economic refugees from the region. The new-comers were crime refugees. A few years ago, I had started one of my columns in the *Miami Herald* like this: "The mayor of Miami ought to erect statues to the Latin American leaders who have done the most for the city's economic progress: Cuban President Fidel Castro, Venezuelan President Hugo Chávez, and FARC Commander Manuel Marulanda." If I were to write it again today, I'd have to change the second part of the sentence to say that the mayor should also erect a statue to the *mareros* and all other criminals who are driving rich and poor alike to leave their homelands and settle down in Miami. The new migrants are exiles from the civil war raging in Latin America.

Investment-drawing and investment-spurning countries

In the new world economy there are countries which attract investment and countries that repel investment, and both come in all political shades. In China, a Communist dictatorship with 1.3 billion people, the proportion of the population living on less than one dollar a day has been reduced from 61 to 17 percent over the past two decades. In Vietnam, another Communist dictatorship, the same thing has happened: since the country began attracting foreign capital — Nike footwear factory is already the country's largest employer, with 130,000 workers — and allowed 140,000 private businesses to open their doors over the past decade, the economy began growing at annual rates of 7 percent, and per capita income has nearly tripled.

On the other hand, Cuba, a Communist dictatorship that has not opened up to the world, remains an economic basket case. Today Cuba has one of the lowest per capita incomes in Latin America, which explains why the Castro regime refuses to allow outsiders to measure its economy by international standards and continues to come up with its own, questionable figures. But some Cuban economic data, which are easy for any visitor to corroborate, speak for themselves. *Granma*, the official organ of the Cuban Communist Party, reported in 2002 that the average income on the island is about $10 per month.[xxiii] "A teacher in Cuba earns $9.60 per month; an engineer, $14.40; and a doctor, $27.*[xxiv] Four years later these figures had barely budged.

*In theory, the Cuban regime provides the population with subsidized food and free medical services that do not exist in other countries and that should be taken into account in any salary comparison. But anyone who has visited Cuba knows that food cards don't cover more than one week of basic needs per month, and that medical services are often available only in hospitals for tourists. Paradoxically, today Cuba lives off the nearly $1 billion in money wired annually by U.S. Cuban-Americans to family members: this has become the largest source of income on the island.

Venezuela, another capital-repellent country, became steadily poorer during the first four years of the Chávez administration, despite the country's fabulous oil boom. According to government figures, the poor increased from 42 to 53 percent of the population from 1999 to 2004, the first five years under Chávez.[xxv] Poverty declined to pre-Chávez levels of 39.5 percent after 2005, but opposition economists question that figure, noting that the country's statistics office had changed its "methodology" after Chávez publicly accused it of reflecting "neo-liberal" standards of measuring poverty. Chávez, for his part, blamed the rise in poverty during his first years in power on opposition-led strikes, which paralyzed the economy, and denied that any methodological changes had affected poverty estimates. Whatever the case, most economists agree that if there was a reduction in poverty, it was the smallest of any similar oil-boom period in Venezuela's recent memory. Chávez's anti-capitalist rhetoric led 7,000 private businesses to close in the first four years of his administration, and triggered a capital flight of $36 billion. Unbelievably, even though oil prices — the Venezuelan economy's engine — rose from $9 to $50 per barrel during Chávez's first five years in power, unemployment increased from 13 to 19 percent.[xxvi]

Despite the bleak headlines from Venezuela in the U.S. media, not all the news from Latin America were bleak, nor were all leftist leaders trying to take their countries back in time. On the contrary, leftist presidents in Chile and Brazil were integrating their countries still further into the global economy, setting up increasingly diversified export industries and creating a solid basis for long-term growth. The striking differences between the economic policies of the leftist governments of China, Vietnam, Brazil, and Chile on one hand, and Venezuela and Cuba on the other, underscore how outdated the terms "left" and "right" have become. Rather, there are countries across the political spectrum that attract investment, and countries of various political stripes that drive off investment. And in virtually all cases, the first group advances economically, and the second group falls back.

The Case of Botswana

When I read a ranking by the World Economic Forum showing that nearly all Latin American countries trailed Botswana in competitiveness, I found it hard to believe. Back when I was a kid, Botswana was one of the poorest countries in the world, the kind of place that appeared on the cover of *National Geographic* magazine to draw world attention to famines or civil wars. And yet, the Forum's competitiveness ranking, a survey of 8,700 executives from 104 countries, rated Botswana ahead of every Latin American country except Chile. The annual ranking, based on perceptions of each country's business climate, including the quality of its institutions and levels of corruption, was led by Finland, the United States, and Sweden. A long list of countries in Europe and Asia followed, including Chile, which ranked 22nd. From there, another long list followed with such nations as Jordan, Lithuania, Hungary, South Africa, and Botswana. Only farther down — much farther down — were any other Latin American countries: Mexico, Brazil, Argentina, and the rest of the region.

A similar study, published by the AT Kearney consulting firm, ranked Latin American countries near the bottom of a 25-nation list of countries evaluated by their attractiveness to foreign investors. This list, based on a survey of 1,000 executives of multinationals, was topped by China, United States, and India. Brazil was ranked 17th and Mexico 22nd. The rest of Latin America didn't make the list.

Intrigued, I called up the chief economist of the World Economic Forum in Geneva. "Why is Botswana ahead of Latin America in your ranking?" I asked Augusto López-Claros. Botswana, he explained, had grown steadily at one of the highest rates in the world since its independence in 1966. Thanks to iron-clad fiscal discipline and responsible economic policies — and, to be sure, considerable help from its diamond production — Botswana had quickly passed from being one of the world's poorest countries to a middle-income nation. Today it has a per capita gross domestic product of nearly $8,800 a year, more than Brazil and nearly as much as Mexico. López-Claros said that, according to his poll, business executives in Botswana complained much less than their counterparts in Mexico, Brazil, and Argentina about such problems as the quality of state institutions, official corruption, and crime. But above all, he said, Botswana offers something rare in many Latin American countries: predictability. It is a country that hasn't changed the rules of the game, despite enduring a devastating AIDS epidemic and being located on a continent that is constantly shaken by coups and regional wars. Stability is inducing domestic and foreign businesspeople to bet on the country's future, he said.

In much of Latin America there was still no consensus around the idea that predictability, legal safeguards, and a receptive investment climate are tickets to long-term prosperity. Few leaders seemed to notice that in Spain elections are won alternately by socialists, conservatives, and socialists again, without causing investors to pack their bags and flee. The same thing happens in virtually all developed countries, but not in Latin American ones, with rare exceptions such as Chile. Politically, Chile may be Latin America's most boring country: it has no messianic leaders grabbing headlines with fiery speeches from the presidential balcony, no revolts at military headquarters, no politicians talking about the need to "re-found" the nation. But therein lies a secret of its success. Chile's relatively high place in the World Economic Forum's competitiveness ranking may be due to its stability: it has had right-wing, middle-of-the-road, and leftist governments, but it has stayed the course. Stability has allowed Chile to grow steadily, and to lead the region in eradicating poverty. From 1990 to 2006, the percentage of poor in Chile dropped from 39 percent of the population to 18 percent, according to official figures.

The Chilean miracle

How did Chileans achieve their stability? In part, Chile's miracle is a by-product of political exhaustion. General Augusto Pinochet's dictatorship was so traumatic, dividing so many families, driving so many into exile, causing so many deaths, that Chileans concluded that they had paid too high a price for their political rivalries. Moderation became more appealing than vindication. But there was also an element of pragmatism — probably absorbed by leading Chilean politicians during their years of exile in U.S. and European universities — which allowed the post-Pinochet center-left and leftist governments to build on what they had inherited rather than trying to start from scratch. After the 17 years of Pinochet's dictatorship, Chilean presidents — Patricio Aylwin and Eduardo Frei of the Christian Democratic Party, and more recently Ricardo Lagos and Michelle Bachelet of the Socialist Party — resisted the temptation to tear down what their political adversaries had built. They put the country before themselves. Having an intelligent, modern left helped Chile achieve a climate of predictability that has steadily improved its economy, and has helped reduce poverty at a record pace.

On June 6, 2003, the day Chile signed its free trade agreement with the United States in Miami, I asked Soledad Alvear, the foreign minister at the time, how she would explain Chile's success. We had been talking about the ups and downs of Chile's neighbors, especially Argentina, which was then going through its worst economic crisis ever. What was Chile's secret? Alvear replied that if she had to pick one factor, she would say it was Chile's decision to pick a development strategy and stick to it. "You can't reinvent a country's strategic objectives with each new government," Alvear told me. "We have established key strategic goals for the country which should be maintained over time. There is a consensus in our society on the country's need to have serious economic policies, fiscal responsibility, and an open economy."[xxvii]

If Alvear is right, Latin America will have a hard time capturing investments without predictability. And one could argue that Latin American countries would not even need much foreign investment if they managed to draw home some of the enormous funds their own citizens keep in offshore banks to protect themselves from instability at home. If Latin Americans have failed to repatriate their offshore deposits, it isn't due to a lack of patriotism or the lack of better investment returns; but because of a lack of confidence that the rules of the game will be maintained.

As late Massachusetts Institute of Technology (MIT) economist Rudiger Dornbush said when asked during a visit to Argentina why that country had so many problems, "Developed nations have flexible rules that are rigidly enforced. You have rigid rules that are flexibly enforced." Indeed, in most economically successful countries, congresses update laws periodically, but once they've done so, governments enforce compliance. In many Latin American countries, the laws are static, but are enforced only sporadically. As long as laws aren't obeyed, or are changed constantly, countries won't be able to attract significant investment, from home or abroad.

The supranational path

So how can Latin American countries succeed in attracting investment, stimulating growth, and reducing poverty? Considering the region's widespread rejection of orthodox International Monetary Fund recipes and the backlash triggered by some corruption-ridden privatizations in the 1990s, it may be time to consider a new option: the supranational path. Although supranationality is not enjoying record popularity in Europe, as evidenced by the 2005 votes against the European Union constitution in France and Holland, it remains one of the most successful development paths in contemporary history. And given the absence of a domestic consensus in most Latin American countries to pursue Chilean-styled sustainable growth-oriented policies, the most effective way to turn countries in the region into investment magnets may be through multinational economic agreements.

As the European Union has learned, supranational agreements help countries discipline themselves. Unlike Chile, many Latin American countries are going through periods of severe political polarization, which prevents them from adopting economic policies that encourage productive, long-term investments. But these countries could still benefit from joining a club of economically responsible nations. Spain, Portugal, and other European Union members achieved much of their current reliability after signing supranational treaties that committed them to honor the rules of the game, and inspired confidence within and outside their borders. What's more, signing on to supranational agreements served as an inoculation against populism and political extremism.

For Poland, the Czech Republic, and other former Eastern Bloc countries, many of which had histories of political turmoil not so different from Latin America's; joining the European Union in 2004 meant — as it had with Spain and Portugal before them — signing a predictability pact. All these countries left behind traditions of political and economic sovereignty, and committed themselves to following responsible economic policies and tough international rules. In a way, supranationality also helped China: the country's Communist regime used joining the World Trade Organization in 2001 as a reason to enact dramatic economic reforms that had little domestic support. All those countries based their development strategies on external agreements. They passed from an era of nationalism to one of supranationalism.

Which supranational framework should Latin America choose? A Free Trade Agreement of the Americas (FTAA) with the United States? A Latin American-European Community? A Latin American Community? And would such a plan be realistic at a time when Chávez and his allies are calling for nationalizations and denouncing free trade agreements with the United States as potentially catastrophic? Obviously, given the political realities, any supranational economic agreement in the region would have to start with a few pro-market countries and then grow gradually with the addition of new ones. A supranational agreement among Latin American nations, even if it started with only a few, would force members to maintain serious economic policies and create strong conflict-resolution mechanisms which would help stimulate investment. To put it bluntly, briefly, and in language no politician would use, Latin American countries would have something that worked wonders in many European countries: a straitjacket.

The main reason to create a Community of the Americas, or a smaller group of like-minded Latin American countries bound by common rules, would not be economic, but legal. Latin America needs a political contract like the European Union's in order to ensure stability. It wouldn't be about creating a supranational government that would make all manner of day-to-day decisions. Rather, it would be about establishing a joint authority to supervise certain fundamental guidelines, such as responsible economic management, democracy, and respect for human rights.

The European Union started small, and managed to create this straitjacket for its members by adopting the concept of shared sovereignty. According to EU regulations: "Sharing sovereignty means, in practice, that member states delegate some of their decision-making power to common institutions they have created to decide specific matters of joint interest democratically and at a European level."[xxviii] To become members of the European Union, countries must comply with concrete parameters of democracy, human rights, and free-market economy, and agree to submit to the community's rules. Unlike an ordinary free trade agreement, the European Union has supranational institutions — such as the European Parliament, European Commission, European Court of Justice, and European Central Bank — that have jurisdiction over specific aspects of decisions made by member countries. In other words, in the European Union no radical populist leader can emerge to stage a military or constitutional coup, not either order the confiscation of foreign companies. If he did, he would be thrown out of the club and would no longer enjoy its benefits. Latin America would benefit greatly from following the European model.

Regional blocs in the 21st century

Supranationality is an economic necessity too, because Latin America will find it hard to compete with the European or Asian blocs unless it musters similar economies of scale. Regardless of a country's politics; why would a multinational corporation make a major investment in Bolivia, with a market of just over 9 million people, when it can do so in the Czech Republic, a nation of similar size that can export to a market of 460 million without customs tariffs thanks to its European Union membership?

The world currently has three giant trade blocs: North America and Central America, with about 25 percent of global gross product; the European Union, with 16 percent; and Asia, with 23 percent, although Asian integration is only just beginning.[xxix] The North American Free Trade Agreement, covering the United States, Canada, and Mexico, has 426 million people. The European Union, with 27 members, has about 500 million. And China has signed a trade agreement with the countries of the Association of Southeast Asian Nations (ASEAN) — which includes Indonesia, Malaysia, the Philippines, Singapore, Thailand, and Vietnam — which aims to launch in 2010 a free trade bloc that would become the largest of its kind by population, though not by output. The Asian bloc will comprise 1.7 billion people, and if India joined it would have 3 billion.

Unless they produce oil or another world-coveted commodity, most Latin American countries whose exports don't have preferential access to one of these three global trade blocs will be left on the margins of world trade. Even if they joined together with other Latin American neighbors to create a purely regional bloc, they would still have a tough time substantially increasing their exports, because the region's markets are relatively small: Latin America has barely 7.6 percent of the world's gross product, and accounts for only 4.1 percent of trade.[xxx] In other words, virtually nothing. As members of the world's largest trade blocs increasingly use their preferential tariffs to do business among themselves, Latin American countries that have no access to one of the three major regional markets could see their share of world trade shrink further. As in the children's game of musical chairs, if Latin America fails to join one of the big world blocs, it will be left without a seat at the table.

Granted, most Latin American leaders say, with good reason, that they would be far more disposed to sign a supranational trade agreement with the United States if Washington did what Europe's richest nations did, and provided substantial economic aid to its poorest neighbors. In Europe, Germany and France spent billions of dollars in the 1980s to stimulate economic development in Spain, Portugal, Greece, and Ireland. From 2000 to 2006 they donated nearly $22 billion for infrastructure improvements in the least developed European Union nations, including the new members from Eastern Europe. However, as several Spanish and Irish officials repeatedly told me, EU economic aid, though valuable, explains only part of the European success, and perhaps the least significant part.

In Ireland, contrary to what I expected, most officials I interviewed said European economic aid had played a relatively minor role in the "Celtic miracle." Rather, the secret of Ireland's success was in submitting supranational rules committing member countries to adhere to democracy and a market economy, and granting them preferential access to a much larger market. According to what I was told in Dublin and later in the former Soviet-bloc nations, what nourished confidence and encouraged the inflow of foreign investment was a combination of guarantees and greater certainties ensured by supranational legal agreements, and access to a much bigger market. In Latin America countries benefit from neither.

But isn't the Brazil-sponsored South American Community a step in the right direction?, I asked many European Union officials. Their reply was invariably negative. When South American presidents met in Cuzco, Peru, to create the South American Community in late 2004, they signed a grandiloquent document packed with good intentions, but they did not create a common legal framework for the region. That alone would have ensured that the project would be taken seriously. The South American presidents made the same mistake as their predecessors, who in previous decades had created —with the same enthusiasm and grandiose rhetoric—such regional institutions such as the Latin American Special Coordination Commission (known by its Spanish acronym CECLA); the Latin American Free Trade Association (ALALC); the Latin American Integration Association (ALADI); and the Latin American Economic System (SELA). In all instances, they signed documents committing themselves to forming a regional community, but without concrete commercial agreements and without creating authoritative mechanisms to resolve transnational disputes.

The European Union did just the opposite of what South America's leaders did in Cuzco. From the outset, in 1952, the Europeans started out by making concrete tariff reduction deals, and establishing resolution mechanisms to solve potential disputes, while leaving the more ambitious goals of overall regional integration for later. Indeed, the EU began as a coal and steel community. Six countries joined a common market in order to pool their coal and steel resources so that they could confront jointly the difficulties of the European winter. After signing their treaty and creating a framework to settle disputes, the Europeans gradually expanded it to include other products. The South Americans, as they had so many times before, started out by signing an overall regional integration treaty with bold statements about the future. But they failed to commit themselves to any specific tariff reductions or mechanisms to handle commercial disputes. The Cuzco agreement made big headlines in the region, but was quickly forgotten. Like many of its predecessors, it was largely economic poetry.

The "community brand"

In addition, as I learned during a visit to the Czech Republic, a supranational agreement could give Latin America a public relations boost. After they joined the EU, former Soviet-bloc countries benefited from an immediate burnishing of their image abroad. They could now take advantage of their new "community brand" among investors and potential export customers. During an interview in Prague, the capital of the Czech Republic, the vice-minister of commerce and industry repeatedly made the point about how much his country's image abroad had benefited from joining a bigger club of successful countries. I had asked Tlapa how a country as small as the Czech Republic, with only 10 million inhabitants, could succeed in attracting investments in a region torn by wars that were making headlines across the world. To my surprise, Tlapa responded that the Czech Republic had benefited enormously from the "community brand." He explained that from the time the Czech Republic announced its intention to join the European Union, even before any documents were signed, his country was seen as a nation that had more in common with Germany than with the Third World. In the global economy, Tlapa explained, one has to go out and sell oneself to the world. The Czech Republic, a new country, a product of the subdivision of the former Eastern bloc after the fall of communism, had a serious marketing problem: it had no "national brand" like Germany's automobiles or Italy's fashion.

"To build a national brand is very expensive. If you hire a public-relations firm, it will cost you a good part of your gross domestic product," Tlapa told me. "But the simple act of joining the European Union gave us a community brand, a guarantee that, now that we are subject to the same rules and the same arbitration courts as other European Union members, investing in the Czech Republic is the same as investing in Germany or Italy. That has made an enormous difference. For many Americans our membership in the EU means a clear brand name for European distribution."[xxxi]

The experience of Europe's least-developed countries of surrendering some sovereignty to a supranational institution has worked well for them. All of a sudden, it became easier for Spain, Portugal, Ireland, Greece, and the new EU members from the former Soviet bloc to leave behind their wild political swings of the past. Nowadays, few foreign investors would stay away from Spain, Ireland, or the Czech Republic due to fear that communists, rightists or socialists would take power. Southern European countries have doubled and, in some cases, tripled their per capita income merely by following EU rules that ensure economic stability.

And Eastern European nations that joined the EU in 2004 quickly became the fastest-growing economies in Europe. Most of these countries received an avalanche of foreign investments in anticipation of their EU membership — so much so that, in 2004, the year of their incorporation, Poland and the Czech Republic already ranked well above Mexico, Brazil, and all other Latin American countries in a United Nations survey of the world's most attractive countries for foreign investors conducted that year.[xxxii] Instead of feeding a senseless nationalism and scapegoating outsiders — be it the International Monetary Fund, the United States, or "capitalism" — Eastern European countries wrapped themselves in the supranational flag of the European Union, and it worked out very well for them.

The Spanish experience

But would Latin America's fiercely nationalistic countries cede sovereignty to a supranational entity? Is this a realistic goal in a region where some leaders still end speeches by shouting "Sovereignty or death"? I posed these questions to former Spanish President Felipe González, the leftist leader credited with Spain's transition from a backward insular country to a modern European state. During his 14 years in office, from 1982 to 1996, González, of Spain's Socialist Workers' Party, had been the architect of Spain's incorporation into the European Union. As a passionate follower of Latin American affairs who knew the region better than any other European leader, he was the perfect person to compare the European and Latin American integration experiences. So when I interviewed him in Argentina, where we were both participating in a conference, I asked him about the chances of European-style supranationalism in Latin America.

At age 61 González still looked like a leftist intellectual-statesman. His outfit was half-bohemian, half-boardroom: black-leather jacket, light blue shirt, blue tie, and Timberland sports shoes. During the two-hour interview, González spoke passionately. He said that one of the key obstacles for adoption of a supranational system in Latin America was the absence of leadership among the region's presidents, and the nationalist and anti-capitalist sentiment in much of its political class. González said Latin America was living in a permanent deception game: politicians won elections with populist promises, and then ruled with orthodox austerity programs. In the meantime, press, intellectuals, and academics continued to embrace a nationalist and anti-capitalist rhetoric that was in open contradiction with global realities and which, in most cases, not even themselves believed. But they repeated it like parrots to win the public's applause.

But didn't the same thing happen in Spain? I asked him. Wasn't there a nationalist and anti-capitalist sentiment in his country when he first took office? Yes, he said, but joining the European Community had allowed Spain to overcome many of these stumbling blocks. At first, Spain's motivation to join the European Community was more political than economic, he said. Spanish politicians and businessmen viewed economic integration with the European Community with trepidation. They believed the plan would bring harsh economic adjustment measures, the loss of national identity, and the danger of being "annexed" by more powerful countries. "It's not that in the beginning there was a social consensus in favor of European integration and then the leaders made the decision to implement it," González explained. "Quite the contrary: Spain's adhesion to the European Community came about more as a result of political leadership than as a result of social support for the idea."

González explained that he had led the debate, and had defined it from the start as a plan of "ceding sovereignty in order to share it, not lose it, and in some cases, to even regain it." The only way to promote modernization in Spain was to exercise leadership. To convince his own Socialist Party to go along, "I would communicate with my party through the public, not with the public through the party. It was the only way to modernize and moderate a party, which had been ideologically overloaded since the dictatorship and reacted badly to the language and content of what I was offering."[xxxiii]

González used the pretext of integration with the rest of Europe to pass economic reforms through Spain's Congress that would have been very difficult to get approved under normal circumstances. Often he would present measures to Congress with little advance warning, or hide them in wider bills, he said. "Latin American presidents should exercise more leadership in the adoption of unpopular measures that produce long-term development. The so-called unpopular policies are in fact unpopular, but they are also ones people are capable of supporting," González said. In Spain, as in Latin America today, there was broad agreement that industries needed to become more competitive. "But the logical social reaction was, 'Let's start with someone else,'" González recalled. "It's always the same story: when it's time to give out, people say, 'Let's start with me.' When it's time to made budget cuts, they say, 'Let's start with someone else.'"[xxxiv]

González agreed with the general idea that Latin America should follow Europe's steps in signing supranational agreements to ensure political and economic stability, as well as democracy and human rights. He conceded that political requirements — such as a "democratic clause" — would sound offensive to many sovereignty-obsessed Latin American leaders. So he proposed a semantic pirouette. Instead of political conditions, "I talk about the need for 'standardization of behavior regarding basic freedoms and democratic functions,'" González said.

Toward the end of the interview González admitted that whenever he talked about these things in Latin America, "the truth is, nobody is convinced." He recalled that on his periodic trips to the region he often told a revealing anecdote about his days in power. Since Spain joined the European Community, the number of daily decisions taken by his country's Council of Ministers had been reduced from an average of 150 to about 15. The reason was that most of the budgetary authorizations that had to be approved by the Spanish cabinet were no longer necessary. They were decided in Brussels. But this had freed the Spanish government from a lot of red tape, and allowed it to concentrate on decisions of a more local nature, where the state's intervention could truly make a difference. "But when I speak of the crisis of the nation-state in Latin America, everybody's hair stands on end," González shrugged, with a smile. "The adoption of supranationality in Latin America would be a difficult project, but not an impossible one. What's needed is a strong dose of leadership," the ex-Spanish president concluded.

"If the Pacific gets together, poor South America!"

Not long afterward I put the same question to Fernando Henrique Cardoso, the former Brazilian president who had launched his country's opening to the world with great success during two consecutive presidential terms from 1995 to 2003. Cardoso had started his career as a left-wing sociologist and harsh critic of his country's rightist military dictatorship. After living in exile from 1964 to 1968, he was arrested upon his return to Brazil, and began his political career shortly thereafter. After being elected senator and appointed foreign minister in 1992, his popularity had soared in 1993 when, as the minister of finance, he managed to stop hyperinflation in Brazil with his "Real Plan." When I interviewed him shortly after he left office, he was still one of the most respected politicians in Brazil and throughout Latin America.

Cardoso agreed immediately with the idea of a regional accord that could work as a straitjacket to ensure political and economic stability. "But time is running against us in Latin America," he said. A few weeks before our conversation China and the 10 ASEAN countries had signed their agreement to accelerate negotiations toward a free trade agreement. And although Chinese President Hu Jintao had just visited Brazil and other countries of South America, promising $30 billion in investments and a spectacular increase in trade, the former Brazilian president was more worried than enthusiastic about the new China–Latin American relationship.

Cardoso was skeptical that China would replace the United States and Europe as Latin America's top business partner, or that China would help significantly to boost the region's economies. "I believe that's only a dream," Cardoso said. "Because sooner or later China will become a competitor." Currently, "China competes mainly with [manufacturing countries] such as Mexico and Central America, but is a huge buyer of agricultural raw materials from Brazil, Argentina, and other South American countries. But soon China is going to start exporting steel and other products of greater value-added, and they're going to compete with all of us."[xxxv]

Cardoso was especially concerned about the imminent creation of a China-ASEAN trade bloc. Even though Brazil, Argentina, and Chile were benefiting enormously from their soaring raw-material exports to China, the bonanza could end soon; once ASEAN countries gained preferential access for their own raw materials to the Chinese market, Cardoso said. "All of Latin America will suffer the consequences of the consolidation of an Asian bloc, but especially the Southern Cone, unless it immediately joins one of the big economic blocs worldwide," Cardoso said. "If the Pacific gets together in a trading bloc, and Latin America's Southern Cone doesn't, poor Southern Cone," the ex-president warned.[xxxvi]

So what should Latin America do, then? I asked him. "We must have a clearer understanding that today's world no longer tolerates a state of splendid isolation. That no longer exists," Cardoso said. Latin America needs investment, and if its countries fail to look ahead and gain access to larger markets, investors will not find it worthwhile to put their money in them. "Why are investors going to China? Why are they even putting their money in Russia? Why do they do that, when many of these countries have less in common with the West than Brazil or Argentina? Because they believe that in those countries they will find stability," Cardoso said. "Today's world requires predictability. The production process is very broad, takes a lot of time, and investments begin to be profitable much further down the road. So I believe we have to understand that that's the way the world works today, and work toward basic agreements for effective integration."[xxxvii]

Would you include a commitment to follow supranational rules among those basic agreements? I asked him. "I believe so," Cardoso answered. "That means creating institutions that go beyond nation-states. I wouldn't go as far as to propose creating a Latin American government, but at least a court that can rule on disputes, allowing agreements to be implemented by a supranational authority."

Just like Spain's former president González, Cardoso warned that the task would be difficult. "Giving up sovereignty is something that comes hard for us," he said. "Because to reach that point, Latin American leaders need to be convinced that such an agreement would be mutually beneficial. And it's not clear that Latin American leaders agree on that. By leaders I don't mean just presidents, or finance ministers, or even foreign ministers. If you go to the Congress, or the media, where these issues are debated every day, you find an impression that an agreement like this could tie us down. It scares them. We need to free ourselves from that fear."[xxxviii]

An inter-American economic charter?

I left the interview with Cardoso pleased that he supported the idea of a supranational system, and worried about the obstacles he saw along the way. But, in general, Cardoso's vision — like González's — left room for optimism. The European Union, after all, had taken several decades to become a reality, and even today — despite its many successes — remains a work in progress. And if the rise of radical populism in several countries makes it difficult to reach a region-wide supranational deal aimed at kindling investor confidence, the process can be started with a few nations, on a limited number of issues, like the European Union did in its beginnings.

One such supranational deal — although less ambitious than integration into one of the three great trade blocs — would be signing an Inter-American Economic Charter, much like the 2001 Inter-American Democratic Charter of the Organization of American States (OAS). The Democratic Charter signed by the 33 OAS member countries in Lima on Sept. 11, 2001, calls for the collective defense of democracy in the region, and requires members to put diplomatic pressure on any government that interferes with democratic processes. The agreement, born after the decision by Peru's then-president Alberto Fujimori to dissolve his nation's Congress, aimed to protect citizens from non-democratic measures taken by democratically-elected presidents. But there is no legal framework that would protect investors from arbitrary decisions by democratically elected presidents who break the rules of the game and tear up existing contracts. An Economic Charter could, for instance, include the creation of a conflict-resolution court, and help create a "community brand" that would encourage investments.

But no matter whether it takes the form of an agreement among a few pro-market Latin American nations or an OAS Economic Charter, supranationality would help protect Latin America from its vicious cycles of boom and bust. It is a political determination that cannot be postponed indefinitely. As we shall see in the next chapter, the startling growth of China and the rest of Asia — an economic tsunami sweeping the world — should prompt Latin American countries to act at once to avoid being left yet further behind.

Notes

[i] "McDonald's revamps menu, expands in China," *China Daily*, August 16, 2004.

[ii] Michael Mortimer, "Foreign investment in Latin America and the Caribbean, 2006," United Nations Economic Commission for Latin America and the Caribbean (ECLAC,) May 2007, Chart No. 2, and interview with the report's author, May 22, 2007.

[iii] Interview with Paulo Leme, Director of Emerging Markets at Goldman Sachs, March 15, 2005.

[iv] World Bank, "World Development Indicators, 2006", p. 73.

[v] Idem.

[vi] UNCTAD Investment Brief: "Foreign direct investment surged again in 2006," Nov. 1, 2007.

[vii] "Corruption, high death toll tear at Rio's police force," *The Miami Herald*, May 2, 2005.

[viii] Interview with Miguel Caballero, *Oppenheimer Presenta*, March 2005.

[ix] "Think Miami's dangerous? Try Latin America," *The Miami Herald*, July 24, 2003.

[x] "United Nations Human Development Report," 2003, Table 31, p. 117.

[xi] National Institute of Statistics and Censuses.

[xii] Interview with Juan Alberto Yaría, Buenos Aires, April 20, 2005.

[xiii] Interview with Oscar Álvarez, Honduras Minister of Security, *Oppenheimer Presenta*, December 2004.

[xiv] Interview with President Tony Saca, *Oppenheimer Presenta*, December 2004.

[xv] "Fostering regional development by securing the hemispheric investment climate," Council of the Americas, November 2004, p. 6.

[xvi] Idem, p. 9.

[xvii] Interview with U.S. Secretary of Defense Donald Rumsfeld, April 5, 2005.

[xviii] Interview with former chief of the Southern Command, General James Hill, January 18, 2005.

[xix] Idem.

[xx] Idem.

[xxi] Idem.

[xxii] "Condo Boom Worries Wall Street," *The Miami Herald*, March 11, 2005.

[xxiii] "Revelan que el salario mensual equivale a 10 dólares," France Press Agency, February 22, 2003.

[xxiv] Associated Press, February 18, 2005.

[xxv] National Institute of Statistics, Bolivarian Republic of Venezuela, "Reporte Estadístico," No. 2, 2004, p. 5.

[xxvi] CEPAL, United Nations Economic Commission for Latin America and the Caribbean, *Anuario 2004*.

[xxvii] Interview with Soledad Alvear, Miami, June 6, 2003.

[xxviii] "The EU at a glance," EU website, www.europa.eu

[xxix] International Monetary Fund, "World Economic Outlook Report," September 2004, p. 191.

[xxx] Idem.

[xxxi] Interview with Martin Tlapa, Prague, Czech Republic, September 1, 2004.

[xxxii] "Global Ranking, UNCTAD-DITE, Global Investment Prospects Assessment" (GIPA), Figure 2, Global Ranking, June 2004.

[xxxiii] Interview with Felipe González, Buenos Aires, Argentina, June 9, 2003.

[xxxiv] Idem.

[xxxv] Interview with Fernando Henrique Carodoso, November 6, 2004.

[xxxvi] Idem.

[xxxvii] Idem.

[xxxviii] Idem.

CHAPTER 2

China's Capitalist Fever

Tall tale: "The state-owned economy, that is, the socialist economy under ownership by the whole people, is the leading force in the national economy. The state ensures the consolidation and growth of the state-owned economy." (Article 7 of the Constitution of the People's Republic of China).

B EIJING — MR. HU, THE CHINESE FOREIGN MINISTRY OFFICIAL WHO WAS my escort during my visit to Beijing, pointed out a huge, rectangular building alongside the second northeastern circuit avenue as our taxi drove us downtown to an interview. "It's the Russian Embassy," Mr. Hu said. For as long as he could remember, he said, it had been the biggest diplomatic mission in the Chinese capital. "But by the end of 2006 they'll finish construction of the new U.S. Embassy, which will become the largest embassy in Beijing," he added, with a smile somewhere between amused and mischievous, as if he still couldn't believe what he was saying. In today's China things are changing so fast that not even its own officials can believe everything they hear, or even much of what they see with their own eyes.

It's no coincidence that the United States was building the largest embassy in China. According to the CIA's National Intelligence Council (NIC), China is rapidly becoming a major world power, and will become the top economic, political, and military rival of the United States by the year 2020. Not unlike what happened in early 19th century Germany and early 20st century America, China and India "will transform the geopolitical landscape, with impacts potentially as dramatic as those in the previous two centuries," the NIC report states.[i] "In the same way that commentators refer to the 1900s as the 'American Century,' the 21st century may be seen as the time when Asia, led by China and India, comes into its own... Most forecasts indicate that by 2020 China's gross national product (GNP) will exceed that of individual Western economic powers except for the United States."

Since China began its shift toward capitalism in 1978, the country has been growing at an average rate of 9 percent annually, and there's no reason to believe its growth rate will decline in the next few years. According to the Chinese government projects, by the year 2020 the country's gross national product will reach $4 trillion, and per capita income will be three times greater than it is now.[ii] That will mean the emergence of a huge Chinese middle class, which will outnumber the entire population of the U.S. and Europe and will transform the world economy. According to China's Academy of Social Sciences, the Chinese middle class — those earning between $18,000 and $36,000 a year — will grow from 20 percent of the population to 40 percent by 2020. That will mean 520 million middle-class Chinese. The global businesses that nowadays produce clothing, automobiles, and news according to the demands of North American consumers will increasingly adjust their production to the tastes of Chinese customers.

The NIC report predicts that multinational companies will become "more Asian and less Western in orientation." It continues: "While North America, Japan, and Europe might collectively continue to dominate international political and financial institutions, globalization will take on an increasingly non-Western character. By 2020, globalization could be equated in the popular mind with a rising Asia, replacing its current association with Americanization."[iii]

Indeed, once you see China you realize these predictions are not exaggerated. The capitalist fever raging in the country is apparent on every street corner. This Communist-ruled country now shelters the world's largest shopping center, where you find the latest lines from Hugo Boss, Pierre Cardin, Fendi, Guy Laroche, or any of the other top haute couture fashion houses even before they debut in Milan, Paris, or New York. The Golden Resources Shopping Mall — its immense English-language sign is in luminous yellow letters —

opened its doors in late 2004 in Zhongguancun, on the east side of Beijing, a quarter few tourists visit. The complex is part of a private business run by Huang Rulun, an entrepreneur who made a fortune in real estate in the coastal province of Fujian. Its five floors cover a total area of 140 acres and house 1,000 stores, 100 restaurants, 230 escalators, and a parking lot for 10,000 cars. The shopping center employs 20,000 people. Soon, construction will begin nearby on 110 apartment buildings, offices, and schools.

When I stopped by one Saturday afternoon, several months after it opened, workers were putting the final touches on an artificial ski slope, an aquarium with six Thai crocodiles, a cinema multiplex, and a huge gymnasium. The owners of the complex say that on weekends there are some 80,000 visitors a day. Touring the entire mall takes four days. I spent four hours there, time enough to convince myself that China is in the midst of a capitalist explosion with few parallels in world history. To my amazement, I later learned that, far from being an isolated enclave of capitalist consumerism within the Communist nation, the Golden Resources Shopping Mall is just one of 400 giant shopping centers built over the previous six years. And that's not all: it would soon lose its title as world's largest mall. Already under construction was the next record-holder, the South China Mall, which was to include a replica of Paris's Arc de Triomphe and streets that mimicked downtown Hollywood and Amsterdam. In fact, by the year 2010 at least seven of the world's 10 largest shopping centers will be in China.[iv]

The building crane: China's new national bird

Today's Beijing is like the New York of the early 20th century: a city that grows by the minute, which is on its way to becoming one of the world's two or three major capitals. Wherever you look, an ultramodern skyscraper is sprouting up. When I visited Beijing in 2005, an estimated 5,000 building cranes were working day and night, more than in any other place on earth, Chinese officials and businessmen assured me. They were probably right. My colleague Tim Johnson, Beijing correspondent for the *Miami Herald* told me, while we were having a drink by his living room window, that when he arrived in China, not one of the five skyscrapers now visible across the street existed. And how long ago had he moved in? "Thirteen months," Johnson said.

China is building as if there were no tomorrow. The pace is so frantic that workers sleep at their construction sites and apartments are occupied before the buildings are finished. In Beijing it's not uncommon to see half-built skyscrapers with lights in some of their windows. The construction boom across China is consuming 40 percent of the world's cement. In general, the buildings are gigantic glass towers similar to the most sophisticated in the West, but with oriental rooftops of contemporary design in the shape of stylized pagodas. The boom is attracting the world's most famous architects, including I. M. Pei, Rem Koolhaas and Norman Foster. What brings them here? Mainly the opportunity to do things they can't do in the United States and Europe because of high labor costs. Just as in New York or Paris at the turn of the 20th century, when labor was at its cheapest; in China today you can construct buildings with carved marble facades and exquisitely ornamented interiors. While buildings in the United States and Europe have become plainer, in part because of rising labor costs, architects in China can let their imaginations run wild, and do pretty much what they want.

There are constructions for every taste, oval, round, or pyramidal. They have only a few things in common: a modern, oriental touch and a colossal size. During my visit I met few Chinese who didn't have a tongue-in-cheek comment about the dizzying transformation of their cities. In Beijing a senior Communist Party official jokingly asked me if I knew what was the national bird of China. No, I said. "The building crane," he announced with a proud grin. In Shanghai, when I expressed amazement to an official about the futuristic look of the city, he joked that I should never blink during my stay in the city, because I might miss the opening of another high-rise.

Everything is immense, ultramodern, squeaky clean and — as the Chinese are quick to note —"the largest in Asia," or "the biggest in the world."

At the base of the skyscrapers along Beijing's principal avenue, Changan Boulevard, is a brand-new Rolls-Royce office. When I passed by, I thought it was a corporate bureau where the company sold jet engines, agricultural machinery, or other capital goods. But I was wrong: when I walked over to take a look, I found out that what Rolls-Royce sold there were its cars. Not far away were Mercedes Benz, Alfa Romeo, Lamborghini, BMW, and Audi dealerships. In China's major cities wealth is in the air, at least for the minority that has gotten rich quick over the past few years. China's dizzying economic growth has not only created a new middle class, but also a new class of super-rich, whose status was legitimated after Parliament amended the Constitution in 2004 to establish that "citizens' lawful private property is inviolable," and that "the state, in accordance with law, protects the rights of citizens to private property and their inheritance."

China's *nouveau riche*

According to the Chinese Academy of Social Sciences, approximately 10,000 Chinese businessmen have $10 million or more in personal wealth. The real number is probably much higher, once corruption and the informal economy are taken into account. China's *nouveau riche*, like their predecessors in the United States and Great Britain in the late 19th century, are eager to show off their wealth. Zhang Yuchen, one of the new millionaires, not only built a replica of the Paris's Château Maisons-Lafitte, erected in 1650 by French architect François Mansart on the River Seine, but he "improved it" — his words — by adding a sculpture garden copied from another French palace, Fontainebleau. "It cost me $50 million because we wanted it to be better than the original," Zhang said.[v] Another supermillionaire paid $12,000 for a table on New Year's Eve at the South Sea Fishing

Village restaurant in the Southern province of Guangdong. The restaurant's remaining tables were going for $6,000 each. When those news hit the Chinese media during my stay in China, another restaurant seeking to ride the publicity wave announced it was pricing its main table at $3,000 on New Year's Eve. Among other delicacies, one restaurant in southeastern China offered a chicken soup prepared with 100-year-old ginseng. The soup alone cost $30,000.[vi]

On Beijing's Changan Boulevard the traffic is just as bad as in the world's other most populated cities, if not worse. Out of 13 million inhabitants in the Chinese capital, around 1.3 million already own cars. Many of those circulating up and down Changan are Volkswagen Passats, Hondas, and Audi A6s — the favorite among top officials and businessmen, with a price tag of $60,000. According to the *China Daily*, the government English-language newspaper aimed at the foreign business and diplomatic communities, sales of luxury cars have soared over the past five years: Mercedes now sells around 12,000 per year, BMW 16,000, and Audi some 70,000. Demand has grown so much that in 2005 Mercedes created a joint venture with a Chinese group to build a factory which would manufacture as many as 25,000 cars a year in China.[vii]

On the streets people often look better dressed than in New York or London, thanks in part to the widespread piracy of top clothing brands. Chinese factories produce a significant percentage of clothing "after hours" — in addition to their clients' orders — and sell them on the black market both home and abroad at a fraction of their normal price. As a result, people in Beijing and other major Chinese cities appear to be constantly renewing their wardrobes, as if the country went Christmas shopping every week. The Chinese have traded the Mao suit for the pirated Armani. Even in the lower-middle-class and poor neighborhoods of Beijing, one sees people in inexpensive, but often new, clothes. The first reaction of the visitor to Beijing is amazement at the speed in which a country that just 30 years ago was famous for its famines has converted from communism to consumerism. As Xu Yilin, a veteran translator who had spent the best years of his life in Cuba translating Mao into Spanish, pointed out to me: "People who come back after four or five years can't believe all the new buildings and avenues they see. In this place, municipal authorities have to re-draw city maps every six months."

A monument to consumers

On my first Sunday in Beijing, before starting on a week of interviews in the Chinese capital, I made the obligatory visit to the Imperial Palace inside the Forbidden City, the majestic complex, five miles around, from which 24 emperors of the Ming and Qing dynasties ruled for centuries until 1911. The Imperial Palace was built in 1406 across from what is now Tiananmen Square, and was retained after the 1949 Communist Revolution as a reminder of China's mighty past. Millions of tourists visit every year. The 14 palaces of the Forbidden City, with names such as the Hall of Supreme Harmony, Palace of Heavenly Purity, or other variations on the same theme, are marvelously preserved even though they are made of wood and have survived several fires. Two things surprised me apart from the immense scale of the palaces in which the emperors and their concubines — at one time as many as 3,000 — lived and played. First, admiring the architectural sophistication of the imperial city, with its red walls and blue-green ornaments, as well as its arched ceilings adorned with sculptures on the vertices; I couldn't help but think that when Columbus arrived to the New World China's leaders had been living in a city as magnificent as this one for nearly a century. The second thing that caught me unaware were the signs in front of each building, which said a lot about China's 21st century communism, or what was left of it. In front of each palace was a wooden sign in English offering a brief history of the building. Beneath the text, in small print, on a blue background in white letters, was a rectangle with the inscription: "Brought to you by the American Express Company." In today's China the Communist Party is in charge of conserving Ming dynasty palaces, while leaving explanations about their historical significance to American Express.

In Shanghai, a commercial capital with a population of 16 million located where the Yangtze River empties into the Pacific, a gigantic monument to Mao still stands, faced toward the horizon. But the most-visited sculpture these days is not Mao's, but a new monument to consumers that the city recently built a few blocks away at one end of Nanjing Road, the pedestrian walkway that passes the city's main shops. There, where hundreds of thousands of people pass by each day, are two life-size bronze sculptures welcoming you to the city's commercial area. Neither is the classic statue of Mao, head held high, red flag raised in the wind, his disciples shouldering their rifles behind him. Rather, it's the figure of a woman walking proudly with her head held high, with two shopping bags in one hand. Next to her is her son, a smiling teenager with a backpack who, instead of a rifle, carries a tennis racket on his shoulder.

The Shanghai government did not officially designate this sculpture a monument to consumers, but local residents gave it that nickname. The commemorative plaque embedded in a rectangular stone two yards wide indicates that the pedestrian walkway was designed by architect Jean-Marie Charpentier in 1999. But there can be no doubt about the sculpture's symbolism: at the other end of the pedestrian walkway, 10 blocks farther along, is another monument by the same artist with the same theme. It depicts a father and daughter, shopping bags in hand. A camera hangs from the father's chest while his daughter apparently gleeful holds a half-dozen balloons. Crowds of Chinese tourists come from across the country every day to have their pictures taken with new digital cameras beside the monument to consumers. Meanwhile Mao stands, gazing out over the river, alone and unnoticed.

China grows more than it says it does

Like many of the officials I interviewed in China, Kang Xuetong, head of Latin American affairs at the Communist Party's Central Committee International Affairs Department, asked me about my impression of China. We were meeting in a protocol room at the Central Committee building, a modern four-story structure with a glass lobby that looked more like a bank than party headquarters. It was one of my most important interviews in China, and one I was very interested in: as in all Communist countries, the Central Committee is the real power behind the scenes, and its officials are often more important than those at the foreign ministry or other government agencies. Kang, an athletic man who preferred to speak in Spanish, was a key player in Chinese–Latin American relations. "I'm impressed," I assured him, with the utmost sincerity. "Annual growth topping 9 percent over several decades, $60 billion in annual investments, 250 million people lifted out of poverty. That's enough to impress anyone."

But rather than welcome my words with pride, as I expected, Kang lifted his hand in in a warning gesture and said, "Yes, but don't lose sight of the fact that we're still a developing nation. We must keep things in context. Investment in China, calculated per capita, is still lower than in Latin America. You can't just look at macro-economic figures. We still have a huge percentage of poor people. We still have many problems. You must keep in mind that any achievement in this country has to be multiplied by 1.3 billion people. And when you do that, what initially looks like a great achievement often becomes insignificant."

In interviews with other officials I couldn't help but notice the same phenomenon: Chinese officials routinely downplay their country's economic accomplishments rather than boast about them. Unlike most countries, where officials brandish favorable statistics to impress visitors and convince them the nation is on its way to grandeur, China's officials did the opposite. When I mentioned this to some of the Western ambassadors I met in Beijing, several agreed that Chinese officials never brag about their achievements. Most likely, they suggested, it's a way to keep others from viewing China as an economic rival or a strategic threat.

The Chinese regime is highly sensitive to world opinion, and it constantly reiterates China's commitment to peace, they said. The government has often gone out of its way to make that clear: in 2004, when it adopted the term "peaceful rise" to describe China's economic boom in its global context, it didn't take long for Chinese officials to sense that the term "rise" might cause alarm abroad. Almost overnight, "peaceful rise" was dropped from China's official vocabulary, and replaced with "peaceful development."

Yet, many Western economists suspect that China's practice of minimizing its economic achievements goes far beyond official comments or government slogans. "As with nearly all economic statistics from China, their reliability is suspect. The Chinese have incentives to fudge," says Ted C. Fishman, author of *China Inc.* on the country's economic boom.[viii] "In the past, the complaint was that officials nudged their numbers up to show they were doing a good job. Now a chorus of doubters argues that the numbers are unduly low," he said. In fact, there are incentives in the Chinese system to misstate economic growth: the central government is exerting growing pressure on investment bankers to channel funds to the country's poorest regions. That encourages China's thriving coastal provinces to reduce their growth figures, not only to get more investment and loans, but also to keep the central government from taxing them more heavily and diverting their money to other regions. Many poor provinces also try to play down their economic progress in order to maintain their status as "impoverished zones" and continue receiving government support.

These may be some of the reasons why national economic figures don't match the total of those reported individually by each city, province, and region. Judging from the total economic output reported by all local governments, the Chinese economy should be 15 percent bigger than the central government says in its reports to international financial institutions, Fishman says. This disparity in statistics has raised so much criticism that the central government has filed charges against 20,000 local officials in the past few years, accusing them of sending fraudulent figures to authorities in Beijing.[ix]

What's more, central government figures represent only the formal economy. If you add in the vast informal sector, China's overall economy is far bigger than is usually reported. By some measures, it is already closing in on that of the United States. The *CIA World Factbook*, a worldwide almanac available online, says that calculated in terms of purchasing power parity — one of two metrics used to measure economic activity, in this case by comparing what money buys in different economies — China's gross domestic product in 2006 amounted to 10 trillion dollars, not too far behind the U.S.'s 12.9 trillion. "Measured on a purchasing power parity (PPP) basis, China stood in 2006 as the second-largest economy in the world after the U.S.," the CIA says.[x] So while official Chinese statistics based on the official exchange rate suggest that the country's economy is a mere 20 percent the size of the U.S. economy, it may amount to nearly 80 percent, and could top it sooner than most people suspect.

The new Communist slogan: privatization

What percentage of the Chinese economy is in private hands? I asked Zhou Xi-an, the National Ministry of Development and Reform official, in my first interview in Beijing. Zhou had welcomed me a few minutes earlier at the ministry building's ceremonial hall, where I had arrived with Mr. Hu, my inseparable escort. In China, foreign journalists must schedule all interviews through the Ministry of Foreign Affairs, which provides entry visas, plans the interviews, and accompanies journalists to them. The peach-colored hall where Zhou was waiting for us was sparsely furnished, but sober and elegant. The setup, however, was uncomfortable for an interview, as I soon found. The chairs in the room were arrayed in a "U," a rectangle with one end open. The two main chairs one for Zhou, the other for his guest were both against the wall across the room from the entrance, facing the open end of the rectangle. Zhou beckoned me to the seat next to his. Behind our respective chairs were two enormous flower vases with orchids, which I soon discovered concealed a man and a woman who would serve as our interpreters. It was the kind of setting used by heads of state for photo opportunities before or after their conversations, except the seats were next to one another, which meant that you had to keep your head turned the entire time. I don't know whether it was meant to torture foreign visitors, but halfway through the interview it certainly felt that way: after nearly an hour of twisting alternatively 90 degrees to the left to look at Zhou and 180 degrees to listen to the translation coming from behind the flower vase, I found myself focused more on avoiding a stiff neck or a twisted back than hearing what Zhou was saying. But from the bits and pieces I got out of the interview, it was clear that China was more profoundly capitalist than I had imagined.

I learned the Chinese government currently controls less than 30 percent of the gross national product, while 60 percent is owned by the "non-governmental" sector and 10 percent is in collective hands. China already has 3.8 million private companies that are "the country's economic development engine, and the fastest-growing source of employment," the English-speaking flower vase located behind Zhou told me.[xi]

"Wow!" I exclaimed. "I never would have thought that 60 percent of China's economy is already in hands of the private sector."

"It's not in the hands of the private sector," Zhou was quick to reply, "It's in the hands of the non-governmental sector."

"And what is the difference between the non-governmental sector and the private sector?" I asked, twisting my neck as far as I could, searching among the orchid petals for some glimpse of the translator's face.

"Well, there are different ways of converting public companies into non-governmental businesses, depending on how the stock is issued," the voice behind the flower vase replied.

"And what's the difference between that and privatizing?" I insisted.

"Actually, not much," the talking flower vase replied, while Zhou smiled mischievously.

Communism without health insurance

The Chinese Communist Party makes all kinds of rhetorical pirouettes to disguise its conversion to capitalism, but visitors soon realize that the reforms begun in 1978 have evolved into a race toward capitalist competitiveness like few seen in history. As in the Industrial Revolution in England, or the start of the 20th century in the United States, the gap between rich and poor is widening at record speeds in today's China. Child labor is visible almost everywhere; work shifts are rarely less than 12 hours a day; millions of workers live packed in dormitories, taking turns to sleep on beds vacated by those working the previous shift; and there's no such thing as a right to free assembly, much less a right to strike. Since 1978 the government has shut down nearly 40,000 businesses deemed to be inefficient. And from 1998 to 2002, state-owned Chinese companies fired no fewer than 21 million workers, more than the entire population of New York State, and nearly twice that of Cuba.[xii]

Even health and higher education, which one might think would be free in a communist system, have to be paid for by average Chinese. University students, except the few who receive scholarships, pay tuition fees that are far from token. Forty-five percent of the country's urban population and 80 percent of its rural population have no health insurance whatsoever, as Vice-Minister of Health Gao Qiang has admitted.[xiii] "Most of them pay their own medical expenses," the Vice Minister said, according to the official news agency Xinhua. Because of the absence of medical coverage, "nearly 48.9 percent of the population cannot afford to see doctors when they fall ill, and 29.6 percent are not hospitalized when they should be."[xiv]

Today's Chinese communism is a state capitalism, a totalitarian regime whose principal goal is to improve competitiveness, whatever the cost. It tolerates no wage demands and uses its might to fire millions of people from inefficient state-owned companies or evict peasants to make way for shopping malls. For now, this model seems to be working. International companies are investing more in China than anywhere else in the world, and although inequality is expanding by leaps and bounds, progress is apparent in the big cities on the country's east coast, though less so for the 800 million people in the countryside. Per capita income has been growing at spectacular rates, the regime has lifted more than 250 million people from poverty over the past 20 years, and everything seems to indicate that it will propel at least 100 million more into the middle class over the next decade.

In Beijing restaurants I didn't see middle-aged waiters. Most were under 21. The servers, nearly always dressed in some uniform selected by the restaurant, are generally people of around 18, often assisted by busboys who are 15 if not younger. These young people live in common dorms, and are often on internships that pay them below the less than the $1 per hour minimum wage. "What time do you start work?" I asked one smiling young woman who served me at the Four Seasons Restaurant on Changan Boulevard. "At 8 in the morning," she answered happily. "And when do you finish your shift?" "At 11 at night, although I do have a break to rest in the afternoon," she answered, smiling at all times. The young woman seemed glad to have the opportunity to work at this restaurant. She told me she had competed with dozens of other applicants perhaps hundreds. She hoped to work there for another two years before returning to her hometown, which was far from Beijing. With a little money saved although in China, tipping is still not common practice she would be able to help her parents, and be left with some money for herself, she said.

Communism: "An ideal for the future"

What's left of communism in China? For several days I'd wanted to ask this question to Mr. Hu, my official escort. I decided to wait until the end of my visit or some special occasion, so as not to sour our relationship. The opportunity arose when Mr. Hu told me, raising his eyebrows as if he were breaking some extraordinary news, that his boss was inviting me to a private lunch the next day. For Mr. Hong Lei, deputy director of information at the Ministry of Foreign Affairs, it was an unusual gesture, Mr. Hu added. Very few foreign journalists have access to him. In keeping with Chinese custom, he referred to everybody as "Mr. Such-and-such," or "Mrs. Such-and-such," even when talking about his own bosses or colleagues. "Do you accept the invitation?" Mr. Hu asked. "Of course," I replied.

Mr. Hong was no more than 35, with an athletic appearance, who came to the restaurant where we agreed to meet dressed in the new uniform of Chinese officials schooled abroad: black-leather jacket, usually from a top Italian designer, over a brown turtleneck sweater. Hong seemed to be Mr. Cordiality himself, and spoke perfect English, partly thanks to the years he'd worked at the Chinese consulate in San Francisco. As always in China, the "private" lunch turned out to be a collective affair, although less crowded than others. Mr. Hong was accompanied by his assistant, Mr. Wang Xining, who couldn't have been more than 30 years old, and I by my ever-present escort, Mr. Hu. After the meal, a delicious menu of no fewer than 10 shared dishes, and after spending nearly two hours talking about the privatizations and other free-market economic reforms China was undertaking, I fired the question that was lingering in my mind all along: "So then," I said, "what's left of communism in this country?"

Mr. Hong's demeanor changed instantly. His smile was suddenly gone, replaced by a professorial look. He adopted the air of gravity Communist officials tend to use when explaining the world to infidels, placed his chopsticks on the table, and said, "We continue to be Communists. But we now think that communism is a long-term goal, which may takes us two or three hundred years to reach." Both of his assistants nodded in silence. Then Mr. Hong added, "During the 1950s, our perception of communism was incorrect. We made the mistake of adopting policies aimed at implementing communism overnight. But, as Marx himself said, communism must take root in a society that has already achieved material well-being."

When I responded with an ironic smile, suggesting that his explanation was a noble attempt to save face after all, it's hard to believe that you will build socialism with capitalist recipes Mr. Hong continued his speech, going into greater detail. Maintaining his newfound solemnity, he explained, "We are building socialism with Chinese characteristics. And at this stage, what characterizes our decisions is pragmatism." In 1997, he said, the Chinese Communist Party plenum had determined that government decisions at all levels should fulfill three requirements, commonly known as "the three criteria." The first was: "Whether the measure leads to improved productivity." The second, "Whether the measure improves people's lives." The third: "Whether the measure contributes to strengthening the nation." And, Mr. Hong continued explaining, "according to our new policy, everything that fulfills these three requirements is good and everything that doesn't is bad. And these criteria have served us very well."

But weren't these explanations an excuse by the Communist Party to keep its hold on power without admitting the utter failure of its ideological model? I asked. Since Mr. Hong had lived many years abroad and was used to dealing with Western journalists, I decided he wouldn't get too irritated by the question, since he had probably heard it before. "Absolutely not. In China we have a one-party democracy, which is what we need," he answered, unflappable. His argument was simple: Communist rule was essential to maintain stability. China, with 1.3 billion people of 55 different ethnicities, harbors so many dormant social conflicts that a multiparty system would be unthinkable, he said. With 800 million people in poverty, "we can't run the risk of unrest," he added.

However, the Communist Party was gradually allowing more room for democracy within its decision-making process, he continued. The party was opening up to the point that it no longer accepted as members only workers, farmers, and the military, but since 2002 it also accepted businesspeople, intellectuals, and employees of multinational corporations. And all decisions were subject to a rigorous process of consultation among all party sectors. China had a democracy, whose sole difference with that of the United States or Europe was that all debates took place among the ruling party's rank and file, he added.

Unable to keep from shaking my head and smiling, I told him that to foreign eyes it was hard not to see China as a country on a rapid march towards capitalism. If 60 percent of the economy was already in private or semi-private hands, and if the Chinese government itself admitted that 100,000 state-owned companies would be privatized in the near future, and if privatization of state companies was "the main economic development engine" — as Dr. Zhou of the National Development and Reform Commission had told me — you didn't need a Ph.D. in economics to conclude that China was leaving communism behind, and was clinging to Marxist rhetoric only to justify its monopoly on power.

Upon leaving the restaurant, on our way down the escalator of the shopping mall we were in, I commented to one of Mr. Hong's deputies that there's a saying in the United States, that if something looks like a duck, walks like a duck, and quacks like a duck, it must be a duck. "We have a similar proverb," the young deputy responded, shrugging his shoulders and smiling. "President Deng Xiaoping used to say it doesn't matter whether the cat is black or white, as long as it catches mice."

The Asian model of democracy

While surfing the Internet in Beijing, I couldn't help thinking with horror that one of the scenarios offered by the CIA's National Intelligence Council report on the future of democracy in China could apply elsewhere in the world, including Latin America and Africa. The NIC suggested that in the next few years "Beijing may pursue an 'Asian way of democracy,' which could involve elections at a local level and a consultative mechanism on a national level; perhaps with the Communist Party retaining control over the central government."[xv] The CIA's think tank made no specific forecasts regarding the export of China's political model to other countries, but in a section on Latin America, it warned about the region's growing disenchantment with democracy and its rising impatience with the crime wave in its biggest cities. "Indeed, regional experts foresee an increasing risk of the rise of charismatic, self-styled populist leaders... [who] could have an autocratic bent,"[xvi] the report said. It would certainly be conceivable that Chávez and other self-proclaimed saviors of the fatherland in Latin America might well embrace this Asian model of democracy state capitalism with leftist rhetoric and limited political freedoms as more palatable than Western-style representative democracy.

In China there is neither democracy nor freedom of speech. The Communist Party runs the government. All newspapers are government-run and controlled by the party's Ministry of Propaganda. While China's newspapers — at least English-language ones — are livelier and more self-critical than their counterparts in the former Soviet Union or Cuba's daily *Granma*, they stress the issues that the government wants to emphasize and censors those it doesn't want talked about. The *China Daily*, which I read front to back every day for several months, offers well-documented, well-written articles, like the best newspapers in the United States or Great Britain. It isn't unusual for the paper to feature stories criticizing this or that government policy, or to run columns calling the government's attention to overlooked environmental problems or corruption, or breaking bad economic or political news.

But the newspaper is clearly aimed at projecting an image of modernity, economic openness, and capitalism, so that its readers in the foreign investment community feel increasingly comfortable with the "Chinese miracle." Good news are played on the front. Bad news, if published at all, are often buried inside, inconspicuous and brief. Moreover, the issues that most worry Chinese leaders are conspicuously absent. You find virtually no news related to international human rights groups' charges about mass executions of criminals, child labor, the Falun Gong religious sect, or China's occupation of Tibet.

One night, browsing the Internet in my room at the Jianguo Hotel in Beijing before going out for dinner, I decided to find out for myself how much information from the outside world you could get in China. I tried to open the Amnesty International home page to see if Chinese people with Internet access — 80 million strong, according to government figures — could learn what the human rights organization had to say about their country. I didn't have much luck: instead of Amnesty International, I got a pop-up saying "This page cannot be displayed." It was the standard sign you get when you can't access a site because of technical difficulties or because the page has expired. I tried accessing another prominent human rights group, Human Rights Watch, again to no avail. The same thing happened when I tried to access Greenpeace, or when I attempted to open www.state.gov, the U.S. State Department page, which contains human rights reports that criticize human rights and environmental abuses in many countries, including China. Increasingly curious, I conducted the same test with Western media. I unsuccessfully tried to enter the *Miami Herald* site, to see if I could read my own columns. *Time* magazine, same thing. BBC, same thing.

Oddly enough, I was able to enter the *New York Times* page. Later that evening I commented on the results of my rudimentary test of China's press freedoms over dinner with a Latin American diplomat.

He explained to me, off-handedly, how censorship works in China: some Internet sites are fully blocked, and others the government allows to be read — so people won't be entirely cut off from the rest of the world — while blocking specific information that might be embarrassing to the regime.

"You can read whatever you want from the New York Times, as long as there are no articles criticizing China," the diplomat told me. When the newspaper publishes an unfavorable article on China, that page magically disappears, while everything else in the paper remains. Whenever hackers create a shortcut or provide a link to censored news, and the new site spreads like wildfire through a chain of e-mails within the country, it takes government censors less than five minutes to block the link, the diplomat said. According to what I later heard from other Western diplomats in Beijing, China has more than 30,000 government censors dedicated exclusively to blocking Internet pages. "Don't forget that if there's something that this country has in excess, it's labor," the Latin American diplomat explained to me that night.

And he probably wasn't exaggerating: a study by the Berkman Center of Harvard Law School sought over 204,000 Internet sites through Google and Yahoo search engines in China, and found that 19,000 were blocked.[xvii] Virtually no sites associated with China that contained the words "democracy," "equality," "Tibet," or "Taiwan" could be accessed inside the country. Even if the Internet pages were reconfigured the next day with a new address, they disappeared within minutes, the group said. According to Amnesty International, in 2004 at least 54 persons in China were either arrested or sentenced to terms ranging from two to 14 years "for expressing their opinions or circulating information on the Internet."[xviii] As if to dispel any suspicions I might have that China is no longer a police state, the Latin American diplomat added casually, "You shouldn't have the slightest doubt that they've already entered your hotel room, gone through all your papers, and made copies of everything you've got on your computer. As far as human rights are concerned, communism is alive and well."

Security without rights

Street crime is not the problem in big Chinese cities like it is in Latin America. Even though I wasn't able to learn more than a handful of basic words in Chinese, both Chinese officials and Western diplomats living in China told me I could safely walk the streets or catch a cab any time of day or night.

No one knows the exact reason for the relative security of major Chinese cities, but everyone suspects it's because the punishment for crimes is draconian, if not barbaric. While the Chinese government does its best to keep information about executions from being leaked abroad, it routinely uses capital punishment as an exemplary measure, and thus makes information about executions public within the country. As a Western diplomat told me, mothers may well be invited to attend their children's executions, and are even allowed to choose the bullets with which they will be killed, so that when they return to their hometowns they will share the horror stories with their neighbors. When I asked other diplomats and journalists in Beijing if this story was true, nearly all said it was impossible to confirm, although many added it was likely. None suggested it was a fabrication.

Amnesty International reports that more people are executed every year in China than all the other countries of the world combined. "According to one estimate based upon internal Chinese Communist Party (CCP) documents, 60,000 people were executed in the four years from 1997 to 2001; an average of 15,000 people per year," Amnesty International said.[xix] That means that every year, the Chinese government executes one person for every 86,000 inhabitants, making China home not only to world's greatest number of executions — no surprise, since it's the most populous country — but also to the second-highest per capita rate of executions as well, after Singapore.

"My Mexican partner was always on vacation"

Before visiting China, I had often asked myself if 450 million Latin Americans could ever compete with 1.3 billion Chinese, who live in a country that offers investors cheaper labor, no strikes, and workers willing to sleep at their factories. But after a few days in China I realized that the challenge facing Latin Americans was actually much greater. A casual conversation with a U.S. businessman suggested that China's competitive advantage goes far beyond cheap labor or limited workers' rights.

On a tourist bus during a visit to the Great Wall, I happened to be sitting next to a 30-something businessman from Indiana, who was accompanied by a Chinese-American who was one of his managers. During the hour-and-a-half trip to the wall the businessman told me his company had been producing plastic construction pipes in China for three years. They used to manufacture the pipes in Mexico, but had decided to switch to China, he said. I told him I wasn't surprised: it was impossible for Mexico to compete with the 72 cents an hour companies pay workers in China. To my surprise, the businessman shook his head, and said the reason his company moved to China had nothing to do with labor costs: it was all about quality. "My Chinese partners constantly reinvest in their factory. As soon as I pay them for a shipment, they buy new equipment, or buy better materials. And they are always available, twenty-four hours a day," he said. "With my previous Mexican partners, it was the other way around: as soon as I paid them, they would go on vacation or buy a luxury apartment in Miami. They wouldn't reinvest in their companies or improve the quality of their materials, like the Chinese. For me, it was an easy decision to make."

Clearly, one can't generalize from one conversation with a businessman during a tourist excursion. Maybe I had run into someone who had the misfortune of dealing with a Mexican partner who was a party animal, or the good luck to hook up with a particularly conscientious Chinese partner. It's also true that, on another occasion, I spoke with a top executive of a U.S. food company who told me that his firm was expanding not only in China, but in Mexico as well. When I asked what had led them to invest in Mexico, he told me that Mexican workers were more dependable than their Chinese counterparts. "Chinese workers are harder-working than Mexicans, but they will also jump ship and move to another company as soon as they are offered a few cents more per hour; so in China you lose a lot of money constantly training new workers. In Mexico you can train a qualified worker, and chances are he will stick with the company for several years," the executive said.

China's impact on Latin America

I had set up a meeting with Dr. Jiang Shixue several weeks in advance, eager to learn how China's best-known Latin America specialist viewed the region, and whether he saw China as an opportunity or a danger for Latin America. Dr. Jiang, who spoke fluent English but no Spanish, is a senior researcher of the Chinese Academy of Social Sciences' Department of Latin American Studies, the state-run think tank which advises the foreign ministry and other government agencies. His department, he said, is the world's largest Latin American study center. With a staff of 55, including 40 full-time researchers dedicated to studying the region, it publishes the only magazine on Latin America written in Chinese.

Dr. Jiang had just written a book titled *Comparative Study of the Development Models in Latin America and East Asia,* which took him five years to research. It included several articles that had already appeared, including "Globalization and Latin America," published in 2003. In it he wrote that globalization "increases the interdependency and economic integration of developed and underdeveloped nations, a process that tends to improve the latter's position in the international arena."[xx] He continued: "Globalization facilitates the influx of capitals and technologies to developing nations, while also giving them an opportunity to expand their markets."[xxi]

But what was even more interesting, coming from a Communist Party think tank, was the paragraph at the end of his essay, which showed a stark difference between China and Latin America: while "antiglobalization sentiment" in Latin America was "evident," in China it was "low."[xxii] While in Latin America, the intellectual and political elites were resisting globalization, Communist China had embraced it enthusiastically.

As soon as he sat down on a couch next to China's red flag in the conference room of what was once the prime minister's headquarters, I went straight to the point that had brought me there: to understand why Asia was growing so much faster than Latin America. "Could you explain your conclusions in more detail?" I asked. Dr. Jiang said he had looked into China's and Latin America's development, and had found major cultural and economic differences. Culturally, China is to this day heavily influenced by the teachings of Confucius, the 5th century B.C. philosopher who stressed education as a pillar of progress. Confucianist philosophy encourages parents to invest time and money in educating their children, calls on people to save money, and stresses obedience to authority, he said.

Chinese people will save their entire lives to pay for the best schools for their children, something rarely seen in Latin America, Dr. Jiang said. Likewise, they tend to respect authority. "One of the things that Chinese businessmen complain about Latin America are the labor strikes. A lot of them say that Latin American workers are on strike all the time," Dr. Jiang told me. But he added that he himself took cultural theories with a grain of salt. "Culture can explain some things, but not all. The way we see ourselves is just another piece of data to be taken into account," he said.

Dr. Jiang's book comparing East Asian development with Latin America focused mainly on economic policies. Learning from the successes and failures of both regions, he had reached several basic conclusions, he said. "First, the economic openness model adopted by East Asian countries several decades ago and more recently by Latin America is superior to previous economic models," he began.

"Now, we can prove that such dependency theory, which was very popular in the sixties, has been fully surpassed." The second conclusion of his book was that "the State should play a major role in economic development. But it should neither interfere too much, nor remain too distant." Other conclusions were that while Latin America had embarked on domestic economic reforms and economic openness simultaneously, China had carried out its economic reforms first — to make its industries more competitive — and only then started opening up to the world. And while Latin America had sought integration with the global economy "rapidly and audaciously," China had done it "gradually and with caution" over the past two decades. In other words, China had moved more slowly, but had stayed in course. The final balance, according to Jiang, was that Latin America's integration into the global economy had been "good in general," but China's had been "much better."

When I left my interview with Dr. Jiang, I couldn't help but think how absurd the situation was. While in Latin America Chávez and his followers were banging the table denouncing "savage capitalism" and "U.S. imperialism," here I was, deep in the heart of Communist China, in front of a prominent government adviser sitting next to a red flag; and hearing that economic openness had proven far superior to state-planned economies; and that the dependency theory blaming the developing world's backwardness on U.S. exploitation had been "fully surpassed." All this was coming only hours after Dr. Zhou, the senior official from the National Development and Reform Commission, had proudly pointed out to me that the conversion of state-owned businesses to the private sector and openness to the world were "the main engine of economic growth" in his country.

It was no coincidence that foreign investment in China had shot up from $40 billion in 2000 to $60 billion in 2004, while foreign investment in Latin America had plummeted from $85 billion to less than $40 billion during the same period.[xxiii] One had to travel halfway across the world from Latin America to see the extent to which the region was out of synch with Asia's booming economies.

China's investments: fact or fiction?

Since late 2004, when Chinese President Hu Jintao made a nearly two-week tour through Argentina, Brazil, Chile, and Cuba on his way to a summit about the Asia-Pacific Economic Cooperation (APEC) in Santiago, Chile, there have been enormous expectations in the region of an imminent boom in Chinese trade and investments. And no wonder. The Chinese president had spent more time in Latin America that year than President Bush had. Then, a few weeks later, Chinese Vice President Zeng Qinghong traveled to Mexico, Venezuela, and Peru, spending more time in the region than U.S. Vice President Dick Cheney had spent in the previous four years.

President Hu promised his hosts a mountain of gold, and his extended visit doubtless showed China's renewed interest in the region. Yet some Latin American presidents or their ministers got carried away by their enthusiasm, and may have read more between the Chinese president's words than the leader intended. Perhaps because he expressed himself poorly or was mistranslated, or due to an overly optimistic interpretation by his hosts, President Hu generated enormous headlines when he was quoted as saying at a November 12, 2004, speech before the Brazilian Congress that China would invest $100 billion in Latin America over the next 10 years. "China to invest 100 billion in Latin America before the year 2014," a euphoric front page of *Folha de São Paulo* shouted out. In Argentina, the newspaper *Clarín* printed a full-page story under the headline, "China vows to invest 100 billion dollars in Latin America." The subtitle said that the Chinese president had assured his hosts that "this figure would be reached over the next 10 years."[xxiv] The excitement over the potential wave of Chinese investment was such that the Argentine media reported a sharp rise in Chinese-language studies in the Argentine capital: the number of students shot up overnight from a handful to over six hundred.

But judging from what I was told by officials in Beijing, a more realistic projection of potential Chinese investment in Latin America over the next few years would be significantly lower. With luck, it will reach $4 billion dollars over the next decade, they said, or less than a twentieth of what South American media had quoted the Chinese president as saying. The Chinese officials I interviewed had been forewarned that I would be asking this question — the Minister of Foreign Affairs had requested I deliver my main questions written in advance, so that they would be better prepared. And most of them smiled when I asked them about the alleged $100 billion investment plans. The figure had been vastly overblown, they said. When I asked Dr. Zhou, of the Ministry of National Development and Reform, about the Latin American press reports about the projected Chinese investments, he responded that the figure was a media "exaggeration." He said: "I read those articles in the media too. As far as I know, none of it is true. I have no idea which was the source for these news stories."

Days later Mr. Hu, my official escort, provided me with a written answer to my question from the Ministry of Foreign Affairs regarding how much China expected to invest in Latin America by 2010. "We will do everything possible to increase investments, which we believe will double the present sum by the end of the decade," the document read. Current direct investments from China in the region, according to the Chinese government, totaled 1.6 billion dollars at the time.[xxv]

"We'll try to increase trade"

But China was much more optimistic about prospects for increasing bilateral trade with the region. According to the Ministry of Foreign Affairs' written answers to my questions, "We will try to increase the volume of bilateral trade one hundred and fifty percent by 2010, breaking the 100 billion-dollar mark." As several officials explained to me later, China's main commercial interest in Latin America was the purchase of raw materials, such as oil in Venezuela, soybeans in Argentina and Brazil, and copper in Chile. If the Chinese economy continued growing at current rates, China would be in need of more and more raw materials. And one of the main priorities of the Chinese regime was to diversify its supply sources so as not to depend exclusively on the United States or the Middle East. For example, China imports 100 million tons of oil per year, nearly all of it from the Middle East. China now wants to diversity its import sources, and was starting to create a strategic oil reserve, like such of the United States, in order to be prepared in case its supplies were disrupted because of instability in the Middle East.

At the same time, as Latin American diplomats in Beijing pointed out to me, another key Chinese goal in Latin America was one that Chinese officials rarely discussed in public: progressively installing Chinese factories in Latin American countries which have free trade agreements with the United States, in order to be able to export to the United States through third countries if Washington ever decided to reduce its huge trade deficit by putting the brakes on Chinese imports. "The Chinese think long-term, and this wouldn't be an unusual scenario," a South American ambassador told me, adding that an influx of Chinese manufacturing plants into Latin America would be great news for the region. Although trade with Latin America, represented only 3 percent of China's foreign commerce, for many Latin American nations the Chinese trade projections were nothing to sneeze at. By 2004 China had already become one of Brazil, Argentina and Chile's top three trading partners. And if China were to choose Latin America as a backdoor channel to secure its status as number one exporter to the United States in years to come, the economic benefits for Latin America would be even greater.

In the short term, judging from what I learned from senior Chinese officials in Beijing and from the Foreign Ministry's written answers to my questions, China's new interest in Latin America may be more political than economic. The Foreign Ministry's letter started out stressing that "We should increase our mutual support in the political arena, in order to jointly face major global challenges at the United Nations and other international fora."

In plain English, the Foreign Ministry was saying that China wants to team up with Latin America to win support for some of its key foreign policy objectives, such as reforming the United Nations, keeping Taiwan from gaining ground in the diplomatic or business arena, and staving off U.S. criticism on issues such as human rights or the occupation of Tibet. The Foreign Ministry letter said that "China wants to establish normal relations with all countries from Latin America and the Caribbean." Since about a dozen Latin American and Caribbean countries still maintained diplomatic ties with what China calls "the province of Taiwan," this could only mean that the Chinese regime wants to push Taiwan out of the region. Deeper economic, political, and cultural penetration in Latin America would help China convince these renegades to cut off relations with Taiwan, and join the convoy of nations who maintain official ties with continental China.

In light of all this, "how much do you realistically expect China–Latin American relations to grow in coming years?" I asked Dr. Jiang of the Institute of Latin American Studies. In general, he replied, he was fairly optimistic. Up until now, Latin America's image in China was pretty bad. "The Chinese press talks about the threat of 'Latin Americanization' when referring to the danger of hyperinflation, chaos, or violence," Dr. Jiang said. "There is even talk of a 'Latin American syndrome' in the sports pages, when sports writers talk about teams fighting. But all that is changing. President Hu's visit was well received by the Chinese press, and now many in China are starting to view the region with different eyes." In addition, President Hu's visit kindled interest among Chinese businessmen: for the first time, several approached Dr. Jiang's institute to get information about Latin American countries. "China will become more and more interested in Latin America because of its strategic interests," Dr. Jiang concluded. "I've held this post for 24 years, and I've never seen this much enthusiasm about Latin America."

Who wins? China, Latin America, or both?

Dr. Jiang was probably right. China was more interested than ever in improving relations with Latin America. But who held the winning hand? China, Latin America, or both?

Clearly, for many Latin American countries China's rise — or "peaceful development," whichever you prefer — may have several advantages. First, China's impressive growth has led the country to become the world's largest consumer of raw materials, surpassing the United States; and has triggered a significant rise in world prices of agricultural goods, oil, and minerals. That has been a blessing for much of South America. To Chile's delight, copper prices rose 37 percent in 2005, and both aluminum and zinc went up 25 percent that year. In a major stroke of good luck for Venezuela, oil prices shot up 33 percent. The same thing happened with Argentine and Brazilian soybeans and other agricultural exports from South America. If China continued growing at its present rates, Latin America would benefit from high international prices on raw materials for years to come. Except for Mexico and much of Central America, whose main exports are manufactured goods, Latin America would find China's voracious appetite for raw materials a blessing.

Second, virtually all Latin American countries — especially Mexico and the Caribbean — could expect to become major beneficiaries of an expected boom in tourism from China. During President Hu's visit to the region in 2004 China announced it would add several Latin American countries to its list of nations allowed to receive groups of Chinese tourists. That could be a gold mine for Latin America's tourist sector: according to the World Tourism Organization, by 2020 no fewer than 100 million Chinese will be traveling abroad every year. An estimated 20 million Chinese already visit foreign countries annually, but the vast majority go to neighboring Asian nations. Increasingly, Chinese tourists —most of them on packaged tours authorized by the Beijing government— are heading toward other parts of the world. If Latin America could promote its beaches and other destinations in China, and capture even a small percentage of the upcoming avalanche of Chinese tourists, they would see their hospitality industries flourish. "If I could get 1 or 2 percent of 100 million Chinese tourists to come to Mexico, I'd be more than happy," Mexico's ambassador to Beijing, Sergio Ley López, told me. "We'd be talking about 2 or 3 million visitors per year."[xxvi]

Third, just as China could benefit from a "strategic consensus" with Latin America in the United Nations, Latin American nations would also find a political alliance with China to their advantage on such matters such as the reform of the Security Council, where Latin America is seeking a permanent seat; and other issues on which developing countries are making demands of the United States and Europe. On many, there is a clear convergence of Chinese and Latin American diplomatic agendas.

However, a "special relationship" with China — like the one proposed by South American officials during President Hu's 2004 visit — might bring as many risks as benefits. First, close trade ties with China could result in an even greater avalanche of China's low-cost goods, many of them pirated and sold in the black market. That could become a nightmare for Latin American industrialists. During President Hu's visit to South America, several Latin American presidents, delighted by China's growing purchases of their exports, gave China a "market economy" status, a legal formula that among other things makes it much more difficult for Latin American countries to file lawsuits against China's subsidized exports, black market goods, dumping, or products manufactured in violation of international labor laws. Will Latin American industries be able to compete with Chinese factories, where people work 12-hour shifts, sleep at their workstations, and earn less than half what Latin Americans do? And how will Latin American industrialists protect themselves against black-market Chinese exports, which — in part because manufacturers there ignore intellectual property rights — sell at much cheaper prices? As I discovered first-hand on the streets of major Chinese cities, it is obvious that the Chinese government does little to discourage the black market.

Two Rolexes for 12 Dollars

On the plane from Beijing to Shanghai I read a recent article from China's official press claiming that the country was making a great progress in its struggle against intellectual property crimes. "The whole country has been mobilized in the campaign against intellectual property rights' infringements,"[xxvii] China's vice-premier Wu Yi said. He announced that the crackdown — launched two months earlier — had already brought more than 1,000 indictments, and said government prosecutors were tracking down producers and vendors of black market goods "in every corner of the country."

But in Shanghai the sale of black-market goods took place openly, under the eyes of police officers. The moment I stepped out of my hotel, an early 20th century palace on the city's main boulevard, I was approached by a street peddler. The man didn't speak a word of English, but he knew enough to do business: "Rolex?" he asked me, discreetly taking a fistful of watches out of his left pocket. When I shook my head no, he removed another fistful of watches from his right pocket, pretending to look around to make sure no one was watching, and asked me again: "Cartier?" When I shook my head again, he continued: "Bulgari?" "Omega?" "Raymond Weil?" I started walking down Nanjing Road, accelerating my pace to get rid of the hawker, who obviously had more brands to offer than I could possibly identify. But the scene repeated itself every half a block. The vendors of pirated luxury watches were asking 200 yuan —$25— per watch. But if you refused, they'd end up offering two Rolexes for $12.

I was even more surprised when, visiting Old Shanghai —the part of the city that had been its economic and trade center under the Yuan, Ming, and Ping dynasties, and which now was a tourist center— I found black-market Rolex watches displayed in stands on the street, in full view of the public. Perhaps China's regime was vigorously pursuing vendors of black-market products in every corner of the country, as the vice-premier had said, but it was doing no such thing in Shanghai, which had become the Mecca of China's black market. Plus, if Chinese authorities were turning a blind eye at home, where they wielded unquestionable power, why wouldn't they do the same thing abroad, where they would find it much easier to claim the wrongdoers were both out of sight and out of reach?

Latin America's "curse": Raw materials

But many Latin American countries faced a much bigger threat from China than an invasion of black-market Chinese knock-offs — a long-term reliance on exports of raw materials. Their new economic relationship with China — whether trade or investment — was based almost exclusively on the extraction and export of raw materials. That could only increase Latin American dependence on primary products, and discourage the region from producing more value-added exports that are sold at higher prices in world markets.

A study by the Goldman Sachs investment bank entitled "A Realistic Look at Latin American and Chinese Trade Relations" concluded that the growth of trade between the two sides was a product of contemporary circumstance. It was not likely to stimulate a durable increase in Latin American exports of more sophisticated goods to China, because Latin American factories lacked the capacity to meet the demands of the vast Chinese market. The study concluded that, unless Latin American countries got to work and enacted the same reforms China had carried out to become more competitive — making labor and tax laws more flexible, and improving their education systems to create a more highly skilled workforce — they would continue to be exporters of raw materials, whose prices would remain below those of finished goods on the world market, and they would fall farther and farther behind.

Nor would the regional investments promised by China, whatever they turned out to be, help much either, because they would be almost entirely aimed at infrastructure improvements intended to facilitate extraction of raw materials. That would do little to push

Latin America to increase value-added production, the study said. China's investment in oil wells in Venezuela, railroads and seaports in Brazil and Argentina, and the copper industry in Chile "is a limited contribution" to the region's technological development or to the diversification and sophistication of its exports, it said. Mexico is of a particular concern: its trade balance with China had deteriorated from a deficit of $2.7 billion in 2000 to $12.4 billion in 2004. This gap seemed certain to widen and was projected to reach a deficit of $16.4 billion by 2010. While Mexico was increasing its metal exports to China, "its total exports to China remained very low, and could not eclipse the country's growing losses of export sales to third markets (such as the United States) or the increasing penetration of Chinese imports in the Mexican market."[xxviii]

The Goldman Sachs study concluded that Latin America was fooling itself if it believed that opportunities with China were a viable substitute for free trade agreements with the United States or the European Union. An economic alliance with China would only perpetuate that status of many Latin American countries as "extraction economies," whereas trade deals with the United States and Europe — especially if both reduced their obscene farm subsidies — would allow the region sell more sophisticated products, which in turn would speed up the region's economic growth.

Was the Goldman Sachs report tainted by a Wall Street view of the world, or was it reflecting a reality? The U.N. Development Program (UNDP), an international agency that cannot be accused of free-market bias, reached a similar conclusion. A UNDP study said Latin America's growing dependency on raw material exports was, in effect, a major economic threat. In its 2005 Human Development Report, the UNDP referred to this phenomenon as "the resource curse."[xxix]

"When it comes to human development, some export activities have better record than others. Oil and mineral wealth generated through exports can be bad for growth, bad for democracy, and bad for development," the UNDP said.[xxx] Half of the combined populations of the 34 largest exporters of oil in the developing world live in absolute poverty, and two-thirds of those countries are not democratic, the report said. It was no coincidence that as oil prices rose, new petro-dictators were emerging around the world, and existing ones were getting bolder.

Latin American countries that chiefly sell agricultural products were also being left behind, the report said. "In value-added manufacturing, Latin America has been losing market share relative to East Asia," the UNDP said. "More than 50 developing countries depend on agriculture for at least one-quarter of their export earnings. These countries are on the downward escalator."

UNDP figures regarding Latin American dependency on raw materials are indeed frightening: primary goods account for 72 percent of total exports in Argentina; 83 percent in Bolivia; 82 percent in Chile; 90 percent in Cuba; 64 percent in Colombia; 88 percent in Ecuador; 87 percent in Venezuela; 78 percent in Peru; and 66 percent in Uruguay. By comparison, primary goods represent only 9 percent of China's exports and 22 percent of India's. The UNDP report concluded that if Latin American countries continue confining their exports to raw materials or low value-added manufactured goods, the region will not reach the current level of development of the United States until 2177.

What's more, there is no guarantee that, even if China continues growing for the foreseeable future, South American countries will be able to continue selling it raw materials as they had in recent years. Under the 2004 trade deal with the 10-member Association of Southeast Asian Nations (ASEAN) — including Indonesia, Malaysia, the Philippines, Singapore, and Thailand — to create the largest free trade zone in the world by 2010; China would soon be buying more raw materials from its Asian neighbors. Most ASEAN countries are agricultural producers, and they were scheduled to begin exporting farm goods to China under preferential conditions in 2007.

Chinese officials readily admit that China will be expanding its trade with its neighbors at the cost of a drop in trade with other parts of the world. When I asked Dr. Zhou, of the Chinese National

Development and Reform Commission, what would be the impact of China's trade with ASEAN on China's overall international trade, he answered, "Currently, ASEAN countries represent 30 percent of our international trade. We hope that, once the free trade agreement comes into effect, that percentage will grow to 40 percent."[xxxi]

The "contagion effect" of Chinese corruption

The greatest danger posed by a special Latin American relationship with China, however, is the possibility of setting back the region's anti-corruption and pro-human rights agenda by decades. Unlike the United States and the European Union, China has no serious anti-bribery laws, and those that do exist are enforced less stringently than similar laws elsewhere in the world. Since the Lockheed bribery scandals in 1977, when the United States passed the Foreign Corrupt Practices Act prohibiting U.S. companies from bribing foreign officials; successive administrations in Washington have made progress in convincing other countries to apply similar anti-bribery laws. Over the past few years — especially after the financial scandals of Raúl Salinas de Gortari in Mexico and Vladimiro Montesinos, Peru's former chief of intelligence — the European Union has joined the fight, signing the antibribery convention of the Organization for Economic Co-operation and Development (OECD), which prohibits tax deductions that countries like France and Germany were giving their businesses on the "commissions" paid in Latin America when bidding for contracts. Although the growing U.S.-European commonfront against bribery still has far to go — the French multinational Alcatel's 2004 bribery scandal in Costa Rica and Sweden's construction giant Skanska's Argentine corruption case in 2007 were just some examples of how much remains to be done — the progress is unquestionable. Since the late 1990s the OECD has approved agreements under which multinational companies will pay increasing fines if they bribe foreign officials, either directly or through subsidiaries.

But Chinese officials and business people are not subject to rules such as the U.S. Foreign Corrupt Practices Act or the OECD's anticorruption agreements. Who will keep them from freely handing out cash to Latin American officials in order to win major bids? Judging by Chinese behavior to date, it will be hard to stop them. According to the Transparency International Corruption Perceptions Index, Chinese companies are among the world's most bribery-prone. In Transparency's ranking of the world's most honest countries to do business in, compiled by surveying multinational corporation executives around the world; China is ranked second to last. [xxxii] According to Transparency's president Peter Eigen, the level of bribes paid by Chinese companies is "intolerable."[xxxiii] Will Latin America be able to avoid a corruption "contagion effect" if its governments dramatically expand their business dealings with China? Barring major changes in China, it's doubtful.

Not only in China's relations with the outside world but domestically as well, corruption is an integral part of its new capitalism. As in many other Communist states, Chinese capitalism was born outside the law. The country's decades-long ban on private property forced people who wanted to make money to operate on the black market. According to the official story told by China's current authorities, the current wave of economic reforms was inspired by the economic success of 18 farmers in the village of Xiaogang, in Anhui province, who had signed a secret agreement — illegal at the time — to work land individually within their co-op. These 18 farmers, who were living in the direst poverty, signed a document with their thumbprints in December 1978, knowing they risked being jailed, or shot, if discovered. It wasn't long, though, before the production on their plots of land had increased dramatically, and the news reached the ears of national leader Deng Xiaoping. Instead of ordering the farmers punishement, as many of his aides expected, Deng requested a study of how they had managed to increase productivity. Soon after, Deng ordered private farm experiments in several provinces. Then, he extended the system to the entire country.

Like the original 18 farmers, millions of other Chinese entrepreneurs started out in business by breaking the law, making use of secret pacts, bribes, and all sorts of shenanigans in order to survive. Fishman, the author of *China, Inc.*, points out that the most frustrating part for many foreign businessmen in China today is their Chinese partners' often blatant disregard for legality. "Chinese businesses grew up in an environment in which extra-legality was the only option," the author says. "If the country's system of bribes, networking, and back-scratching remains the norm for decades to come, it will have a pervasive influence on the companies entering the market; who will at the very least demand a free hand (from their parent companies) to deal with the Chinese market in the same way the Chinese businesses do."[xxxiv] And if U.S. companies will face internal pressures to relax their ethical standards when doing business with China, there is no reason to believe that the same thing will not happen in Latin American countries, where anti-corruption standards are already less strictly enforced.

The potential for contagion is also evident in the human rights field. When Chinese authorities speak of a "strategic consensus" with Latin America to counterbalance U.S. influence in world affairs as one of their top goals for the region; they refer among other things to China's securing Latin American support in defending itself against accusations of human rights violations at the United Nations. If Latin America joins in defending China against such accusations, as Argentina and Brazil have begun to do under the banner of "non-intervention" in other countries' internal affairs, it would not only set back the cause of human rights in China, but would create a dangerous precedent for Latin America. Repressive Latin American governments in the future will increasingly use the same "non-intervention" principle to keep others from criticizing their own wrongdoing. A political alliance with China may be just as hazardous to Latin America's democracies as to its economies.

The Achilles' heel of the Chinese miracle

For the moment, China's economic boom seems unstoppable. According to Chinese government forecasts, the country will continue growing at more than 7 percent annually over the next 10 or 15 years, increasing average per capita income from $1,740 in 2006 to more than $3,000 in 2020. In business centers like Shanghai, per capita income in 2020 will top $10,000 per year. If Latin American economies fail to grow substantially, residents of big Chinese cities will surpass those of most Latin American capitals in personal income, according to the National Commission of Reform and Development projections.[xxxv] And if forecasts from both the Chinese government and the CIA's NIC are correct, the Chinese economy will have easily overtaken Europe and India by the year 2020, and will be on its way toward becoming the world's number one power in the decade or so that follows. According to some enthusiasts, like Professor Oded Shenkar of Ohio State University, author of *The Chinese Century*, China could become the greatest economy in the world even sooner, between 2020 and 2025.[xxxvi]

Will these prophecies come true? After interviewing dozens of officials, academics, and businesspeople in China, I have no doubt that — barring unexpected events — China will become a major world power in the not-so-distant future. My only reservation about these forecasts is that they are based on snapshots of present data, and history, as ever, is full of surprises. If a Russian visionary had said as recently as in 1987 that the Soviet Union would cease to exist, that the Soviet Communist Party would become something like a retirees' social club, and that Poland and the Czech Republic would be Cuba's main accusers on U.N. human rights panels, he would have been considered a lunatic. If a Chinese academic had predicted during Mao's Cultural Revolution that the main tourism attraction in Shanghai early in the 21st Century would be a monument to consumers, he would have been branded an intellectual basket case, and sent to a communal farm for re-education. Just like previous predictions that Japan would be the biggest super-power, or that the world was heading toward a new Ice Age, the predictions that China is destined to be the world's next superpower could end up being highly speculative.

Many things could happen in China. There could be a political uprising among the 800 million farmers who have received little more than breadcrumbs from the new economic boom, and who might begin to view harshly the gap that separates them from those who own top-of-the-line Mercedes and spend $37,000 on a New Year's dinner. It already happened once, during the student uprising of Tiananmen Square in 1989, and there's no guarantee it won't happen again. Judging from the Chinese government's most visible concerns, there could be a religious revolt involving one of the dozens of ethnic groups in the country. It's no accident that the Chinese government is more worried about Falun Gong, the religious sect that is violently repressed every time it stages a public protest, than about any political group.

Even without social unrest, the economy could collapse because of the fragility of China's banking system. Big Chinese banks are drowning in bad loans that can't be restructured, and they could topple over like dominoes. Moreover, even barring political or economic catastrophe, the mere evolution of the China's political system could lead to growing conflicts within the ruling elite. As the years go by, China's business tycoons, many of whom already have local Communist Party and police officials on their payrolls, could forge their own alliances within top party or government officials at the national level. This could lead to a system of feudal barons with their own security services, who — as has happened before in China's history — end up fighting with one another, or teaming up against the government.

If I had to predict, I would say China will continue to grow in coming years, although at less spectacular rates than in the past two decades. The reason is simple: much of China's current dynamism is due to the current generation of people emerging from communism, who are enthusiastic converts to state-run capitalism. They are willing to work as hard as necessary, under almost any conditions, in order to buy themselves apartments or the latest consumer gadgets. But their children and grandchildren will not share the same drive. The novelty of being able to replace the Cultural Revolution's drab uniforms with black-leather jackets and blue jeans will be old and — as happens with immigrants in industrialized nations — newer generations won't be as eager to work around the clock, or sleep at their workstations, for some of the world's lowest salaries. If there are no surprises along the way, China will continue to be the world's factory, but it will be less competitive than it is today. The capitalist fever, like all fevers, will be over. In the meantime, however, China will have a growing impact on Latin America — beneficial to many in the short term, but potentially dangerous to all in the long term.

NOTES

[i] *Mapping the Global Future: National Intelligence Council's 2020 Project,* National Intelligence Council, 2005.

[ii] *China Daily,* "Country salutes extra foreign investment," January 31, 2005.

[iii] *Mapping the Global Future: National Intelligence Council's 2020 Project,* National Intelligence Council, 2005, p. 12.

[iv] "China, New Land of Shoppers, Builds Malls on Gigantic Scale," *The New York Times,* May 25, 2005.

[v] "China's elite learns to flaunt it while the new landless weep," *The New York Times,* December 25, 2004.

[vi] "$37,000 dinner hard to stomach? Not for the rich in China," *Singapore Sunday Times,* February 6, 2005.

[vii] "Low gear for the luxury car market," *China Daily,* February 7, 2005.

[viii] Ted C. Fishman, *China Inc.,* Scribner, p. 9.

[xix] Chi Lo, *The Misunderstood China,* Singapore, Pearson Education, 2004, p. 22.

[x] *The World Factbook,* CIA, 2007

[xi] Interview with Zhou Xi-an in Beijing, February 2, 2005.

[xii] "Reforming China's Economy: A Rough Guide," Royal Institute of International Economics, www.riia.org

[xiii] *Xinhua,* January 10, 2005.

[xiv] Idem.

[xv] *Mapping the Global Future: National Intelligence Council's 2020 Project,* National Intelligence Council, 2005, p. 13.

[xvi] Idem, p. 78.

[xvii] "China's Internet Censorship," The Associated Press, December 3, 2002.

[xviii] "People's Republic of China Controls tighten as Internet activism grows," Amnesty International, Document, January 28, 2004.

[xix] "People's Republic of China: Executed. Accord-ing to the law? — The death penalty in China," Amnesty International, March 22, 2004.

[xx] Jiang Shixue, "Globalization and Latin America," Institute of Latin American Studies, Chinese Academy of Social Sciences, No. 5, 2003, p. 2.

[xxi] Idem.

[xxii] Idem.

[xxiii] "Overseas Investment on the up," *China Daily*, February 1, 2005, and "La inversion extranjera en América Latina y el Caribe," CEPAL, 2003.

[xxiv] *Clarín*, November 13, 2004.

[xxv] *China Daily*, Xinhua, February 8, 2005.

[xxvi] Interview with Sergio Ley López, Beijing, Thursday, February 3, 2005.

[xxvii] "Progress on IPR protection in China," *China Daily*, January 14, 2005.

[xxviii] "A Realistic Look at Latin American and Chinese Trade Relations," Goldman Sachs, December 3, 2004.

[xxix] Idem, p. 6.

[xxx] "Human Development Report, 2005," United Nations Development Programme (UNDP), p. 124.

[xxxi] Interview with Zhou Xi-an, Deputy Director of the National Development and Reform Commission, Beijing, February 2, 2005.

[xxxii] Transparency International, *Corruption Perceptions Index*, May 14, 2002.

[xxxiii] Idem.

[xxxiv] Ted C. Fishman, *China Inc.*, p. 63.

[xxxv] Interview with Zhou Xi-an, Deputy Director of the National Development and Reform Commission, Beijing, February 2, 2005.

[xxxvi] "China Poised to overtake U.S. in 2020s," *China Daily*, February 9, 2005.

The Irish Miracle

Tall tale: "The model that has failed is the capitalist model."
(Hugo Chávez, president of the
Bolivarian Republic of Venezuela, April 17, 2005)

DUBLIN, IRELAND – IT DIDN'T TAKE ME LONG TO FEEL AT HOME IN THE Irish capital. As I walked down the street from my hotel on my first day in Dublin, something in the air was familiar. Strange, I thought, having never been to Ireland. There's no Irish blood in my veins, nor do I recall ever having any particular interest in the country beyond reading the works of Oscar Wilde and James Joyce when I was growing up in Argentina. But I always suspected the Irish were the Latin Americans of Northern Europe, or at least, that the two cultures had a great deal in common.

And I wasn't wrong. Ireland, traditionally agrarian and Roman Catholic, is home to a people long celebrated as hard drinkers, poets, musicians, globetrotters, admirers of all things bohemian, more gifted at improvisation than at teamwork. Historically, they are the poor cousins of their British neighbors, with whom they have endured much the same love-hate relationship that many Latin Americans have with the United States.

Ireland, like many Latin American countries, has traditionally been better known for its glories in the arts, literature, and sports than in science, technology, or business. Mention Ireland and the names that come to mind are writers such as Wilde, Joyce, W.B. Yeats, Samuel Beckett, and George Bernard Shaw, painters like Francis Bacon, or — more recently — dancers and musicians like the Celtic dance group Riverdance, Enya, the Chieftains, or U2 with its lead singer,

Bono. But when you ask whether the country has produced any figures of a similar caliber in the sciences, the Irish look at each other for help, trying to come up with a good example. During my conversations with Irish people at my stay here, at least, none suggested a world-known name.

My suspicions about the similarities between the Irish and Latin American characters — or at least their stereotypes — were confirmed when I discovered, with alarm, that I was running late for my first appointment with a government official. The appointment was scheduled for 4 P.M. the day of my arrival. I had been delayed at my hotel room by a telephone call, but fortunately the hotel was only a block from the Department of Foreign Affairs, where the interview was to take place. At 4 P.M., I took off running, and arrived breathlessly at the Ministry's building on 74 Hartcourt Street at 4:10.

Once there, I asked for the public relations officer with whom I had arranged the meeting. I was somewhat surprised that he wasn't already in the lobby, nervously checking his watch and waiting for me. But no. I called him from downstairs and he arrived a few minutes later. When I apologized profusely for my tardiness, he answered with a conspiratorial smirk: "Don't worry. The appointment was at 4 P.M. Irish time." In other words, it wasn't a big deal: this was not Switzerland, or any other country known for its cult of punctuality. As we were riding up in the elevator, he explained to me that "Irish time" allowed for flexibility in the time of appointments, as if the concept were totally alien to a Latin America–born visitor. So when I learned that, in addition to being great poets, dancers, and sportsmen, the Irish aren't punctual either, I realized this was an ideal place to look into whether Latin Americans could learn from Ireland's economic miracle.

Twelve years is nothing

In the 12 years ending in 2003, Ireland, which not long before had been one of the poorest countries in Europe, had become one of the world's richest. By 2006 Ireland's per capita income had reached $43,600 — higher than that of Germany and Great Britain, and the second-highest in the European Union after Luxembourg.[i] The Celtic Tiger was roaring.

When I visited in 2003, Ireland had just been chosen as "the best country in the world to live in" by The Economist Intelligence Unit, the *Economist* magazine's research group; beating out such favorites from previous years as Switzerland, Norway, and Sweden.[ii] How did the Irish manage to go from an impoverished agricultural society to a technology powerhouse, tripling their annual per capita income in little more than a decade? How had they managed to leave behind centuries of political instability, social conflict, and economic sluggishness to become the country with the fourth-highest per capita income in the world? And, what was even more intriguing, how had the Irish managed to surpass economically the British, who had always looked down on them?

These questions are all the more relevant at a time when, as we will see in Chapter 5, "cultural theories" of development, which credit geographic, religious, and historical factors for the prosperity of some nations and the backwardness of others, are so popular in U.S. academic circles. According to adherents, poverty in Third World countries can often be explained by their tropical climates, which facilitate the spread of disease, and by their Catholic traditions, which allegedly discourage individual entrepreneurship and independent thinking. When deciding to visit Ireland and look into the country's recent past, I wanted to know if Latin America could prove such cultural theories wrong and become an economic miracle over the next decade, just as Ireland had done.

Not long ago, Ireland was an economic disaster. In the late 1980s unemployment hovered around 18 percent, inflation hit 22 percent, and public debt skyrocketed. As would be the case 10 years later in many Latin American countries — briefly confirming the darkest predictions of anti-globalization activists — Ireland's economic opening had resulted in the closure of automotive, textile, and shoe factories, which threw tens of thousands of people out of work. Like many Latin American countries, Ireland was financially strangled by its foreign debt and was a source of massive emigration. Around 90 percent of the government's tax receipts had to be spent on foreign-debt interest payments, which left virtually nothing for development projects or social programs for the poor. Ireland's poverty levels were close to those of Third World countries. Like them, Ireland had a stagnant economy, largely dependent on remittances sent by the growing Irish immigrant community in the United States. By 1987 the most popular joke in Ireland was the same one that Latin Americans had heard many times before: "Would the last Irishman to leave the country please turn out the lights?"

But the country I found upon arriving in Dublin 15 years later looked nothing like that picture. The Irish economy had grown an average of nearly 9 percent a year during most of the 1990s, one of the highest rates in the world. Per capita income had risen from $11,000 in 1987 to more than $35,000 in 2003. Individual earnings soared, from 40 percent lower than the European average to 36 percent higher over the same period. Although the wealthy have benefited the most from the Irish economic boom, former Prime Minister Sean Lemass's prediction that "a rising tide lifts all boats" had come true: Unemployment fell to 4 percent, and extreme poverty to 5 percent.

Ireland was now one of the world's top technological and pharmaceutical centers. It had managed to become a platform for exports to the European Union, Africa, and Asia from major multinationals in the information and pharmaceutical sectors. Among the companies with major research and development centers in the country are Intel, Microsoft, Oracle, Lotus, Pfizer, Merck, American Home Products, and IBM. Around 1,100 multinationals have set up shop in Ireland in the past few years, and together they export products worth around $60 billion a year. Despite its tiny population of not even 4 million, Ireland exports one-third of all the computers sold in Europe and — even more surprising — is the largest exporter of software in the world, surpassing even the United States.[iii]

In Dublin signs of progress were everywhere. Even though it is one of the most expensive capitals in Europe and its economy has lost momentum due to growing competition from India and China, the Dublin I visited was a boomtown. On Grafton Street — the pedestrian walkway crossing the downtown area — I found myself surrounded by people carrying two or three shopping bags at a time from the area's luxury stores. Although there were fewer foreigners than in London, many of the waiters in the downtown restaurants were Italian, Spanish, or South Asian. Ireland was no longer a country that people were forced to leave; it had become a magnet for new immigrants. Many of the Irish men and women who had gone to the United States were returning home, joined by young Spaniards, Italians, and Greeks who would come to work for a year or two and earn more than they could in their native lands.

Late-model cars lined the side streets. Construction projects were under way all around. Avenues across most of the city were being widened by teams of workers — creating major traffic jams — to make way for construction of the Luas, a $1 billion trolley system that would tie together much of the city. At the seaport, a mega-tunnel was being built to make it easier for trucks to come and go. In all directions construction cranes loomed. Dublin was definitely on a roll.

Recipe for progress

"Which was the secret behind the Irish miracle?" I asked everyone I interviewed in Dublin. Government officials, businessmen, and labor leaders credited a combination of several factors: a "Social Partnership" agreement between corporations and workers, European Union aid, the elimination of red tape and other obstacles that discouraged investment, deregulation of the telecommunications industry, a wide-ranging amnesty for tax evaders, cuts in individual and corporate taxes, a strong investment in education, and the fact that successive governments had stayed the course despite missteps at the beginning of the country's economic opening.

For many, the key factor behind the "Celtic miracle" was the 1987 agreement between business and labor. Despite the crisis that had shaken the economy during the initial attempts to open the economy, when the shutdown of assembly lines at Ford, Toyota, and several textile companies drove unemployment up to 18 percent; the government and much of Irish society concluded that the country's domestic market was too small to sustain an economy of protected national industries. An auto industry, for instance, capable of producing cars that were as good and as cheap as imported ones would require a market greater than a country of 4 million could offer. There was no choice but to move forward with economic openness, continue slashing public spending, and lowering corporate tax rates to attract foreign investments; no matter how much social trauma those reforms would cause in the first few years.

The government decided that the country's priority should be an agreement with labor unions under which they accepted tighter wage increases now, in exchange for more substantial increases later, once the economy started growing. Hence, the first Social Partnership was signed in 1987 by the government, business owners, and workers. Under the agreement, the government agreed to reduce corporate taxes; business associations agreed to maintain employment; and labor unions agreed to defer demands for wage raises until the economy recovered. The initial pact was signed for a three-year period. It has been renewed ever since.

"We did all this without help from the International Monetary Fund," said Kieran Donoghue, planning director of the Industrial Development Agency of Ireland, the country's equivalent of an industrial development ministry. "Simply put, we reached the point where we decided that national capitalism had been a failure, because the political and business elites were only betting on safe investments, things like real estate or land, instead of taking risks and investing in job-creating industries. So we decided to gamble on an economic opening, an American-style capitalism that would stimulate risk-taking and reward entrepreneurs."

In the beginning, the Social Partnership worked only halfway. The economy did start growing, but growth didn't translate immediately into more jobs or any other social betterment. After two years labor unions started getting nervous: they said while they had made big sacrifices, the new growth was largely benefiting the rich. But government economists argued that growth hadn't yet reduced unemployment significantly because Irish factories were still only utilizing idle capacity they had inherited from the crisis years and could easily raise output without any more hiring. That would not last forever, they said. Patience was needed. Shut your eyes, hang on, and stay the course.

To speed up growth, the government ordered a general amnesty for tax evaders. In Ireland, as in much of Latin America, tax evasion was pervasive, in part because taxes were so high — as much as 58 percent for high-income individuals and 50 percent for corporations — so a significant part of the population cheated. The government now gave tax evaders six months to come clean. The results were staggering. While government economists had originally expected that the tax amnesty would bring $45 million into government coffers, the country received some $750 million. Before long it became evident that the new policies were working: in 1993 unemployment began to decline, at first slowly and in subsequent years at an increasing speed. By the end of the 1990s, the same country that not long before had been losing 30,000 workers a year to massive emigration had halted the outflow of people, and was now the net recipient of 40,000 foreign workers per year.

Without a doubt, Ireland's admittance into the European Union in 1973 and the EU's economic aid in the years that followed helped accelerate the country's economic growth. But most government officials and academics I talked to agreed that, contrary to what outsiders might expect, European subsidies were not the most important factor in the Irish miracle, nor did they have an immediate effect. Ireland's economic opening had begun long before the country became an EU member. It dates from 1965, when — after decades of political nationalism and commercial protectionism — Ireland and the United Kingdom signed the Anglo-Irish free trade agreement.

"Until then, we had been a backward, isolationist country. Our way of expressing independence from Great Britain had been to seek self-sufficiency and import substitutions," Brendan Lyons, vice-minister of foreign affairs, told me in an interview. "The only thing we managed to create was an inefficient national industry." In 1973, when Ireland joined the EU, its potential market expanded from 4 million consumers to 300 million. "Entering the European Union allowed us to both reduce our dependency on Great Britain and to become a staging ground for U.S. investments aimed at exporting to the European Community," Lyons explained. The following years weren't easy, he added, referring to the factory shutdowns and social problems which had continued until the first Social Partnership was signed 15 years later.

Of course, EU aid helped make the transition more bearable. But debunking one of the favorite themes of Latin American politicians — that the region needs a U.S. Marshall Plan because the Irish miracle was made possible only thanks to generous EU subsidies — Irish officials assured me Europe's economic aid was never a determining factor in their country's success story. The EU, they said, had for years given generous "cohesion funds" and "structural funds" to Ireland, just as it had to Spain, Portugal, and Greece. Richer European countries had voted for these aid packages to, among other things, stem a mass influx of workers to the more industrialized EU countries. From 1989 to 1993 alone, the EU gave Ireland $3.4 billion for bridges, roads, telephone lines, and other infrastructure works, as well as to subsidize its most vulnerable farm sectors. According to EU figures from 1994 to 1999, Ireland received a second package of about $11 billion.

"Without those funds, it would have been very difficult to get back on our feet," Lyons admitted. "At the time, we had to cut government budgets in order to heal our economy. Without European Union help, the social cost of those cuts would have been a much greater one. But the Irish miracle would have happened anyhow." The country would have recovered thanks to structural reforms it had launched to attract investment, including the business-labor pact and the corporate tax cuts, he said. Recovery would just have been messier and would have taken longer, he said.

Taking a book down from the small library in his office, Lyons looked up some figures to back up his claim. EU subsidies to Ireland began in 1973, but the country didn't get off the ground for another 15 years, he said. EU aid to Ireland had risen substantially by 1992, after the Maastricht accords, and yet they never represented a significant portion of Ireland's gross national product. Most academic studies about the impact of EU cohesion and structural funds concluded that they contributed an average of 0.5 percent a year to the country's economic growth during the 1990s — by no means negligible, but for an economy that was growing at an average of nearly 7 percent a year, far from the key to success.[iv] Rather, the EU help had made the necessary sacrifice more tolerable during the transition to Ireland's full integration into the global economy.

More technicians, fewer sociologists

What else had Ireland done to grow so much, so fast? I asked Irish officials. After mentioning the Social Partnership, most cited the country's battle against red tape and other obstacles to foreign investment, which helped transform Ireland into one of the world's most investor-friendly countries. Today, to start a company in Ireland you need follow only three legal procedures; the entire process takes an average of 12 days, according to a World Bank report.[v] By comparison, opening the same company in Mexico would take seven legal steps and 51 days, and in Argentina 15 bureaucratic steps and 68 days. Compared with Latin America, Ireland is a paradise for foreign investors.

Another key factor in Ireland's success in attracting high-tech and pharmaceutical firms was government support for university research and for developing products with commercial potential. After slashing corporate taxes and deregulating the telecommunications industry, which sharply reduced the cost of international long-distance phone calls and Internet connections, Ireland focused its energies on attracting the world's biggest computer companies. To be able to offer them a large pool of skilled labor, successive governments invested heavily in the '80s and '90s to increase the number of graduates in science and technology by creating two new universities and giving more money to the ones already in existence.

Before it joined the EU, Ireland, like virtually all Latin American countries today, produced plenty of social science graduates. But, when it decided to compete within the global economy, Ireland concluded that it needed more scientists and technicians and fewer sociologists. During the 1990s the number of university students pursuing careers in science and technology more than doubled. The number of computer science students alone increased from 500 in 1996 to 2,000 in 2003, according to official figures.

"After we entered the European Union in the '70s, we launched a deliberate state policy to channel more resources into engineering and science schools," said Dan Flinter, president of Enterprise Ireland, a kind of Ministry of Planning within the Irish government. "We did it by founding two new universities specifically tailored to these degrees."

From elementary school onward, Irish teachers — following Department of Education guidelines — try to steer their students into pursuing technical careers, several parents of school-aged children told me. For instance, a typical homework assignment might be to analyze a U2 rock concert from dozens of technical angles, such as the manufacturing of the podium where the musicians play, the acoustics in the auditorium, and the mathematics behind ticket sales and administrative expenses. Another assignment might demand that students perform an in-depth technical analysis of their favorite soccer teams, including stadium construction, accounting, and administration.

The nationwide focus on technical education has had an enormous cultural impact, to the point that Ireland's main newspapers dedicate several pages a day to education news, including expert debates on how the best schools in the country are ranked and critiques of elementary schools, high schools, and universities. Much as newspapers in other countries devote significant space to music, art, and television reviews, Irish papers do likewise with school reviews.

The government has provided strong backing for scientific or technical research and development with business potential. Flinter, the man in charge of the Irish economic planning agency, told me that his main responsibilities include identifying promising R&D projects at universities and contributing funds to help them materialize. On average, Enterprise Ireland each year invests government funds in about 70 projects at various universities to develop products with business potential, he said. At the time we met, the agency had just created an investment fund in partnership with private businesses for the development of a computer program with cell-phone applications. "What does this mean?" I asked. "It means that, together with other partners, we gave a team of researchers at Trinity College one million euros for them to develop a specific application for a program used to play games on cell phones," Flinter said. "We give the research team six to nine months to develop the application, then we do the testing, and then we go out and offer the product to cell-phone companies."

As the number of projects increased and several Enterprise Ireland–backed start-up businesses become commercial successes, the agency started making money by selling its shares in the new formed companies. Often, it recovered its original investment and made a profit. In a good year, Enterprise Ireland was making $100 million from the sale of stock in its start-up firms. That sum represented a third of the total budget of the 900-employee agency, and helped pay for its 34 commercial offices around the world dedicated to promoting Irish exports.

One of the things I found most interesting in Flinter's story about his agency's role in Ireland's growth — for its potential of imitation in Latin America — was how it made use of Irish immigrants in the United States to draw U.S. investment dollars. The United States is home to 30 to 40 million Irish citizens and people of Irish heritage. Many Irish-Americans are descendants of those who emigrated because of the great famine of 1840. Many are now successful executives at some of the world's biggest multinationals. Successive Irish governments decided that, as a matter of state policy, the country would try to milk relations with Irish-Americans as much as possible, particularly targeting highly successful business people. Officials at the Irish Embassy in Washington, for instance, were asked to look in the Web pages of major multinational corporations for Irish names among their top executives, and to contact them immediately.

"We used our embassies abroad to identify and approach the people of Irish heritage who interested us the most," said Donoghue, of the Industrial Development Agency. "We are lucky that so many Irish-Americans have reached top positions in U.S. corporations. We invite them to social events at our embassies, make contact with them, and then give them a presentation on the advantages of investing in Ireland, or Irish companies."

Of course, just because a top executive of a multinational happens to be of Irish descent does not guarantee that he or she will return the embassy's calls, much less encourage corporate investment in Ireland. But in today's competitive world, where countries spend millions on public-relations agencies just to get potential investors to give them a few minutes of their time, exploiting ethnic bonds can indeed open doors. There are far more chances that an executive of Irish origin will answer the Irish embassy's phone calls than someone of German or Guatemalan descent, Donoghue remarked. And once the Irish officials got their foot in the door, they had a good product to sell.

"Obviously, we were wrong"

As a journalist used to interviewing Latin American union leaders, who are most comfortable leading the charge against free market reforms; I was curious about how Ireland had convinced its labor leaders to sign a wide-ranging pact with their adversaries in the business world. Had they actually participated voluntarily in Ireland's economic opening, which triggered so many shutdowns in the early stages? Or had they been pressured to do so, either with carrots or sticks? I soon learned that, like their peers in Latin America, the leaders of the Irish Congress of Trade Unions (ICTU), the biggest umbrella group for Irish labor unions, had tenaciously opposed free trade in the early '70s. The trade-union coalition had been the main supporter of the "No" vote during the 1972 referendum on whether the country should join the European Union, arguing — accurately in the short term, as it turned out — that free trade would bring massive layoffs in automotives, textiles, and shoemaking. But the "Yes" vote won the referendum by a wide margin, and Ireland joined the EU in a matter of months.

Two decades later, Irish workers had made a 180-degree turn. The ICTU was no longer blindly opposing globalization or free trade. Rather, it had become an organization focused on negotiating the best deals it could for its members within Ireland's free market economy, and that rose from relative obscurity every three years to renegotiate the Social Partnership with representatives of business and government.

Few Irish people today know what the ICTU does, or even where it's based. It took my cabdriver, a veteran Dublin cabbie, quite a while to find the trade-union headquarters. He had a vague notion of what the ICTU was, but he'd never seen the building, and didn't know quite where it was. It turned out to be one of several four-story town houses, each an exact copy of the next, on Parnell Square, in Dublin's historic downtown area. Years ago, the neighborhood had been an upper-middle-class residential area, but more recently it had been taken over by Asian and African workers. The union headquarters was just another house, distinguished only by a sign next to the door. Obviously, it wasn't a major reference point in the Irish capital, or even a place cabdrivers were familiar with.

Oliver Donohoe, a former activist of the "No" cause in the 1972 referendum, who was now a top ICTU official, greeted me at the door. He invited me into the conference room, which had obviously once been a family dining room. The place was modestly furnished. The only decorations were posters from international union conventions, many of them unframed and stuck to the walls with tacks. Once we were seated, I asked Donohoe how he felt now, in hindsight, about the Irish labor unions' opposition to free trade and integration with the European Union in the early 1970s. The veteran union man answered with a resigned smile: "Obviously, we were wrong."

According to Donohoe, the trade union had focused its opposition to free trade on well-founded fears that integration with the European Union would end up destroying many Irish industries and leaving thousands of workers in the street. What the ICTU didn't foresee at the time was that Ireland's economic opening would create many more jobs — and with higher wages — than those lost in the early stages of the process, he said. As the years passed, the ICTU gradually changed its position. "Once we lost the referendum and the country joined the European Union, we started working with the European Trade Union Confederation. Very soon, we realized that European integration could work in our favor," he explained.

The watershed for the Irish labor movement came in the mid-1970s, when the European Union began to demand that all member countries provide men and women with equal pay. The Irish government opposed the measure, arguing the country needed more time to adjust to the new rule. All of a sudden, the Irish labor movement found itself aligned with the European Union.

Irish labor unions found — to their surprise — that Europe's supranational institutions could be their strongest allies in the struggle for better working conditions in their own country. "That was a turning point in our political stands," Donohoe recalled. "From then on, we supported trade integration, and voted in favor of a broader integration with Europe in each of the referendums that followed," he added. Irish unions had discovered that economic openness, with all its problems, could lead to more advanced social policies, like those prevailing in Europe's most industrialized nations.

Toward the end of our interview, when I asked Donohoe whether most Irish workers were benefiting from the "Celtic miracle," he shrugged his shoulders. As if he were recognizing an indisputable fact, but at the same time not wanting to turn his back on the union struggles to which he had dedicated his life, he said, "In general terms, yes, there can be no doubt. Even though the gap between rich and poor has grown, the living standard of poor people has risen. The idea that a rising tide will lift all boats turned out to be true. If I had to sum up our position, I would say that the economic growth has benefited workers, but not enough."

What, then, were the Irish labor movement's main demands nowadays? A few days after my interview with Donohoe, I read an article in the *Irish Independent* newspaper about the status of negotiations for a new Social Partnership that left me shaking my head in amazement. According to the newspaper, the SIPTU, one of the largest unions in the Irish labor congress, had decided at its annual meeting to demand the government to reduce the workweek to 30 hours, with flexible working hours. At the meeting, the union leadership had described the current schedule of 40 hours a week as abusive. For a country that a few decades ago had more in common with the Third World than with its richer European neighbors, which just 15 years ago had suffered under an 18 percent unemployment rate; the current labor demands looked like solid testimony to the country's economic progress.[vi]

The trauma of progress

In recent years Ireland's economic growth had brought about a marked improvement in its standard of living — and higher wages. Low labor costs, which had been a key inducement for foreign investors coming to Ireland in the '80s and '90s, were a thing of the past. Today China, India, and the former Soviet Bloc countries of Eastern Europe were offering much lower salaries and skilled labor forces. Yet, contrary to anti-globalization theories claiming that economic openness is always a "downward race" that forces countries to reduce wages to be able to compete with poorer competitors, Ireland came out on top. At the start of the new millennium, it not only had a relatively low 4 percent unemployment rate, but had also increased the salaries of many of its workers by creating better-paid jobs.

Take the case of the Apple Corporation's plants in Ireland. In 1977 Apple employed 1,800 people at its Cork factory. Some years later, when competitors began to produce similar products more efficiently in other countries, Apple transferred a large part of its Cork operations to the Czech Republic and Taiwan, where labor costs were much lower. Did Cork's economy collapse when its main employer left town? Not at all, as I was told. According to company executives, the Apple factory in Cork was transformed into a regional research and service center for all of Europe, with 1,400 employees, most of them university graduates and nearly all of them with better-paying jobs than the previous staff. Many workers from the dismantled factories were retrained. In other cases, new people were hired. The change was traumatic for many, but the final result had been a greater injection of capital for the city.[vii]

Of course, economic progress brought the Irish new problems: the cost of housing soared (by some measures, property prices quadrupled in the ten years ending in 2005), traffic on the streets of Dublin and other cities had become increasingly chaotic, and the arrival of new immigrants was placing a heavy burden on schools and hospitals. But these were development-related troubles most poverty-ridden countries would gladly exchange for the unemployment, crime, and misery with which they contend.

The Irish model and Latin America

Latin America's nationalist-leftist politicians and protectionist industrialists who see globalization as a threat argue that the Irish miracle cannot be used as an example for the region, because Ireland benefited from several extraordinary circumstances. There certainly are some factors that helped Ireland, such as EU economic aid, that doesn't exist in Latin America, and is unlikely to exist in the near future. Ireland received more than $15 billion in aid from the EU at a critical point in its transition to an open economy. Although the funds were not the most important cause of Ireland's success, they did allow the country to ease social pressures of economic adjustment. But Latin America has not received, nor is it likely to receive in the near future, such generous help from the United States.

Second, Ireland — unlike Latin America — enjoys a natural advantage: the Irish speak English. That has helped the country not only to find suited people to staff customer-service operations for major U.S. companies — which transferred their call centers first to Ireland and then, in more recent years, to India, in order to reduce labor costs — but has also allowed Irish workers to deal with U.S. or British supervisors in their own tongue. While Caribbean nations enjoy that advantage, Latin America as a whole doesn't, even though many of its nations have bilingual elites. Third, just as labor leader Donohue told me, Ireland had been lucky to have a community of more than 30 million Irish-Americans in the United States, who would not only send millions in remittances a year to the country of their ancestors, but who would also turn out to be excellent business contacts in helping channel investments to the country. Latin America has about 36 million compatriots living in the United States, but most of them are low-paid workers, without the economic status of Irish-Americans in big multinational companies.

Still, Latin America could learn a lot from the Irish success story. A good many Latin Americans have indeed reached top positions in the U.S. and European corporate worlds. Carlos Gutierrez, a Cuban raised in Mexico, was chief executive of the giant Kellogg's food corporation before being named U.S. secretary of commerce; Alain Belda, a Brazilian, was CEO of Alcoa, the largest steel company in the world; and most heads of multinational companies' Latin American operations are Latin Americans. There is no reason why Latin American embassies in Washington could not do the same things the Irish had done, and use their own diasporas to their advantage.

On the way to Dublin airport to catch my return flight, I couldn't help but conclude that the "Celtic miracle," regardless of whether it should be the economic model for Latin American countries, could certainly be an inspiration to them. As Mexican academic Luis Rubio said, "Ireland shows that the limitations are not economic, but mental and political."[viii] He added, "The Irish looked at themselves in the mirror and realized the obvious: their country was falling behind not because the rest of the world was conspiring against it, or because the past was sacred, or because imports had displaced their local producers, or because they lacked capital or investment or export opportunities, but plainly and simply because they themselves were immobile... Once [the Irish] were willing to face their shortcomings and organize themselves to take advantage of their potential, the economic opportunities opened up almost magically."[ix]

Of course, while there are many differences between Ireland and Latin America, the similarities between the Ireland of two decades ago and the Latin America of today are startling. Those similarities show that predictions that Latin America is doomed to backwardness because of history, religion, and culture may be as mistaken as they turned out to be in Ireland. Not long ago Ireland was a poor, largely rural Catholic country renowned for its poets, musicians, and drunks; as well as by its people's lack of punctuality, meager respect for laws, and political violence. There is no biological reason for Latin American countries to be doomed to failure, just as there wasn't for Ireland. By taking some cues from Ireland's success, Latin American countries could prosper sooner than even the most optimistic of their analysts imagine.

Notes

[i] *The World Factbook*, CIA, 2007

[ii] "The World in 2005", *The Economist*, November 27, 2004.

[iii] *The Economist*, October 16, 2004.

[iv] "A Survey of Ireland", *The Economist*, October 16, 2004, p. 5.

[v] *Doing Business in 2004. Understanding Regulation*, World Bank, Country Tables.

[vi] "Union sets target of 30-hour work week", *Irish Independent*, August 28, 2003, p. 10.

[vii] *The Economist*, October 16, 2004, p. 7.

[viii] Luis Rubio, "Irlanda: otro mundo", *Reforma*, Mexico, March 27, 2005.

[ix] Idem.

CHAPTER 4

The "New Europe"

Tall tale: "After the Soviet Union's fall... socialism has been resurrected! Like Karl Marx, we too can say: The specter is once again haunting the world!" (Hugo Chávez, President of the Bolivarian Republic of Venezuela, August 14, 2005)

KRAKÓW, POLAND — MY FIRST DAY IN POLAND, FROM A PROFESSIONAL point of view, was a bit rough. I realized I was off on the wrong foot when, during my first interview with a top Polish official, I declared with enthusiasm that I had come to write "about Eastern Europe's economic boom." (I was sincere enough, but I also hoped to win his confidence.) To my surprise, he seemed both perplexed and annoyed. His expression then switched to one of bewilderment — as if he were talking to an alien from outer space — until he picked up my business card from the table and read it. Only then, after seeing the words, "Latin American Editor, *The Miami Herald*," under my name, did his demeanor soften. In a condescending tone, he said, "Look, allow me to make a suggestion: Don't go around Poland saying that you are writing about Eastern Europe, because a lot of people in this country aren't going to like it. Poland is in *Central* Europe, not Eastern Europe." Poland, the Czech Republic, Slovakia, and Hungary no longer have anything to do with the artificial division of the region made during the Soviet era, he explained. Now these countries have gone back to what they had always been: Central Europe. Nowadays, he added, when you speak of "Eastern European" countries, you are referring to the least-developed nations in the region, such as Ukraine and Belarus. I asked him to forgive my ignorance. Evidently, I had come to write about one region and had found myself in another, at least in the view of its officials.

The countries of Central Europe, or "the New Europe" — as then-U.S. Defense Secretary Donald Rumsfeld had called them, referring to the former Soviet-bloc countries that were now embracing capitalism with almost religious passion — were so proud of their new status as emerging economic powers that they had even changed their region's name. The term "Eastern Europe" had been exiled from their vocabulary a few years earlier, and officials were dusting off their countries' past accomplishments in order to portray their poverty in the 20st century as a historical aberration, a parenthesis in an otherwise glorious history.

Soon after my first blunder, I found myself in a similarly embarrassing situation when I interviewed Witold Orlowski, chief economic adviser to Poland's then-president Aleksander Kwasniewski, and asked him how relatively small countries such as Poland and its neighbors had managed to attract more investment than much bigger nations such as Mexico, Brazil, or Argentina.

Orlowski seemed puzzled by the question. You couldn't compare Poland and its neighbors with Latin America, because "Central European" countries had been advanced nations in the past, with high education levels. Some, like the Czech Republic, were among Europe's richest before World War II, he explained. "We are European countries that, because of a bad joke of history, ended up inside the Soviet bloc. We were industrialized countries that became poor when we ended up within the Soviet camp." What was happening now, the revisionist argument went, was that countries in the region were beginning to recover their old splendor.

I had decided to visit Poland and the Czech Republic after reading a report by the United Nations Conference on Trade and Development (UNCTAD), which concluded that those two countries were likely to draw significantly more foreign investment over the next few years than Mexico, Brazil, or any other Latin American country. UNCTAD had polled executives of 335 multinational companies about where they planned to invest in the next five years. No Latin American country even showed up among the top five choices. The first place, predictably, was China, followed by India, the United States, Thailand, and, in a tie for fifth place, Poland and the Czech Republic. The highest-ranked Latin American country was Mexico, which shared seventh place with Malaysia.[i] The rest were far behind. What were Poland and the Czech Republic doing to be so much more attractive to foreign investors than Latin America?

"The best moment since the 16th century"

Like many Latin American nations, Poland is a middle-income agricultural-industrial country. It is highly nationalistic, deeply Roman Catholic, very bureaucratic, and fairly corrupt. Its per capita income is roughly that of Mexico or Argentina, and it shares with them a general cynicism toward its political class, a history of political violence, and a passion for soccer. According to Transparency International, the Berlin-based nongovernmental group that publishes an annual corruption perception index of 133 countries, Poland is about as crooked as Mexico, and has higher levels of corruption than Brazil, Colombia, and Peru.[ii] Not a month goes by without a major corruption scandal exploding in the Polish media. Prime ministers are changed frequently, either because they are accused of taking bribes or because Congress fires them for incompetence. In that sense, the front pages of Polish newspapers look much like those of Latin America's. And the Poles' sense of humor about corruption is also similar to that of most Latin American countries: when a recent poll found that 90 percent of Polish drivers admitted bribing a police officer to avoid a ticket, the running joke was that the other 10 percent had lied.

Many Poles I spoke to blame the corruption on their country's recent past. During the Communist era the Polish people — who were the black sheep of the Soviet bloc, to the point that Joseph Stalin once said that bringing communism to Poland was like trying to saddle a cow — boasted that thanks to their personal creativity they enjoyed a higher standard of living than most of their Communist neighbors. Poles would say that theirs was a country of empty shops and full apartments. The secret to survival then was *pokombinowac* — the knack of having a "connection" in government stores, so that Poles could buy things that were not on display in shop windows. Corruption was a survival skill, and it spread to every corner of the economy. Many of those habits had persisted in the post-Soviet era. Even today, with the equivalent of $15 one can often get a cop to forget all about a traffic ticket, and there are go-betweens and fixers who can expedite any legal procedure, from paying a bill to setting up a corporation.

Like many Latin American countries, Poland often defines itself politically by its mistrust of its nearest imperial power. In today's Poland, amazingly, the most admired leader is the late U.S. President Ronald Reagan, the conservative Republican whose arms spending helped hasten the collapse of the Soviet Union. Throughout history, Poland had been invaded by both the Russians and the Germans several times. And just as many Latin Americans sympathize with Russia or Cuba simply because they represent counterweights to the United States, many Poles are pro-American simply because the United States can put the brakes on Russia or Germany. "One tends to think highly of those who are not your neighbors," a Polish official pointed out to me. "Poland is probably the most pro-American country in the former Eastern Europe, and the former Eastern Europe is much more pro-American than Western Europe." So when President Bush asked for international support after the U.S. invasion of Iraq, it was no surprise in this part of the world that Poland was among the first countries to respond, sending more than 2,500 troops and taking charge of one of Iraq's main military regions.

Despite those similarities, I noticed a big difference between today's Poland and many Latin American countries: in Poland there is optimism in the air. Like many of its former Eastern-bloc neighbors, Poland feels reborn. Its economy has been growing at annual rates of nearly 6 percent, partly because of a boom in foreign investment attracted by low labor costs, tax breaks, and a highly educated population. Even though unemployment was still nearly at 20 percent when I visited the country, it was starting to drop. Like its neighbors in the "New Europe," Poland seemed fairly certain to continue to grow at a similar or higher rate over the next few years. Foreign investment had more than tripled from $4 billion per year in the 1990s to $12.6 billion in 2006.[iii] "Poland can look forward to many, many years of very high growth," Orlowski, chief economic advisor to the Polish president, told me. Helena Luckzywo, an editor at the *Gazeta Wyborcza*, went one step further: "This is Poland's best moment since the 16th century," she said.[iv]

There are signs of progress throughout Kraków, the old Polish capital, now a center of industry and tourism. I got there a few months after Poland entered the European Union, and the climate was joyful. Even though joining the EU had caused the prices of some products to rise, Kraków's main plaza, known for its majestic 13th century St. Mary's Basilica, was filled with shoppers. On Rynek Glowny, a principal downtown thoroughfare, Italian and German tourists as well as Poles could be seen coming and going from stores, shopping bags in hand, or sitting at cafés eating chocolate. For many Poles, one of the small, everyday delights of post-Communist life was being able to eat *czekolada*, as they call chocolate. No wonder: after the declaration of martial law in 1981, the regime had imposed ration cards, and only children were allowed chocolate. Today Poles are gobbling up *czekolada* as if they were making up for all the chocolate they had not been able to eat before. The cafés of Kraków's main plaza offer chocolates in every size, shape, and color.

Two new five-star hotels, the Sheraton and the Radisson, had just opened a few blocks from the main plaza. Not far from there, two gigantic shopping centers were being built: Kazimierz Gallery and Kakowska Gallery. Outside the city several multinationals, including Philip Morris, Motorola, and Valeo, had just put manufacturing plants into operation.

Poland's comparative advantage

Poland, like most of its neighbors, is benefiting from a flood of investments from "Old Europe," drawn by low labor costs, highly skilled professionals, and low corporate taxes. "Our huge comparative advantage is that we provide highly skilled workers at much lower wages than Germany or France," Orlowski explained. Production costs in Poland average 30 percent lower than in Germany, 27 percent lower than in Italy, 26 percent lower than in England or France, and 24 percent lower than in Spain.[v]

European multinationals such as Siemens, Volkswagen, and Fiat have moved many of their factories to Poland, and General Motors announced it would close two Opel car plants in Germany, which employed 10,000 people, to open a new one in Poland. GM didn't have to give many explanations: while many car workers in Germany make $38 an hour, a comparably skilled Polish worker earns $7. German manufacturers have moved to Poland en masse, which prompted former German Chancellor Gerhard Schroeder — in a fit of rage that drew criticism from the German media — to accuse the companies of being "unpatriotic." Schroeder demanded that former Eastern-bloc countries raise their corporate taxes, since, he said, low tax rates were the main reason German factories were relocating.

Some foreign businessmen who have been arriving in the country over the past few years, like British entrepreneur Richard Lucas, are among the most enthusiastic about the Polish "miracle." Lucas, a youthful-looking 37-year-old who wears blue jeans and a worn-out shirt, is one of the many foreigners who arrived in Poland after the collapse of the Soviet-bloc, eager to ride the capitalist wave. Lucas told me he arrived in Kraków at age 24, fresh out of Cambridge University, and has since started eight businesses; three had gone bankrupt, and five were doing very well. His various businesses' total income was "11 million a year," he told me. "Dollars?" I asked. "Yes, dollars," he answered, without smiling. The last business in which he had purchased a significant block of shares was the economic newsletter *Emerging Europe*.

I met with Lucas in one of the conference rooms of the magazine's headquarters, which apparently had been a residence until not too long ago. The newsletter, one of several English-language publications that cover the former Eastern bloc for foreign businesses, had prospered thanks to the robust international interest in the region. As we climbed the stairs of the house, I could see about two dozen young people — mostly Poles — writing in English on their computers. Lucas told me he had hired 12 people in the past few months and the magazine now had a staff of 35 full-time writers. Paid circulation had climbed from 100 subscriptions to 500 over the past two years, and most were going to multinational corporations that paid more than $500 for an annual subscription, he told me. To Lucas, "emerging Europe" was no wishful thinking.

Poles see the avalanche of foreign investments as a clear sign that their future is growing ever brighter. The tourism brochure I found at the front desk of my hotel said that Poland "has gone from being a country of people lining up to leave, to a country of people lining up to get in." This is an exaggeration, of course, given that the country continues to have the highest unemployment rate in the European Union. Many young professionals who are having a hard time finding work in Poland are taking advantage of their EU citizenship to move to Ireland or Spain. But in general, I found Poles to be cheerful about their future. "During the Communist era, everything in this country was black and white. Now, we have become a country full of colors," I was told by an engineer with whom I struck up a casual conversation in a café. As he spoke, he gestured toward the signs lit up along the street and in the store windows, displaying goods of all colors and shapes. It was a vivid comment on Poland's progress.

Granted, part of the current optimism stems from an instinctive rejection of the old system. Most of the population has bad memories of the Soviet era — endless lines, no heating, and food rationing, among other things — to the point that the three political parties that are critical of the new capitalism take pains to distance themselves from the Communist past, and have recycled themselves with names such as the Democratic Left Alliance, Social Democratic Party, and Polish Peasant Party. Even so, altogether they get no more than 15 percent of the vote. The vast majority of their members are retirees with pensions inherited from the old regime, or low-skilled workers who were left jobless when their companies were privatized and are now too old or too tired to retrain for new jobs. They are a minority, albeit a visible one. Today they walk through the streets gazing at storefronts filled with products they never dreamed of seeing, but without a penny to buy them with.

The best aid is conditioned aid

When did Poland take off? I asked several officials, businessmen, and academics. Contrary to what I had thought, the Polish economy started improving well before it joined the European Union. Up to five or six years before the integration was made official in 2004, the mere prospect of EU membership had created a climate of trust that almost immediately was met with an inflow of investment.

To Poles and foreign investors, EU membership meant that Poland would soon be used as a platform — a place from where they would be able to take advantage of low production costs to export goods to Europe's market of 450 million, with no customs barriers. EU membership would also have a concrete legal effect: it would guarantee would-be investors that, if there were a dispute that couldn't be resolved satisfactorily by Poland's justice system, it could be brought before the European court.

But judging from what I heard from the Poles I interviewed, the most important reason for investor confidence even before Poland joined the European Union was the expectation that it would soon be required to comply with rules that guarantee political and economic stability and protect investors from populist misadventures. In fact, from the time the country first confronted the opportunity of joining the EU, Polish politicians — eager for the support of EU member countries — began to enact economic reforms that were painful in the short run, but necessary. The fact that the EU would soon be giving Poland some $2.5 billion dollars per year in cohesion funds to build highways, schools, hospitals, and other infrastructure — like the money Spain, Greece, Ireland, and other countries had received when they entered the economic community — helped make privatizations and other unpopular reforms much easier to sell. However, what surprised me was the near-unanimity with which Polish political leaders had welcomed the fact that European economic aid would come with strings attached — a stern EU insistence on honesty, transparency, and economic discipline. In other words, the supranational legal system would force Polish politicians to behave.

Bogdan Wisniewski, the chief executive of Optima, a computer assembly company that employs 200 people outside Kraków, said the case of Poland's corruption-ridden highways was a good example. Highways like the one from Kraków to Katowice, which passes through the city of Olkusz, had long been poorly maintained, when they were maintained at all. A series of democratically-elected administrations hadn't been able to provide the necessary maintenance because of political cronyism and corruption; work was awarded to construction companies that never followed through on their contracts. The local press had jokingly named this highway after the minister of infrastructure who in 2003 had announced a new tax to repave it, but after collecting the money had never done anything to improve the road, as far as anyone could tell. But this would change, Wisniewski assured me. "When previous administrations opened up the bidding on a license, it was always won by someone, and that someone never built a highway. Now, finally, we have rules and obligations that our politicians are legally bound to follow," the businessman told me. "Cheating will be more difficult than before. The European Union will give us funds to build highways, but with conditions that we follow stringent bidding regulations. Politicians won't be able to influence the bidding process, as happened before.

The company that wins the license will build the highway. And the same thing will happen in every sector of the economy."

Similarly, Thomasz Barbaiewski, a physicist at Kraków University, told me that Polish companies traditionally hired "go-betweens" to take care of customs problems. Barbaiewski was one of many business people who enjoyed certain privileges during the old Communist regime, and who continued to be successful under Poland's new capitalism. Before the fall of communism in 1989, when former dockworkers' union leader Lech Walesa came to power, Barbaiewski had earned only $30 a month as a university professor. But as a scientific researcher he had been periodically sent abroad, which had allowed him to earn fees in dollars that were worth a fortune in his country. Today his university salary has risen to around $1,000 a month, and he made another $10,000 per month as a consultant to information companies. Of course, the cost of living had risen: while in the Communist era you could buy a car for $1,500, now it was hard to find a car for under $12,000. Even so, the fact that a sizable part of the population now felt that better living was within reach had generated a wave of optimism. Barbaiewski, like other Poles I spoke to, said he was hopeful that Poland's entry in the EU would make things better, because it would help reduce red tape and corruption.

Recounting one of his many everyday horror stories about Polish bureaucracy, Barbaiewski told me that a few months earlier he had ordered a book from the United States through Amazon.com. The package had arrived in Poland within 48 hours via Federal Express, but was then held up three weeks by customs, he said. As had long been the Polish tradition, officials were likely delaying delivery of the package in hopes that somebody would show up with a bribe to speed up the process. "Now that we're part of the European Union, we'll see fewer bureaucratic hurdles of this sort, at least as far as Europe is concerned," he told me. "Since a book imported from another European country won't have to go through customs, there will be fewer opportunities to demand bribes."

An example for Latin America?

So what do Poland and the Czech Republic have that Mexico, Brazil, and Argentina lack? I wondered. As with Ireland, most of the experts I talked to cited EU adhesion as one of the key factors in Central Europe's fledgling success, but not the only one. Many said the sudden opening of a market that had been virtually shut to private investment for decades had itself unleashed an avalanche of investment.

"Imagine what would happen if Cuba opened up overnight: that's exactly what happened here," said Richard Lucas, owner of the *Emerging Europe* newsletter. "Economic growth in these countries is largely a consequence of pent-up demand. Here we saw in the past 15 years what it took a century to happen in other countries."

Although a backlog of opportunities from decades of Communist-era restrictions is a factor that applies only to former Soviet-bloc countries, most of the other conditions behind Central Europe's growth were fully or partly applicable to Latin America. For example, just like Ireland, Poland had made the most of its huge *émigré* community in the United States and elsewhere in Europe, which after the 1989 fall of communism had started returning home as investors or tourists. "They say Chicago is the biggest Polish city in the world," Lucas joked. "All the ex-Communist countries have enormous diasporas, and tens of thousands of emigrants are now coming in to buy a little apartment in Kraków, or just to visit the land of their ancestors."

Kraków's Jewish quarter is one of the best examples of how Poland had turned nostalgia, curiosity, and even tragedy into a tourism opportunity. The Jewish ghetto of Kazimierz, just a few blocks long, had been the site of events portrayed in *Schindler's List*, the famous Steven Spielberg movie about the German businessman who had saved hundreds of Jews from dying in the nearby Auschwitz concentration camp by insisting they worked at his Kraków factory. Although virtually all of Kraków's Jewish population were killed in the Holocaust — according to my guide, barely 100 Jews are left nowadays, of whom nearly all had come from Russia and other countries after the war — the old Jewish ghetto had become the city's main tourist attraction. There were guided tours to the seven synagogues of Kazimierz, all but one of which had been converted to museums, and the flood of tourists had attracted vendors of all kinds to their main entrances. There were so many cafés, bars, restaurants, and stores opening up that real-estate values had skyrocketed over the past few months. I saw five Jewish restaurants within a three-block radius, with names like "Aleph" and "Arka Noego," which I guessed meant Noah's Arc, and paintings on Jewish themes and literature about Schindler and Auschwitz were for sale in almost every shop. Overnight, the Jewish quarter had become the "in" place for young Krakowians — and a significant source of income for the economy.

The same thing was happening in the neighboring Czech Republic, a much richer country that, as Czechs constantly reminded visitors, had been among the seven most industrialized nations in the world before World War II. In Prague, perhaps the most beautiful capital of Europe, nearly everything was geared to attracting Czech expatriates and tourists from other countries. The Jewish neighborhood, the 9th-century castle, the Stare Mesto old-town area, everything had become a tourist attraction, which was drawing nearly 5 million visitors a year to a country with a population of just 10 million.

There was even a Museum of Communism. According to a brochure I found at the front desk of my hotel, it was located on the first floor of the majestic Savarin Palace, "right over the McDonald's, next door to the Casino." It was hard to resist the temptation to visit a museum to communism located atop a McDonald's. It was in the heart of Prague's business district, in a sea of signs advertising U.S., French, and Spanish stores. The museum had been founded in 2002 by Glenn Spicker, a 35-year-old American who, after opening a jazz club and café in Prague, thought it might also be good business to create a tourist attraction commemorating the hardships of life under communism. So he began to rummage through Prague's pawn shops and antique stores, spending $28,000 to buy about 1,000 articles of memorabilia from the Communist era, from statues of Marx and Lenin to lamps for secret-police interrogations and chemical-proof suits.

For the equivalent of $7, visitors can tour several salons, including one dedicated to the "cult of personality," which features posters, books, and statues of the founding fathers of communism, and another featuring a torture chamber reconstructed by several former Soviet-era political prisoners. The last room was dedicated to the 1989 Velvet Revolution, which signaled the beginning of the end of communism. But what was most interesting about the museum was how sharply it contrasted with its surroundings. While inside the museum you saw films, photographs, and reconstructions of scenes of daily life in the Communist era — long lines of people in dark, threadbare clothes waiting to purchase tiny rations of food or telephones that never worked — visitors glancing out to the streets through half-opened windows could hear the bustle of the street, where crowds of people in colorful clothes could be seen walking in and out the McDonald's and other stores. Who would have imagined that scene in the early 1980s?

Science and technology

In addition to carrying out economic reforms and making the most of their diasporas, Poland and the Czech Republic took pride in the fact that they were growing in part thanks to their highly skilled labor forces, the product of high-quality educational systems. According to their officials, an emphasis on engineering and other tech-related careers, plus intensive training in English, had helped transform the former Soviet bloc into one of the world's most desirable industrial locations.

The Czech Republic began providing incentives to study engineering, computers, and technology several years before joining the EU. The Czechs knew that the best way to raise their standard of living was to attract investment in sophisticated industries that demanded highly skilled — and thus well-paid — workers. For that, they would need a good education system. So in the mid- '90s the Czech government started to increase its budget for science and technology institutes. Soon Czech spending in the field exceeded the European average. The Czech Technological Institute of Prague, with an extraordinary 104,000 students, has become Europe's largest technological study center, according to Czech officials. "Our highly skilled labor force is more important to attracting investment than the government's economic incentives to foreign companies," said Radomil Novak, director of Czechinvest, the government agency that helps bring in foreign investment.

Novak — whose 150 employees do everything from promoting investment opportunities to helping potential investors find real estate and make their way through red tape — showed me a brochure with the latest educational statistics from the OECD, according to which 8.1 percent of higher-education students in the Czech Republic major in math, statistics, and computer science, compared with Britain's 6.4 percent, France's 5.5 percent, Germany's 4.8 percent and the United States' 4.1 percent.[vi]

Similarly, six or seven years before joining the EU several Central European countries had begun investing heavily in English-language instruction. Over the past decade, English replaced Russian as the main foreign language required in most Czech schools, and it was being taught at full speed. On the streets of Prague I found myself surrounded by older people who couldn't understand a word of English. But most young people could readily give me directions in English, some with amazing fluency. Virtually all former Eastern-bloc countries have made intensive foreign-language instruction obligatory, and the vast majority of students were choosing English. About 88 percent of students in Slovenia and Rumania, 86 percent of Estonian students, 80 percent of Poles, and 64 percent of Czechs were studying English.[vii]

They didn't make the switch just because English is fashionable. Rather, the choice was a response to the demands of investors who need English-speaking employees for their regional call centers. The German giant Siemens, one of the first big investors in Central Europe, adopted English as its official corporate language in 1998 to facilitate the communication among its different European subsidiaries. When word got out among Central European countries that foreign-owned factories preferred to hire people who spoke English, young people began studying the language almost immediately. Starting in 2004, when most students could already communicate in English, the Czech Ministry of Education started requiring instruction in two foreign languages.

Tax breaks

Of course, if a German official heard Czechinvest's director Novak claim that foreign multinationals were moving to Poland in search of skilled labor instead of economic incentives, he would be furious. In fact, while they offered low-cost, qualified labor, Central European countries also offered huge tax and operational incentives in their quest to attract industries from "old Europe."

While corporate taxes in Germany and the United States hover at about 40 percent, the Czech Republic has a rate of 28 percent, Poland and Slovenia 19 percent, and Hungary 16 percent.[viii] Many former Eastern-bloc countries have also simplified their tax systems, creating a flat income tax. That movement began in 1994, when Estonia announced it was adopting a single tax rate of 26 percent. When Estonia started raking in investment, Lithuania and Latvia quickly followed suit. During my trip to Poland and the Czech Republic, the main opposition parties in both countries declared themselves in favor of tax simplification, and no one ruled out adopting a single-rate system in the near future in order to attract even more investment.

Tax incentives aside, the former Eastern bloc had gone almost overnight from being among the most rigid and bureaucratic systems in the world to being some of the most investor-friendly economies. According to the World Bank, to open a domestic or foreign-owned business in Poland or the Czech Republic requires only 10 bureaucratic steps, generally completed in 31 to 40 days. A startup in Brazil takes 17 steps and 152 days; in Argentina, 15 steps and 32 days; and in Paraguay, 17 steps over 74 days.[ix]

The Czechs say their first economic priority has been to become a place that welcomes investment. It seems to have worked. When I visited Prague, DHL had just announced that it was moving in its technology centers from Great Britain and Switzerland and building a technology center for all of Europe in Prague. The $700 million dollar regional center would require about 400 technicians initially, a workforce that eventually would grow to 1,000 highly trained professionals. Czech officials were citing the DHL deal as "clear evidence that the Czech Republic has the greatest potential to become the new center of Europe's technology industry," according to Czechinvest president Martin Jahn. At the same time, Accenture, the technology service multinational that employs 100,000 people in 48 countries, was building its new European financial administration headquarters in Prague. At the new Accenture offices in the Czech capital around 650 employees — mostly university graduates, fluent as a group in a total of 23 languages — were preparing to handle clients across all of Europe.

Jaroslav Mil, president of the Confederation of Industry of the Czech Republic, laughed and made a disparaging gesture when I asked him whether the Germans weren't right in saying that a great deal of the Czech Republic's success was due to its low corporate taxes. Like many members of the "New Europe" business class, Mil saw the Germans and French as symbols of times past. In his view, the countries of Western Europe were doomed if they continued to cling to their four-week vacations, their 35-hour workweeks, and their retirement age of 55. They were never going to be able to halt the exodus of their businesses if they continued to be "socialist" countries, he said. The future was in "New Europe."

"'The new members of the European Union have a new mentality, a more pragmatic one," Mil told me. "First, you've got to bake the cake before you can pass it around. We are definitely a more pro-free market, less bureaucratic, and we have much more potential than the countries of 'Old Europe.'" Wasn't it somewhat rude for him to refer that way to his richer European partners and neighbors? I asked. "No. I don't have any problem with using the term 'New Europe,' he answered. "'Old Europe' has the problem."

Mil's pessimism about the future of "Old Europe" was shared by many business people and intellectuals in the Czech Republic, a view that wouldn't change much after Germany's 2005 election of pro-market Chancellor Angela Merkel, or France's 2007 election of economic reform-minded President Nicolas Sarkozy. Nor was it far from the somber predictions of the NIC, the CIA's long-range think tank, about Germany, France, and the other rich countries of Western Europe. According to the NIC study, "the current welfare state [of Western Europe] is unsustainable and the lack of any economic revitalization could lead to the splintering or, at worst, disintegration of the European Union, undermining its ambitions to play a heavyweight international role."[x] The study by the NIC's futurologists added that "the EU's economic growth rate is dragged down by Germany and its restrictive labor laws. Structural reforms there — and in France and Italy to lesser extents — remain key to whether the EU as a whole can break out of its slow-growth pattern. A total break from the post-World War II welfare state model may not be necessary, as shown in Sweden's successful example of providing more flexibility for businesses while conserving worker rights. Experts are dubious that the present political leadership is prepared to make even this partial break, believing a looming budgetary crisis in the next five years would be the more likely trigger for reform."[xi] While Merkel and Sarkozy were eager to turn things around, the conventional wisdom in New Europe continued to be that they won't be able to beat the system.

Not everybody I spoke to in Prague was so pessimistic about "Old Europe," or so optimistic about the new one. Thomas Klvana, a Czech economics columnist who writes for major media in his country, told me that the economic "miracle" of central Europe would be short-lived. "Our economies are still very rigid compared to Asia's. This wave of foreign investment that started a few years ago is starting to slow down, because our labor costs are already rising. In a year or two our competitive edge will be practically worn down," he said.

But Roberto Maciejko, head of the Boston Consulting Group office in Warsaw, which had completed a broad study of European competitiveness, offered a very different view. "Central Europe will become Europe's China," he told me. "European companies that want to be competitive in this part of the world will have to consider moving their operations to Central Europe." According to Maciejko, multinationals decide to invest in a country based on three main factors: political and economic stability, labor costs, and transportation costs. If stability persists, European companies that make goods cheap to transport, such as textiles or computer chips, will probably continue to invest in China. But European companies that produce cars, steel, furniture, tires, or heavy machinery, all of which are much more expensive to transport, will gradually choose to invest in Central Europe. In his view, the new paradigm of investment in manufacturing industries will be, "if it's light, go to China. If it's heavy, go to Central Europe."

A "Polish threat" in Latin America?

Will Central Europe's economic growth affect Latin America? I asked Maciejko. "Probably," he answered. First, "New Europe" will attract a growing share of global investment capital. In a world of limited capital and fierce competition for it — where China, India, and the United States absorb the lion's share — it is possible that "New Europe" will take much of the rest. "A great deal of the competition for investments is a question of image, public relations, and success stories. And, right now, 'New Europe' has all three," he said.

Second, in terms of trade, "competition from 'New Europe' could displace many Latin American countries from the markets of Germany, France, and other 'Old Europe' countries," he said. When it comes to products like steel, car parts, and general machinery, Germany, France, and Spain will find it more convenient to replace Latin American suppliers like Mexico and Argentina with new ones in Poland and its neighbors, now their EU partners.

Finally, the countries of "New Europe," just like South Korea, will become medium-sized industrial powers that will create their own multinationals in the near future. Over the next five years, as more foreign companies move into Central Europe, we will also see a growing class of businesspeople, managers, and other qualified personnel there, he said. That will pave the way for the emergence of Central European multinational firms, which will go on to manufacture increasingly sophisticated products for the world market, he said. The result of all this will be that Germany, France, and Spain will import increasingly advanced products from Central Europe, while buying lesser value-added products from countries located further east, such as Ukraine and Belarus.

In other words, "Latin America could be shut out from the European market," Maciejko said. "Latin American companies should offer much more sophisticated services if they want to remain competitive. If they offer cheap products, they'll be defeated by China. And unless they become much more competitive in high-end technology, they'll be displaced by Central Europe."

Who was right? The skeptics like Klvana, who claimed that the former Eastern Europe wouldn't be a threat to other emerging countries because its increasingly well-paid labor force would soon be as uncompetitive as that of "Old Europe"? Or the enthusiasts, like Maciejko, who saw ex-Eastern Europe as the new China?

I put that question to Gerry McDermott, a professor of the Wharton School at the University of Pennsylvania, who has written comparative studies on the development of Latin America and former Eastern-bloc countries. McDermott, who travels several times a year to both regions, was clear: "Latin America is going to have problems competing with the 'New Europe,'" he said. Poland, Slovakia, the Czech Republic, and their neighbors are already attracting many companies that used to produce car parts and industrial tools in Spain and Portugal. Soon they will start attracting firms that are now in Latin American countries such as Mexico, Brazil, and Argentina. "The new members of the European Union not only offer cheap labor, but they also have much more to offer in terms of research and development, education, economic and political stability, and good infrastructure. They are far ahead of our Latin American brothers," he said. "If foreign companies are going to think about manufacturing biotechnology, or computer products, or machinery to sell in the European market, they are likely to look first to Poland, Hungary, or the Czech Republic."

The Latin American niche

What can Latin America do, then? If China is winning the race for production of low-and-medium-cost manufacturing goods, and "New Europe" is winning the competition for production of more sophisticated products, and India and Ireland are increasingly ahead in services, what's left for Latin American countries? Should they go on exporting cheap raw materials, as in colonial times? Nearly all experts said the same thing: "Latin America should exploit its comparative advantage of being geographically close to the largest market in the world, and in the same time zone." Which is, in fact, an enormous edge. Just as the proximity to "Old Europe" is one of the main advantages held by Poland and the Czech Republic because it cuts freight costs, proximity to the United States is a great long-term advantage for many Latin American countries. And in a global era, when multinationals locate their data processing and call centers wherever is most convenient to them, being in the same time zone as the United States and Canada confers an advantage that's far from negligible.

"If you compare Argentina and Poland in 1989, both countries were very much alike: both were Catholic nations of around 38 million people, both had histories of hyperinflation and corruption, and both were trying to make a transition from centralized to market economies," McDermott told me. "And the Argentines were further along: they had a much more advanced market economy and a solid democratic tradition, with more organized political parties than the Poles. And yet, the Poles pulled ahead." There were many reasons for Poland's recent success, but one of the main ones was its integration with the EU market. Latin America, he said, urgently needs a similar process, with supranational rules and economic aid that will flow in return for responsible economic behavior.

Notes

[i] *Global Ranking,* UNCTAD-DITE, *Global Investment Prospects Assessment,* (GIPA), Figure 2, Global Ranking, June 2004.

[ii] *Transparency International,* Corruption Perceptions Index, 2003.

[iii] Global Development Finance, 2007, World Bank, May 29, 2007

[iv] "Glum Days in Poland", *The New York Times,* January 26, 2005.

[v] *Capturing Global Advantage,* study by the Boston Consulting Group, July 14, 2004.

[vi] *Education at a Glance,* OECD Indicator, 2003.

[vii] "After Babel, a new common tongue", *The Economist,* August 7, 2004, p. 41.

[viii] Comparative study by the United States Embassy in Prague, 2004.

[ix] *Doing business in 2005: Removing Obstacles to Growth,* World Bank and the International Finance Corporation, September 2004.

[x] *Mapping the Global Future: National Intelligence Council's 2020 Project,* National Intelligence Council, 2005, p. 61.

[xi] Idem.

CHAPTER 5

The "Fundamental Commitment" that never was

Tall tale: "I will look south... as a fundamental
commitment of my presidency."
(George W. Bush, Miami, Aug. 25, 2000)

—

WASHINGTON, D.C. — DURING A CLOSED-DOOR CONFERENCE HERE at the Inter-American Development Bank (IDB), which I attended as a panelist in early 2005, Roger Noriega, then assistant U.S. secretary of state for Inter-American Affairs, was asked if it wasn't the right time for the United States to provide more generous economic aid to its neighbors to the south and participate more actively in regional development. Among the officials, academicians, and journalists from three continents were participating in the colloquium was Robert Pastor, former director of Inter-American Affairs under President Jimmy Carter, and at the time of the conference director of the Center for North American Studies at American University in Washington, D.C. Pastor suggested Noriega that the United States follow the example of the European Union (EU), with the wealthiest nations channeling aid funds to the poorest in exchange for pledges from recipients to adopt responsible economic policies. Anticipating Bush administration objections to "helping-hand" solutions — both within the White House and among most American voters, the notion prevails that providing economic aid to irresponsible countries is both counterproductive and wasteful — Pastor explained to Noriega that what he was proposing was aid conditioned upon responsible economic behavior. In other words, the United States and Canada would help finance infrastructure and education projects in Mexico, while Mexico would reform its energy, tax, and labor policies to enable long-term growth. This way, Pastor argued, everybody would win. The United States would help close the income gap with its neighbor and benefit in turn from a reduction in illegal immigration. And Mexico would have strong reasons to enact reforms that would accelerate economic prosperity, just like Spain, Ireland, and other countries that had benefited from EU economic aid.

Noriega, born in Kansas of Mexican descent, had cut his political teeth as an advisor to ultra-conservative Senator Jesse Helms during the Central American wars of the 1980s. He shook his head firmly, ruling out the idea right off the bat, as if it were utter nonsense. "Obviously, unless Latin America and the Caribbean are capable of making more efficient use of the $217 billion in income from their annual exports to the United States, another 20 billion in U.S. investments, and another 32 billion in remittances to the families of Latin Americans living in the United States; no amount of foreign aid will make a substantial difference in reducing poverty and stimulating economic growth," said the State Department's senior Latin American affairs official.[i] "What we're sending to the region now is infinitely greater than what we would be able to send in foreign aid. The key to sustained economic growth is adopting a reform agenda that leads to greater economic openness, promotes investments, and expands free trade."[ii]

I left the meeting convinced that the Bush administration, absurdly, had closed its mind to any plan that would include a greater U.S. financial commitment to growth in Latin America. For Bush and his advisors, the sole solution to the region's problems was free trade. The president had made it the cornerstone of his policy toward Latin America. Virtually, every time Bush was asked about the future of the region, he would offer a stock reply centered on free trade, even when the question concerned North America. At a 2005 summit in Waco, Texas, Bush was joined by the heads of state of Mexico and Canada in announcing a "Security and Prosperity Partnership of North America." But during the closing ceremony, when a Canadian journalist asked Bush whether he believed the new alliance could be the first step toward creating a North American Community patterned after the European Union, the president said no: "The future of our three countries will best be served by establishing trade relations with the rest of the hemisphere... I envision a union based upon free trade within a commitment to the market, democracy, transparency and the rule of law." [iii] Bush would not consider a more sweeping plan, either with Mexico alone or with Latin America as a whole.

Free trade: A sure path to prosperity?

But would it be reasonable to hope that free trade might catapult Latin America into the First World? Or was it totally naïve? The European Union success story seemed to suggest the latter: Much more than free trade was needed to close the income gap between rich and poor countries. True, free-trade agreements gave smaller countries preferential access to larger markets. But access would matter little if those smaller countries had nothing to export, or couldn't do so competitively. Something more was needed.

The European Union agreed on a customs union that not only covered the free movement of goods and persons, but also promised an entire system of economic aid, as long as poorer countries carried out long-term structural reforms and became more competitive. And while opening the borders to the free movement of labor would be unthinkable in the foreseeable future in the Western Hemisphere — the income gap between north and south alone, which was much more profound than within even the expanded EU, would guarantee an immigration stampede — other aspects of the European model might well be worth emulating. In Europe, rich countries such as Germany and France had given the poorest a supranational political framework, which among other things assured the rich that their economic aid would not be squandered. For less developed countries, supranationality would provide a legal mechanism for conflict resolution and a regional framework to stimulate confidence abroad. The result would be more foreign investment and a greater competitiveness. This was much, much more than the free trade agreements offered by the United States could give.

To be fair, the U.S. free trade agreements with Mexico and Chile have turned out to be excellent business arrangements for both Latin American countries, albeit not necessarily in all economic sectors. The figures were overwhelming and proved that whoever had opposed these trends in Latin America was terribly mistaken. From 1994, when the North American Free Trade Agreement (NAFTA) came into effect, to 2004, Mexico went from having a trade deficit with the United States of $3.15 billion to a surplus of $55.5 billion. [iv] Few times in the history of modern commerce has there been such rapid growth in exports from one country to another. That is why, a decade after the treaty took effect, many more voices in the United States than in Mexico were demanding renegotiation. Likewise, during the first year of the 2004 free trade agreement between Chile and the United States, Chilean exports to the U.S. grew 32 percent, U.S. exports to Chile, 35 percent, and the trade balance remained highly favorable to Chile.[v]

However, free trade did not magically deliver prosperity to Mexico. Trade turned out to be more of a guarantee against economic crises than an engine of development. Perhaps because of the U.S. economic slowdown, or the absence of economic reforms that might have enabled Mexico to compete on a better footing with China and other Asian nations, the Mexican economy has been stagnant since 2000. The income gap with the United States widened once again, triggering a surge in illegal immigration and protests from neo-isolationists in Washington. NAFTA had been a commercial success, but Bush's formula for Latin American progress was clearly inadequate.

It wasn't just Bush. Free trade had become the cornerstone of U.S. economic policy over a period of decades, after Washington concluded that economic aid to the region in the 1960s and '70s had done little to generate economic improvement. Already during Bill Clinton's administration, the White House mantra for the region was "Trade, not aid."

When I pointed out to U.S. officials that economic aid with strings attached could be good policy, as the Europeans had found, they insisted that the Bush administration had increased aid to the region through the Millennium Fund that the president had unveiled at a U.N. anti-poverty summit in Monterrey, Mexico, in 2003. They said the fund, aimed at reducing poverty in the poorest countries in the world that were democratic and free-market oriented, represented a 50 percent increase in U.S. foreign aid. But it was a trick answer, because only a very small percentage of that aid was intended for Latin America. The fund's total amount, $5 billion, was to be distributed among 15 countries with annual per capita incomes of less than $1,435. Of the 15 beneficiaries, only three were in Latin America: Honduras, Nicaragua, and Bolivia. Median-income countries like Mexico, Brazil, Peru, or Argentina wouldn't get a penny, despite having pockets of extreme poverty that in several cases are larger and more populous than many of the countries that did benefit. The policy of handing out money to poor countries instead of poor regions had met with resistance inside the U.S. government. Donna Hrinak, U.S. ambassador to Brazil, told me in an interview in Brasilia: "This is going to work against us [the United States]." [vi] The "this" was a major aid package for three countries that together account for less than 5 percent of Latin America's population. Attempting to sell it as an aid package for the entire region, as the Bush administration was doing, was a clumsy gambit that would never be taken seriously.

"The next war won't start in Tegucigalpa"

It is no secret that after the terrorist attacks of September 11, 2001, Latin America essentially fell off the map for the United States. During my first trips to the U.S. capital following the attacks, I wrote a column suggesting, half-seriously, that post-9/11 Washington was interested only in countries that had names starting with the letter "I": Iraq, Iran, and Israel. Everything else was, and continued to be, secondary. Every time I found myself in a conversation regarding the need to pay more attention to Latin America, U.S. officials would respond that the United States was at war, and the region was not involved. The U.S. government's first priority — practically its only priority — was to prevent or forestall another terrorist attack. The rest of the world could wait.

The war mentality in the White House became evident during an interview in Washington with one of the hawks in the Bush administration. I asked him if the United States wasn't making a serious mistake by paying so little attention to Latin America. I pointed out that no one doubted that the president's priority was to defend national security. "But isn't it in Washington's own best interest to make a greater effort to contribute to a Latin American economic development, among other things, to create a cordon of security around the country that would help keep terrorists out?" I asked. The official looked at me as if he were talking to a tourist from another galaxy, removed his glasses with one hand, looked at me patronizingly and said, "My friend, that's all well and good. But if there's going to be a third world war, it isn't going to start in Tegucigalpa." The comeback was witty and might even seem funny, but at heart it reflected the new political climate in Washington, where the war on terror became the unassailable explanation for a thoroughgoing refusal to embrace Latin American economic development as a U.S. policy goal.

"The most important region in the world"

In nearly three decades of writing about relations between Washington and Latin America, I had heard all kinds of statements from American administrations as to how very important Latin America was to the United States. But none was as emphatic — and as empty — as the one I heard from then-Secretary of State Colin Powell during a State Department ceremony in September 2003.

I had been invited to a ceremony in a State Department ballroom in which Roger Noriega would officially take charge as assistant secretary of state for Latin America. In the room were about 200 people, the cream of the tiny Washington world of ambassadors, academicians, and heads of non-governmental organizations (NGOs) involved in the region. The crowd was festive, and no wonder: whatever what one thought of Noriega — a hard-line conservative Republican — he was the first chief of Latin American affairs at the State Department to be confirmed by the Senate since 1999. His two predecessors, Otto J. Reich and Peter Romero, had been forced to serve as "interim" officials because they never received Senate approval. The general belief in Washington was that until Noriega's appointment that day, U.S. policy toward the region had been adrift because no official had full governmental authority to facilitate a dialogue between the Bush administration and Latin American countries.

In this festive setting, when Powell took the microphone to say a few words of official welcome to Noriega, he made a surprising statement that went unnoticed in the media. "There is no region in the world more important to the people of the United States than this hemisphere," he said.

Was he serious? If that were true, why didn't the U.S. government act accordingly? Powell was fooling his audience, or fooling himself. It was true that from a trade, immigration, drug trafficking, environmental, and, increasingly, oil-producing perspective, no region in the world had a greater impact than Latin America on day-to-day life in the United States. The U.S. already exported more to Latin American and the Caribbean than to all 25 nations of the European Union. Canada and Mexico were among the top U.S. trading partners, and the U.S. sells more to Mexico than to Great Britain, France, Germany, and Italy combined, and more to the Southern Cone of South America than to China. Of this country's four chief energy suppliers — Canada, Saudi Arabia, Mexico, and Venezuela — three are in this hemisphere. And no countries have greater impact on such domestic issues as immigration, drugs, or the environment than Mexico, El Salvador, or Colombia. Yet, everyday reality proved that Powell's speech was no more than lip service.

If Latin America was indeed the most important region in the world to Powell, why hadn't the Secretary of State visited the region with some regularity? According to the State Department, at the time of his no-region-in-the-world remark Powell had made 39 trips abroad since taking office in 2001, but only nine to Latin America or the Caribbean. If Latin America was so important, why hadn't he accepted invitations to talk about the region before Congress? Why didn't the State Department assign more officials to the region? During the first Bush administration, the Russia Office of the State Department had 11 officials, while the Brazil desk had four and other South American nations had one or two. And if Latin America was so essential, why had the U.S. stood by in 2001 while the Argentine economy crashed, when a gesture of support from the administration to the International Monetary Fund could have averted the country's worst economic crisis in recent history?

And why hadn't the U.S. restarted the immigration negotiations that were so important to Mexico?

For the CIA, an irrelevant region

You didn't have to be a scholar to answer these questions: President Bush, a former governor of Texas who claimed an affinity with Mexico, and Powell, the son of Jamaican émigrés, had personal ties to the region. But the "hardliners" who held the reins of power — Vice President Dick Cheney, Defense Secretary Donald Rumsfeld, and National Security Advisor Condoleezza Rice, who later succeeded Powell — saw Latin America as a backyard that might have to be helped out when necessary but never at the cost of neglecting other regions that were much more crucial. For the hardliners — or realists, depending on where you stood — it was important that Latin America grow economically in order to prevent surges of illegal immigration, environmental problems on the border, upticks in drug trafficking, or coups that might interrupt the U.S. oil supply. But in the end, within the new global context the region was an irrelevancy. That context was defined by the war against Islamic terrorism and the emergence of China — and very likely India — as the signature economic and military powers of the 21st century. In the final analysis, Bush adopted the worldview of his closest advisors.

The Bush administration's perspective differed little from the one reflected in the forecast produced out by the National Intelligence Council, the CIA's long-range study center, on the world of 2020. The NIC report, published in 2005, noted on its cover that it did not necessarily reflect the opinion of the U.S. government but was the result of an ambitious research project for which independent experts had been hired from academic, business, and political circles. The research, which lasted over a year, had resulted in a document titled "Mapping the Global Future," and Latin America very nearly did not appear on that map.

The study said that by 2020 the center of gravity of the global economy will have shifted several degrees toward Asia, because Western markets will be saturated and new business opportunities will be found in the East Asia and India. Over the next few years the Chinese middle class will have doubled in size. Responding to demand pressures, multinational companies will increasingly adapt to the gigantic Asian consumer market, changing not only their business culture profiles but also the design and taste of their products, the study concluded.[vii]

Within that new worldwide context, the NIC study painted Latin America as a marginal region in which perhaps only Brazil will stand out, although not enough to produce a locomotive effect and stimulate development among its neighbors. "Brazil, Indonesia, Russia, and South Africa are moving toward economic growth, although they are unlikely to exercise the same political clout as

China or India. Their economic growth undoubtedly will benefit their neighbors, but they will hardly become economic engines in their regions — a key element in Beijing's and New Delhi's growing political and economic power," it said.[viii]

"A region of advances and reversals"

What, then, could Latin America expect? Although the final NIC report said little in this regard, a preliminary study for the same project predicted that the region would experience an uneven progress within a general context of stagnation. That preliminary study, titled "Latin America in 2020," was one of several regional analyses by independent experts hired to contribute to the global study after a conference organized by the NIC in Santiago, Chile, in mid-2004. The outlook it offered for the region was "a mixture of lights and shadows."[ix]

The study concluded: "Few countries [in the region] will be able to take advantage of opportunities for development, and Latin America, as a region, will see the gap separating it from the most advanced nations of the planet grow wider." The authors continued: "Some situations will improve but always within a cycle of oscillations, ups and downs, advances and reversals. And those countries and regions that fail to find an economic, political, and social direction will be plunged into crises and experience reversals. All this will take place within the framework of mounting regional heterogeneity." The region will be composed of three groups of nations: the first will comprise the most successful countries, including Chile, Mexico, Brazil, Costa Rica, and Uruguay, which will consolidate their democracies and join the global economy by 2020. The analysts were skeptical about the prospects for Brazil to exercise regional leadership. They suggested it will attempt to consolidate its leadership role, but its efforts will be "a project that will advance somewhat but not as much as predicted at the start of the new millennium." Brazil's "complex domestic political and social processes" will stand in the way of much-needed economic reforms without which the country would not begin emerging as a world power by 2020, it said.

The second group of countries will be those that tend toward authoritarianism, the study said. They include Bolivia, Guatemala, Venezuela, and Paraguay, where "there are certain tendencies away from democracy and toward a new militarism in the years ahead." The third group consists of the region's failed states or regions with no effective government, in which central authority of any kind is likely to collapse, while there is an escalation of internal conflict, institutional fragmentation, and proliferation of mafias or "de-facto powers," such as drug trafficking or organized crime gangs. "This failed-state scenario includes cases like Haiti and some areas — not necessarily countries — of the Andean region," the study said.

The dangers that lie ahead

What are the main dangers threatening Latin America? First and foremost, according to the NIC's regional study, is the steady decline of security. The futurologists were alarmed by the dangerous absence of governmental authority in such areas as the Boyacá and Caquetá departments in Colombia, Venezuela's borders with Brazil and Colombia, and the Cochabamba area of Bolivia. They also suggest that insecurity may provoke a public clamor for authoritarian solutions, as we have already seen with the election of a president in El Salvador who promised to wield a "super-heavy hand" against the country's *maras* gangsters. "Insecurity and crime indicators have shown an upward trend for many years," the study noted, "reflecting the increase in poverty and inequality in most of the countries. Personal insecurity will be a leading issue in Latin American societies and, in a like manner, an issue of growing political and electoral importance. This phenomenon will give 'heavy-handed' politicians and candidates access to mayoralties, governorships, and presidencies in the region."

Second, the NIC analysts warned of an increase in informal labor, which in many Latin American countries already accounted for two out of every three workers: "Current projections anticipate that job creation in the next 15 years will take place increasingly in the informal sector," largely because of rigid labor laws that discourage businesses from hiring new workers and the inefficiencies of the state sector. As a consequence, widening segments of the population, lacking access to social benefits or credit, will be increasingly marginalized. "This phenomenon has institutional consequences that impinge on long-term political and economic prospects. The retirement system of the future faces serious sustainability risks due to the sprawling informality as today's pensioners are supported by a smaller number of taxpayers and the fiscal reserves will prove inadequate for tomorrow's pensioners," the study states. Likewise, the growth of the informal economy will increasingly affect the capacity of states to collect taxes, which can further weaken the state's contribution to national life.

Third, the NIC regional study warned about possible indigenous revolutions. "The next 15 years will see a growth of cultural contradictions in Latin American society resulting from the emergence of new ethnic and regional influences. The most resounding expression of this phenomenon will be the indigenous movement, whose influence is expected to grow particularly in the Andean region, Central America, and the south of Mexico... Indigenous movements, advocates of old social values and historic claims, will depend on the degree of inclusion that existing societies and powers give them... Where political and economic exclusion rigidities prevail, indigenism will evolve into more radical expressions that will openly confront the social, political, economic, and cultural institutions of the European structures prevailing in Latin America. In these potential situations, issues of historical identity and [demands for] compensation will overshadow economic growth expectations." the report stated. Put more plainly: If countries don't do more to integrate their native peoples economically, we will enter into a period of ethnic struggle against white or mestizo power.

As for relations between Latin America and Washington, the study suggested that the Americas could find themselves essentially partitioned along the Panama Canal. "The informal border along the Panama Canal will deepen; countries to the north will be more influenced by the American evolution, whereas those to the south will strengthen their subcontinental identity — especially as Brazil aspires to regional leadership."

The general pessimism of the NIC document, while contrasting with the Bush Administration's public statements, reflected fairly well the predominant thinking in Washington. Internal documents at the Southern Command of the United States Army, which with 1,500 officers has more people dedicated to Latin America than all other U.S. government agencies combined,[x] also predicted a future filled with uncertainty. The Southern Command had already drafted in 2003 an internal document that warned of growing dangers to democracy in the region over the next 15 years.

The document, according to people who have seen it, included a graph with five maps of the Americas corresponding to different cycles in recent regional history; democratic countries were colored green and totalitarian red. In 1958 nearly the entire region was green: only Paraguay, Peru, Ecuador, Colombia, Venezuela, some Central American countries, and Cuba were red. In 1978 nearly the entire region was red, with only Colombia, Venezuela, and Guyana green. And in 1998, at the high point of democratization of the Americas, the map was entirely green with just one tiny red dot — Cuba. The fourth map, in 2003, already showed signs of danger: a great deal of the region, including Argentina, Paraguay, Bolivia, Peru, Ecuador, Colombia, and Venezuela was colored yellow as "countries in danger" of falling into totalitarianism or radical populism. The final map, from the year 2018, was totally blank, with only a great question mark covering the entire region from Alaska to Tierra del Fuego. It wasn't exactly an optimistic outlook.

The perspective of big multinational companies was not much more encouraging. A study for the Defense Department by the

New York–based Council of the Americas — which comprises major U.S. multinationals operating in Latin America — noted with alarm a drop in investment across the region over the past few decades. Even though in 2005 the U.N.'s Economic Commission for Latin America and the Caribbean (ELAC) jubilantly announced that investments had grown 44 percent over the previous year, reversing five consecutive years of decline, the net movement continued to be negative: foreign investment was still 20 percent less than in 1999. The Council study, "Fostering Regional Development by Securing the Hemispheric Investment Climate," attributed the fall in investments to several factors, including a decline in productivity, low standards of education, political and bureaucratic obstacles, corruption, and — above all — insecurity. Productivity indexes had fallen over the past two decades, and the same thing was happening with education. As for corruption, the study compared the ratings of Latin America and Asia on Transparency International's Corruption Perceptions Index over the past four years, and again Latin America fared poorly: in 2002 average corruption in the region had risen to 60 points, while in Asia it had dropped to 43. "Of course, patterns such as these weigh heavily on the minds of investors," the Council stated.[xi]

"The century of the Americas"

Judging from President Bush's statements during his first months in office, it seemed Latin America was poised for a much brighter future. During a campaign speech in Miami on August 25, 2000, candidate Bush had promised, "Should I become president, I will look south not as an afterthought, but as a fundamental commitment of my presidency."[xii] Until 9/11 Bush — who since his days as governor of Texas had courted the Hispanic vote — was consistently going well beyond his predecessors in his pledges to seek closer ties with Latin America.

Curiously enough, as confirmed to me by several regional heads of state who met repeatedly with Bush, the man who became the most reviled U.S. president in Latin America in recent history was also the one who, on a personal level, seemed to have felt closest to the region, at least until the day of the 2001 terrorist attacks. At the start of his term Bush had made unprecedented gestures toward Latin America, particularly Mexico. He was the first president to dedicate an entire campaign speech to the region. Once elected, he broke with tradition by making his first official trip not to Canada, but to Mexico. The Canadians were furious, but Bush wanted to send a message that his country was going to start looking southward. The first presidential summit he attended was the Summit of the Americas in Quebec, Canada, in April 2001. There, together with 32 Latin American and Caribbean presidents, he signed a declaration proclaiming the 21st century "the century of the Americas."

On September 5, 2001, a week before the terrorist attacks, Bush received Mexican president Vicente Fox in the White House and honored him with the new administration's first gala dinner for a foreign visitor. Once again the Canadians, who in previous years had enjoyed this social and diplomatic privilege, were hopping mad. During his banquet speech that night, at the height of the political idyll between the two leaders, Bush told Fox: "For the United States, there is no more important relationship in the world than the one sustained with Mexico." [xiii] I was in Washington, watching the scene on TV, and I couldn't help but smile while imagining the looks on the faces of Canadian and British ambassadors when they heard those words.

Why had Bush made overtures to the region? It was a combination of ideology, family pride, and political need. To Bush, unlike Clinton, free trade with Latin America wasn't an abstract notion but a concrete policy whose benefits — more commerce and more investment — he had seen for himself during his time as governor of Texas, one of the states that benefited most from the free trade agreement with Mexico. Bush believed in free trade because he had seen it work. He also had a personal interest in the success of the U.S.-backed Free Trade Area of the Americas (FTAA) project: the initial idea was floated during the presidency of his father, George H.W. Bush, under the banner of an "Americas Initiative." If it had come to pass, the FTAA would have been part of the Bush family political legacy. Finally, the brand-new president knew all too well from the razor-thin election in 2000 that a successful overture to Mexico and Latin America would bring him Hispanic votes when he ran for re-election four years later.

How Bush became an "expert" on Latin America

At the time of the Quebec summit in April 2001, the White House was making an effort to portray Bush as an "expert" on Latin America. He could mumble a few phrases in Spanish — learned in Texas — and even crack some jokes with his Latin American peers when they informally greeted each other. But he needed an interpreter when he sat down with them to discuss matters of state, and used simultaneous-translation earphones to listen to speeches in Spanish. As several Latin American presidents told me, Bush liked to brag that his brother Jeb, governor of Florida, is married to a Mexican woman and that he therefore has Mexican-American nephews. He was a Latin American gringo, he would joke.

As so often happens in politics, much of Bush's supposed interest in Latin America was the product of domestic political calculation. During the 2000 campaign, he had been strongly criticized for his near-total lack of experience in foreign policy. He had practically never been out of the country; nor had he ever held any position that might have required him to deal with international affairs. That left him extremely vulnerable when facing his rival, the then-Vice President Al Gore. For his part, Gore had traveled around the world during his eight years in the White House and had been in charge of several delicate international negotiations. The gap between Gore and Bush, when it came to knowledge of global politics, was immense. Worse yet, Bush had made a fool of himself in a media interview during the campaign when he had been unable to identify several Asian leaders and had gotten their names wrong.

Desperate, Bush's image consultants rummaged around in his past, searching for anything that might allow them to present him as knowing something about foreign policy, Bush aides told me privately years later. What they found was that he had made a few official trips to Mexico either as governor of Texas or for some weekend social event. Problem solved. A few days after the unfortunate interview in which Bush mixed up the names of Asian heads of state, his campaign began presenting him as an "expert" on Mexico, and by extension — why not? — on Latin America. Eager to help, Bush started to polish what little Spanish he knew and to cultivate his contacts with Mexico and Latin America. By the time the November 2000 elections rolled around, the future president had even convinced himself he was an "expert" on the region.

Of course thin as it was, Bush's Latin American commitment fell apart in a matter of hours September 11, 2001. His determination to launch a war on Iraq without the consent of the U.N. Security Council would make him the most hated world leader in the eyes of a vast majority of Latin Americans. By late 2003, after the U.S.-led invasion, a whopping 87 percent of Latin American opinion-makers rated Bush negatively, according to a Zogby International poll. Bush's often-proclaimed love for the region had waned just as quickly: the president himself — as we shall see in Chapter 9 was disappointed by what he saw as a lack of support from Mexico and much of the region after the terrorist attacks. Already, in a September 20, 2001 address to a joint session of Congress, Bush — who two weeks earlier had pronounced Mexico the country's "most important" bilateral relation — declared: "America has no truer friend than Great Britain." [xiv] Everything had changed.

The attack that left nearly 3,000 people dead in the Twin Towers of New York City and the Pentagon was a grievous blow, consistently described by the U.S. media as the worst suffered on American soil in the country's history. Unlike the 1941 Pearl Harbor air raid that brought the U.S. into the Second World War, this was no attack on remote military facilities in the Pacific Ocean, but a strike at the heartland of U.S. business and government. Moreover, U.S. officials characterized it as a frontal assault on the U.S. way of life, an expression of a plan to replace Western culture with a theocratic order based on a radical interpretation of Islam. Given such a threat, no effort could be spared to defend the country. The nation's friends would be those who stood alongside it, White House officials argued.

"Madame Secretary" and her 20 minutes per day

To be fair, the post-September 11 Bush did not pay much less attention to Latin America than his predecessor had. Under the Clinton administration, Secretary of State Madeleine Albright had made 72 trips abroad, of which only 10 were to Latin America. Albright never appeared before the Senate Foreign Relations Committee to speak specifically about the region. In fact, the last secretary of state to appear before the full committee to talk about Latin America was Warren Christopher in January 1995. Before him it had been nine years earlier that a secretary state — George Schulz in February 1986 — had testified about the region to the Senate panel, according to congressional historians.

During her book tour to promote her memoirs, titled *Madame Secretary*, I scheduled an interview with Albright in Miami to ask her something that had always intrigued me: How much time did secretaries of state dedicate to Latin America? Albright was born in Prague to a family that had fled first from the Nazis, then the Communists, and which had arrived in the United States when she was 11 years old. Though she was the first woman to serve as the country's top diplomat, Albright had never been a Washington superstar. More an academic than a politician, she had never built the network of personal relations in Congress or the media was necessary to become a real power in the Clinton administration. She was an intelligent woman, but not at all charismatic.

I had interviewed her once before, during the Americas Summit in Chile in 1998, at the hotel suite where she was staying. She had received me late at night together with two of her advisors, and I remember she took off her shoes during the interview and put her bare feet up on a chair. Albright's eyes would light up and she'd speak passionately when referring to Eastern Europe, above all when she mentioned then-Czech president Vaclav Havel and others who had led the struggle for democracy in her homeland. She had written her doctoral dissertation on the Soviet diplomatic service and had cut her teeth in the diplomatic world working for President Jimmy Carter's Polish-born national security advisor, Zbigniew Brzezinski, another exile from the Soviet bloc. Latin America wasn't a subject that fascinated her.

When we started discussing this issue in Miami, Albright criticized the "militaristic focus" of Bush's foreign policy and his "lack of attention toward Latin America." She insisted she had been much more attentive to the region. Really? What proportion of her time on an average day had she dedicated to Latin America, I asked. Albright raised her eyes, trying to remember, and after reflecting for a few moments she answered: "I dedicated 20 percent, perhaps 25 percent of my time." However, this was not reflected in the pages of her autobiography. After the interview, when I started reading *Madame Secretary*, I found that of 29 chapters not one was dedicated to Latin America. The book was centered on Eastern Europe, the Middle East, Western Europe, China, and Russia. Of 562 pages, you could count those dedicated to Latin America on your fingers. And out of these, the vast majority referred to two countries: Cuba and Haiti. In the index, Cuba appeared on 18 pages, Haiti on 12. Mexico had six mentions and Brazil four, one of them an appearance on a list of countries that voted in favor of a UN resolution on Haiti.

Albright — like Henry Kissinger, Brzezinski, and practically everyone in charge of U.S. foreign policy — was a product of the Cold War. In her Eurocentric worldview, Cuba had been important because of its alliance with the Soviet Union, which had turned the island into a potential springboard for an attack on its chief enemy, the United States. Haiti was important because it was a country in chaos that at any moment could unleash a desperate new wave of illegal immigration to the United States. The other countries of the region, no matter how large, occupied a remote place in the minds of those who directed the State Department.

"Latin America marginalized itself"

Albright told me that Latin Americans were to blame for their own irrelevance on the world stage, partly because they didn't participate more actively in major international issues. When I asked her what advice she had for Latin American countries, she said that, for their own good, "they should play a more active role on the world scene." And what did that mean? The former secretary replied that, during her time in office, she had often felt frustrated by the lack of cooperation from Latin America during international crises. The main difference between Latin American and European diplomats was "the latter's degree of interest in other parts of the world," she said. "Latin Americans are interested in North-South relations, and not too much in other parts of the world." She recalled, for example, that when she had been ambassador to the United Nations from 1993 to 1997, the United States, Europe, Canada, and Australia took part in a political coordination group to try to coordinate their votes, while Latin American countries convened their own, separate group. They had marginalized themselves, she said.

"I thought we should have a group in the U.N. that would be the 'Americas Group.' But it couldn't be done," Albright said. In effect, as U.N. diplomats later told me, Albright had unsuccessfully tried to create an "Americas Group" in the mid-1990s. Mexico and Brazil did not back the idea, fearful that Washington would end up dominating the other members. "We should be natural allies in the development of our relations with other parts of the world, "Albright continued. A hemispheric group in the U.N. "would be a much more natural alliance than one with Europe," she added. "Other steps, such as the creation of a Latin American military force that could participate in peacekeeping efforts around the world, would give the region much more international influence."

It seemed reasonable that a greater Latin American participation, for example in peace missions around the world, might make the region's support more valuable internationally, although the frequent service of troops from equatorial Africa as U.N. peacekeepers had not noticeably enhanced that region's global influence. But more important, her vision remained blinkered: for her, Latin America's role in the world seemed to depend on its acceptance of Washington's agenda. I thanked her for the interview and said goodbye. But I couldn't stop thinking the obvious: What about Latin America's own agenda, with such major issues as poverty and education? Was the United States willing to provide conditioned aid, as several countries in Europe had done with their poorer neighbors? Albright was placing all the emphasis on the lack of cooperation from Latin American countries, and it was obvious she hadn't given much thought to the absence of a sustained commitment from Washington to its neighbors to the south.

Clinton's priorities: Cuba and Haiti

Albright's boss, Bill Clinton, hadn't been much more generous than Bush with the time allotted to the region. During his first four years in the White House he didn't set foot in Latin America, something that the Bush administration — which made several trips to the region during its first four years — later reminded the world. Judging by what's between the lines of his book, *My Life*, Clinton never gave much time or mental energy to Latin American affairs. The book, a 957-page cinderblock that tells the story of his meetings with world leaders, dedicated just 10 pages — about 1 percent — to regional issues and his conversations with Latin American leaders. In the book, for which he received an advance of $10 million, Clinton even confused the name of the Latin American president whom he claimed to admire the most: He repeatedly referred to the former Brazilian president as "President Henrique Cardoso," or "Henrique," when his name is Fernando Henrique.

What two countries in the region did Clinton mention most often? The same ones as his secretary of state — Cuba and Haiti. The index contains 29 references to Haiti and 21 to Cuba. Mexico has only 15 mentions, Brazil 5, and Argentina 5, and they are almost always tangential allusions. Was it an accident that Cuba and Haiti had captured more of the former president's attention than Mexico, Brazil, or Argentina? Or had his editors suggested this as a way to ensure greater sales in the United States? Neither, I'm afraid. For decades now, Cuba and Haiti have been accorded unusual prominence on Washington's regional agenda.

Some U.S. officials privately joked that for the White House, there were three kinds of countries in Latin America: Cuba, Haiti, and "the R.O.L.A. countries" — acronym for The Rest of Latin America. More than anything, the priority assigned to Cuba and Haiti derives from domestic policy issues. Haiti was a decisive issue for African-American legislators in Congress, who had made it the centerpiece of their international agenda. As for Cuba, the Cuban-American vote in Florida and New Jersey is key to winning those two states in any presidential election. "Cubans can't elect their own president in Cuba, but they've been doing it every four years in the United States," as one Democratic politician told me.

Perhaps the one exception to this geographic myopia in the White House was Colombia, which had become one of the world's top recipients of U.S. economic and military aid. Between 2001 and 2005 Colombia received $3 billion from Washington for the war against drugs and narcotics-funded guerrillas and paramilitary groups. The aid enabled President Álvaro Uribe to win a significant reduction in kidnappings and homicides. Neither Democrats nor Republicans could afford to vote against aid packages to Colombia: Chávez was arming to the teeth in neighboring Venezuela, buying some $2 billion worth of arms from Russia, Spain, and Brazil. Colombia was no longer a drugs-only issue for the U.S. Congress.

Alarmed by Bush's gains with the Hispanic electorate in the 2000 election, Democrats took steps toward assembling a more ambitious program for the region. John Kerry's presidential campaign in 2004 introduced a strongly positive agenda toward Latin America, even though Kerry knew little about the region. According to Kerry's public statements and what he told me in two interviews, the Democratic senator proposed to form a "Community of the Americas" that would include a Social Investments Fund of $500 million per year for small businesses in the region. This was a small-scale version of what had been done in Europe, but it would be a start. He also proposed the creation of a "security perimeter for North America" integrating the immigration and customs policies of Mexico, Canada, and the United States, and a threefold increase in funding for the National Endowment for Democracy in order to promote human rights in the region.

Fencing with immigration

With the United States gearing up for the 2008 presidential elections, the Democratic Party's Hispanic vote promoters got an unexpected gift from Bush: pushed by his party's anti-immigration wing on the eve of the 2006 mid-term elections, the president signed a bill to build a 700-mile fence along the 2,100-mile U.S.-Mexico border to stem the in-flow of undocumented migrants. Some estimates put the cost of construction of the fence at $37 billion: up to $30 billion for electronic surveillance, plus another $7 billion for the physical construction.[xv] The outlay was more than twice that year's total foreign investment in Mexico, and would do very little to stop large numbers of unauthorized Mexicans from entering the United States. (It also did little for Republicans in the 2006 mid-term elections: they lost both houses of Congress, and their fieriest anti-immigration candidates were defeated.)

The anti-immigration movement — whose most prominent spokesman was isolationist-populist TV anchorman Lou Dobbs of CNN — argued that Islamic terrorists could take advantage of gaps in border controls with Mexico to infiltrate the United States, and that a wave of Latin American immigrants was straining schools, hospitals, and public services nationwide. In 2004 Samuel Huntington, director of the Academy for International and Regional Studies at Harvard University, lent an air of academic respectability to anti-Hispanic opinion-makers with his book *Who Are We?* Huntington, who in 1993 had written the best-seller *The Clash of Civilizations*, argued in his latest book that the United States was in danger of being buried under an avalanche of Hispanics. "The most pressing, serious challenge to the traditional identity of the United States comes from the persistent high level of immigration from Latin America, especially Mexico, and the birth rates among these immigrants," he wrote. "Will the United States continue to be a country with a single language and a predominantly Anglo-Protestant culture? By ignoring this question, Americans are passively accepting their gradual transformation into a country of two peoples with two different cultures and two languages."

Mexican immigrants, he said, aren't assimilating into the United States as Europeans did, and in the future may even reclaim territories that the United States seized from Mexico in the 19th century. Huntington noted with concern that Spanish-language television channels in Miami were reaching a bigger audience than their Anglo competition, that "José" had replaced "Michael" as the most popular name for baby boys in California, and that Mexican-Americans support Mexico's national soccer team when it plays against the United States. "Mexican immigrants constitute a major potential threat to the cultural and political integration of the country," he wrote.

The arguments were dubious: the history of Latin American immigration shows that by the second generation immigrants are integrated into U.S. society and speak perfect English. I could see it first-hand every day: although many immigrants in Miami do not speak English, their children and grandchildren do. And Miami has become an international business center precisely because it has a bilingual professional class able to navigate perfectly in both cultures, home and abroad. Huntington's stance is not well grounded in reality. As for terrorism, not one 9/11 terrorist had entered the United States from Mexico. Of course that could happen in the future, just as terrorists could enter from Canada or from anywhere with air or sea connections to the United States.

Granted, many critics of illegal immigration were neither racist nor isolationist. Often, when I have written columns about the immigration crisis, I would get irate letters from readers in California, Texas, and Arizona, inviting me to visit them to see first-hand the impact of unchecked immigration on their communities. Their roads, schools, and hospitals were clogged, they said. Some said they had taken family members to hospital emergency rooms, only to wait for hours or to be turned back altogether because there were more serious emergencies to be taken care of — often involving undocumented workers. Why should a tax-paying American be denied proper treatment because an illegal alien was ahead in line? Even though the tax issue was debatable — by some measures, undocumented aliens pay fortunes in value-added taxes and other forms of taxation — the readers were not bigots. They were law-abiding citizens, seeking to correct serious problems that affected their daily lives.

But the idea that the United States could stop the flow of undocumented foreigners with fences is naïve at best. Since the early 1990s, when Washington began building a 14-mile fence along the border in California, illegal immigration had soared. The fence did nothing but shunt immigrants to crossing points farther east. A 700-mile fence would only force them to seek more dangerous places to cross. Even if the U.S. built a 2,100-mile fence along the entire border — both physically difficult and unfathomably expensive — immigrants would find ways in. They would dig tunnels, cross the 7,000-mile Canadian border, or continue entering very comfortably through U.S. airports. A 2006 Pew Research Center study found that, unbeknownst to a U.S. public fed with TV images of migrants sneaking through the desert under cover of darkness, nearly half of all unauthorized aliens enter through major U.S. airports with tourist, business, or study visas, and simply stay on after their visas expire. In U.S. immigration circles they are known as "overstayers." To them, and the many who will follow them, a fence along the border has no effect.

As long as the income gap between the United States and its southern neighbors remains as wide as it is — annual U.S. per capita income averages $44,000, while in Mexico it is $7,000, according to World Bank figures — there will be no fence high enough to keep migrants out. Other unilateral U.S. measures to stop migration flow have failed as well. According to one study by Princeton professor Douglas S. Massey, the United States increased its U.S. Border Patrol budget by 383 percent since the mid-1990s; meanwhile illegal immigration more than doubled. Clearly, the stricter enforcement urged by some politicians and journalists didn't work.

So what can Washington do?

In responding to illegal immigration Washington has a number of options — beyond paying more attention to the region in general and creating a blueprint for a Community of the Americas. The most difficult one to sell to the American public would be legislation to create a North American Investment Fund, like that proposed in a 2006 bill sponsored by Texas Republican Senator John Cornyn. The money would be used to build roads and broadband Internet lines in southern Mexico, the source of most U.S. migrants. Under the plan, half of the money would be paid by Mexico and the rest by the United States and Canada, and funding would be linked to Mexico's adoption of sensible economic policies.

The investment fund would address one of the key shortcomings of the 1994 North American Free Trade Agreement (NAFTA) — its failure to address the problem of poverty in Mexico's south. While NAFTA spawned considerable foreign investment in northern Mexico, where investors built manufacturing and assembly plants near the U.S. border, it didn't do the same in Mexico's poverty-ridden and largely rural south. People from southern and central Mexican states began moving first to northern Mexico and later to the United States. Mexican government plans to promote development in southern Mexico failed — even though wages are often one-third those of northern Mexico — because, among other things, the area has no highways on which to ship goods to the U.S. market. Roads in southern Mexico lead only to Mexico City, one of the most congested places on earth.

American University regional expert Pastor, the former Carter Administration official who had confronted under-secretary of state Noriega at the 2005 IDB meeting, told me that with the right infrastructure southern Mexico could become a magnet for investment, and that would reduce the incentive to migrate. "If you build the roads, the ports, the communications in southern Mexico, foreign investment will come," said Pastor, an author of the investment fund bill. And if U.S. public opinion resisted giving Mexico matching grants, money could be made available through low-interest loans, he said. Indeed, most Americans have long forgotten this, but when then-president Clinton provided a $50 billion financial bailout of Mexico in 1995 — a move bitterly criticized in some quarters — Mexico repaid its debt in full, ahead of schedule.

There are other ways for the United States to promote job-creation and stability in Mexico and other Latin American countries, some of which would benefit the U.S. directly. One idea, originally proposed by Brazil, was kicked off by Bush during his 2007 trip to Latin America: a joint U.S-Brazil plan to produce sugarcane ethanol in Central American and Caribbean countries, which would both help reduce America's dependence on Middle Eastern oil and boost Caribbean Basin economies. Bush's ethanol alliance with Brazil, a world leader in renewable energy, which replaced most of its oil imports by converting its cars to sugarcane-based ethanol, was part of his 2007 State of the Union pledge to reduce gasoline usage in the United States by 20 percent by 2017. While Bush's overall plan also included stepping up production of corn-based ethanol in the United States, a questionable move that environmentalists and many economists fear will lead to higher food prices and hurt the world's poor, most experts agree that sugar-based ethanol is a relatively clean and efficient alternative to fossil fuels.

Another idea whose time may have come is a hemispheric health-care deal, whereby the more than 100 million U.S. baby boomers who will retire over the next 30 years could use their medical insurance to get lower-cost, more personalized health care at U.S.-certified hospitals in Mexico, Central America, or other countries in the region. Even if at the start such a program would be mostly used by U.S. Hispanics — many Latinos, my family included, use vacations in Latin America to get dental work or other medical procedures for less than what they pay in health-plan deductibles in the United States — medical tourism would give a tremendous boost to the region, while helping Washington control rising health-care costs and helping to reduce the giant U.S budget deficit.

Mexico and Central America could become, like Spain, a second home to millions of retirees from northern countries looking for warm weather, a cheaper cost of living, and personalized health care.[xvi] Some of this is already happening; more than 1 million Americans already live in Mexico, many of them retirees who moved there in recent years, according to a recent report in the *Dallas Morning News*. I often run into them on flights to and from Mexico. They live in places such as San Miguel de Allende and Los Cabos, far from crime-ridden Mexico City, and they couldn't be happier. If Washington found ways to make it easier for them to use their U.S health insurance in certified Mexican hospitals, their numbers would soar, and both Mexico and the U.S. Treasury would greatly benefit.[xvii]

Like medical tourism, educational tourism could be a huge area of opportunity. The number of Americans studying abroad has more than quadrupled over the past two decades, to 206,000 in 2006. Yet in part because few U.S. colleges offer exchange programs in Latin America, relatively few students go to the region: more than 60 percent choose Europe — Britain is the most popular destination, followed by Italy and France — while only 8 percent go to Latin America.[xviii] Part of the reason, experts told me, is that European universities offer English-language classes that allow U.S. students to claim credits at universities back home. Latin America is not yet in the game, but — given its affordable cost of living — could be turned into a much bigger destination for American students.

When it comes to volunteer aid to the region, Washington would find it hard to compete with Cuba these days. Cuba has more than 30,000 doctors and teachers in Venezuela alone, and several thousand more in other countries in the region, according to Venezuelan government reports. (The U.S. Peace Corps, by comparison, had 2,194 volunteers in the entire region in 2006.) But the United States could use its competitive advantage — as a country with a powerful reputation for modernity and cutting-edge technology — to launch a hemispheric English-language teaching program through the Internet. There would be nothing frivolous about this: while China has started teaching compulsory English in all public schools starting in third grade, most Latin American countries — including Mexico — don't start teaching English until the seventh grade.

The United States could offer free English lessons through the Internet, run by established U.S. universities. And as Argentina, Brazil, Uruguay, and other countries are in the process of buying millions of $150-dollar laptop computers for their schoolchildren from U.S. or Indian manufacturers, there would be a golden opportunity to help speed up Latin America's competitiveness. Many Latin Americans would sign up to enhance their job skills. The United States would enhance its image as a world power whose language is the lingua franca of the 21st century, and could regain some of its faded luster as modern democracy that cares about its neighbors.

The boom in family remittances

Yet another factor could become a major engine of development if Washington steered it in the right direction: remittances. Money wired home by Latin American immigrants is becoming a principal source of foreign income for several countries, hitting a record $62 billion in 2006, a figure much higher than the total of all International Monetary Fund (IMF) and World Bank loans combined, according to the Inter-American Development Bank (IDB). Total remittances to Latin America exceeded the average foreign investment in the region for the three previous years. That phenomenon alone could change the region's economic and political map.

On the plus side, remittances mean direct cash for poor people, which can act as a powerful engine for development in the most deprived regions. According to IDB studies, remittances could have an enormous multiplier effect if the 60 million Latin American informal workers and farmers who are receiving them opened up bank accounts, entered the formal economy, and became credit-worthy. An experimental IDB project in Mexico, Colombia, Ecuador, and El Salvador found that those who started receiving money transfers into their bank accounts could qualify for loans of up to $25,000 to buy homes, start businesses, or pay for education. IDB economist Fernando Giménez told me that using money wires to guarantee credit could increase the number of Mexicans with access to commercial mortgages by one-third. "Believe it or not, in a country like Mexico, with 100 million people, there are only about 9,000 commercial mortgages per year," Giménez said. "We hope to increase that number by one-third almost immediately, and by much more than that once the program becomes more popular."

Washington could provide technical help to help channel a sizable part of the $62 billion in remittances into credit unions in remote rural areas of Latin America, which in turn would start giving out long-term loans to peasants. The U.S. government, working with recipient countries in the region, could also provide technical assistance to create tuition packages, whereby migrants in Los Angeles or Miami could invest in the education of the children they left behind in their home countries, instead of sending cash that may end up being used for the purchase of a new television set or state-of-the art sneakers. "The beauty is that none of these things would cost a lot of money," says Manuel Orozco, a remittances expert with the Inter-American Dialogue in Washington, D.C.

But the boom in remittances comes with dangers. Politically, U.S. interests could threaten to block these transfers as an instrument of political leverage to influence Latin American elections. That has already happened in El Salvador, where supporters of President Saca — with the help of a conservative American congressman — used the threat of remittance controls as a propaganda tool to win the 2004 elections. During Saca's campaign, his right-wing ARENA party warned that if leftist candidate Shafick Handal of the Farabundo Marti National Liberation Front (FMLN) won, the resulting rift in Salvadoran-U.S. relations might prompt Washington to impose controls on the flow of family remittances from 2.3 million Salvadorans living in the United States.

A typical pro-Saca television spot, aired in the closing days of the campaign, showed a middle-class Salvadoran couple receiving an anguished phone call from their son in Los Angeles. "Mom, I wanted to let you know that I'm scared," the young man says. "Why?" his mother asks. "Because if Shafick becomes president of El Salvador, I may be deported, and you won't be able to receive the remittances I'm sending you," he replies. Meanwhile, Salvadoran officials said in the closing weeks of the campaign that, thanks to the ruling party's good relations with the United States, the George W. Bush Administration had repeatedly renewed the Temporary Protective Status for tens of thousands of undocumented Salvadorans in the United States. Those renewals, ARENA supporters claimed, would end if Handal became president. Saca also got an assist from Republican Congressman Thomas G. Tancredo of Colorado, who said in Congress just before the election that if the FMLN won, "it could mean a radical change" in U.S. policy on remittances to El Salvador.

Did the U.S. interfere in the Salvadoran election? Probably not as much as China and Cuba tried to interfere in favor of Handal, as then-Salvadoran President Francisco Flores told me in an interview a few weeks before the elections. One of Handal's top campaign officials later confirmed to me that, as Flores claimed, an organization affiliated with China's Communist Party had sent several containers with computers, T-shirts, and other items for use in Handal's campaign. Still, thanks in part to the remittance campaign, Saca won with 58 percent of vote, versus 35 percent for Handal. It could happen. Could the Salvadoran example repeat itself in other countries? El Salvador is the country that depends the most on U.S remittances — 28 percent of its adult population receives money from relatives in the United States. And it didn't work in Nicaragua's 2006 elections, nor was the strategy used by Mexico's ruling National Action Party in that year's elections, but few in the region doubted that the scare tactic could be used in the future.

The greatest danger of remittances, however, is that some countries are getting accustomed to the revenues and have begun taking them for granted when they make their economic plans, just as they once depended on a continued flow of new international borrowings. A study by Columbia University predicts that the flow of remittances will drop over the next few years, as more Latin American immigrants bring their families to the United States and, accordingly, stop sending money home. "In the 1980s and '90s, most Mexican migrants were young men, age 20 to 25, who were looking for job opportunities," Columbia's researcher Jeronimo Cortina told me in an interview. "Now we're seeing more women and children among migrants, and that's part of a family reunification process that will result in fewer remittances." Something similar happened in Turkey, when remittances from Turks living in Germany grew enormously during the '80s and '90s, topping out at $5 billion in 1998. Then they began to drop, as family reunification accelerated in Germany.

Reasons for hope

Although the history of the United States in Latin America has had many dark chapters — from the military interventions in Cuba, the Dominican Republic, and Mexico in the early 20th century to today's cold shoulder — and although promises out of Washington already ring hollow to many Latin Americans, there are some reasons to believe that a greater U.S. partnership with the region is possible, perhaps even inevitable.

Wednesday, June 18, 2003, is a date that may go down in history as a turning point in the history of U.S.–Latin American relations. That was the day when the U.S. Census Bureau announced that the country's 38.8 million Hispanics had become the largest U.S. minority group, surpassing the 38.3 million African-Americans. Hispanics now accounted for 15 percent of the U.S. population. And their numbers would keep growing by leaps and bounds. By 2007 the Census Bureau was reporting the country had 44 million Hispanics, and 40 million African-Americans.

Most important, the Hispanic vote was becoming increasingly essential to presidential elections, both because of its size and its geographic distribution. While Hispanics had accounted for only 5 percent of the 95 million voters in 1996, they accounted for more than 8 percent of 122 million voters in the 2004 election, and — according to pollster John Zogby — could reach 10 percent of an expected 130 million voters in 2008. In a country where the past two elections were decided by the thinnest of margins — just 500 votes in 2000 — the Hispanic vote will be increasingly decisive. What's more, Hispanic voters are concentrated in the states with the most electoral college weight: California, New York, Florida, Texas, and Illinois.

One of the most potent Hispanic political weapons is that, unlike African-Americans, who vote almost uniformly for Democratic candidates, the Latino electorate cannot be taken for granted by either party. It is a "swing" bloc capable of deciding any close race.

In the past, the Democratic Party took 80 percent of Hispanic votes simply because they automatically identified with the Democratic support for organized labor and poor people in general. But this changed in the 2000 elections, when the Republican Party under Bush began advertising in Spanish and captured 35 percent of the Hispanic vote. In the 2004 elections Bush broadened that base even more, winning 40 percent of Hispanic voters, according to Democratic Party estimates, or 44 percent, according to CNN and Republican exit polls.

"It was the greatest performance of all time by a Republican candidate among Latino voters," Sergio Bendixen, one of the main Hispanic population pollsters for the Democratic Party, told me at the time. "This is a wakeup call for the Democratic Party in the 2008 elections. Republicans are stealing a group of voters the vast majority of whom, for socioeconomic reasons, should be Democrats. From now on, the Democratic Party is going to fight a lot harder to win the Hispanic vote."[xix] Steffen Schmidt, a political scientist at Iowa State University who specializes in the Hispanic vote, agreed: "The [2004] election put the Hispanic community with one leg in each political party, which will give it an extraordinary political advantage in future elections," he said. [xx]

And what guarantee is there that U.S. Hispanic voters, who tend to be more assimilated to their country of choice than newly-arrived immigrants, will press for closer ties to Latin America? I asked several experts. Nearly all agreed that the plunging cost of international telephone calls, satellite television, and the Internet — in addition to affordable air travel — is bringing the Latin American diaspora much closer to its countries of origin. Today Mexicans, Argentines, Colombians, and Venezuelans can see from their homes in Los Angeles, New York, or Miami the same live news programs that their relatives are watching in Mexico City, Buenos Aires, Bogotá or Caracas.

Plus, via Internet millions of Latin Americans read newspapers from their native countries every day — often at the expense of their own U.S. hometown newspapers. I know that first-hand: even though my column appears in Miami both in English and in Spanish before it does in Latin American newspapers, hardly a week goes by when I don't get an e-mail from a U.S. Hispanic reader who has read it in his native country's newspaper. Thanks to free trade agreements with Mexico and Central America, many U.S. Hispanics make a living importing or exporting goods to their native countries. They are members of a new generation of transnational families with one foot on each side of the border. This is a new phenomenon, a result of the technological revolution, which has tended to bring the Latino community much, much closer to Latin American countries.

According to pollster Bendixen, the 2004 elections proved that "the most disputed vote in future elections will be that of recent immigrants, and that's the group most interested in subjects like free trade or the issues of Latin American countries. It is the vote of people who are wiring money to their relatives, who communicate with them daily, who watch television from their countries by cable or satellite."[xxi] A national poll by Zogby International and the *Miami Herald* just before the 2004 elections confirmed the growing interest of Hispanic voters in Latin America: 52 percent of Hispanic registered voters said U.S. policy toward Latin America was a subject they considered "very important"; another 32 percent found it "somewhat important."[xxii] As Zogby told me later, "That's new. In a close election, the candidate who ignores Latin America is going to be in trouble."[xxiii]

Along with the increasingly powerful Hispanic vote are powerful economic reasons why we may see a positive U.S. hemispheric agenda — based on growing trade, energy, and health-care cooperation — prevail over the current, fear-driven agenda focused on terrorism, drugs, and illegal immigration. If the consolidation of European and Asian trade blocs continues, the United States will have a much greater need of its own to intensify its economic integration with its neighbors to the south. "The recent expansion of the European Union and the creation of a free trade bloc between China and the Association of Southeast Asian Nations in 2007 will force the United States to broaden its trade agreements in order to maintain its international competitiveness," [xxiv] I was told by Richard Feinberg, former director of Latin American affairs for the National Security Council during the Clinton administration.

Why? Because, Feinberg explained, trade blocs in Europe and Asia will increase the competitiveness of those regions by combining the technology of their richest members with the cheap labor of the poorest. The United States will not wish to be left behind, and it will have to seek similar arrangements with Latin America. Just as German companies are moving their plants to Poland or the Czech Republic to manufacture cars more efficiently and at lower prices, so the companies of Singapore will start producing their goods in China under the Asian free trade agreement. If the United States doesn't do likewise with Latin America or some other region of the world, its companies will no longer be competitive, he said. A regionalization of the global economy, plus the growing weight of the Hispanic vote, could end up prevailing over the anti-economic integration mood of parts of the United States.

As the late Mexican Nobel laureate Octavio Paz once told me in an interview, "Geography is the mother of history." Nationalists could scream as much as they want about their neighbor, but they would not be able to make it disappear; nor could they prevent their region's economies from becoming increasingly intertwined. That was in 1994, and I was talking with Paz at his Mexico City apartment about the noisy opposition by Mexican nationalists to that year's free trade deal with the United States and Canada. Were he alive today, he would likely say the same thing about U.S. isolationist tirades against closer ties with Mexico and the rest of Latin America.

Notes

[i] Roger Noriega's presentation at the Inter-American Development Bank's Europe-Latin America-U.S. Forum held on February 15, 2005, in Washington, D.C. This speech was not made public, but Noriega later gave the author permission to quote him.

[ii] Idem.

[iii] Press conference given by George W. Bush together with Mexican president Vicente Fox and Canadian Prime Minister Paul Martin in Waco, Texas, March 23, 2005.

[iv] Trade balance between Mexico and the United States. Economic Secretariat of Mexico, with data from the World Bank.

[v] Tyler Bridges, "Free trade helped Chile, data show", The Miami Herald, February 17, 2005.

[vi] "Huge U.S. aid package may bypass most of Latin America", The Miami Herald, February 9, 2003.

[vii] Mapping the Global Future: National Intelligence Council's 2020 Project, National Intelligence Council, 2005 p. 47.

[viii] Idem, p. 21.

[ix] Latin America in 2020, National Intelligence Council, Global Trends 2020 Project, Conclusions from the workshop held in Santiago, Chile from June 7-8, 2004, p. 2.

[x] General James Hill on the television program Oppenheimer Presenta, November 13, 2004.

[xi] Fostering Regional Development by Securing the Hemispheric Investment Cimate, Council of the Americas, November 2004.

[xii] "Bush's stated commitment to Latin America faces big hurdles", The Miami Herald, December 17, 2000.

[xiii] President Bush's speech during gala dinner in honor of president Vicente Fox, September 5, 2001.

[xiv] State of the Union Address by President Bush to Congress, September 20, 2001.

[xv] Andrés Oppenheimer, "How to make better use of $37 billion border fence fund," The Miami Herald, Nov. 23, 2006

[xvi] Data from the Institute of International Education, New York, November 2006.

xvii Since I first read about this idea in Walter Russell Mead's Power, Terror, Peace & War, I discussed it with Mexico's President Felipe Calderon, Costa Rican President Oscar Arias and several other Latin American leaders, and they responded enthusiastically. Their countries could not only provide first-rate medical tourism services, but also nursing homes where large numbers of American retirees could live year-round, they said.

xviii Data from the Institute of International Education, New York, November 2006.

xix Interview with Sergio Bendixen, March 22, 2005, in Miami.

xx Interview with Steffen Schmidt, November 2, 2004, in Atlanta.

xxi Interview with Sergio Bendixen, March 22, 2005, in Miami.

xxii "Hispanic voters will affect foreign policy," The Miami Herald, April 11, 2004.

xxiii Interview with John Zogby, October 1, 2004.

xxiv Interview with Richard Feinberg, March 23, 2005.

CHAPTER 6

Argentina's Maradona syndrome

Tall Tale: "Kirchner says that, in the world today, 'Argentina
is regarded with different eyes'."
(Headline from Argentina's daily *Clarín*, May 7, 2005).

—

BUENOS AIRES — WHEN PRESIDENT BUSH TRAVELED TO ARGENTINA
in November 2005 for the much-anticipated Fourth Summit of the
Americas, he came with the expectation that after years of planning
and months of negotiation the 34 assembled heads of state from
throughout the hemisphere would take the final steps toward
signing a historic U.S.-backed agreement creating a free trade zone
stretching from the Yukon to Patagonia.

Bush had not counted on a formidable adversary, a man he had
probably never heard of. It was an Argentine sports legend named
Diego Armando Maradona, once the world's biggest soccer superstar and now a cultural idol of enormous popularity. How Maradona
emerged as a fiercely anti-American political force and moved
Argentina's president Néstor Kirchner to turn against this sweeping
economic initiative only hours before the summit opened is an
instructive tale in the infuriating vagaries of populism and policy in
the Argentine Republic.

The demise of the Free Trade Area of the Americas came
without warning. At about 8 P.M. on November 2, 2005, less than 48
hours before Bush's scheduled arrival at the seaside resort of Mar
del Plata, where the summit was taking place, and after six months
of negotiation over a final summit document that most delegates
thought was ready to be signed, Kirchner introduced a provision
that effectively killed the plan, which had been the cornerstone of
U.S. policy toward Latin America since 1994.

I was lucky enough to spend five hours inside Mar del Plata's heavily guarded Costa Galana Hotel, where the summit negotiations were being conducted. My presence was courtesy of a Latin American minister who helped me sneak in by claiming that I was a member of his country's delegation, and lasted until I was kicked out by four security officials who told me journalists were not allowed in the hotel. My conversations with U.S., Canadian, Mexican, and other pro-FTAA officials there made it clear that they were livid over the sudden collapse of the negotiations. "It came as a total surprise," a senior U.S. official told me. "Their intention seems to be to destroy FTAA."

The free trade area, originally launched by President Clinton in Miami in 1994, was originally scheduled to start on January 1, 2005, but that deadline had passed, largely because of objections from Brazil and Argentina to U.S. agricultural subsidies. The White House hoped the Mar del Plata summit would lead to re-launching FTAA talks early in 2006. Instead, Argentina introduced a paragraph stating that "the necessary conditions are not in place to reach a balanced and equitable hemispheric free trade agreement." In other words, Argentina, which as host country chaired the meeting, had taken the issue off the agenda.

Why did Argentina kill the FTAA talks? Diplomats at the Costa Galana told me Kirchner changed his mind at the last minute because he didn't want to be upstaged by Venezuela's Hugo Chávez, and — more importantly — by Diego Maradona. I was incredulous. I knew that Chávez enjoyed strong popularity among Argentines, who were now going through an anti-American phase and celebrated the Venezuelan leader's tirades against "imperialism." But Maradona? The story, I learned, was that Chávez and Maradona — who after his retirement as a soccer player had become Argentina's most popular TV talk-show host — were scheduled to lead a huge anti-Bush protest at a soccer stadium near the summit's auditorium. The rally was timed to coincide with the conference's opening ceremony, and the tension was building, as Chávez vowed to upstage the official conference with his own "counter-summit." En route to Argentina, he issued a pledge: "In Mar del Plata, we will bury FTAA."

The counter-summit was organized by a pro-Kirchner congressman and — as promised — stole the media limelight. Chávez spent two hours live on nationwide television speaking to a crowd of 40,000 at a stadium amid Cuban and Venezuelan flags, while the speeches of other visiting presidents — including Bush's — went largely unnoticed. Most were not even broadcast at the press center, where more than 1,000 journalists covering the official summit were glued to television sets watching the live broadcast of Chávez's speech, with Maradona applauding at his side.

Maradona had been treated for drug addiction in Cuba for five years after the U.S. government had denied him a visa for drug rehabilitation in the United States. That was when he became a zealous fan of Fidel Castro. Earlier the week of the summit, his TV show "La Noche del Diez" had aired the first part of a five-hour Maradona interview with Castro and had drawn a near-record audience, almost as much as all the other major networks combined. A day later, Maradona's photo with Castro was all over the front pages. Asked by a Cuban government reporter about Bush, Maradona had responded, "He's a murderer." His statements were well received in Argentina. A poll by the pro-government leftist daily Página 12 showed that 58 percent of Argentines opposed Bush's visit, and only 10 percent wanted the country's foreign policy more closely aligned with that of the United States.

Argentina, which had been one of the region's most pro-U.S. countries only a decade earlier, had become one of the most anti-American countries in the world, other polls showed. Enrique Zuleta Puceiro, who conducted the Página 12 poll, said the U.S. war against Iraq and the TV images of poverty-ridden black residents of New Orleans in the aftermath of Hurricane Katrina had led many Argentines to reject not only Bush, but the United States as a country. "America has definitely ceased to be the promised land that many [Argentines] saw five years ago," Zuleta told the newspaper. In

186 | SAVING THE AMERICAS

that context, if ever there was a battle of ideas within Kirchner's mind, the populist side won. Judging from what I saw in Mar del Plata, the summit had come down to a face-off between Bush and Maradona, and Kirchner plainly didn't want to join the losing side.

At his inaugural speech in the Mar del Plata summit, addressing Bush and 31 other heads of state from a corner of the podium, Kirchner lashed out at the United States, the International Monetary Fund (IMF), and his country's foreign creditors. I was standing next to senior U.S. officials, and after Kirchner finished one of them said, "He has just antagonized almost everybody in the world who could possibly help him." As the summit ended, the consensus among Latin American diplomats there was that Chávez, with indispensable help from Maradona, had gotten his wish: after 11 years of FTAA negotiations, for the first time participating countries had failed to agree — or even to pretend to agree — on advancing the free trade talks. Years later, even Bush Administration officials would concede that, as Chávez predicted, the decade-long campaign for a hemispheric free trade plan pretty much died in Mar del Plata.

A country of extremes

Argentina's wild swing from U.S. worship in the 1990s to zealous anti-Americanism a decade later was fully consistent with the nation's history of extreme political cycles, just as Kirchner's last-minute decision to sabotage the hemispheric free trade talks was no exception to its presidents' record of unpredictable behavior. The Maradona Syndrome — the country's tendency to follow charismatic leaders of dubious authority in politically inconsistent directions — had been a constant in Argentina's tumultuous history. Indeed, if Latin American politics has a well-earned record of unreliability, Argentina may well be its most reliable example. For decades, Argentina was a country of wild political mood swings, in which each newly elected president blamed his immediate predecessor for everything that has gone wrong, and then set the country off in the opposite direction. As a result, despite periodic flirtations with progress, Argentina was getting nowhere.

It was nearly two years before the Mar del Plata fiasco that I first met with Argentine president Néstor Kirchner and his wife, Senator Cristina Fernandez de Kirchner, at a 2003 summit in Monterrey, Mexico. After two lengthy conversations with them, my first thought was that Argentina was one of the countries that would benefit the most from a supranational accord that would prohibit indulging in those constant policy shifts. Left to his own devices, it seemed clear, Néstor Kirchner would do nothing to halt the pendulum swings that took Argentines every decade or so from collective euphoria to mass despair and back again.

A curious propensity toward single-mindedness seemed to lead Argentines every few years to passionately adopt the very political stands they had opposed with the same zeal in the past. Those swings had given the country a reputation for irresponsibility that many Argentines were the first to acknowledge, but from which they could not free themselves. Kirchner, from what I heard that night in Monterrey, was carrying on the tradition of lashing out against what his predecessors had said — positions he himself had supported before he became president.

Kirchner, it was plain, is no master of public relations. As I discovered, tact is not his forte. I met him for the first time on January 12, 2004, at the Camino Real Hotel in Monterrey, where he and 34 other hemispheric leaders were attending that Summit of the Americas. When I encountered him in the hotel lobby, I approached him respectfully, introduced myself, and politely requested an interview. Kirchner was at the peak of his popularity: he had a 70 percent approval rating at home, where the media referred to his huge popularity as the "K phenomenon," and he strutted as if he had the world at his feet.

I greeted him with a cordial "nice to meet you, Mr. President," and introduced myself by name, suggesting that he might have read some of my articles in the *Miami Herald* or *La Nación* in Argentina, or seen one of my commentaries on CNN or my television program, "Oppenheimer Presenta". "Would you be so kind as to grant me an interview?" I asked.

Kirchner adjusted his double-breasted blazer with one hand, spent a moment looking down on me from his six-foot-two height and said, without a trace of a smile: "Yes, yes. I know very well who you are. And let me tell you, I don't like what you write one bit!" His reply caught me off guard. In my three decades of journalism, I had never come across a president — or any other public figure — who responded to a friendly approach with a scolding. On the contrary, like many journalists I am used to politicians who greet me effusively, pretending to be great admirers of my work, or at least claiming that they follow my articles closely. (A Mexican minister once gave me a big hug and said, "Andrés, so good to seeeeeee you! I read you every week in the *New York Times*," when I've only written one article in my life for that newspaper, and that was more than 20 years before.) Although politicians generally lie when they praise journalists, it is part of the ritual — the same ritual by which journalists, when asking politicians for interviews, tell them their statements are of crucial importance and that the public can't wait to hear them.

But Kirchner was no ordinary politician. He didn't seem to have the slightest interest in getting on my good side. That could mean only one of two things: that he was an honest man — who actually said what he thought — or that his vanity prevented him from charming a U.S. reporter for the good of his administration or his country.

"Why don't you like what I write?" I asked. "As far as I know, I've never treated you badly." It was true: I had criticized Kirchner's confrontational style, especially when he needlessly lashed out at international financial institutions, the United States, and Spain, all of which he blamed for his country's December 2001 financial debacle. I had also written that while Kirchner may have done well by coming across as a tough negotiator, he ran the risk of falling into the same old Argentine syndrome of blaming others for the country's problems, and never forcing the country to take responsibility for itself. But I had always ended my columns by giving him the benefit of the doubt, pointing out that Kirchner was no Chávez, but rather a former provincial governor suddenly thrown into the national ring who would most likely mature in time.

"Why are you being so hard on me?" I asked him, raising my eyebrows without abandoning my smile. By then, two or three of Kirchner's cabinet ministers had gathered around us, including then-foreign minister Rafael Bielsa, who had left another conversation sensing that he was missing out on a tasty scene. Kirchner, still looking down on me with a mixture of anger and irritation, responded: "You have said that I'm a demagogue. And I don't like people who call me a demagogue!" He spoke thrusting his chin, almost throwing out his chest, like football players after a clash on the field.

"Excuse me, Mr. President, but I've never called you a demagogue," I replied, flashing the friendliest smile I could muster. Guessing what Kirchner was probably referring to, I added: "The one who called you a demagogue was [celebrated Peruvian writer] Mario Vargas Llosa, on my television show. But take it out on him, not me!"

At that moment, one of his aides approached to hand him his cell phone and the president moved a few yards away to take the call. I was left waiting, chatting with the foreign minister. After a while, Kirchner came back, smiling for the first time. He handed me the phone, and said: "The last friend you've got in Argentina would like to say hello." I took the phone, intrigued, and on the other hand heard his cabinet chief, Alberto Fernández, greeting me. I had met him years before, when I interviewed him several times for a book I wrote on corruption scandals involving U.S. multinationals in Latin America. After exchanging greetings with Fernández, I told Kirchner, again trying to downplay the melodrama, that not everyone hated me in Argentina. "I still have my mother down there," I pointed out, laughing, hoping that would soften him up. A smile flitted across his face and, returning to his previous attitude, he told me we'd see about an interview later on. Then he about-faced and walked away, his foreign minister trailing him.

Presidential tantrums

The Argentine president's attitude, as I learned later, was no isolated event. It was part of his personality. While other countries pay millions of dollars to lobbyists in Washington to improve their images and attract investment, Kirchner seemed not to care at all about what the rest of the world thought. He even seemed to derive personal satisfaction out of not showing interest in what the world's richest countries might say about him. Whenever journalists questioned him about this, he said his job was to solve the problems of Argentina, and that's what he dedicated all of his time to. Most Argentines, frustrated by the poor results of their attempts to open their economy to the world during the 1990s, applauded him. What might be considered bad manners outside Argentina was regarded there as an expression of national bravado mixed with homespun irreverence. During his first visit to Spain in July 2003, Kirchner had castigated major investors at a meeting at the headquarters of the Spanish Federation of Business Organizations. Some 20 Spanish magnates and CEOs were present, including César Alierta of Telefónica, Alfonso Cortina of Repsol YPF, and Jesús de Polanco of the publishing giant Prisa. According to the Argentine newspaper *Clarín* and the Madrid daily *El Mundo*, Kirchner told the Spaniards they couldn't complain about the freeze on public service rates — Spanish companies largely controlled the Argentine public services that were affected — because they had already earned quite enough money in Argentina in the 1990s and plainly were not in the country "to dispense charity."[i]

The Spaniards were appalled. Argentina had stopped repaying much of its foreign debt in late 2001, and frozen the rates on public services provided by their businesses, yet Kirchner blamed them for the problems the country was going through. If Kirchner's strategy was to negotiate from a position of strength, the tactic was understandable but dangerous, since it could prompt more than one multinational to pull out of the country. But if he really believed what he was saying, his speech was even more disturbing. At the end of the meeting, the chairman of the Federation of Business Organizations, José María Cuevas, told Kirchner: "Mr. President, you've set our nerves on edge."[ii]

Hours later, Kirchner told the newspaper La Nación, "My speech was raw but dignified. I believe that not all but many Spanish businesses benefited greatly during the [Carlos S.] Menem government [Kirchner's predecessor], and it had to be said. Now they have to respect the rules of the game in our country."[iii] The following day, El País, Spain's most influential newspaper, carried the front-page headline: "Kirchner accuses businessmen of taking advantage of Argentina." An editorial observed that "what he did was not useful in terms of opening up new horizons," and noted that his haughty attitude had been compared by someone attending the meeting to "that of the typical Argentine we all know so well." The Madrid newspaper ABC, which generally reflects more conservative sectors, said that day: "His message was motivated by electoral issues. He was interested in sending a message to Argentines about getting tough with Spanish businesses. He didn't give them any guarantees, and he didn't make any commitment to look after their interests."[iv]

I became a close witness of the Argentine president's unpredictability a few months later. In October 2003, after accepting an invitation from the Miami Herald to be the main speaker at the newspaper's annual Americas Conference, Kirchner failed to show up, without offering any excuses. As one of the organizers and moderators of the gathering, attended each year by hundreds of U.S. businessmen, I had been involved for months in the process of inviting him.

Some weeks before, through both his office in Buenos Aires and the embassy in Washington, Kirchner had confirmed that he would be attending. The publisher of the Miami Herald at the time, Alberto Ibargüen, had written a letter of invitation that I personally handed to Kirchner's chief of staff, Alberto Fernández. After his attendance was confirmed, the Herald announced he would be keynote speaker at the conference, which would also be attended by the presidents of Ecuador, El Salvador, and Nicaragua, the presidential chief of staff in Chile, and Roger Noriega, then-head of the State Department's Latin American operations. The newspaper, happy to have Kirchner among its invited presidents, was publishing his photograph atop those of all the other participating presidents almost daily, as guest of honor.

But 48 hours before the event I learned almost by accident that Kirchner wasn't planning to attend. During a phone interview on an unrelated issue, foreign minister Bielsa had mentioned, almost in passing, that the president would most likely not be traveling to Miami. I was astonished. "Can't be!" I said. "Kirchner has already confirmed through his office." Bielsa told me that was the rumor in the presidential palace. Alarmed by the news — attendees had spent hundreds of dollars for a seat at the luncheon where Kirchner would be speaking — I asked the foreign minister whether he was officially informing me of this, or whether he was offering it as a private comment, off the record. "The latter," Bielsa answered. Confirmation could come only from the president's office, he added.

For the next 48 hours, conference organizers made frantic calls to the presidential office and the Argentine Embassy in Washington. No one in Argentina answered the calls, and the ambassador in Washington, whose intentions seemed irreproachable, said he couldn't get any answer from the president's chief of staff. Two days before the conference, we held a meeting at the *Herald* to decide what to do. Three hundred businessmen had already bought tickets for the luncheon. What were we going to tell them? Perhaps we should announce immediately that Kirchner had cancelled, somebody said. But how could we do that, when we had no official confirmation? What if he came after all? We decided to wait until the next morning, the day before the conference. That day, Argentina's newspapers quoted unofficial sources that Kirchner would not make the trip to Miami. Responding to a flurry of calls from Argentine journalists, Ibargüen issued a press statement saying that President Kirchner had not notified conference organizers about the cancellation of his visit and that Ibargüen therefore had heard with "surprise" and "concern" the unofficial reports about his possible decision to cancel the trip.

Finally, the afternoon of the eve of the event, I received a call from Alberto Fernández, Kirchner's chief of staff. He told me, yes, the president wouldn't be traveling "due to an injury to his foot" sustained several days earlier. "Injury to his foot?" I asked. The Argentine newspapers had said nothing about the presidential foot. I told Fernández that Argentina was going to look bad. Could he send somebody else in his place? Fernández agreed, and in two hours — with little time remaining before the last scheduled flight of the day left for Miami — he informed me the government was dispatching Vice President Daniel Scioli. Scioli, the most cosmopolitan of top Argentine officials, had little power — according to the Argentine press, he had no regular access to the president — but his presence was better than an empty seat. The next morning, Scioli spoke. At lunch, when Kirchner was supposed to speak, the president of Nicaragua took his place.

Months later, Kirchner stood up more important figures than us, including Russian President Vladimir Putin and Carly Fiorina, then-CEO and board chair of Hewlett-Packard. Kirchner had scheduled a meeting with Putin at the Moscow airport, on the way to China on June 26, 2004. But Kirchner arrived from Prague two hours late, and Putin had meanwhile been obliged to stick to his plans and fly to St. Petersburg to inaugurate a railroad extension there. Argentina's official news agency Télam quoted the Argentine ambassador in Moscow, Juan Carlos Sánchez Arnaud, that "a storm front" in the Czech Republic had delayed Kirchner's flight from Prague. However, some time later, journalist Joaquín Morales Solá reported that there had been no such storm front, but rather a dinner conversation in Prague that lasted too long. Morales Solá indicated that, according to Russian diplomats, "the president of Argentina let himself be carried away by an after-dinner conversation in another country," and Putin hadn't wanted to wait for him more than 40 minutes.

Months later, a top Argentine official who been on that trip told me what really happened: Kirchner had stayed behind, sightseeing in Prague, fascinated by the city. "Even today, he still says it's the most beautiful city in the world," the official told me. When Kirchner finally arrived in Moscow, he and Putin exchanged perfunctory greetings by telephone. "The truth is, foreign presidents bore him. Foreign policy is the part he enjoys least about his job. His priority is to lift Argentina out of poverty," the Argentine official told me admiringly, as if one thing had nothing to do with the other.

Also in mid-2004, Kirchner stood up Carly Fiorina, at the time the most powerful businesswoman in the United States. On July 27 Fiorina — on a South American tour to analyze investment projects — went to Casa Rosada, the presidential palace in Buenos Aires, for an appointment she had made with Kirchner. But after waiting more than 45 minutes for him to appear, she left, offended. Two days later the *Financial Times* reported: "Speaking to journalists, Fiorina said that South America's second-largest economy had become very important for her company... But is Hewlett Packard so important for Néstor Kirchner, the country's left-wing president? He was supposed to meet Fiorina on Tuesday in the presidential palace. But he kept her waiting so long that her patience gave out. Welcome to Argentina, Carly."[v]

Immediately thereafter, Fiorina left for Chile, where she was received by then-president Ricardo Lagos, and Brazil, where she was welcomed not only by President Luiz Inacio Lula da Silva, but also by his Minister of Development, Industry and Commerce, Luiz Fernando Furlán. Both accompanied her to HP's offices in São Paulo, where Fiorina declared that her company would double in size in Brazil over the next three years.[vi]

In late 2004 Kirchner sent a low-level aide to the airport to receive the president of China, who — according to the Argentine press — had promised to announce giant investments. A week later, he canceled a dinner he was going to host in honor of the president of Vietnam, claiming he didn't feel well. "Every time a foreign president comes, we all start trembling," a top foreign ministry official told me at the time, referring to how frequently the president broke his appointments. In mid-2005, just 12 days before the Latin America visit by South African president Thabo Mbeki and 40 businessmen from his country, Kirchner's administration asked that the trip be postponed "due to scheduling conflicts." Argentine officials said Kirchner wanted to throw himself into the October 2004 legislative campaign elections. "The gesture surprised the South Africans, who had to reprogram the leader's Southern Cone tour," the newspaper *Clarín* reported.[vii]

A matter of temperament

In Argentina, some political analysts tore their hair out over Kirchner's apparent contempt for the outside world, but they were a minority. The "K style" was an attitude with elements of pride, defiance, and independence, something that a great many Argentines admired. In a country where many believed in slogans like "Argentina Superpower," and where Congress celebrated the suspension of foreign debt repayments in 2001 with jubilant shouts of "Argentina! Argentina!" as if they had won an international tournament, polls showed that the "K style" was fueling the president's popularity. The country's foreign policy was viewed unfavorably by only 11 percent of Argentines.[viii]

How to explain Kirchner's aversion toward the outside world, or his lack of understanding that the countries that progress the most are those that welcome deep integration with the global economy? When I asked two presidential Cabinet members the same question in separate interviews, they explained to me that this wasn't an ideological rejection but a question of temperament. "Kirchner is a BAR," one of them explained to me. "BAR?" I asked, with no clue what he was talking about. The official explained that in the Patagonian province of Santa Cruz, where the Kirchners hail from, BAR stands for "Born and Raised" in Patagonia. It distinguishes them from the migrants from Buenos Aires or the northern provinces. People "Born and Raised" in Patagonia were proud of their roots and naturally distrustful of anyone from the outside. And there was an explanation for this phenomenon: Santa Cruz is an oil-producing province of 200,000, more than self-sufficient, and boasting some of the most magnificent natural beauty in the country. According to this explanation, Kirchner, who had been governor of Santa Cruz for 12 years, was simply displaying the inherent localism — or isolationism — of his fellow provincials.

Before taking office as president, Kirchner had viewed Buenos Aires the same way many inhabitants of Buenos Aires view New York: important, but remote. He had practically never traveled abroad, spoke no foreign languages, and wasn't much interested in exploring the rest of the world. Why would he? as Kirchner said to one of his economic aides, who later told me the story. When foreign companies want to look for oil, they come to Santa Cruz. "He's a man obsessed with domestic records. Every day, at 7 P.M., he checks the national reserves, the energy stocks, and the state of the treasury, but he doesn't have any intellectual curiosity about why some countries do better than others," a former top foreign ministry official told me. "During meetings with other heads of state, he frequently checks his watch. Those meetings bore him."

The economy and captive votes

The "K style" went over well in Argentina, thanks to terrible memories of the '90s, when the country had idolized the international economists who urged greater and greater economic openness, without warning that openness without controls on corruption and cronyism could be disastrous. Besides, there was logic to the president's strategy of focusing on domestic affairs. Argentina had suspended repayments on its foreign debt of $141 billion in 2001, and it would be futile to try to sell investors on a country that had just starred in the biggest financial default in recent history and had yet to settle with its empty-handed lenders. To top it off, the way Argentina had gone into default — with the full Congress chanting "Argentina! Argentina!" — was scandalous. In early 2002, days after the suspension of foreign debt payments, Argentina was in total chaos: amid violent street riots, it had a succession of five presidents in the course of one week, and hyper-devaluation had sent per capita annual income plummeting overnight from $7,500 to $2,500. At an academic conference I attended in Miami on January 20, 2002, regional specialists discussed with the utmost seriousness whether Argentina should be considered a "failed state," the diplomatic term reserved for countries, like Angola, Haiti, and Sudan, that had lost the capacity to exercise basic governmental functions, such as maintaining order or collecting taxes.

Eduardo Duhalde was the last of the five interim presidents after the 2002 protests — which, according to ousted president Fernando de la Rua, may have been funded by Duhalde's political faction within the Peronist party. He managed to restore peace by promising to hold elections and by claiming the country had been an innocent victim of disastrous austerity policies imposed by the International Monetary Fund. Blame went to global financial organizations and their close ties with the Menem government in the '90s, Duhalde said. It was time to "return to our ways," he claimed. Luck was on Duhalde's side, just as it later would be on Kirchner's: beginning with Duhalde, Argentina benefited from a worldwide rise in commodity prices and massive soybean purchases from China. Those factors allowed the country to emerge from its crisis more quickly than most economists predicted. Argentina soon found itself in its best international economic environment in many decades: high commodity prices, low international interest rates, a growing world economy, and a voracious appetite in China for Argentine soybeans. The country's economy, which had fallen 4 percent in 2001 and a whopping 11 percent in 2002, rebounded with 9 percent growth in 2003. Over the three years ending in December 2006, largely thanks to an extraordinarily benign world economic climate, it would continue growing an average of nearly 9 percent a year, according to World Bank figures.

Like Kirchner after him, Duhalde had been a provincial governor with little interest in world affairs. He revived the most unsavory elements of Peronism — political patronage and populist rhetoric — and blended them with the longtime practice of Mexico's former ruling Institutional Revolutionary Party, in which presidents from the almighty party pass the baton to one another in every election, creating a hereditary democracy. After Duhalde took office in January 2002, the number of Argentines receiving direct government subsidies increased from 140,000 to nearly 3 million, according to the New Majority Studies Center, a Buenos Aires think tank. "The Peronist party is not winning more votes because it has more supporters, but because it has more people who depend on its subsidies," Rosendo Fraga, the think tank's president, told me in a Buenos Aires café. "The level of poverty in Argentina has risen from 30 to 60 percent, and political patronage is more widespread than ever."

Duhalde fashioned a safety net to save Argentines from the turmoil caused by the 2001 crisis and named it the Heads of Household Plan. It provided $50 monthly subsidies to 1.7 million unemployed. Critics of the plan pointed out that the beneficiaries were not always unemployed, and that ruling Peronist party officials were doing nothing more than buying the loyalty of beneficiaries. According to a study by Martín Simonetta and Gustavo Lazzari of the Atlas Foundation, a pro-market non-profit, about 20 percent of voters now depended for their livelihoods on state subsidies, and thus constituted a "captive vote." As Simonetta told me, "In Argentina, since the Heads of Household Plan came into effect in 2002, the percentage of voters who can be considered captive voters has doubled. The federal government uses this as a political recruitment mechanism in rural areas and towns. The more people are recruited, the bigger the subsidy plans grow." As a result, politics in Argentina increasingly took place "on a slanted playing field," where "there is unfair competition between the government and the other candidates," Simonetta said.[ix] Plus, a World Bank study raised serious doubts about the plan's effectiveness. According to this study, coordinated by Sandra Cesilini, having local governments, rather than independent agencies, give out the subsidies "favors patronage and corruption."[x]

Meanwhile Duhalde was openly backing his candidate, Kirchner, in the April 2003 elections. Taking a page from 20th-century electoral custom in Mexico, which critics described as a "six-year hereditary dictatorship," Duhalde proclaimed a few days before election day that Kirchner would win, and sent his most popular ministers to appear on television alongside the candidate. As predicted, Kirchner won, albeit with just 22 percent of the votes.

Years later, after the Argentine economy had bounced back from its 2001 collapse, Buenos Aires *Herald* ex-editor James Nielsen said the economic debacle and sudden impoverishment of millions of people had transferred economic power from the private sector to the political class, who now had more power than ever to determine who would be privileged and who would be poor. Much of the population accepted that new class of corrupt officials, reasoning that at least they had resurrected the economy. That acceptance enabled the coalition of patronage-dispensing politicians, old-guard labor leaders, anti-capitalist crusaders, and business-sector cronies, who benefited much more from the current system than from freer competition, to run the country as they pleased. Argentina's governing model was one of "the political administration of poverty," which would do little but enrich the political class, increase corruption, and condemn the country to stagnation, Nielsen said.

"I hope to change this system"

In one of my visits to Buenos Aires in 2005, during an interview with then-minister of economy Roberto Lavagna, I found out that at least one powerful member of Kirchner's cabinet was very much aware that political subsidies were a recipe for economic backwardness. During the interview Lavagna — who later left the government to run as an opposition candidate in 2007 — assured me that the Heads of Household Plan would soon be dismantled. "I hope to change this system. I'm trying to convince the government to turn this emergency measure into an unemployment program that offers assistance for a limited time, let's say one year, during which the beneficiaries would have to seek jobs and get training," Lavagna told me.[xi] Interesting! "But does President Kirchner agree?" I asked him. Lavagna nodded. "The president accepts the idea. The only question is, when do we start," he said. "Most likely, this will happen after the legislative elections in October 2005."[xii]

Although Lavagna shared Kirchner's habit of blaming everyone else for the country's ills, he understood better than most in the government how necessary it was to attract foreign investment. Now that Argentina had recovered from the 2001 economic collapse and was growing again, it needed to increase its investments from 21 percent of GDP to 24 percent to continue growing at the current rates. That wasn't much, Lavagna said, but it was essential to the nation's sustained growth.

Later, when I left Lavagna's office and commented enthusiastically to several friends that Argentina would soon dismantle its political subsidies' system and launch an offensive to seek foreign investment, many of them looked at me with a skeptical smile and asked, "And you believed them?" Was I so naïve as to think that Kirchner would disband his army of subsidized unemployed, which also acted as shock troops in pro-government demonstrations or harassing multinationals that dared criticize price controls? Did I really think Kirchner would do that before the 2007 presidential election, in which he was likely to nominate his wife Cristina as government-backed candidate to succeed him? Their suspicions proved right. The day after I published my interview with Lavagna in the *Miami Herald*, an unidentified official from Kirchner's office told reporters the president had not approved the economy minister's plan.[xiii]

Lavagna had been one of Argentina's leading voices confronting the International Monetary Fund and foreign creditors, but by 2005 he was beginning to fear the country would pay dearly for its poor reputation among foreign investors. The country risk continued to be sky-high, as if there had never been any economic recovery, he told me.

"How unimaginably stupid," Lavagna said, getting up from the conference table where we were speaking and walking to one of two computers on his desk. Pulling up a Web page with the latest financial news, he showed me headlines about a constitutional coup that had just happened in Ecuador amid bloody protests. Ecuador's president Lucio Gutiérrez had been ousted and was heading for the Brazilian Embassy, while Congress named the country's vice president to replace him. At least three protesters were dead, dozens wounded. Yet, as Lavagna showed me on his computer, the country risk for Ecuador was still much lower than that of Argentina. Pointing to a J. P. Morgan country risk table on his screen, Lavagna said, "Tell me if this isn't completely absurd: right now, with tanks in the streets, Ecuador's country risk is 722 points, while Argentina's is 6,130." The difference in country risk between Ecuador, even while embroiled in a bloody national crisis, and Argentina, in a period of tranquility and recovery, was testimony to the high price Argentina continued to pay for the confrontational policies and rhetoric of its rulers.

The long-awaited interview

Kirchner made good on his vague promise of an interview two days after our encounter in the hotel lobby during the Monterrey summit. In a nearly empty hotel bar at around 3 in the afternoon, recorder in hand, I sat down to ask him about his foreign and domestic policies. Did it really make sense to boast about putting an end to the Menem Administration's "carnal relations" with the United States, instead of pursuing independent policies — whether Washington liked them or not — without publicly antagonizing Washington? I asked. Did it make sense to announce restoration of full ties with the Castro dictatorship right after 75 Cuban journalists and peaceful dissidents had been sentenced to 25 years' imprisonment? Wasn't he rewarding repression with his announcement? Had he done the right thing by supporting Bolivia's Evo Morales, the coca farmer leader who at the time was leading violent riots against the government? Hadn't Kirchner also interfered in the internal affairs of Uruguay by supporting the candidacy of left-wing opposition leader Tabaré Vázquez? And hadn't he helped legitimize Hebe de Bonafini, extremist leader of Argentina's Mothers of the Plaza de Mayo group of victims of the 1970s dictatorship, who was now a supporter of armed struggle and had applauded the 2001 attacks on the United States? What kind of message was he sending to the world with these shows of support? I asked.

I was especially interested in Kirchner's human rights views, because I had viewed with great concern his shift on an issue that, ironically, he had ostensibly turned into one of his government's top priorities. Kirchner had portrayed himself as a champion of the victims of the 1976–83 military dictatorship, and routinely described his press critics as former supporters of the regime. But he couldn't do that with me: I had left the country after the 1976 military coup, and had publicly criticized the dictatorship from the start. In fact, my only article for the New York Times was an op-ed column published in 1978, in which I had strongly criticized human rights violations in Argentina and the U.S. media's benign view of Gen. Jorge Rafael Videla's pro-market military government.

What concerned me about Kirchner's policy was that, by ignoring civil and human rights abuses in Cuba — and later Venezuela — he was undermining the newly established regional principle of collective defense of democracy. Amnesty International, Human Rights Watch, and other major international human rights groups had been fairly successful in recent years in convincing Latin

American governments that you could not be a champion of human rights at home while ignoring violations abroad. If Argentina didn't raise its voice about rights abuses elsewhere, who would come to the country's own rescue tomorrow, if its own democracy were threatened? As former Mexican foreign minister Jorge Castañeda had once told me, "The best way to secure respect for human rights at home is by ensuring international condemnation of human rights violations abroad, no matter where they take place. If the human rights principle is undermined internationally, sooner or later it will be undermined domestically."[xiv]

Kirchner's answers during the interview weren't as bad as I had expected. What he said into the recorder fell within the parameters of democratic thinking, even if he was a bit too anchored in old-guard 1970s blame-the-rich ideas. But, unlike Chávez, Kirchner did not a come across as a would-be messiah. Asked how he defined himself politically, Kirchner told me, "I believe in the major themes of economic liberalism, but I'm progressive within economic liberalism. I believe in liberalism with justice and equity."[xv]

When we got to the subject of Cuba, I asked why he, a vocal critic of Argentina's dictatorships, had warmed up relations with Cuba's. Raúl Taleb, Argentina's new ambassador to Cuba, had just announced normalization of relations. "Look, we support the people's right to self-determination," Kirchner said. "We don't like to interfere in other nations' domestic affairs. The situation in Cuba is very special for many reasons. The problems of the Cuban people must be solved by the Cuban people," he added. "Precisely," I responded. "The Cuban people must solve their own problems. But how are they going to do that when they can't vote, or have an independent newspaper, or anything like that?" Besides, I added, terms like "non-interference' and "people's self-determination" had long been used by both right- and left-wing dictators to prevent international monitoring of rights abuses in their countries. In today's world, when it comes to human rights many democracies are putting the principle of "non-indifference" to abuses way ahead of that of "non-intervention" in other countries' affairs. Was Kirchner aware that Cuba was imprisoning people for the "crime" of distributing mimeographed copies of the U.N. Charter?

Kirchner reiterated his stand about the need to respect the country's self-determination, adding at the end that "each one has a view on the subject. I believe that recent events in Cuba [the 25-year sentences of dissidents) had negative repercussions. They weren't exactly among Fidel's best moves."[xvi]

The subject of Cuba didn't seem to inspire much passion one way or the other. I asked a final question anyway. Now that Argentina was developing closer relations with Cuba, would it speak only to Fidel Castro on the island? Or would it also talk to the opposition, as Castro had with ultra-leftist groups during his visit to Buenos Aires in 2002 and on each of his trips abroad? "You can never be so demanding in real life," Kirchner responded. "We'll see." His answers suggested he wasn't so naïve as to admire the Cuban dictatorship. But he didn't seem to have any notion of the harm he was doing to the cause of human rights by tacitly supporting the idea — shared by a good part of Argentine society, judging from polls — that there is such a thing as a benevolent dictatorship.

Changing the subject, I asked him whether he had supported Morales's candidacy during a visit to Bolivia, as the Argentine press had reported. Kirchner replied that, contrary to press reports, "I never told Evo Morales that we were going to support him. I'm not interfering in Bolivia's domestic affairs. What I told Evo Morales was that I thought it was essential for him to abandon any notion of insurrection.... But I am not going to support a candidate from another country, that's absurd. It would constitute an unacceptable interference."[xvii] Yet that was precisely what he did with Uruguay's leftist candidate Tabaré Vázquez, I pointed out. In fact, Uruguayan then-president Jorge Batlle publicly stated that Kirchner had thrown his support behind Vázquez, who later won the presidential election. Kirchner, annoyed at this question, put Batlle's accusations into perspective. "In Uruguay there's a pretty tough political struggle between the traditional parties and the [left-wing] Broad Front. It is very polarized. And the mayor of Montevideo [Mariano Arana] invited us, Mesa, Duhalde, and Lula, so he could present us with the key to the city. And one of President Batlle's aides came out saying — he was overruled later — that we were interfering in domestic affairs. Absolutely not. I don't interfere."

Had he not helped legitimize Hebe de Bonafini, the self-proclaimed Argentine human rights leader who had said she was "happy" about the 9/11 attacks on the United States, by inviting her periodically to the presidential palace? I asked. "I feel great affection for her," Kirchner answered. "Politically, we have always been in different camps. [But] she was a housewife who was destroyed by this loss [of her son], and she turned into a revolutionary militant, as she herself says. And as a representative of all the mothers who suffered so much, I will always receive her whenever she comes to see me. That doesn't mean I agree with all her stands. If I had to agree with every person who comes into my office, I wouldn't be able to receive anyone."[xviii]

Was Kirchner annoyed when the press painted him as an ally of Brazil, Venezuela, and Cuba? "Well, it neither bothers me nor doesn't bother me, because everyone knows what it is. The only true axis I can think of in South America is that of Brazil-Argentina, or Argentina-Brazil." He added that Argentina had not signed any major joint agreements with Venezuela and Cuba, "but just because we haven't signed any doesn't mean that I agree with isolating Chávez, or any other president. On the contrary, I believe that dialogue is essential."[xix]

I left the interview mildly impressed with Kirchner. Judging from what Kirchner told me that day — albeit well before he signed key economic agreements with Chávez and gave the Venezuelan president significant political support in 2007 — he seemed more democratic and tolerant than many of us believed. Perhaps he was a man with an arrogant, confrontational personal style who, in the end, had a subtle, thoughtful intellect. However, my initial optimism about Kirchner was confounded the following night, when I had another long conversation, more extensive and private, once the summit had come to an end.

Late-night with the Kirchners

It was about 11 P.M. I had just sent my column to the *Herald*, ate dinner in my room, and went down to the hotel lobby to see if there were any officials left to talk to. When I popped my head into the bar, I saw Kirchner sitting at a table with his wife Cristina and foreign minister Bielsa. They were having coffee, killing time while their luggage was brought down, waiting for the presidential airplane to be readied for their return to Argentina. I went over to greet them and stood next to the table long enough for them to have no choice but to invite me to sit down with them. In a little while we were talking about the topics that had caught everyone's attention at the summit. Since this was a private conversation, off the record, I never published what Kirchner said, nor will I at this time. I shall simply relate what I said, and the impression his answers made on me.

It was a conversation that left me worried. During our informal chat, Kirchner seemed to go beyond being just a "progressive within economic liberalism," edging closer to the old-guard reactionary left that blamed all of the world's ills on U.S. imperialism and international financial institutions. During our conversation, we returned to the subjects of Venezuela, Cuba, Bolivia, Uruguay, and Argentina itself. This time, with no recorder between us, Kirchner insisted time and again on blaming the United States, the IMF, the free-market reforms of the 1990s, and his predecessor, Menem. Some of the things he said were true; the United States had indeed left former Bolivian president Gonzalo Sanchez de Losada high and dry after getting the country to accept a huge sacrifice by destroying its coca fields. Other things, such as blaming the IMF for Argentina's economic fiasco, were debatable, but still within the scope of serious political debate. But when, issue after issue, Kirchner pointed his finger at anybody but his own country, I started to get worried. Noting that he was either bored or not overly interested in hearing my opinion, I decided to confine my role to that of indulgent questioner, and reserve my opinion for the end of the evening. So after 40 minutes of conversation, during which Lavagna and two or three of Bielsa's aides had joined us, I expressed my point of view.

"Mr. President," I said, "many of the things you say are true. It is undeniable that the United States has a dubious history in the region, especially in the early 20th century But we must also acknowledge that over the past three decades Washington has learned some lessons, and has often backed democracy and human rights in the region. If you'll allow me some constructive criticism, your government often comes across as eager to do exactly the opposite of whatever was done in the '90s, whether good or bad." Kirchner looked at me with a stony face, with an air I perceived as distrustful. I continued, "It's not good for countries to make a U-turn with every new government. Constant policy flip-flops generate domestic and foreign distrust, which results in fewer investments, more capital flight, less growth, and more unemployment. Countries that do well, such as Spain, Ireland, or Chile, are those that stay the course. They are countries where you see the left, right, or center winning elections, and nobody changes the course. You won't see investors fleeing in panic from Spain or Chile before an election, for fear that one party or the other will win."

As Kirchner listened in silence, I continued: "Argentina is a country of constant political zigzags," I told him. As far back as Argentines can remember, there have been practically no extended periods of stability. Its history has been characterized by extremes. The search for a middle ground has been the exception, not the rule, so much so that, while the rest of the world sees moderation as a virtue, Argentina considers it a sign of weakness. Argentina is the only country I know where even a major centrist party proudly bears the name 'Radical Party.' Wasn't that absurd in the 21st century, when most countries compete to showcase themselves as moderate and pragmatic in order to attract investment? I reminded Kirchner that a few decades ago the Radical Party — which, paradoxically, represented the urban middle class — had splintered, and those who had spun off reorganized themselves as the "Intransigent Radical Party," as if to ensure that no one would think they would succumb to such vices as moderation, open-mindedness, or consensus-building.

Argentina had successively gone from the nationalist populism of Perón in the 1950s to recalcitrant anti-Peronism in the 1960s, to the brief return of Peronism — now allied with the left — in 1973, to an anti-Peronist right-wing military dictatorship in 1976, to weak democratic governments in the '80s, to free-market crony capitalism under Menem in the '90s, to the current government, which claimed everything done in recent decades had been worthless. Summing up, I said I applauded his criticism of Menem government corruption. But it was one thing to attack corruption and specific policies, and quite another to attack the whole concept of economic openness and the need to attract investment, which was exactly what was helping countries as diverse as China, India, Poland, and Chile to reduce poverty at a record pace

Kirchner didn't listen, or at least he gave the impression of not having listened. He shrugged, looked down his nose at me and responded with his standard lecture about the "barbarities" of Menem's free-market policies, not even mentioning my argument that no country can advance if it changes direction all the time. A few minutes later it was time to said good-bye. I left the table feeling I had failed miserably in my attempt at constructive criticism. My only consolation was that, as I was leaving the hotel bar, Kirchner's wife Cristina said something along the lines that I was right that countries should try to maintain basic state policies over time, but that I needed to understand the depth of Argentina's 2001 economic disaster, how much it had affected people's lives, and the fact that society had emerged from the crisis longing for a dramatic change in course. I wasn't convinced by her arguments, but at least she had listened to mine.

The view from Washington

My conversations with the Argentine president weren't the only surprise of the Monterrey summit. The other was the coverage by the Argentine media, which reported that the meeting between Kirchner and Bush had been a resounding success. "Government improves U.S. relations," declared *La Nación* on January 15. The front-page article reported that "yesterday, the government rated as a 'total success'" Kirchner's participation at the summit. The country's highest-circulation daily, *Clarín*, led with the headline, "Bush renewed his support, but asked for a clear signal regarding [foreign] debt."[xx] In a news analysis, it said, "Kirchner maneuvered well during his second meeting with the White House chief in seven months."[xxi]

But senior Bush administration officials who were at the meeting told me a completely different story later. True, Kirchner's meeting with Bush had been civil, and even positive, one White House official told me. But in his speech to the summit a few hours later, Kirchner blamed the United States for practically everything that was wrong with the region, demanding a Marshall Plan for Latin America. Within hours, the positive climate had vanished. Midway through Kirchner's speech, Bush removed his simultaneous-translation earphones.

Otto Reich, at the time White House special envoy to Latin America, told me in an interview that "the reaction of the U.S. delegation was one of incredulity, given the antiquated rhetoric of the Argentine president. It was a Third World speech straight out of the '60s."[xxii] Reich added: "What had such a negative impact on the perception of the U.S. delegation was that Kirchner's speech had taken place at the closing session of the Summit of the Americas," which Kirchner chaired as head of the country that would host the following summit, the Mar del Plata meeting in November 2005. "The summit had been dedicated to promoting development, and during the entire day-and-a-half there had been discussions about things like creating jobs by cutting through red tape and other state-imposed barriers to new business. And instead of talking about how to generate growth and employment by reducing state intervention, we find someone who's still thinking in terms of dependency theory."[xxiii]

Buenos Aires never heard about the terrible impact that Kirchner's presentation had had on the U.S. delegation. On the contrary, Argentine government officials returned home with a triumphant air, as if they had managed to side with both God and the Devil, without paying any price for it. For the few journalists who were talking to officials from both countries, Argentina was kidding itself. U.S. delegates were telling us that, after his closing-session speech in Monterrey, Kirchner could forget about having a friend in the White House. And so it was. Months later, Kirchner made his first official trip to the United States, visiting New York City and Washington. But despite efforts by the Argentine Embassy to arrange an interview with Bush, then-Secretary of State Colin Powell, or then-National Security Advisor Condoleezza Rice, the Bush administration wouldn't give him the time of day.

Reich said he tried in vain to convince Bush's office that the president should receive Kirchner, if only for a moment. No dice, Bush's office replied. "People in President Bush's office were saying: 'Why the heck does he want another meeting? We're going to have another nice get-together and then, who knows, he'll come out with another speech against us?'" the official said. It would be more than a year before Bush and Kirchner met again, at the 2005 Summit of the Americas in Argentina. And there, far from improving, the relationship took yet another turn for the worse, and reached its lowest point in recent memory.

The partition of the Americas

The 2005 hemispheric summit in Mar del Plata had clearly marked a temporary — perhaps not so temporary — partition of the Americas. One bloc was made up of the United States, Canada, Mexico,

Central America, Chile, and other countries that either had free trade deals with Washington or were about to sign them. Another bloc was Brazil, Argentina, Uruguay, and Paraguay, which had resolved to stay out of future negotiations as long as Washington didn't relax U.S. agricultural subsidies. Then there was oil-rich Venezuela, which openly advocated replacing free trade with the United States with a new anti-American alliance centered in Caracas.

After Mar del Plata, Argentina would gravitate increasingly closer to Venezuela and farther from Washington. Domestically, while never going as far as Chávez in Venezuela, the Kirchner government unilaterally rescinded foreign-controlled utility company contracts, imposed price controls on key products, and took other measures that orthodox economists criticized as a dangerous reversion to economic nationalism. In its international relations, Argentina's tilt toward Chávez became much more evident. Officials explained it to me as an economic — not political — decision. By early 2007, with oil prices at more than $65 a barrel, Chávez had more money at his disposal than ever. He bought up $3.5 billion in Argentine bonds at above-market prices, which gave the Kirchner government a much-needed influx of funds at a time when few foreign investors were willing to put their money in Argentina. That was only one instance of Chávez's generosity toward Argentina, officials said: among other things he had agreed to rescue bankrupt dairy giant Sancor and invest in 600 state-run gasoline stations. Plus, he vowed to build a monumental $20 billion natural-gas pipeline from Venezuela to Argentina, and create a $7 billion Banco del Sur, a South American development bank that, Chávez said, would be much better suited than the Washington-based IDB to alleviate poverty in the region. While Washington talks, Chávez puts money in the table, Argentine officials said.

Naturally, Chávez's largesse wasn't free: increasingly, Kirchner had to reciprocate with political support for Venezuela and for Chávez's ego-trips. At a 2006 meeting Kirchner chaired of Mercosur — the trade bloc then comprising Argentina, Brazil, Paraguay, and Uruguay — the group welcomed Venezuela as a new member, and one of the expanded bloc's first measures was to throw its support behind Venezuela's bid for a U.N. Security Council seat (which ultimately failed.) Then, in 2007, Kirchner allowed Chávez to come to Argentina on the eve of Bush's visit to neighboring Uruguay, and to stage — much as the Venezuelan had done in Mar del Plata nearly two years earlier — a huge Bush counter-rally. Once again, addressing more than 30,000 leftist sympathizers waving Cuban, Venezuelan, and Argentine flags, Chávez stole the limelight from Bush's long-awaited Latin America trip, denouncing the U.S president's "imperial excursion" to the region and calling him a "coward" and "a political cadaver." Kirchner did not attend the rally, but had invited Chávez for a meeting earlier that day, giving the Venezuelan president the chance he needed to steal the show from Bush hours before the U.S. president's arrival in Uruguay. It was no surprise that Bush, in his March 2007 visit to Brazil, Uruguay, Colombia, Guatemala, and Mexico, decided to skip Argentina altogether.

"An adolescent country"

How do you see Argentina's future? I asked Manuel Rocha, the U.S. chargé d'affaires in Buenos Aires from 1997 to 2000. "Dark," he replied. I had sought out Rocha's opinion not only because he had been a senior official of the U.S. Embassy, but because he had spent much of his diplomatic career in Latin America — most recently as ambassador to Bolivia until 2002 — and was a passionate student of hemispheric affairs. Why was he so pessimistic? "Because there's no consensus within the ruling class on a common national project. There's tremendous division within the ruling class. In Chile you can talk with somebody on the left, on the center, or on the right, and you'll find that in terms of economic policy there's not much disagreement. In Argentina, when you discuss economic policy you can't find any basic consensus, not even within the Peronist party." According to Rocha, this was due to "the ineptitude of an immature political class, which hasn't lived up to the standards of a country like the one it has, in part because of the [populist] legacy of Peronism. And, also, because of the ineptitude of the business class." As for the inability of Argentine business leaders to understand the need to modernize and compete in a global economy, he added, "They just don't get it."

But didn't Argentina have one of Latin America's most sophisticated intellectual, political, and business classes? Isn't it the South American country with the most avant-garde theaters, operas, museums, conferences, and book fairs? "They are sophisticated people, but only in appearance," Rocha said. "They wear British clothes, but if you compare them to a guy from Hong Kong, Singapore, or even a ranking member of the Chinese Communist Party, all three are more sophisticated than an Argentine politician or businessman. That's because Argentina has a very individualistic, every-man-for-himself culture, where everyone is out to get rich as fast as he can, by any means possible."

Rocha cited the case of Maradona's famous goal — celebrated by his countrymen to this day — during the 1986 World Cup in Mexico. In a match against Britain's national team, Maradona faked a head shot — legal in soccer — while slapping the ball into the net with his hand, which is utterly illegal. The referee didn't notice it, and counted it as a goal. When journalists after the game asked Maradona whether he had slapped the ball with his hand, he smiled and said, "the hand of God." To this day, Argentines celebrate his wit. Many years after Maradona's retirement, and even after the former star had been charged with tax evasion in Italy and had gone in and out of drug rehabilitation clinics in Europe and Cuba, a 2005 poll asked Argentines who was the celebrity that best represented Argentina. Maradona came in first with 51 percent of the vote, followed by Kirchner with 31 percent.[xxiv] "It's a wonderful country, with a tremendous amount of talent, where despite the talent people applaud the guy who scores a goal with his hand," Rocha said. "They applaud slyness, rather than hard work and discipline." It was no coincidence that Kirchner got huge applause in Argentina for blaming the IMF, banks, creditors — almost everybody outside the country except Argentines — for the debt suspension, the former diplomat said.

Rocha attributed much of Argentina's "immaturity" to the legacy of General Juan D. Perón, the populist nationalist who drew much of his political inspiration from his time in Benito Mussolini's Italy. "Peronism created a relationship between the individual and the state that makes the individual dependent on the state. Argentines expect the state to solve all their problems, and to take care of everything. In Argentina, instead of John F. Kennedy's 'Ask not what your country can do for you; ask what you can do for your country,' people ask, 'What can my country do for me?' Therefore, when there's someone to blame, they blame the state, the IMF, capitalism, or the free market model, but never even consider taking responsibility for their own actions. It's an immature, adolescent country. And it won't get out of its crisis because of its inability to take the most basic steps, like respecting contracts."

In the strictest sense, Rocha's view on Peronism is so widespread outside Argentina that Secretary of State Condoleezza Rice herself — apparently without noticing that she was criticizing the founder of Argentina's ruling party — said in testimony before Congress on May 12, 2005, that Perón, like Chávez today, had been a "populist" president whose "demagoguery" hadn't done his country any good. Even in neighboring Chile, foreign minister Ignacio Walker saw himself forced to apologize to the Argentine government upon taking office for having written a November 2004 article in the daily *El Mercurio* in which he said "the real wall separating Chile and Argentina isn't the Andes mountain range, but the legacy of Peronism and its perverse logic." Walker referred to Kirchner's Peronist party as a movement with "authoritarian, corporative, and fascistoid features," and added, "Since Perón came into power in 1945, Peronism and militarism have managed to systematically destroy Argentina."[xxv]

But isn't it possible that Kirchner is doing things in stages? I asked Rocha. Clearly, the Argentine president was no cosmopolitan, up to date with the latest world economic trends. But to deal with the economic havoc left by the 2001 crisis he may have decided that he had to put his house in order before even beginning to seek investment or to integrate his country into the global economy. In fact, the Kirchner government's strong-arm tactics have worked, in one respect at least: he did secure major relief in the repayment of Argentina's debt, and that was nothing to sneer at. "I'd like to think that's true, but I'm afraid it isn't the case. We're talking about people in positions of leadership in Argentina whose ability to understand what is happening in the world is nil," Rocha concluded.

"They've been saved for the time being"

James Walsh, U.S. ambassador to Argentina from 2000 to 2003, saw the country with slightly less pessimism than his predecessor, but in the end his vision wasn't markedly different. Walsh had close ties to Argentina, where he had studied as an exchange student in the province of Córdoba at age 17. He returned as a young U.S. diplomat in the late 1960s. During his latest stint, as ambassador, he had had to deal with the biggest political crisis in the country's recent history: the succession of five presidents in one week. "I was the guy who went to the presidential palace every day with a diplomatic note that read: 'The government of the United States is honored to recognize the new government of Argentina,'" he recalled in a telephone interview after his retirement. "A newspaper took a picture of me leaving the presidential palace for the fourth or fifth time on a Saturday morning, without a tie, and wrote half-jokingly that presidential succession had become so routine that the U.S. ambassador was delivering diplomatic notes of recognition in leisure wear."

To Walsh, Argentina's adolescent, crafty character was truer of the capital than of the country as a whole. During his years in Córdoba, he had never seen the same glorification of the every-man-for-himself culture that he later witnessed in Buenos Aires. "When you travel around the country, you find out that the concept of honesty, the worth of one's word, does indeed exist. In Córdoba, saying that someone is crafty is not a compliment. In Buenos Aires there's a different attitude: the same concept is seen as something appealing, positive." But Walsh agreed that both Kirchner's government and —judging by the polls — most Argentines were living out a fantasy, celebrating their economic growth in 2003, 2004, and 2005 as if it were the start of an era of prosperity. Like almost all U.S. diplomats and foreign businesspeople, Walsh saw the near 9 percent economic growth rates as the product of external factors that wouldn't last. "They've been saved for the time being, but the fact is, sooner or later interest rates are going to go up, the prices of raw materials are going to drop, and the bubble will burst," Walsh told me.

And how did Duhalde and Kirchner's officials respond when you told them these things? I asked. "Half of them told me that they agreed, that they've got to do something about it, and then nothing happened. And later, when the economy started to improve [in 2003], you started hearing people make comments like 'See, we didn't have to do any of that stuff they were advising us to do.' And that's foolish, because of course they had to carry out all those institutional and structural reforms they were being advised to. Because if you don't make those changes when things are going well, how are you going to do it when the economy starts to fall, as it will sooner or later? When you're on top, that's the time to make those reforms." Obviously, Kirchner wasn't making the necessary reforms. "From what I can see now, at a distance, reading Argentine newspapers, a great deal of this optimistic rhetoric is a mirage," Walsh said.

Kirchner's pressure on the media

Part of the problem was that much of the Argentine press had lost its nerve. With a few exceptions, such as the daily La Nación or the magazine Noticias, Argentine media now almost always reflected the good news fed to them by the presidential palace, with little or no questioning. Press advocates said that whoever dared to criticize

— especially on television — got angry phone calls from the government, often from the president himself. A top television executive told me that Kirchner had complained personally to him because one of his channel's leading anchors had smiled skeptically while announcing a government plan. Kirchner was the most media-obsessed president in recent history, and the one who became the angriest over trifles, other Argentine journalists told me. I had seen something of that first-hand in my first meeting with him, except that since I was a writer for a U.S. newspaper his rancor wasn't something that could alter my professional life. But for Argentine reporters, who often worked for companies that depended financially on government advertising, presidential tantrums were no small matter: they often resulted in calls to their bosses, and in their dismissal or demotion.

As time passed, reports of government "squeezes" on journalists became more frequent and more public. Kirchner tolerated criticism in the opinion pages of newspapers, but less so in the news-filled front pages. The U.S. human rights group Freedom House, which annually analyzes press freedom around the world, rated Argentina as "partly free," and ranked it 105th of 195 countries.[xxvi] The Inter-American Press Association (IAPA) concluded that although there was a free press, "with restrictions," there were also "disturbing and serious trends and facts that, if they continue over time, could cast a shadow on the horizon of press freedom." Aside from threatening phone calls, the estimated $46 million a year the government spent in advertising was being politically manipulated, it said. The independent daily *La Nación*, for instance, received the same quantity of government ad revenue as the pro-government *Página/12*, even though *La Nacion*'s circulation was 10 times bigger. In conversations with some of Argentina's top journalists, I felt even those who played by government rules were beginning to resent Kirchner's pressures. "Now everyone follows his lead. But wait until he drops to 49 percent in the polls, then everyone will go after him," a well-known journalist told me, reflecting a widespread sentiment. Here, as on other fronts, Kirchner was playing with fire.

"Argentina is doing well, but not going in the right direction"

Euphoric over the economic recovery and challenging those who had criticized him for not carrying out market reforms to achieve long-term growth, Kirchner proudly proclaimed on December 30, 2004, that Argentina's economic growth had taught "a lesson in life to forecasters who had predicted a dark future."[xxvii] He seemed convinced that Argentina's economy was roaring not because of a general expansion of the world economy and China's massive farm purchases, but because he had disregarded the IMF's orthodox prescriptions. Couldn't everyone see how Buenos Aires shops were full again, unemployment was falling, and industries were warming up their engines for the first time in many years?

In June 2005, when Argentina successfully renegotiated most of the nearly $100 billion in default bonds — the world's largest debt renegotiation — Kirchner's supporters boasted that his tough-guy stance had worked: Argentina got a nearly 75 percent discount on the price of the bonds. According to Lavagna, this meant savings of $67 billion in debt payments and a green light for Argentina to return to credit markets for the first time since 2001. To be sure, the country had emerged from the crisis, but it would be a long time before international investors would return in a big way. And the economic bonanza would not last. As the world economy began cooling, Argentina's prospects became more uncertain. By 2007, World Bank forecasts showed that Argentina's near 9 percent growth rates would slow to 7.5 percent that year, 5.6 percent in 2008, and 3.8 percent in 2009.[xxviii]

Kirchner had managed both to give his countrymen the self-confidence they needed after their worst economic crisis in decades and to negotiate better payment conditions for a nation in default. But he had failed to integrate the country into the global economy and put it on a path toward long-term growth. He had wasted the best international economic environment Argentina had enjoyed in five decades — some economists say a century — for carrying out economic and educational reforms that could have turned Argentina into a sustained success. Instead of recognizing that Argentina was growing thanks to external factors, and seizing the moment to start preaching the need to compete in the global economy, Kirchner had ended up sitting back and celebrating.

On a 2005 trip to Buenos Aires, I ran into a senior government official in a restaurant at Puerto Madero, the fancy riverside promenade whose enormous silos and hangars had been converted a few years earlier into elegant restaurants. When we sat down for coffee, I told him what I thought. Without a doubt, Argentina was better off than in 2001. But, in a global economy where China, India, and other countries are competing for investments and export markets, it's not good enough to compare yourself with your recent past – you must also compare yourself with others, I said. Otherwise, you will get fewer investments, the country will export less and will become poorer. Argentina is doing well, but is not going in the right direction, I told him. If it didn't take advantage of the world economy's favorable winds now and if it failed to seek greater competitiveness and promote education, science, technology, and everything else that would allow it to sell more sophisticated goods abroad, its future was bleak.

The official nodded, and replied: "You are right. But you have to understand that the 2001 crisis was so devastating that it's still very hard to talk about tomorrow." For those living abroad, it was easy to see what Argentina needed to do, and they were probably right, he said. But people living in Argentina were still in a state of shock over the worst economic collapse in the country's history. "Before the ship can sail, we have to repair the leaks in the hull," he concluded. It was a good metaphor, as we were sitting in a riverside cafe watching boats pass by. I told him he was partly right, and that I would take his insight into account when writing about the Kirchner government in the future. But it was also true that if the ship didn't leave port while the tide was high, getting under way once the tide was out might be impossible.

NOTES

[i] "Duro reproche de los empresarios españoles," *El Mundo*, July 18, 2003.

[ii] Idem.

[iii] "Dura reunión de Kirchner con empresarios," *La Nación*, July 18, 2003.

[iv] Idem.

[v] "Waiting Game," *Financial Times*, July 29, 2004.

[vi] "HP pretende dobrar de tamanho no Brasil em 3 anos," *O Estado de São Paulo*, web edition, August 4, 2004.

[vii] "Por lo de la campaña [electoral], Kirchner no recibe al presidente sudafricano," *Clarín*, May 31, 2005.

[viii] Larry Rohter, "Argentine leader's quirks attract criticism," The *New York Times*, December 27, 2004.

[ix] Andrés Oppenheimer, "El peligroso aumento del voto cautivo," *El Nuevo Herald*, July 2, 2004.

[x] Idem.

[xi] Interview with Roberto Lavagna in Buenos Aires, April 20, 2005.

[xii] Idem.

[xiii] The number of Heads of Household program beneficiaries fell by 40 percent — or about 861,000 people — in 2006, as Argentina's economic growth reduced the number of unemployed who were eligible, but the government simultaneously granted a life-long automatic pension to 850,000 retirees who had never paid social security. "In the end, the size of the captive vote has remained pretty much unchanged," Atlas Foundation researcher Gustavo Lazzari told me in 2007.

[xiv] Interview with Jorge Castañeda, Mexico City, September 23, 2003.

[xv] Interview with Néstor Kirchner, Monterrey, Mexico, January 13, 2004.

[xvi] Idem.

[xvii] Idem.

[xviii] Idem.

[xix] Idem.

[xx] *Clarín*, January 14, 2004.

[xxi] "Entre Bush y Kohler, el presidente buscó consolidar su poder político," *Clarín*, January 15, 2004.

[xxii] Interview with Otto J. Reich, in Washington, D.C. January 21, 2005.

[xxiii] Idem.

[xxiv] "San Martín y Maradona, los que mejor representan al país," *Clarín*, March 31, 2005.

[xxv] "Nuestros vecinos argentinos," *El Mercurio*, October 2, 2004.

[xxvi] *Global Press Freedom 2007*, Freedom House.

[xxvii] "Los argentinos dieron una lección," *La Nación*, December 30, 2004.

[xxviii] *Global Development Finance*, 2007, World Bank, p. 9, Table 1.1

CHAPTER 7

Brazil: the Colossus of the south

Tall tale: "Brazil is the country of the future, and always will be."
(Traditional Brazilian joke)

BRASÍLIA – WHEN I INTERVIEWED BRAZIL'S FOREIGN MINISTER CELSO Amorim at his huge office in Itamaratí, the Ministry of Foreign Relations' headquarters in the Brazilian capital, what caught my attention most wasn't anything he said, but something I saw on the wall. Amorim, a career official who had served as foreign minister under former president Itamar Franco and, more recently, as ambassador to London, was the quintessential Brazilian diplomat: urbane, cosmopolitan, fiercely nationalistic. Like most of his colleagues at Itamaratí, he spoke good English and several other languages. But that didn't prevent him from insisting that the interview be carried out in Portuguese, after I foolishly told him I had been studying it for two years. During the hour-long interview around a small coffee table in a corner of his immense office, Amorim said nothing I hadn't heard before. And yet I was glad to have made the trip to Brasília when I saw the enormous tapestry hanging on the wall behind his desk at the far end of the room. It said everything about President Luiz Inacio Lula da Silva's government, and about Brazil.

It was a map several yards wide that showed the world upside down. Brazil was at the center, with Africa over to one side, taking up most of the tapestry, while the United States and Europe were far below, in the remote south, almost falling off the map. After the interview was over, as we walked toward the door of his office, I couldn't help pointing to the map and joking that I finally understood why President Lula's government was so nationalistic: its foreign minister spent his days working under a map that placed Brazil at the center of the world, with the United States and Europe deep at the bottom. Amorim shrugged, and explained matter-of-factly that he had inherited the map from his predecessor Celso Lafer, who had held the job under Cardoso. The tapestry, as far as he knew, had always been there.

As I later learned, the tapestry was the work of Brazilian artist Madeleine Colaço, based on a world map by an ancient Italian cartographer, and indeed had been there as long as anybody at Itamaratí could remember. It was nothing that the foreign minister or any of his aides had installed, or for that matter paid much attention to. In fact, as I learned afterward, Brazil is full of upside-down maps, or at any rate maps that are upside down compared with traditional maps produced by the Northern Hemisphere countries that had colonized the rest of the world. When I visited the editor of the daily *O Estado de São Paulo*, on his desk was a paperweight with an upside-down world. At Brazil's Varig airlines office, I came across a poster with the world upside down. For Brazilians, it was an old joke that had long ago become part of the nation's geopolitical folklore, to the point that nobody but foreign visitors noticed it.

Was there any justification for this Brazilian superiority complex, aside from the country's international prominence in soccer, music, and street festivals? Or were these delusions of grandeur? Brazil was by far the largest country in South America, with a gross domestic product totaling more than half that of the rest of the sub-region. But until the end of the Cardoso administration, it had been an insular power, proud of itself but isolated from its neighbors and the rest of the world. No wonder: not only did Brazilians speak a language different from that of all its neighbors, but geography had forced the vast country to focus on what its diplomats called the "quest for consolidation of the national space." With more than 8.5 million square kilometers (the fifth-largest country in the world) and a population of 190 million, it was a continental country, much like the United States, Russia, China, and India. U.S. diplomat George

F. Kennan at the turn of the 21st century had already included Brazil on his list of what he called "monster countries," not only because of its size, but because of its economic weight. Unlike the United States, however, which has only two neighbors (Mexico and Canada), Brazil borders 10 countries, a fact that historically has demanded both diplomatic skills and internal unity to maintain peace and keep its national identity vibrant. At the same time, because of the size of its economy — the world's 10th largest — and its vast superiority over its neighbors, Brazil had always looked north and east in its search for markets sizable enough for its production capacity, and sought to avoid being contaminated by the chronic instability of its geographic neighbors. Until the late 1990s South America had never been a priority for Brazilian governments.

Even the jokes one heard in Brazil well into the '90s reflected Brazil's scant affection for its neighbors — above all, the Argentines. According to a joke I heard in São Paulo after the Brazilian devaluation of 1999, which prompted a sharp cut in its imports from neighboring countries and paved the way for Argentina's 2001 economic crisis, then-president Cardoso had appeared on Brazil's national television to deliver the following message: "My fellow Brazilians: I have good news and bad news. The bad news is that we will have to devalue the currency, which will cause thousands of Brazilian businesses to shut down, massive layoffs, unemployment, and poverty, which means that there will be tough times ahead for our country." He then paused, and added, with a mischievous smile: "The good news is, the same will happen in Argentina."

But starting in the 1990s with the collapse of the Soviet bloc, when the two-superpower international regime was replaced by one consisting of a single superpower and several regional powers, Brazil began seeking out a leadership role in South America as a necessary step toward establishing itself among the world's emerging second-tier powers. As part of its plan, Brazil started actively campaigning for a permanent seat on the United Nations Security Council, for which it needed the support of its South American neighbors.

Accordingly, it set out to create a new South American bloc, which it would lead. President Cardoso organized the first Summit of South American Presidents on August 30, 2000, in Brazil — the first step in a campaign for regional leadership that his successor, Lula, would make an even higher priority during his first term in office.

The idea of playing a leadership role in the region was not new in Brazil, even if it had never been actively pursued. The country's policy-makers had been discussing regional integration since the early 20th century, when the Baron of Rio Branco, the intellectual father of Brazilian diplomacy, proposed in 1909 "to contribute to the union and friendship between South American countries," adding that "one of the pillars of this endeavor should be the ABC alliance" — Argentina, Brazil, and Chile.[i] Little happened for another eight decades, until Brazil, Argentina, Uruguay, and Paraguay created the South American Common Market, or Mercosur, in 1991.

Since then, Brazil's economy had become increasingly connected with those of its Mercosur neighbors. Not only did its trade with Mercosur countries rise significantly, but Brazil also started replacing Middle Eastern oil imports with energy supplies from its neighbors, which was a clear sign of confidence in the regional partnership's future. Brazil began buying oil from Venezuela and Argentina and natural gas from Bolivia. It collaborated with Paraguay in building the Itaipú dam, which furnishes electricity to nearly all of Brazil's southern and southeastern states. And after the NAFTA free trade deal involving Mexico, the United States, and Canada went into effect in 1994 and Brazil saw a dramatic rise in Mexico's exports to the United States, the Brazilian foreign ministry decided the country needed strong ties to a critical mass of economies in the region if it intended to avoid ending up in a geographic no-man's land in the new world economy, while North America, Europe, and Asia created separate regional trade blocs. So Brazil decided to bet on plans for a South American Union.

Bye-bye Mexico, welcome "South America"

The 2000 Summit in Brasília, attended by 12 South American presidents, was much more than a symbolic meeting. It was Brazil's debut on the regional stage with a new geopolitical project — formalizing South America as an acknowledged region. Former foreign minister Lafer did not conceal Brazil's intention to become the region's leader, arguing that Mexico and Central America had become virtual satellites of the U.S. and were therefore no longer part of what Brazilians until then had called "Latin America." For Lafer, Mexico and Central America were already on the other side of the border. "The future of that part of Latin America depends more and more on what happens in the United States," he said. "South America, on the other hand, has ... its own specificity."[ii]

Very soon, Brazil began to rewrite history and to redefine the region's geography in a way that essentially excluded Mexico and Central America, leaving Brazil as the undisputed regional leader. Perhaps that was because securing worldwide recognition as a regional power prevented it from sharing the spotlight with Mexico, or because Argentina's 2001 economic collapse left Brazil — by default — as the only substantial power on the continent. Whatever the reason, the fact is that Itamaratí officials began to preach a new interpretation of hemispheric history. In the late 1990s Brazilian diplomats started spreading the notion that "Latin America" did not exist. Instead, the hemisphere comprised three regions: South America, Central America, and North America. Brazil's geographic revisionism banished Mexico from the Latin American region and relegated it to a secondary role in U.S.-dominated "North America." That automatically left Brazil the remaining region's undisputed leader.

I first heard Brazilian officials debunking the concept of "Latin America" in 2000, when Brazil's ambassador to Washington, Rubens A. Barbosa, brought up the issue almost casually during a conversation in Washington. Barbosa was a heavyweight in Brazilian diplomatic circles: he had been appointed envoy to the United States by Cardoso and was later confirmed by Lula, one of the rare instances when Lula's new leftist government retained senior officials left from the prior government. "We are entering the 21st Century in a new economic landscape," Barbosa told me, "in which the business community perceives Latin America as divided into three areas: North America, Central America and the Caribbean, and South America." He said that South American countries, with 340 million people and an economy that was becoming a hub of international commerce and investment, shared geography, history, and values that set it apart from their neighbors to the north. South American countries also "share values: they share a commitment to build a better future through the consolidation of democratic institutions, sustained economic growth, and the struggle to combat social injustice," Barbosa said.

Latin America: an obsolete concept?

Three years later, Brazil ramped up its geographic revisionism and declared that "South America" was a natural region, whereas "Latin America" was a 19th century fabrication intended to respond to political imperatives rather than reflect geographic realities. "The concept of Latin America is obsolete," Ambassador Barbosa said at a 2003 panel on Latin America's future in Miami, adding that it had been created in the mid-19th century by a French sociologist. "He invented that concept after Emperor Maximilian was installed in Mexico, at a time when the French wanted to justify a military expedition to Mexico in order to expand their empire from there to the south. But things have changed a lot since the 19th century, and today we have a new geography in the region, one that makes the concept of 'Latin America' totally outdated," Barbosa said.

I was sitting next to Barbosa at the panel, and looked at him with bewilderment (more out of ignorance than anything else, because

I had never heard that the term "Latin America" had been a French coinage.) Noticing my amazement, the Brazilian ambassador went into further detail. He explained that the region was currently divided into three blocs that weren't just economic but political as well. "When I talk about breaking up the concept of 'Latin America,' I am also reflecting what the United States is doing. One can't talk about U.S. policies toward 'Latin America,' because there is no such thing: there are policies for different countries or groups of countries. Not even the State Department calls us 'Latin America.' It calls us 'the Western Hemisphere.'"[iii] I replied that the State Department's Office of Western Hemisphere affairs is probably named that way because it also includes Canada, and therefore could not possibly be named "Office of Latin American Affairs." But Barbosa had piqued my curiosity.

Was he right? Was the concept of "Latin America" a relatively recent invention of a Frenchman that was embraced by the United States because it responded to the political interests of an imperial power? A few days after the Miami conference, I called up Barbosa and asked him for the name of the famous Frenchman. He got back to me a few days later and told me it was Michel Chevalier, a traveling intellectual and senator. It turns out Chevalier was an advocate of France's imperialist dreams in the Americas, and wanted to prove that France — not the United States — was the country with the greatest historical affinity with the region. Chevalier argued that the countries to the south of the United States were "Latin" and "Catholic," whereas the United States and Canada were "Protestant" and "Anglo-Saxon." The logical conclusion of his division of the Americas was that France, the main "Latin" power in the world at the time, was destined to lead its sister nations in the Americas. (Years later, Spain would coin a term to suit its own aspirations of regional leadership, which is used by Spaniards to this day: "Ibero-America").

Chevalier had managed to convince Napoleon III to set up Emperor Maximilian in Mexico as a first step toward what he hoped would become a French empire in the New World. In his books *L'Expédition du Mexique* (1862) and *Le Mexique ancien et moderne* (1863), he made a passionate argument in favor of a "Latin" empire in the Americas. This empire would elevate the presence of France in the world and act as a wall of containment to what Chevalier called "English America on the continent" or the "Anglo-Saxon and Protestant empire" of the United States.

Chevalier openly proclaimed his intentions. In a text whose title translates as "Reasons for a European, or just French, intervention in the affairs of Mexico," he wrote: "The [French] expedition has as its stated goal: the intention to act as the starting point of the political regeneration of Mexico [...] and the need to finally build, in the interest of world political equilibrium, a dam to contain the invasive spirit that has possessed the Anglo-Americans of the United States for the past many years."[iv]

To shore up the French presence in America, Chevalier said France had a special reason, different from that of England and the northern European countries, to intervene in the new continent — France was one of the "Latin nations." The consolidation of Latin nations was essential to France's future. Preventing the United States from taking over the hemisphere's Latin countries had to be a priority for his country. France "stands out in literature. [It excels] in the sciences and the arts, its industry is increasingly fertile and its agriculture is bound to have a great future, its army is numerous and well-respected. But if the Latin nations were to disappear from the world stage one day, France would find itself irremediably weak and isolated. It would be like a general without an army, almost like a head without a body."[v]

The alternative vision of "Latin America"

Still, the idea that Chevalier originated the concept of "Latin America" — argued in a 1965 monograph by U.S. historian John Leddy Phelan — has been increasingly disputed. In a 1998 essay in

Spain's *Revista de las Indias*, titled "On the origin and dissemination of the name 'Latin America,'" historian Mónica Quijada argued that Chevalier had never actually used the term "Latin America." Rather, he spoke of the "Latin people of the Americas," and the existence of an America that was "Latin" and "Catholic." According to Quijada, the first people to use the term "Latin America" were Latin Americans themselves: essayists like friar Francisco Muñoz del Monte of the Dominican Republic, or Santiago Arcos and Francisco Bilbao of Chile, and, above all, José María Torres Caicedo of Colombia, who began to use the term as a geographic reference in the early 1850s, some years before Chevalier's writings. And their motive was not to justify European domination, but to resist U.S. imperialism.

"'Latin America' is not a label imposed on Latin Americans by foreign interests, but a name coined and consciously adopted by Latin Americans themselves, as an expression of their own yearnings," Quijada writes.[vi] Hispanic Americans adopted the term at a time when the United States seemed determined to create an empire that would spread farther and farther to the south. In the 1850s Washington was attempting to build a canal in Central America to join the Atlantic and Pacific oceans. In the middle of that decade, Washington's foreign policy provoked even greater alarm in the region when the U.S. pirate William Walker proclaimed himself president of Nicaragua, with open support from U.S. President Franklin Pierce. That, on top of the annexation of vast territories in Mexico by the United States following the occupation of Texas by U.S. settlers, "led many Hispanic-Americans to turn their eyes toward the old unionist dream of that great liberator, Simón Bolívar," Quijada writes. "The main reason that inspired the reappearance of those ideals was the need, felt by many, to oppose the growing power and aggressive policies of the United States."[vii]

Curiously enough, the first known mention of "Latin America" as a geographic region is in a work of poetry, Quijada says. The poem is "The Two Americas" by Colombian Torres Caicedo. In the ninth stanza, it reads: "The race of Latin America / confronts the Saxon race." Later on, Chevalier's books and the founding of the *Latin American Review* in Buenos Aires would contribute considerably to the widespread use of the term, which by the end of the 19th century was the way the region was most often referred to internationally, she says.

If Quijada is correct, Brazil's geographic revisionism loses much of its claim to historical accuracy. Although the term "Latin America" is rather novel, as the Brazilian ambassador to Washington pointed out, it was probably not born out of imperialist intentions. On the contrary: it had emerged from the Hispanic Americans' intention to distinguish themselves from their Anglo-Saxon neighbors to the North, and to build bridges with European countries in the defense of a common religion and shared values.

In Washington, Haiti counts as much as Brazil

Just as for decades Brazil ignored the rest of Latin America, so the United States ignored Brazil. The Bush Administration's State Department has so few in-house experts on South America's biggest country that it had to bring in an outsider, William Perry, to advise the Bureau of Western Hemisphere Affairs on Brazil-related issues. The problem, as several former U.S. ambassadors to Brazil pointed out to me, is that very few officials on the sixth floor of the State Department — where the assistant secretary for Western Hemisphere Affairs works — speak Portuguese, or know much about Brazil. Perhaps because of Brazil's self-sufficiency, national pride, and relative indifference to what Washington might or might not say about most issues, Brazil has never been a posting eagerly sought by career-minded Foreign Service officers. It didn't help that Brazil, unlike other Latin American countries, never revered its U.S. ambassadors as virtual imperial proconsuls.

Due to the shortage of experts on Brazil, the main posts at the State Department's Brazil Desk have generally been filled by specialists in other parts of the world, who were assigned to Brazil because of some political or personal misstep. Peter Hakim, the president of Inter-American Dialogue, a middle-of-the-road Washington think tank on hemispheric issues, told me a long-running joke at the State Department. Whenever a diplomat committed a blunder, his colleagues would tell him, "They're gonna send you to the Brazilian Affairs office."

At the U.S. National Security Council, the White House office that advises the president on foreign policy, the situation wasn't much different. Richard Feinberg, director of the NSC Office of Latin American Affairs in the first Clinton Administration, once told me, half-amused, half-horrified, that the office had only two officials at the time: "One was in charge of Haiti, and the other one, who was me, was in charge of all the other Latin American countries." During the second Clinton Administration and later under Bush, the office was expanded to six officials, but the disproportion in the territory each covered continued to be huge: in 2004 one full-time official was in charge of Haiti and Cuba, while another took care of Brazil, Argentina, Uruguay, and Paraguay — the Mercosur countries. In other words, the White House office advising the president on Latin America assigned the same staff to two Caribbean countries whose total population was less than 19 million, with a gross product of $43 billion, as it did to four South American countries with a total population of more than 240 million and a combined gross product of over $1.4 trillion.

So Washington never paid Brazil the attention it deserved as the region's most important country. Former Secretary of State Colin Powell spent nearly four years in office without once setting foot in Brazil. He finally visited two months before leaving office so that no one could say that he hadn't gone to the biggest country in South America during his entire tenure. As Hakim told me with a hint of frustration, when Inter-American Dialogue with the support of congressional leaders in 2003 invited all 450 members of Congress to travel to Brazil during the year-end recess, all expenses paid, to make them aware of the importance of the South American giant, just over a dozen responded with some degree of interest, and only one ended up going.

Lula, Wall Street, and revolution

To be sure, Lula's statements during the 2002 election campaign didn't convert any officials in Washington to the cause of paying greater attention to Brazil. Hardly a week went by in which Lula didn't say something to infuriate Bush Administration conservatives who were monitoring the leftist candidate's campaign. A few months before the election, when I interviewed Lula in Brasília, he was still referring to the U.S.-backed hemispheric FTAA trade deal as "a plan to annex the Brazilian economy to that of the United States." He proposed defaulting on Brazil's external debt and breaking ties with the International Monetary Fund — a position he changed only shortly before the election — and proudly proclaimed his support for Cuba's dictatorship. Of course, much of this was done to secure the enthusiastic support of the radical wing of his party and keep it more or less content while he built bridges with Brazil's business class and hinted about moving toward a market economy. But his statements often fell like a cold shower in the White House, and especially in Congress.

When I asked Lula in Brasília about Washington's fears about his ties to Cuba, he replied, "I've been in Cuba many times over the past 20 years, and I consider myself to be a friend of Cuba and an admirer of the Cuban people. They are a people with enormous self-esteem who haven't backed down when there were problems and adversities, and who pay a very high price for it." Intrigued, I asked him how he knew what the "Cuban people" wanted, if they hadn't been able to vote freely in four decades. Besides, how could a union man like himself, who had fought against dictatorships in his own country, continue to support a dictatorship that didn't allow independent labor unions? Lula backed off, but only a little: "Obviously, the fact I'm a friend of Cuba doesn't mean that I or the Workers' Party agree with everything they do. On one of my last trips, I had the opportunity to tell Fidel Castro publicly that for us, Cuba is not a model, just as the United States and France are not models."[viii]

After winning the election and taking office on January 1, 2003, Lula surprised the world with a dramatic shift toward the center. But he had a problem, as his own advisers recognized in private: he talked too much. When I returned to Brazil in February 2003, more than a month after his inauguration, the daily buzz in the Brazilian press was the new president's verbal incontinence. Not a week went by without his saying something that caused a misunderstanding with the United States, Europe, or somewhere else in the world. Some of the things he said were charming and ingenuous, and won him applause at home. During an official visit to London for a meeting of "progressive" leaders, he said, "If there's one thing I admire about the United States, it is that the first thing they think about is themselves, the second thing, themselves, and the third, themselves. And if they still have some time left over, they think a little more about themselves."[ix] Other times, his statements were more hostile and provoked diplomatic incidents.

Once I happened to stand in the middle of one of Lula's outbursts, one that brought him a lot of criticism in the Brazilian press. I had interviewed then U.S. trade representative Robert Zoellick — the man in charge of FTAA negotiations for the Bush administration, who in 2007 became president of the World Bank — about Brazil's criticism of the U.S-backed hemispheric free trade plan, and he had given me an uncharacteristically strong answer. Zoellick said Brazil, as a sovereign country, could do whatever it wanted, and added — sarcastically — that if Brazil wasn't interested in doing business with the United States, "they can do business with Antarctica." When my story in the *Miami Herald* was reprinted the next day in Brazilian newspapers, Lula said he would not deign to respond to a statement made by "a subordinate of a subordinate." His comment set off an avalanche of criticism in the Brazilian press, not only because Lula had turned the debate into a personal issue — instead of rebutting the argument — but also because he was mistaken: as U.S. trade representative, Zoellick held cabinet rank within the U.S. administration.

During a February 2003 visit to Brasília I found a climate of general support for Lula, although I did hear concern over his careless statements. I was staying at the Tennis Academy Hotel, a series of cabanas surrounded by tennis courts where I had been advised to stay, given that nearly all the newly appointed cabinet ministers in the new government were staying there while looking for housing in the Brazilian capital. It turned out to be a great choice: when I asked the concierge, almost out of curiosity, how much they charged for tennis lessons, he said it was the equivalent of one U.S. dollar, which — compared with $40 per hour in Miami — was a steal. (In the days that followed, between one interview and another, I took several tennis lessons, and joked with my interviewees that I wasn't sure that my trip would help me understand the Lula phenomenon any better, but it would certainly improve my game.)

One night I invited William Barr, a diplomat who had just retired as head of the political section of the U.S. Embassy in Brasília, to join me for dinner. He had decided to stay in the city as a political consultant and private businessman. "What's your opinion of Lula's first few weeks in office?" I asked him. "Good, but he talks too much," Barr responded. "Lula has always given speeches to suit every particular audience, without really considering the broader implications of his statements. The problem is that now, he is the president."

Six months after taking office, Lula had given over 100 public speeches, most of them extemporaneous. *Veja*, Brazil's most influential weekly magazine, indicated that this habit was a remnant from the president's days as a union leader, and cautioned that it was exposing him to unnecessary problems. "Within the world of labor-union meetings, words carry enormous weight, nearly as much as actions. He who makes the best speech can win the public over," *Veja* said. "But in government, winning over the public is just the first step."

Lula and "the American dream"

Like many political analysts, I had always thought — mistakenly, as I've come to learn — that despite its general arrogance and clumsiness in foreign affairs, there was one thing the Bush Administration had done well in Latin America: it had swallowed its ideological prejudices and made friendly gestures toward Lula, despite the leftist candidate's frequent statements criticizing the United States. In fact, during the 2002 campaign, when many in Brazil expected the United States would do everything possible to prevent a Lula victory, the Bush administration did exactly the opposite. It surprised everybody with a seemingly sophisticated position toward Lula's candidacy, which ended up benefiting him enormously, and — to some degree — helping him win the election.

During the campaign, Lula's biggest challenge had been to win the centrist vote. Unlike his predecessor, and many other Latin American presidents who had come from the left, Lula wasn't a middle-of-the-road social democrat at the time, but the leader of a hard-line socialist party. In 1989 he had declared that "the agenda of the Workers' Party is socialist. Socialism is the party's final goal."[x] Until a few months before the 2002 elections, he repeated his mantra that the FTAA was "a mechanism of annexation to the U.S. economy," and that "Brazil has to break away from the International Monetary Fund." As the election approached, Lula's rivals stepped up their fear campaign, accusing him of being a radical leftist who would turn the country into a new Cuba. In the United States, 27 members of the U.S. Congress had joined that fear campaign, sending an open letter to Bush warning that Brazil would join with Cuba and Venezuela in forming a new "axis of evil" in Latin America.

At this key moment, when many expected the Bush Administration to remain silent, or make a comment explicitly or tacitly suggesting that Lula might pose a threat, exactly the opposite occurred. Donna Hrinak, the U.S. ambassador, made a surprising statement: Asked whether the Bush administration was fearful of a Lula victory, she said no. Her own father, like Lula's, had been a steel worker, she said, so she understood the Brazilian leftist candidate very well. What's more, Hrinak said, she admired Lula because he worked his way up from an impoverished childhood — he had been forced to drop out of high school — to become a candidate for the presidency of South America's biggest country. "Lula," the ambassador said, "is the personification of the American dream." That statement made front-page headlines in Brazil, and instantly wrecked his rivals' campaign claim that a Lula victory would put Brazil on the road to Marxist revolution and lead to a dangerous confrontation with the United States. From that moment on, Brazilian business leaders who had kept a prudent distance from Lula reconsidered their apprehension. If the conservative Bush administration had expressed approval of Lula, many businessmen thought, it was likely that Washington knew something they didn't know about the left-wing candidate. If he was acceptable to the United States, he couldn't be that bad for Brazil's business community.

However, as I came to learn years later while conducting interviews for this book, my original perception that the White House had handled the situation brilliantly was erroneous. Indeed, when I asked Hrinak in 2004, soon after she left Brasília and retired from diplomatic service, whether she had consulted with her bosses in Washington before making her famous "personification of the American dream" comment, she told me she hadn't. "Really?" I asked her, astonished. Had she taken such liberties without consulting with the State Department? "Really, I didn't consult Washington. I said what I believed was the least prejudicial thing I could say in the heat of the campaign about Lula. I obviously didn't want to say anything negative. And it's not that we had decided to endorse him, but I didn't just want to say, "We won't make any comment on any candidate." I wanted to say something more upbeat, because there was a lot of speculation in the Brazilian press about our opposition to Lula. So I came up with the 'American dream' thing," Hrinak told me.[xi]

Was there opposition to Lula in the Bush administration?" I asked her. Hrinak answered that she never knew whether Powell or Condoleezza Rice opposed Lula, but opposition was growing among Republicans in Congress, as shown by the letter signed by 27 members. How had her immediate bosses in the State Department reacted after her "American dream" statement? According to Hrinak, Otto Reich, the State Department's top official in change of Latin American affairs at the time, said nothing directly to her, but sent a message through his second in command — Kurt Strubel — that she shouldn't make any more statements about Lula. Apparently, a Republican congressman had complained to Reich about the apparent U.S. support for Lula.

Asked about it, Reich confirmed the story, adding that in the wake of Lula's election the State Department considered that the net result of the ambassador's intervention had been positive. "What she did is something we never do: she intervened in a campaign in favor of a candidate, and that caused problems in Washington, both in the White House and in Congress [...] We got a lot of complaints," Reich recalled. "All we did was to remind her that she had to maintain absolute neutrality."[xii]

Between the Workers' Party and Wall Street

But, whether it was thanks to the Bush administration or in spite of it, the United States had come out on top. Lula won the election by a wide margin and immediately made a turn to the center that surprised much of the world. He appointed a pro-market economic team that put the business class at ease and pleased Wall Street and maintained his predecessor's economic policies. Shortly thereafter, speaking at a steel plant in the state of Espirito Santo hours after returning from a summit of Latin American presidents, he said, "I'm tired of hearing Latin American presidents always blaming imperialism for the Third World's misfortunes. That's nonsense."[xiii]

Despite criticism from his Workers' Party's radical wing that his free market policies cost them in the 2004 municipal elections — where the party lost the mayoralty of São Paulo and other cities — Lula vowed to stay the course. "If there's one thing this government has done well, it's economic policy," he said. Referring to the 2004 election results, he added, "The Workers' Party can't hide behind criticism of this policy in its efforts to find excuses for its defeat."[xiv] The numbers prove him right: in his second year in office, the economy grew 5 percent, the highest rate in 10 years; Brazil's country risk dropped to its lowest level in seven years; exports reached a record $95 billion; employment rose by 6 percent.

In 2005, before corruption scandals rocked his administration, Lula had achieved what few would have imagined: he had become a model for pragmatic leftists, someone who could be at the same time a star guest at the World Economic Forum in Davos, Switzerland, where the world's richest and most powerful gathered, and at the Global Social Forum of Porto Alegre, where the anti-globalization movements assembled. Lula continued to criticize U.S. policy and the absence of democracy in both the United Nations and international financial institutions. But he was aware that China, India, and other developing countries were competing to attract foreign investment, and knew that Brazil couldn't be left behind. Somehow, even though most of his closest advisers came from the left, he had achieved a remarkable balance in his administration. "Lula has entrusted his foreign policy to the Workers' Party, and his economic policy to Wall Street," said Moisés Naim, editor of Foreign Policy magazine in Washington. While Lula prided himself on spending time trying to strengthen economic and political ties with China, Russia, South Africa, and other emerging powers — arguing that Brazil would benefit from a more multipolar world — his guiding star wasn't ideology, but economic pragmatism.

A conversation between Lula and the U.S. ambassador who replaced Hrinak, John Danilovich, says much about the Brazilian president. According to the private conversation, which the ambassador later shared with me, he and Lula were participating in a ceremony commemorating the 50th anniversary of Brazil's first

Caterpillar factory, held at the U.S. heavy machinery company's plant in the city of Campinas, in São Paulo state. The event took place not long after the announcement that Lula would receive the president of China, Hu Jintao, a few weeks later, amid media speculation that China was going to invest billions of dollars in Brazil. After the event, as Lula and Danilovich were walking out, the U.S. ambassador told the Brazilian leader, "Mr. President, you've had great success in achieving economic agreements with China, India, and several other countries. I hope you won't forget the United States." Lula stopped and, looking Danilovich in the eye, told him with a smile that Brazil was indeed making great efforts to increase trade with China, India, and South Africa. "But if you believe for one moment that I'm not absolutely certain that our most important relationship and our most important business partner is the United States, then you must think I'm very much a fool." The ambassador returned his smile and answered, "No, I don't think you're a fool at all."[xv]

Brazil's three goals

With Lula, Brazil took its ambitions for regional leadership to another level. Judging from what I heard from top Brazilian officials, the country's strategy had three stages: first, creating the South American Union, which was formally inaugurated in a solemn ceremony in Cuzco, Peru, on December 9, 2004; second, making sure that Brazil would join the U.N. Security Council by 2005 or 2006; third, negotiating a free trade agreement with the United Sates from a position of strength — as an emerging world power with a seat on the Security Council — by 2006 or 2007.

Once the first stage of the plan was carried out with the creation of the South American Union, and Brazil was positioned as South America's leader and the main U.S. interlocutor with the region, Brazil embarked alongside Japan, Germany, and India into an all-out effort to reform the U.N. charter and create new seats on the Security Council. Those four countries, and several others, wanted to join the major league of world politics, on an equal footing with the United States, Great Britain, Russia, and China. Now Brazil needed its regional leadership in South America more than ever. Brazil's openness toward the rest of South America was motivated more by politics than economics.

This, of course, troubled Argentina, its proud neighbor to the south. Before its financial meltdown in 2001, Argentina had hoped to share South American leadership with Brazil — much as happened in Europe, where Germany and France shared regional leadership for decades. But Argentines had always suspected that Brazil was promising more integration than it was willing to concede. Argentina had always been more enthusiastic than the Brazilians about Mercosur, the regional common market. In the 1990s, during the ascendancy of the regional bloc, Argentina even phased out its national passports and replaced them with new ones whose covers — like those of European Union member countries — carried the name of Mercosur. Argentina also enthusiastically promoted teaching Portuguese in its public schools. And in 1994 Argentina had amended its constitution to include a regional integration clause recognizing Mercosur as a supranational body. Under the 1994 Constitution, integration treaties with neighboring countries would take precedence over national, provincial, and municipal laws.

Brazil never entirely reciprocated. In Brazil, for Mercosur regulations to take precedence over domestic laws when the two were in conflict, it was and is necessary for Congress to ratify the regional rule and approve it as an international treaty. "They want to lead, but without sharing sovereignty," said Diego Guelar, a former Argentine diplomat who had been an ambassador to Brasília and Washington in the 1990s. "They don't have a 'European' vision of the South American community. They talk, but they don't act."[xvi] To Argentines, the Brazilian devaluation of 1999 had been a betrayal that had seriously hurt Argentina's exports, and had been one of the factors that led to country's economic crisis of 2001. But Guelar conceded that Brazil's regional leadership was not part of a cynical plan to push Argentina out of the picture, but because Brazil had simply grown too strong to fear its neighbor to the south . "At the beginning, the idea was to create an area of integration in which Brazil and Argentina would be like Germany and France are in Europe. It was a relationship between equals. After the Argentine collapse in 2001, that was no longer possible. But this was because reality set in, not because of some evil Brazilian plot," Guelar said.[xvii]

Even though Argentina's Kirchner Administration soon proclaimed it would repudiate Menem's "carnal relations" with Washington and replace it with closer ties to Brazil, the love affair between the next-door neighbors wouldn't last long. Two years after Kirchner took office, Argentina was already complaining about the behavior of its "Big Brother." According to Argentina's daily *Clarín*, which enjoyed preferential access to the Kirchner government, the Argentine president was overheard saying at a social function shortly after the death of Pope John Pope II: "If there's a spot in the World Trade Organization, Brazil wants it. If there's a seat in the United Nations, Brazil wants it. If there's work to be done at the U.N. Food and Agriculture Organization, Brazil wants it. They even want a Brazilian Pope."[xviii]

In Brazil, even the past is uncertain

Would Brazil become a South American world power? Or would its dreams of greatness collapse under the weight of political scandal, internal splits, and the distrust of its neighbors? Even before Venezuela under Chávez began to eclipse Brazilian leadership in 2006 with its petrodollar largesse, a series of corruption scandals in 2005 had weakened Brazil's diplomatic offensive. Lula's all-powerful cabinet chief José Dirceu and Workers' Party president José Genoíno, among others, resigned after reports that Lula's party had bribed several legislators $12,000 a month in exchange for their support. Lula's party, which won the 2002 elections thanks largely to its anti-corruption stance and the reputation for honesty it had gained in the past from its handling of local government affairs, was now on the defensive, accused of falling into the same corrupt practices of the administrations it so harshly criticized. Even if Lula managed to overcome the scandals and win the 2006 elections — as he did, by a landslide — many Brazilian experts doubted that he would be able to maintain the domestic support he needed to help the country emerge as a world power.

Even at the height of Brazil's new activism in South American affairs during the first years of the Lula government, Brazil never dared play a leading role in efforts to solve the region's most controversial issue: the war in Colombia. Indeed, while Lula's Brazil sent troops to Haiti, helped formed a group of friendly nations to mediate in a political crisis in Venezuela, and played the leading role behind creating the South American Union, it never launched a regional initiative to help bring about peace in Colombia. How could Brazilian officials complain about the presence of U.S. military trainers in Colombia if their own country — the region's powerhouse — was sitting idly by, without offering any solution to help Colombia win its war against guerrillas, paramilitary groups, terrorists, and drug traffickers? That was an issue foreign diplomats and academics raised when asked about Brazil's regional leadership.

It's a valid question. "Brazil is the only country that could make a difference in Colombia, but it's not doing it. There is no political will on the part of the Brazilians," retired Colonel John Al Cope, a professor at the U.S. Army's National Defense University in Washington, told me. When I asked a former Brazilian foreign minister why his country never wanted to help end the bloodiest war in the region, one taking place in a country next door, he explained that the Brazilian military had always opposed taking a more prominent role in Colombia for fear that the Revolutionary Armed Forces of Colombia (FARC) guerrillas that operate along the two countries' border would spill the conflict onto Brazilian territory. That made sense from a domestic policy point of view, I responded. But it undermined Brazil's new aspirations to be the undisputed regional leader.

Skeptics about Brazil's future said that in the aftermath of the 2005 corruption scandals everything coming out of Brazil should be taken with a grain of salt. Brazil may be an unrivaled powerhouse in the region, but it was also the land of unfulfilled promises, they said, as the old joke has it, fated perpetually to be the country of the future. Despite its enormous geographic and economic dimensions and its great achievements — such as being a world pioneer in sugar-cane ethanol production, and selling renowned Brazilian-made Ebraer planes in the United States and Europe — Brazil continues to be the Latin American country with the widest income gap and some of the world's highest levels of bureaucracy and corruption. As Brazilian congressman Antônio Ferreira Vianna (1832–1905) said more than a century ago, "O Brasil só precisa de uma lei: uma lei que diga que é preciso cumprir todas as outras," or "Brazil needs only one law: a law that says that all other laws should be obeyed."

There are always predictions that, sooner or later, inequality will trigger a revolt of the country's poor. In Brazil's intellectual circles it was common — at least until the recent economic boom in India — to refer to the country as "Belindia," where a small minority lives in a First World country similar to Belgium, while the huge majority lives in extreme poverty, as in India. While most economists are upbeat about Brazil's future, few will bet on it. As the former president of the Central Bank of Brazil, Gustavo Franco, said when asked if he could guarantee the country's long-term economic stability: "No Brasil, mesmo o passado é incerto!" or "In Brazil, even the past is uncertain."

Brazil's giant leap forward

But by 2007 a dispassionate look at Brazil during Lula's second term allowed for much more optimism than Brazilians' eternally self-deprecating humor would encourage. While not growing by spectacular rates — an expected 4.2 percent in 2007, 4.1 percent in 2008, and 3.9 percent in 2009, according to World Bank projections[xix]—

there were reasons to believe Brazil was on a path of solid, sustained growth. Granted, Lula had yet to adopt major economic reforms, such as streamlining the social security system and cutting the country's Kafkaesque red tape, which is a major disincentive to foreign investors, and there was little likelihood he would carry them out in the remainder of his term. But his leftist government had helped Brazil overcome the country's biggest problem: the stigma of economic uncertainty. At the moment when Lula was first elected and decided to preserve the best of the Cardoso government's economic policies, Brazil had taken a giant step forward. Much like Chile when it elected its first socialist presidents, Brazil had joined the club of serious nations that don't make wild economic swings that scare away domestic and foreign investors. And that was paying off: during Lula's first four years in office, per capita income had risen 1.4 percent a year and poverty had dropped by a combined 15 percent, in part thanks to massive social programs.

Even if Lula had done nothing during his administration but stay the course, his most glittering achievement would have been to demonstrate that — despite the traumatic examples of Fidel Castro in Cuba and Salvador Allende in Chile — Latin America's biggest country can bring forth a responsible, non-populist left-wing government. In mid-2005, when his popularity dropped significantly after his top aides were charged with corruption, Lula said: "Don't expect any populist economic moves from me just because we have elections coming up a year from now [...] We don't want to build a solid foundation for one-year growth. This nation [...] should have a 10- or 15-year sustainable growth cycle if it is to one day become a truly developed country."[xx]

Unlike Latin American presidents who had little interest in the outside world, Lula — like Cardoso before him — was well aware of the need to become increasingly competitive in the world economy. When asked during his National Radio program, "Café com o Presidente" — Coffee with the President — whether he was traveling too much, Lula cited the remarkable increase in Brazilian exports since he became president. "What's happening is that, in this globalized world, a country with Brazil's potential for production [...] can't remain seated on its chair, waiting for people to come and discover it. Either we are daring and tuck our products under our arms, going out to sell them to the world, or we lose this war in a globalized world," he replied.[xxi]

My main cause for optimism about Brazil, despite its recurring political crises, is based on something I heard from an academician during a television show I hosted featuring an interview with ex-President Cardoso. We were taping the show at a studio in Miami, and Cardoso — speaking via satellite — had spent much of the show criticizing Lula, his long-time political rival, who as an opposition leader had made Cardoso's life miserable during his presidency. When I asked Cardoso, who was now in the opposition, whether he agreed with Brazil's recent decision to demand that airport officials photograph and fingerprint Americans coming into the country, in reprisal for similar measures in the United States, Cardoso shook his head, and said that was a "childish" measure on Lula's part, which would only hurt his country's tourist industry. Likewise, when asked about various Lula foreign policy decisions, Cardoso responded that they were the likely result of his successor's lack of experience, or ignorance of world affairs.

But then, toward the end of the program, I asked the former president to rate Lula's efforts in foreign policy on a scale of one to 10. Cardoso raised his eyebrows, as if weighing his answer, and, with a mild shrug, answered: "Seven ... eight." Soon afterward, as the show was coming to a close and I asked the invited guests at the studio to comment on whatever they felt was most interesting in what Cardoso had said, one of them said something that got me thinking. Guillermo Lousteau, a professor of Latin American studies at Florida International University, said what had impressed him most was the former president's rating of his successor. "In Argentina it would be unimaginable for [current president] Kirchner to give a seven or an eight to [ex-president Eduardo] Duhalde, or for Duhalde to give a seven or eight to [ex-president Fernando] De la Rúa, or for De la Rúa to give a seven or eight to [ex-president Carlos S.] Menem, and so on and so forth," Lousteau said. Probably, the same could be said of presidents from most other Latin American countries. Despite all the political noise you heard every day in Brazil, something had changed in that country. And it was for the better.

NOTES

[i] Celso Lafer, *La identidad internacional de Brasil*, FCE, Mexico, 2002, p. 63.

[ii] Idem, p. 68.

[iii] Rubens Barbosa, during the Workshop for Journalists & Editors of Florida International University, Miami, May 2, 2003.

[iv] Michel Chevalier, *Le Mexique ancien et moderne*, 1863, pp. 387, 391.

[v] Idem, p. 404.

[vi] Mónica Quijada, "Sobre el origen y difusión del nombre 'América Latina,'" *Revista de las Indias*, No. 214, 1998, pp. 595-616.

[vii] Idem, p. 605.

[viii] Andrés Oppenheimer, "Brazilian candidate out of touch on Cuba," The *Miami Herald*, August 22, 2002.

[ix] "Lula's loose talk imperils U.S.-Brazilian honeymoon," The *Miami Herald*, July 20, 2003.

[x] *Veja*, October 30, 2002.

[xi] Telephone interview with Donna Hrinak, Miami, December 22, 2004.

[xii] Interview with Otto Reich, January 5, 2005.

[xiii] *Veja*, April 20, 2003, p. 40.

[xiv] *Veja*, December 8, 2004.

[xv] Interview with Ambassador John Danilovich, in Miami, January 11, 2005.

[xvi] Telephone interview with Diego Guelar, December 22, 2004.

[xvii] Idem.

[xviii] *El Nuevo Herald*, quoted in "Las pugnas internas de América Latina," May 8, 2005.

[xix] *Global Development Finance*, 2007, World Bank, p. 9.

[xx] *Veja*, "Palavra do Presidente," June 8, 2005.

[xxi] *Café com o Presidente*, May 16, 2005.

CHAPTER 8

Chávez's Narcissist-Leninist Revolution

Tall tale: "Venezuela is growing socially, morally, even spiritually."
(Hugo Chávez, president of the Bolivarian Republic of Venezuela,
during the closing ceremony of the U.S.-Venezuela Macro Business
Round Table, Caracas, July 1, 2005)

▬

CARACAS — FEW TIMES HAVE I SEEN SO MANY NEWS REPORTERS RAISE
their eyebrows in unison as when Venezuelan President Hugo Chávez
made his royal entrance at the inaugural session of the third Latin
America-European Union Summit in May 2004. Chávez was followed
by an entourage of personal videographers, photographers, palace
chroniclers, ministers, vice ministers, bodyguards, and special guests. I
was in the Convention Center of Guadalajara, Mexico, with a group of
European journalists in an area reserved for media and special guests,
watching the arrival of the 58 delegations that attended the summit.

French President Jacques Chirac, German Chancellor Gerhard
Schroeder, Spanish Prime Minister José Luis Rodríguez Zapatero,
and nearly all their European colleagues had just entered, each
flanked by perhaps two or three aides. But when Chávez entered
with head held high and gaze fixed on the horizon, he arrived at
the head of a gigantic contingent. The Europeans nearby looked
at me with a mixture of perplexity and amusement. Did he think
he was Napoléon? I shrugged. What could I say? Chávez's narcissism was no news to those of us who followed him closely, but for
most European reporters who had come to Latin America for the
first time with their presidents, it was a bizarre scene that reaffirmed
their moldiest clichés about Third World leaders.

After the summit's opening ceremony, the various presidential
speeches had been so boring that, with nothing better to write for

my next day's column in the *Miami Herald*, I decided on an experiment: in light of the reaction of European journalists to Chávez's outlandish delegation, I wondered how big his delegation was compared with those of other governments at the summit. Was there any relation between the size of a country's entourage and its gross national product? That was how I learned that the Venezuelan delegation was, indeed, the summit's biggest: he had brought 198 people in the new presidential Airbus A319 CJ he had just bought in France for $59 million.

As the Guadalajara newspaper *El Informador* reported the next day, much of the Venezuelan retinue consisted of Chávez's personal reporters and cameramen. Just as Cuba's president-for-life Fidel Castro did at all the summits — not this one, because Castro dismissed the European Union as "an accomplice to the crimes and aggressions against Cuba" — Chávez had flown in a small army of private chroniclers to record every detail of his speech against the International Monetary Fund and "savage neo-liberalism."

For their part, French President Chirac had shown up with a delegation of 90, German leader Schroeder around 70, and Spanish Prime Minister Rodríguez Zapatero 48, according to officials who accompanied them. Some Eastern European leaders, whose economies were among the fastest-growing in the world, had come with delegations that could fit into a car. Juhan Parts, the prime minister of Estonia, which topped some lists of the world's most successful economies, arrived with five people. And instead of making grandiose political speeches, the Estonians spent their time meeting businesspeople and trade officials from other countries to identify investment opportunities. So, half-jokingly, I wrote a column presenting a novel approach to measuring a country's economic development — it is inversely proportional to the size of its delegations at international summits.

How else could you explain Chávez, who was wasting the biggest economic windfall in his country's recent history and bringing a delegation of nearly 200 people? In part, it was because Chávez, much like Castro before him, relied heavily on media spectacle. Their popularity depended on making headlines, creating conflict, constantly playing the role of victim and champion of various causes, always at center stage, in part to distract public attention from vexing domestic issues, in part to build their image as larger-than-life heroes. The summit at Guadalajara was no exception. After seeing Castro at international summits for several decades and now, seeing Chávez, I knew the ritual by heart. It was always the same movie, with slight variations in the script.

In Guadalajara, Chávez used the opportunity to denounce a conspiracy of "coup plotters"—allegedly backed by the United States, Colombian paramilitary groups and the Venezuelan opposition — who sought to "destabilize the Venezuelan government and create chaos, for the purpose of bringing about a foreign invasion." His argument was peculiar, considering that it came from a former lieutenant colonel who had led a bloody coup attempt on February 4, 1992, and who since then had not only boasted of his attempt to overthrow the government, but — once he was president — had institutionalized the use of red berets and declared February 4 a national holiday to commemorate his failed attempt. Now Chávez was asking for "international solidarity" to prevent further coups. He used his 20-minute slot at the summit to harangue for over 35 minutes against "you, the rich" — pointing out German chancellor Schroeder — for allegedly being responsible for poverty in Latin America. The Europeans shook their heads. The delegation from Estonia wasn't even listening. Its members were glued to their cell phones, seeing what new factory they could attract to their small country, which was undergoing a phenomenal economic boom.

Predictably, the next day Latin American newspapers led their coverage of Guadalajara with Chávez's speech, his tirade against the IMF, and "you, the rich." They did not know yet that Chávez's Narcissism-Leninism had set off the greatest capital flight in Venezuelan history, that poverty had risen from 43 percent of Venezuela's population in 1999 to 53 percent in 2004, while extreme poverty — people living on less than $1 a day — jumped from 17 percent to 25 percent, according to the government's own figures.[i] A year later, when those figures from the Venezuelan National Institute of Statistics were published, Chávez appeared on television to say that even though they were official figures, they weren't credible. "I'm not going to say that [the data] are false, but the instruments they're using to measure reality aren't suitable," because "they're measuring our reality as if this were a neo-liberal country," Chávez said in April 2005, during his program, "Hello, Mr. President." The government considered prohibiting its statistics agency from issuing further figures based on international standards, replacing them with Cuban-style numbers that are impossible to corroborate independently, but record oil prices soon bailed him out: in 2006, Venezuelan poverty rates began to decline to pre-Chávez levels.

Elected dictatorship or authoritarian democracy?

In August 2004, a few months after the summit, I traveled to Venezuela to see the Bolivarian Revolution with my own eyes. How would Chávez win the election? Were the opposition's accusations true, that Venezuela was swiftly becoming a Cuban-style dictatorship? Or was the Venezuelan political class, defeated at the polls, exaggerating the threat in hopes of discrediting a traditional populist who made radical speeches but who, despite all his flaws, respected elections and won them?

When I boarded my flight to Caracas, the question in my mind was whether I would land in a country that had turned into Nicaragua in the 1980s, or into Cuba, with its revolutionary propaganda posters everywhere and its streets renamed for real or imaginary martyrs of the official mythology. To my surprise, I found neither one. Rather, I found myself in a more peaceful version of 1980s Beirut, a city geographically and politically divided into two halves, where the residents of one side rarely dared to enter the other. There was an East Caracas and a West Caracas.

Curiously enough, Chávez and his self-proclaimed Bolivarian Revolution had done some pretentious things — like changing the country's name to the ponderous "Bolivarian Republic of Venezuela," which had obliged all government agencies to reprint their stationery — but they had not done the first thing that revolutionary regimes usually do: change the names of streets.

In Cuba, I often found plazas renamed for Che Guevara, Ho Chi Minh, and other Marxist guerrilla fighters or Cuban soldiers who had fallen in some battle long forgotten by the rest of the world. In Nicaragua under the Sandinistas, the parks had been rechristened with the names of Marx, Lenin, and other icons of the Communist era. Even in Mexico, where the party that inherited the Mexican Revolution of 1910 had governed for seven decades until losing power in the 2000 elections, the main avenues of the capital bore names like "Reform," or "Revolution." Yet Chávez had done nothing of the sort in the more affluent neighborhoods of Caracas. After touring Los Rosales, Altamira, Chacao, and other middle- and upper-class zones of East Caracas, I didn't find many changes from the last time I had been there several years before, at the start of the Chávez government.

"Chávez didn't mess with street names in that part of the city," a friend said, surprised at my amazement. In fact, Chávez hadn't messed much with the names of streets in more working-class quarters of West Caracas such as Catia, Petare, or El Centro, either. Even though he had changed the name of Venezuela and had over 17,000 Cuban doctors and teachers working in the poorest parts of the capital and the rest of the country, he had not succumbed to the temptation to modify the names of the great avenues — or at least, not yet. As opposition mayor Alfredo Peña explained to me, if Chávez had wanted to, he could have immortalized his revolutionary heroes by renaming the great avenues with a wave of his hand.

So then, if this was heading into dictatorship, why didn't Chávez just get it over with? I started asking that of everyone I interviewed in the following days. One of the first people I saw was Teodoro

Petkoff, one of the few Venezuelan political leaders who could still analyze the reality of his country without being blinded by emotion. Petkoff, a former guerrilla fighter who, after entering the political arena, had been a founder of the Movement Toward Socialism and then minister of planning, and now led the independent newspaper *Tal Cual*. In his small office, late at night, I said I was surprised to see that the streets of Caracas still had their old names, as if nothing momentous had happened.

Petkoff raised his eyebrows and looked at me as if he were speaking to someone who had just flown down from Jupiter. He told me there were no visible signs of revolution in Venezuela simply because there had been no revolution. "The only revolution that has taken place in Venezuela is the one in Chávez's head and in the heads of some of the widows of communism in American and Latin American universities," Petkoff told me. "Besides passing a land reform that was never implemented, he has done nothing revolutionary. He hasn't established a single-party system, hasn't suppressed the opposition, or nationalized foreign companies."[ii] A process of "Cubanization" would have been very difficult, if not impossible, in Venezuela, Petkoff added. Unlike what had taken place in Cuba, Chávez hadn't been able to create a party or military apparatus that could control the population. Not that he didn't want to: among other things, he had formed neighborhood groups of political control that he had named "Bolivarian Circles" after the "Committees for the Defense of the Revolution" in Cuba, and he was gradually appropriating more television time for his endless speeches to the nation. He even had his own television program, "Hello, Mr. President," in which he served as director, host, interviewer, political analyst, singer, and — whenever he was traveling — tour guide. But it was a case of narcissism more than communism, Petkoff said. Venezuela wasn't Cuba. There was a tradition of democracy and free speech that would make it very difficult to impose a closed dictatorship. "Here there's a process of weakening the institutions in order to toughen a strongman, but this isn't Cuba," Petkoff maintained.

Other analysts with whom I spoke gave me diametrically opposite views. The reason Chávez hadn't changed the names of the streets was because his revolution was a gradual process, rigorously planned and closely advised by Castro, that envisioned several stages in which the traditional bastions of power would be beheaded. The names of the streets hadn't been changed yet because the time wasn't ripe, some critics explained.

The facts were in plain sight, they said. First, after winning the 1998 elections Chávez had used his political capital to change the Constitution and create a legal system that would allow him to run — and win — future elections. Then, in 2001, he had pushed through laws on land, hydrocarbons, and banking. When these measures triggered massive opposition protests and later a nation-wide strike, Chávez had decapitated the main business organization, Fedecámaras, and had then done the same with the most important labor organization, the Venezuelan Workers' Federation (CTV), and PDVSA, the independent state monopoly that was by far the biggest contributor to the national budget. In April 2002 he had purged the military hierarchy after a murky military rebellion in which — depending on whom you choose to believe — Chávez either resigned under duress only to return to power 48 hours later, or was unseated by the coup plotters. In 2004, after emerging victorious from a plebiscite on his mandate, Chávez ordered the Supreme Court to be expanded from 20 to 32 members, filling it with loyalists and assuring control over an institution that in the future would have the last word on any further disputes regarding freedom of the press and electoral legislation. That same year he had a media law approved that gave the government *de facto* powers to censor the press. In other words, he had removed all of his real and potential enemies, one by one, until he had gained control of the three branches of government and, to some degree, of all the elements of power in the country.

"It's just a question of time before he changes the names of streets," said Alberto Garrido, a former university professor, columnist with the newspaper *El Universal,* and author of several books about Chávez. "What we're seeing now is what Chávez himself has called a period of transition," Garrido said during one of several conversations we had. "Chávez hasn't created a new state, but he has been gradually co-opting the existing state: he has already taken over control of Congress, the Supreme Court, the electoral council, etc." Anyone who didn't want to see this reality was kidding himself, because Chávez had never concealed his intentions, Garrido added. In effect, the president had repeatedly said that he would remain in power until 2021. He had declared numerous times that representative democracy was a system that "does not work for Latin American governments," and from the beginning of his political career had announced that the revolution would be carried out gradually, step by step, Garrido indicated.

When Chávez was in the Yare prison, following his imprisonment for his bloody coup attempt, he had already written a long manifesto in which he indicated it would take 20 years in power to bring about a revolution in Venezuela. The document, titled, "On How to Escape this Labyrinth," was published from prison in July 1992. It said Venezuela needed a "civilian-military fusion," and that "the strategic goal of the Simón Bolívar National Project is placed on a far-off horizon, 20 years after the initial scenario."[iii] And only five years had passed since Chávez had taken over as president, Garrido pointed out. "From the outside, the institutions, like the streets, carry the same names. But don't be fooled, because everything is changing, although many times it's not something you can see right away," he assured me.

Was Venezuela's political system an elected dictatorship or a hybrid democracy with a charismatic leader? In the days following my interviews with Petkoff and Garrido, when the referendum of August 15, 2004, was held, I could reach my own conclusion: Venezuela was neither a closed dictatorship — at least for the time being — nor a hybrid democracy. It was, rather, an authoritarian democracy that was gradually being undermined by a sly populist.

The arrogance of the past

Chávez held an enormous advantage: His speech against the Venezuelan "oligarchy" had a strong foundation. Venezuela had been for decades a model of "kleptocracy," where corrupt governments and fawning businessmen had divvied up the oil profits at will and with absolute contempt for an impoverished majority. As in many other nations, oil had ruined Venezuela, turning it into a nation where nothing was produced and everything was purchased abroad, even the unnecessary. During the previous oil boom in the 1970s, Venezuelans had even imported hospitals prefabricated in Sweden, complete with heating equipment and snow plows, for cities like Maracaibo that have never known cold weather. The "Saudi Venezuela" of the '70s had destroyed national industry and generated a "give-me-two" phenomenon, after the famous phrase used by Venezuelans who traveled to Miami and bought two of everything, just in case. The business class, which lived almost entirely off the generosity of the state, boasted that the country had the world's highest per capita consumption of Johnnie Walker Black Label premium scotch, and the greatest number of private airplanes in Latin America.

I saw Venezuela for the first time in 1984, as a newly hired reporter for the *Miami Herald*, and I remember being shocked by the economic and social blindness of its ruling class. The oil bonanza of the 1970s had come to an end two years earlier, but Venezuela continued to throw money away as if nothing would matter. The government subsidies were astronomical. A great many of them were not for the poor, but to keep up the sumptuous habits — including subsidies for whisky imports — of the upper and middle classes.

Around that time, I wrote an article from Caracas about how you could buy a U.S. Buick Century car assembled in Venezuela for $9,000 there, much cheaper than in Miami. The reason was simple: Venezuela subsidized imports of automotive parts. Gasoline was dirt-cheap — 15 U.S. cents for the equivalent of a gallon — because the government sold it for less than production cost, paying the difference with exports. A bottle of Johnnie Walker Black cost $18, much less than in the United States, because the government gave whisky importers the same preferential exchange rate it granted importers of medicines. A round-trip airplane ticket from Caracas to Margarita Island, 260 kilometers northeast of the capital, cost $18 on Aeropostal, the state airline. I couldn't believe it, until I made the trip myself in a plane that was just as nice as those of any international airline.

Since it was cheaper to import products than to produce them in Venezuela, before long the national industries collapsed. The country's reserves plummeted from $20 billion in 1981 to $8 billion in 1988, but by the end of the decade Venezuela imported almost twice as much as its neighbor, Colombia, which has nearly twice the population. "Venezuelans refuse to accept the fact that they're no longer the rich country they once were," a U.S. diplomat told me, as I reported from Caracas in 1989. "Everyone is living as if there were no tomorrow."[iv]

The business class behaved with an arrogance that visitors found hard to swallow. During a trip to Caracas I had the chance to interview a businessman from one of the wealthiest families in Venezuela, the Boultons. This man, who was very busy, agreed to talk in the barbershop of his private club. When I arrived, he was sitting in the barber's chair with three people around him. While the barber cut his hair, two manicurists worked on his hands, one on each side. I introduced myself and told him I would wait until he was finished. To my surprise, the man answered me in English, telling me to stand in front of him, next to the mirror, so we could do the interview right then and there. "OK, no problem," I answered him in Spanish. When I asked him the first question, he answered me again in English. Uncomfortable because we were speaking a foreign language in front of his personal groomers, I asked the next question in Spanish but he again answered in English, either because it was easier for him or because he didn't want anyone to understand what he was saying — a curious choice, since the interview would be published locally in the next few days — or because he wanted to assert his membership in a class that was distinguished even by language from that of his servants. In any case, it was an absurd and uncomfortable situation — I questioned him in Spanish, he answered in English, while the barber and manicurists pretended they weren't trying to understand. Somehow, it exemplified the arrogance of quite a few members of the Venezuelan business class.

In 1989 former President Carlos Andrés Pérez, who governed during the oil boom of the 1970s, had won election with a populist campaign, promising to return the country to the prosperity of his predecessors. As expected, a few weeks after he got into power he had no choice but to do exactly the opposite of what he had promised: he slashed government spending and some subsidies, including those awarded to urban transportation. The rising bus fares set off a riot, leaving at least 350 dead and thousands wounded. As no politician had spoken honestly to the public, telling them they couldn't spend what they didn't have, it wasn't surprising that thousands of Venezuelans felt betrayed and had taken to the streets.

I returned to Venezuela a few hours after the February 1992 coup attempt led by then-lieutenant colonel Chávez. Five battalions of armed forces had surrounded the presidential residence, La Casona (The Big House), as well as several government agencies, attacking them with cannon fire and hoping to force Pérez's surrender. At least 56 people, including 14 presidential guards, died in combat. Hours later, the Associated Press reported at least 42 more deaths, nearly all of them civilians struck by stray bullets. When I reached Caracas the next day, the uprising had been quashed. The government announced the leader of the coup attempt had been a man called Lieutenant Colonel Chávez, who identified himself as a member of a so-called Bolivarian Military Movement that intended to impose a military government in Venezuela.

"They had a recording prepared for broadcast on television that announced formation of a military junta," presidential spokesman

José Consuegra told a press conference the following day. "They had seized Channel 8 [the state-run channel] and were about to put it on the air," but the 14 rebel soldiers manning the television station were unable to do so because of technical difficulties, Consuegra added. The rebel troops had managed to take control of the building, but they didn't know how to broadcast the tape. When the journalists asked what kind of government Chávez had intended to install, the government spokesman answered: "A right-wing regime."[v]

As I recall, what impressed me most about my trip to Venezuela after the attempted coup in 1992 was the passivity — almost complacency — with which most Venezuelans reacted. Some of us who had seen South American military dictatorships up close during the '70s were horrified by what had just happened. Venezuela was one of the oldest democracies in Latin America — its last military regime had ended in 1959. And instead of repudiating the bloody coup attempt, many Venezuelans shrugged, or said the government deserved it. In my room at the Caracas Hilton, watching a televised session of Congress at which the events of the past few hours were being debated, I was amazed that the legislators — who should have been the first to defend democracy — were making fiery speeches that, rather than lay aside their political differences to condemn the attempted coup, focused criticism on the current government. Former president Rafael Caldera, a center-right opposition senator at the time, demanded a "rectification of the government's economic policy." I couldn't believe it: he was tacitly justifying the coup plotters and lashing out at Pérez's budget cuts, as if the country could continue living off its oil wealth from the '70s. Soon afterward, Caldera demanded Pérez's resignation. Populism seemed to course through the veins of Venezuelan politicians of all stripes.

Can't you see you are playing along with a coup plotter? I said to my friends and quite a few of the people I interviewed in Caracas. Most of them told me that I was the one who was wrong, because in Venezuela there was no danger of a repetition of the kind of dictatorships that had taken over in Chile, Argentina, and other countries of the region a few years earlier. The Venezuelan military was different, they said. Its members didn't come from the upper classes, as in other Latin American countries, but were working-class in origin, and more knowledgeable than anyone else about the country's problems because they alone had hands-on experience in zones the private sector didn't even enter. The Venezuelan political class was no model of democracy either, argued many intellectuals and politicians of the democratic left who would eventually become members of the Chávez administration (and, later, his toughest opponents).

From the arrival of democracy in 1959, leaders of both main parties — Democratic Action, left of center, and COPEI, right of center — had divided up power between them as if the country were a ranch they co-owned. The leaders of both parties drew up the lists of deputies and senators and appointed governors, mayors, and members of municipal legislatures. The concept of primaries to elect candidates for public position was practically unknown, and just recently had begun to be put into practice — timidly, and in limited cases. Most of the 190 members of Congress hardly knew what districts they represented: their names were placed on random lists by the leadership of their party, and their loyalty was to the leaders who named them.

President Pérez was seen as a leader who spent too much time traveling around the world, using Venezuela's oil wealth to promote grandiose international political projects, and too little time taking care of the country's problems. In fact, when the coup attempt caught him by surprise, Pérez, 69 years old at the time, had just arrived from one of his trips to the United States and Europe. The media criticized him regularly for making 34 trips abroad during the two first years of his second administration, from 1989 to 1990. And in 1991, the year before Chávez's coup, the president had kept up his annual rate of some 17 international trips. In the previous few months he had been trying to resolve the crisis in Haiti, the armed conflict in Colombia, the Cuban crisis, internal wars in Central America, and disputes within the Organization of the Petroleum Exporting Countries (OPEC.) "He should quickly name a prime minister and dedicate himself full-time to what he likes best. What does it matter if Venezuela gains a seat on the United Nations Security Council, when our cannons can hardly reach La Orchila Island [off the coast of Venezuela]. We could hardly play a relevant role in the global context," the Caracas newspaper *Economía Hoy* said just a few days before the military uprising. As would happen to Chávez years later, the oil bonanza had gone to Pérez's head.

In late 1993, Caldera won the elections by promising the sky, and took office a second time early the next year. He was 78 years old and walked leaning backward, as if his head were permanently behind his heels. One of his first acts in government — which would change the country's history — had been to give a presidential pardon to 30 officers who had participated in the February 1992 attempted coup or another in November that same year. Not long afterward, he rolled out the red carpet for some of the leaders of the failed coups, including Chávez. That reception was a totally irresponsible act that set a terrible precedent for Venezuelan democracy: if a group of officers who had caused at least 56 deaths were freed and received by the president after just a few months behind bars, how would others be deterred from following their example in the future? Shortly afterward, Chávez and his followers were appearing regularly in the media and treated as heroes. Caldera's government was falling to pieces, amid erratic economic measures and growing accusations of nepotism at the highest levels. One of his sons, Andrés, was the president's chief of staff, while the other, Juan José, was head of the ruling party. The president's son-in-law, Rubén Rojas Pérez, led the presidential guard and was one of the president's military advisers. The Caldera government was a family affair.

Meanwhile, Luis Miquilena, a former leader of the Communist Party of Venezuela and founder of the Revolutionary Party of the Proletariat, who had long proposed a civilian-military leftist alliance, had taken the recently-released Chávez under his wing. With

Miquilena advising his every political step, Chávez ran for office in 1998 dressed in a military uniform and vigorously justifying his 1992 coup attempt. "Go ahead, let them call me pro-coup. Let those who believe the coup was justified raise their hands," he would say in his campaign speeches, making the crowd raise their arms in unison.[vi]

But during the campaign Chávez was also careful not to present himself as a Castro-styled revolutionary. "Me, a Communist?" Chávez would ask reporters with a scornful smile. When I interviewed Chávez two months before the 1998 elections and asked him about Venezuelan and Colombian intelligence reports claiming that he had close ties with Colombian rebels, Cuba, and Libya, Chávez responded, "For the past five years, they have been trying to destroy me politically and morally, and have been making up all kinds of stories about me. These stories are completely, totally false." Chávez denied he was a radical leftist, adding that his fiery speeches against the free market were inspired by Pope John Paul II's ideas, and were merely rhetorical devices arising from "the head of the electoral battle."[vii]

On election day, December 6, 1998, Chávez swept the polls with 56 percent of the votes, against 40 percent for his main rival, Henrique Salas Rohmer, and 15 percent for former Miss Venezuela, Irene Sáez. By then the country had split in half, and Chávez would polarize it even further over the next four years, as he railed daily against opposition parties, the media, the Catholic Church, the "oligarchy," and any other group that dared criticize his government. During his first years in office that criticism grew each day, because Chávez's disastrous management had achieved an economic miracle in reverse: despite a new boom that benefited from the precipitous rise in the price of oil from $9 a barrel when he took office to a record of about $50 in 2004, the Venezuelan president had managed to impoverish the country as few before him ever had. Over 7,000 factories had shut down since his administration began.[viii] Capital flight had surpassed $36 billion, the economy had shrunk over 20 percent,[ix] and urban unemployment had risen from 15 percent to 18 percent.[x] According to Ricardo Hausmann, former head economist at the Inter-American

Development Bank, the number of poor had grown by 2.5 million since the beginning of the Chávez Administration.[xi]

The April "coup"

The Bush Administration's clumsiness was a bonanza for Chávez when a short-lived military uprising forced him to leave office for 48 hours in April 2002. In a rare case of business-labor solidarity, the business coalition Fedecámeras and the Venezuelan Workers' Federation united to back the national strike of PDVSA workers, and the resulting general strike spawned the largest protests in Venezuelan history. Hundreds of thousands of people, unionized workers incited by their unions and non-union workers encouraged by their employers, turned out before the presidential palace, Miraflores, on Thursday, April 11, to demand Chávez's resignation. At 1 P.M. the column of protesters who had congregated before a PDVSA building began to head toward the presidential palace. The army — its generals would later say — refused to follow Chávez's orders to put down the crowds. Once the demonstrators reached downtown, paramilitary sharpshooters or groups of armed *Chavistas* shot at them, either to disperse them or to answer gunfire from anti-Chávez metropolitan police. The bloody battle that followed left at least 19 people dead and dozens wounded. That night, the top military command rebelled against Chávez. At dawn the president announced publicly he had agreed to "abandon" power. "I told them, 'I'm leaving,' but I demand respect for the Constitution," he said, suggesting he be replaced by the president of the National Assembly, who was a follower of his.[xii] A few minutes later, the general in charge of the armed forces, Lucas Rincón, an ally of Chávez's, announced on television that the military had asked the president to resign, and that "he accepted." At the same time, Rincón said that business leader Pedro Carmona would act as interim president, at least for a short time, until the order of constitutional succession could be established. But on that afternoon, Friday the 12th, whether because of megalomania, stupidity, or both, Carmona surprised the world by suspending both Congress and the Supreme Court of Justice, and proclaiming himself interim president until elections could be held the following year.

The Bush Administration, instead of immediately condemning an obviously unconstitutional transfer of power—even if Chávez resigned, his replacement should have been the leader of Congress—looked the other way. What's worse, it blamed Chávez for the events that led to his overthrow. While the presidents of Mexico, Argentina, and other Latin American countries, who by coincidence were attending a summit in Costa Rica, condemned Carmona's self-coronation as president, White House spokesman Ari Fleischer said at noon on Friday the 12th, a few hours before Carmona's formal takeover, that "Chávez had fallen after government supporters, following his orders, shot at unarmed protesters."[xiii] It wasn't far from the truth, but it neglected to mention that Carmona was not Chávez's legal successor. State Department spokesman Philip Reeker said that "Chávez has resigned from the presidency," and that "before resigning, he fired the vice president and the cabinet." Reeker attributed the events to "Chávez's anti-democratic actions" over the previous three years.

On Sunday, April 14, Chávez was reinstated by loyalist military officers, and international criticism of the United States' role in the coup began to build. Chávez charged that he had been the victim of a U.S. plot, and growing numbers of opinion-makers around the world speculated that the Bush Administration had encouraged the coup. Some of the allegations were hard to take seriously, among them Chávez's claim that a U.S. warship had approached the coast of Venezuela at the time of the military rebellion to provide support for the coup plotters. But many others were valid, such as one made by Democratic U.S. senator Christopher Dodd, a chief Congressional critic of the Bush Administration. Dodd correctly deplored the fact the coup hadn't been immediately condemned by the Bush Administration, and demanded an internal investigation of the State Department's role in the affair. Speculation grew when the *New York*

Times reported that Otto Reich, head of Latin American Affairs at the State Department, had spoken by phone with Carmona during the events, advising him not to disband the National Assembly or other constitutional bodies. If that conversation had taken place, it raised questions of whether Reich had been in contact with Carmona long before, perhaps even offering advance approval of his takeover.

Carmona later denied that there had been any such conversation, and the Bush Administration said — after Chávez was back in power — that the man who called Carmona to demand that Congress not be disbanded had been the U.S. ambassador to Venezuela, Charles Shapiro. Weeks later, the internal investigation requested by Senator Dodd determined there had been no U.S. involvement in Chávez's overthrow. On the day before the coup, Thursday, April 11, the State Department had issued a communiqué during the street violence in Venezuela, stating that the United States vigorously condemned "any unconstitutional efforts from either side" in the conflict. Once the Venezuelan high military command had rebelled, and Chávez's resignation and the firing of the vice president and congressional leader were announced at dawn on April 12, "both the State Department and the embassy worked behind the scenes to persuade the interim government to hold early elections and obtain the approval of the National Assembly and the Supreme Court." The investigation added that "when the interim government, contrary to the advice of the United States, dissolved the National Assembly and the Supreme Court, and adopted other anti-democratic measures, the State Department worked through the O.A.S. [Organization of American States] to condemn these events and to restore democracy and constitutionality in Venezuela."[xiv]

"Did Chávez political opponents ask for help from the [U.S.] embassy or the State Department to remove him from power through anti-democratic or unconstitutional means? The answer is no," the State Department's internal investigation concluded. "The opposition informed their American interlocutors regarding their intentions or those of others, and the officials of the United States systematically responded to these accounts with statements that opposed any effort to remove Chávez from government by anti-democratic or anti-constitutional means."[xv]

Some time later, after he had left his post and retired from the U.S. Government, I asked Reich whether the Bush Administration hadn't been too hasty in taking Chávez's resignation for granted. The Venezuelan president now claimed he never resigned. How did Reich and his colleagues in Washington know he had? "Rincón, the commander in chief of the Venezuelan armed forces, had come out to say [on television] that Chávez had resigned, and Rincón was a man who had been appointed by him. Besides, we had an ambassador from a Western country who had called [U.S. Ambassador] Shapiro to tell him that he had just spoken to Chávez, who had asked for his assistance so that nothing would happen to his family. The new Venezuelan authorities made preparations for him to travel to Cuba and meet his family there," Reich recalled. All night, ambassadors from Britain, Spain, and other countries communicated with Shapiro to tell him that Cuba's ambassador to Venezuela, Germán Sánchez, was asking that members of the diplomatic corps accompany Chávez to Cuba to guarantee his safety, a U.S. official who reported to Reich at the time told me. According to Reich and his aides, there was no coup, and the media distorted what had actually occurred, because at the time the statements of the Bush Administration were made at noon on Friday, April 12, no illegal actions had been taken in Venezuela: "There was an uprising of Venezuelan military officers and the Venezuelan people after Chávez had given an unconstitutional order [to suppress the crowds] and the military refused to carry it out," and the president had resigned. "Carmona did not illegally come into power until after 4 in the afternoon on that same day," Reich said.[xvi]

A few hours before Carmona's takeover on the afternoon of April 12, Reich said, he heard from Ambassador Shapiro that Chávez's interim successor intended to dissolve Congress and declare himself president. "When Shapiro called and told me that Carmona was going to proclaim himself president, I answered, 'He's proclaiming himself what?' I couldn't believe it. Then, I asked Shapiro to call Carmona himself — I didn't want to speak to him — and tell him that if he broke the constitutional thread and proclaimed himself president, he could not count on the support of the United States. I don't really recall whether I used the word sanctions, but I clearly remember telling him that there would be consequences if they took that step. And I expressed to Shapiro that he should make it crystal-clear during the conversation that he was speaking on my behalf, and on behalf of the government of the United States. That was around midday. At two in the afternoon, Shapiro called me back, saying that he had spoken to Carmona, he had conveyed the message, and that Carmona had answered that 'We know what we're doing.' I think those words will go down in history as one of the stupidest things he could have said."[xvii]

By the time the State Department's internal investigation appeared, several months after the events, Chávez was already going around the world denouncing, as if it were incontrovertible truth, Washington's instigation of the coup. Speculation had become official history in Venezuela, and would soon be taken up by Venezuela's supporters abroad. With time, it would become accepted by most governments. What's true is that Bush had given Chávez a huge propagandistic gift: he could now boast his own credentials as a victim of U.S. "imperialism," and compare himself to the late Chilean president Salvador Allende. Even though the United States had not supported the coup, it had hesitated and tacitly accepted an unconstitutional presidential succession. As Senator Dodd pointed out, "having remained silent during the illegal overthrow of a government is a fact of extreme concern and will have profound implications on hemispheric democracy."[xviii]

CHÁVEZ'S NARCISSIST-LENINIST REVOLUTION | 267

Chávez's 2004 victory

I am not convinced — unlike much of the Venezuelan opposition — that Chávez won the August 15, 2004, referendum on his mandate by rigging the election results. Although the opposition denounced a "gigantic" cybernetic fraud, my conclusion from covering the vote in Caracas that day was that — in the absence of conclusive evidence to the contrary — the Carter Center and O.A.S., which had monitored the vote and ruled there were not enough irregularities to alter the result of the vote, deserved the benefit of the doubt. Still, from what I saw during my stay in Venezuela, there had undoubtedly been "environmental fraud" in the election process in the months leading to the vote. Chávez had resorted to all kinds of tricks — some legal, others not — to hold down the opposition turnout on election day. While those obstacles didn't invalidate his victory, they did take away much of its luster, and should have been brought to the world's attention by international election monitors, I concluded.

How did Chávez win? Through a combination of petro-populism, a poorly-run opposition campaign, government intimidation, and measures he took throughout the electoral process to keep anti-Chávez voters from the polls. The referendum on Chávez's mandate had been convened by the opposition under Chávez's own Bolivarian Constitution, which permitted Venezuelans to call a plebiscite to remove any elected official as long as they gathered a sufficient number of signatures, estimated at the time at 2.4 million. After the opposition organized a "super sign-up" in 2003 and collected over 3 million signatures on forms printed by the state, the government retroactively changed the requirements for validating the signatures, voiding about 1 million and bringing the total below the required minimum. In May 2004, after a wave of protests and under pressure from the Carter Center and the O.A.S., the National Electoral Council, dominated by Chávez loyalists, agreed to allow the verification, one by one, of nearly a million signatures it had invalidated.

Even then, the government set up all kinds of obstacles: it limited the number of voting centers, forms, and the days and hours when opponents could sign them, and it announced 38 new criteria by which signatures could be invalidated. Simultaneously, the government let it be known that it would carefully examine the list of those who had signed the petition for the referendum, and that government employees or businessmen who had contracts with the state should not expect the government to continue to give them the same treatment. In other words, those who signed would be subject to reprisals. As the first denunciations of the arbitrary firing of opponents who had signed the petition began to appear in the press, the government announced that those who "repented" could sign a new form demanding to be removed from the list. Still, the opposition managed to gather enough signatures all over again; even after the government invalidated hundreds of thousands, it surpassed by a wide margin the number required for a referendum. The National Electoral Council had no choice but to hold a vote on August 15 that year.

But that was only the beginning. As the referendum date approached, Chávez set up additional hurdles to deter foreign monitors, requirements that were so onerous that the European Union withdrew its observers days before the vote. The Carter Center and the O.A.S. stuck with their commitment, albeit with strong reservations. In the meantime, Chávez progressively began to make use of television "chains" — live broadcasts of his speeches — almost daily, without allowing his opposition a fraction of his air time. According to opposition television stations, at least 203 presidential speeches were broadcast on national television in 2003, and the radio and television stations had to broadcast 91 presidential speeches in 2004, nearly all of them just before the referendum. Often, the speeches lasted for hours. During them, Chávez accused the independent nongovernmental organization Súmate — which was monitoring the referendum process — of working for the Bush Administration, because it had accepted $53,000 from the National

Endowment for Democracy to monitor the referendum. The NED, a nonpartisan organization funded by the U.S. Congress, had contributed for several decades to election monitoring in Mexico, various South American countries, Asia, and Africa, by paying among other things for the rental of cell phones and computers with which election monitors could do their job. The accusation was ridiculous, since Súmate was not making partisan propaganda, while Chávez was sending military missions with pro-government propaganda signs to the most impoverished neighborhoods of Venezuela while opening bragging of having brought 17,000 Cuban doctors and teachers into the country to assist his "revolution" in the months leading up to the referendum.

In some cases the obstacles set up by the government were so childish, they were laughable. Among the 300,000 Venezuelans who wanted to register abroad to vote — many of them anti-*Chavistas* living in the United States — only 50,000 managed to comply with the cumbersome list of government requirements that grew longer each day. In cities where most Venezuelans were hostile to Chávez, people who wanted to vote were left waiting for hours without being able to do so. At the Miami consulate, a low-level employee of the diplomatic offices finally came down in mid-morning to tell the crowd of would-be voters stranded on the ground floor that, unfortunately, the building elevator had broken down. After a long wait, many went home, convinced they would never be allowed to vote.

"We're going to Fort Apache"

The intimidation of voters, from what I could see in Caracas, wasn't subtle. A few days before the referendum, I requested an interview with Alfredo Peña, mayor of Caracas, one of many politicians who had supported Chávez at first and now took part in the opposition. I had met Peña more than 10 years before, when he was editor of the Caracas newspaper *El Nacional*. Toward the end of the 90s, when I wrote that I was afraid that Chávez would become an authoritarian military strongman like so many others in Latin America before him, Peña had chided me for not understanding the working-class nature of the Venezuelan armed forces, and the Chávez phenomenon in particular. Soon afterward, he had been sworn in as Chávez's spokesman and head of his cabinet, a key position in the new administration. However, his honeymoon with the new president didn't last long: within four months he had grown disenchanted with the growing militarization and authoritarianism of the government, and he was replaced by the president himself with a trusted military man.

Since then, Peña had crossed over to the opposition and won the mayoralty of Caracas by an overwhelming majority. But he had a geographic-political problem: City Hall was in El Centro, in the heart of *Chavista* territory, surrounded by buildings where the toughest sectors of Chávez's government were concentrated. Next to City Hall was the Ministry of Foreign Relations, and across from it the Congress and the headquarters of the Libertador Municipality, whose mayor was accused by the opposition of responsibility for a paramilitary riot squad that handled the government's dirty work. One block away was the Vice Presidency building, where José Vicente Rangel, one of the brains behind the Chávez administration, went about his business. Two blocks away was Miraflores Palace, where Chávez himself lived.

I began to understand Peña's problem when, innocently, I got into a taxi at my J. W. Marriott hotel in East Caracas and asked the driver to take me to City Hall in El Centro. The taxi driver turned around in slow motion, as if he wasn't sure he had heard me right. When I repeated my destination, he smiled nervously and told me he couldn't take me there. What's more, he recommended I not go at all because it was too unsafe. Soon afterward, Peña sent his son to fetch me in a bulletproof SUV, with three City Hall cops inside armed to the teeth and two more vans escorting us. "We're going to Fort Apache," Peña Jr. told me, smiling. "Don't be afraid."

As we crossed the city, going from the Venezuelan version of East Beirut to West Beirut, I couldn't help but be amazed at how the landscape was changing. On the east side of the city the great majority of posters were in favor of "YES," exhorting people to vote for the early removal of Chávez from office; every two or three blocks a "NO" poster could be seen. As we entered West Caracas, the number of "YES" posters gradually declined, then disappeared altogether. In El Centro, virtually all posters called on people to vote "NO" on the proposal to oust Chávez from power. The unpainted downtown buildings were covered with big signs bearing slogans like "Bush Out," "Imperialism Out," "kNOck Them Out," "NO until 2021," and "Hey, Hey, Chávez is here to stay." Even on a wall at the headquarters of the armed forces — in theory, an apolitical institution — an enormous "NO" banner was hung. Practically every 10 yards of construction had a pro-Chávez slogan, and there wasn't a single opposition poster in sight. "Here, if you paint a "Yes" sign, you're risking your life," the mayor's son explained.

We entered City Hall through a small, bulletproof door, nearly hidden to one side of an open-air parking lot where the mayor was waiting for me. Peña wanted at all costs to guide me for a visit to City Hall, and his motive was soon clear: it was a fortress under siege that already had been attacked several times. All the windows were protected with bars, and all ground-floor doors were blocked with tree branches or iron bars that had obviously been hauled in fast to stave off an attack. According to Peña, the Chavista riot squad — security staff at the Libertador Municipal Building across the street — merely waited, sitting around the plaza until they were ordered to put down opposition protests or events. The building had been attacked with firearms and stones on 26 occasions. Peña took me inside the cafeteria, an enormous hall with a rectangular table that seated at least two dozen people, so he could show me the bullet holes in the wall. Five City Hall police officers and two civilians had already been wounded by bullets coming from the plaza, he explained, pointing at a blood stain on the window curtain. Some of the best paintings in the City Hall collection, including one by Armando Reverón, probably the country's most famous painter, had bullet holes in them. Finally, Peña showed me the *piéce de résistance* in the menu of violence perpetrated by the Chavista mob: his own chair in the executive offices' dining room, pierced by a bullet through the middle of the back. "If I had been eating here that day, I wouldn't be alive to tell the tale," Peña said.[xix]

Obviously, Peña and other opposition leaders had little room for maneuver. They had no access to the TV channels Chávez controlled, no money to hand out as the government did, no control over electoral institutions, and no authority to change the rules at their convenience. Often they couldn't even bring supporters together in facilities like City Hall that they controlled. Government intimidation was everywhere. "Those who attacked my office 26 times are armed Chavistas, government employees. We already know them, because they're the same ones you see sitting there in the plaza," the mayor concluded, taking me to the window and inviting me to poke my head out, but not too far.

The greatest electoral intimidation, however, took place through the new electronic voting system inaugurated by the government for the plebiscite. It had never been tested anywhere. While threatening to fire public officials who signed the referendum petition and to deny government contracts to businessmen who signed it, the government announced the new voting system would have "fingerprint snapshot" machines that would record each voter's prints. Theoretically, that would prevent anybody from voting more than once. With the new electronic voting system, Venezuelans could vote "YES," to remove Chávez, or "NO," for him to stay, on a computer screen and receive a ballot that registered their vote. Immediately, official media spread the word that thanks to the "fingerprint snapshot" machines the government would know precisely how each citizen had voted; therefore, people should not be misled into believing their votes were secret. Similar warnings seemed more plausible in light of press reports shortly before the referendum that the voting machines would use software from Bitza, a U.S. company of which the Chávez government held 28 percent. After the *Miami Herald* revealed that the company was registered in the state of Florida, Bitza announced it would buy out the Venezuelan government's shares. But millions of citizens couldn't help regarding the new electronic voting system with distrust, and fearing for their future if they voted "YES."

But despite Chávez's legal maneuvers and widespread voter intimidation, what helped him the most on election day was the avalanche of petrodollars his government was able to campaign with. The president spent between $1.6 billion and $3.6 billion from PDVSA — the Venezuelan state's petroleum monopoly — in the months before the vote, in the form of temporary scholarships of more than $150 per month to hundreds of thousands of young and unemployed people. These were mostly education scholarships, but also scholarships that didn't include any obligation to study. Chávez was swimming in petrodollars. In a country where oil accounted for 80 percent of exports and was the state's main source of income, Chávez had loads of money and was spreading it around in cash, essentially to buy votes.

So it was no surprise that at the end of the day, the National Electoral Council gave Chávez 59 percent of the votes, compared with 41 percent for the opposition. The opposition said the results were impossible, given that exit polls coordinated by Súmate had given the anti-Chavista vote an 18 percent lead. How could Chávez have won by nearly the same percentage? opposition leaders asked, implying that the final results had been rigged at some top-secret cybernetic center. But the O.A.S. and the Carter Center, after some verbal sparring with the government, recounted votes at random and were convinced Chávez had indeed won. The president had met the challenge, using all kinds of tricks during the electoral process, but he had won.

The informal economy's vote

Walking through Caracas the next day and seeing thousands of informal workers who seemed to have taken over the city selling trinkets in the streets, I concluded that Chávez's triumph was probably due to the vote of the informal economy workers. Indeed, the opposition's political campaign had been aimed at those who had formal jobs, or had once had them, or hoped to have them some day. But for the millions of Venezuelans who operated in the informal economy — selling on the streets or working off the books in all kinds of businesses — and whose numbers had swollen as a result of the factory closings during Chávez' first years in power, the opposition's recipes were empty words compared with the $150 in cash the Chávez government was handing out.[xx]

For a young man selling made-in-China plastic sandals on the streets of Caracas who had entered the labor market under Chávez and had never held a formal job, it meant little if some opposition politician or intellectual said that thousands of factories had shut down since the start of the administration, that urban unemployment had risen steadily, that over $36 billion had fled abroad in the past five years, or that Venezuela had dropped to the bottom of global competitiveness rankings. Those figures meant something to those who hoped to get a formal job or upgrade the one they had, but they said little to the street vendor or informal sector worker. Those millions of marginalized people weren't bothered much by Chávez's corruption and waste, or by his awarding government contracts without bids, paying $59 million for a new French plane that listed for $42 million, or wearing watches worth thousands of dollars. Hadn't his predecessors done the same? In Saudi Venezuela, none of that was surprising.

Perhaps many street vendors and other informal workers in Venezuela had told pollsters that they would vote against Chávez because he seemed like a clownish character to them and because they realized the government was chaotic, with things changing daily for no better reason than some whim of the *Comandante*'s. Over the previous five years, Chávez had hired and fired no fewer than 59 ministers. According to a tally by the newspaper *El Universal*, if you added in those he had transferred from one ministry to another, he was up to 80 ministerial appointments, including six ministers of finance, six of defense, six of commerce, and five of foreign relations. Not a week passed without Chávez announcing some social plan of enormous scale, a gigantic public work, or a continent-wide initiative, which would be completely forgotten within hours. It was hard to take him seriously. But at the moment of truth, when the electorate cast their votes, perhaps they concluded the cash Chávez was giving them meant more than the opposition's arguments that the country would achieve long-term growth only by creating conditions for more investment, or that government handouts would plummet once the oil boom had ended, leaving the country poorer than before. Many thought it was better to have one bird in hand than a hundred in the bush.

Petrodollars and the continental revolution

Following Chávez's win in the 2004 referendum and the U.S. government's acceptance of his victory, the future of US.-Venezuelan ties would largely depend on whether Venezuela would continue — or increase — its support of political violence in Latin America, U.S. officials told me privately. According to them, the Bush Administration had given plenty of evidence of its goodwill toward Chávez: for five years, it had silently withstood his daily diatribes against Bush's "imperialism" and "savage neo-liberalism." The President of the United States had never answered back, and his ambassadors to Caracas had maintained a policy of turning the other cheek, they said. What's more, during the first years of Chávez in power, U.S. Ambassador John Maisto had been fiercely criticized by Venezuela's opposition for publicly maintaining that the world should not judge Chávez by his rhetoric. "Don't watch what he says, but what he does," Maisto repeatedly told reporters, adding that the Venezuelan president, despite his revolutionary rhetoric, had not confiscated any foreign companies, shut down television channels, or — even more importantly for Washington — interrupted the flow of oil to the United States.

However, within the State Department and the White House concern was growing over intelligence from several Latin American governments that Chávez was supporting radical groups in their countries. From the start, he had been criticized by Andrés Pastrana's administration in Colombia for allegedly supporting FARC guerrilla fighters. In 2000 Colombia filed a formal protest and temporarily withdrew its ambassador from Caracas after Olga Marín, a top FARC leader, was invited to speak to the Venezuelan National Assembly. Although Chávez responded that he personally had not authorized Marín's invitation, Colombia's then–foreign minister, Guillermo Fernández de Soto, complained in a communiqué dated November 28 of that same year that, besides constantly criticizing the Colombia plan and predicting the "Vietnamization" of South America due to U.S. military aid in Colombia, Chávez had allowed "the participation of FARC representatives in a conference ... in Venezuela under the auspices of the government, and with the presence of government officials."[xxi]

It wasn't long before the then-president of Bolivia, Hugo Banzer, told me in a telephone interview that Chávez was supporting the extreme-leftist indigenous followers of Felipe Quispe, who had just carried out a violent strike that left 11 dead and 120 wounded. At Banzer's suggestion, given that he didn't want to appear in public making any accusations, I interviewed his presidential chief of staff, Walter Guiteras, who confirmed that "President Banzer has expressed his concern to President Chávez over his intervention in the internal affairs of our country." Around the same time, the government of Ecuador had told Washington of its fears that Chávez was supporting Colonel Lucio Gutiérrez, leader of the military and indigenous coup that had overthrown Jamil Mahuad's government. Asked about these accusations, the then-head of the State Department's Latin America office, Peter Romero, a Democrat who came out of the Clinton administration and had been ambassador to Ecuador, declared in an interview that "there are signs of Chávez government support of violent indigenous movements in Bolivia" and "groups of rebel officers" in Ecuador.[xxii] Chávez immediately denounced Romero as "an international agitator," and the Venezuelan foreign minister referred to him as "Pinocchio."

But intelligence reports of Chávez's links to violent groups in the region wouldn't stop. Soon after, Argentina's State Secretariat of Information (SIDE) received information of two diesel-fuel sales contracts by the government of Venezuela — worth more than $350,000 each — awarded to a lawyer linked to Hebe de Bonafini, the leader of the pro-Castro branch of the Mothers of Plaza de Mayo group. And in 2002 the magazine *U.S. News and World Report* published a long report indicating that, despite Chávez's categorical denials, there was "detailed information" that Colombian rebels had camps inside Venezuela, and that "maps actually pinpoint the location of the camps, and first-hand testimonies describe visits by Venezuelan officials." The main FARC training camp in Venezuela was in the mountains of Perija, near the village of Resumidero, according to the magazine, which added that one of the top Colombian guerilla commanders, Rivándo Márquez, could be found there with about 700 rebels. Citing defectors, the magazine indicated that FARC also had a smaller camp within a two-day walk in the town of Asamblea, near the city of Machiques, and a clandestine radio broadcasting station about 50 kilometers from there on the border with Colombia. One of the witnesses interviewed by the magazine had spent seven months at one of the camps. He said he had seen Venezuelan officials arrive by helicopter. Another defector indicated that his unit had carried out ambushes against Colombian army columns and then found safe haven in Venezuela.[xxiii]

Was Chávez behind all that, or were Venezuelan officials acting without his knowledge? Nearly all top Colombian officials insisted that the green light came from Venezuela's presidential office, but they said so in private. From the start of the Álvaro Uribe administration to the kidnapping of FARC "foreign minister" Rodrigo Granda in Venezuela in early 2005, the Colombian government had declined to say anything more in public that might upset its relations with Venezuela. Colombia had enough problems with its internal war without opening up a new front with a neighbor that had the capacity to increase enormously its support of the Colombian guerrillas. When I asked President Uribe in 2004 whether Chávez was supporting the FARC, he would not say yes or no, commenting only that it was a "complicated" subject. By then, at least one top ex-general of Chávez's had confirmed the presence of FARC camps in Venezuela.

But the information was vague. The once all-powerful minister of the interior, Miquilena, would say later, after he had broken with Chávez, that accusations that the Venezuelan government was providing financial or military aid to rebels in Bolivia, Ecuador, or the FARC in Colombia were "totally false," although he recognized that there was frequent contact with the guerrillas for certain limited purposes: "We made contact with the FARC and the National Liberation Army to free Venezuelan hostages. Even when they kidnapped the brother of [O.A.S. Secretary General] César Gaviria, the relatives asked Chávez to intervene with the guerrillas to free him [...] The only thing we did was support the [Nicaraguan] Sandinista Liberation Front. During the [2001] elections in Nicaragua, we gave the Sandinistas some money for posters and things like that. But it was less than 20 million Bolivars [the equivalent of $27,000]. And it wasn't sent in cash: it was printed propaganda materials." Had Miquilena overseen this personally? "Yes."[xxiv]

In fact, although Chávez emphatically denied that he was giving aid to violent groups or leftist political parties in other countries, there were numerous indications that he was doing so, and they came from various sources. According to General James Hill, chief of the U.S. Southern Command, Chávez funded not only rebel indigenous groups in Bolivia, but also the FMLN in El Salvador. Venezuela had become a Club Med for violent groups in Latin America, a place where they could meet, rest, and plan the continental "revolution," while the government looked the other way. Chávez routinely fueled rumors about his ties to the FARC and the ELN by insisting that Venezuela was resolutely "neutral" in the Colombian armed conflict, and by refusing to describe the Colombian guerrilla fighters — who frequently attacked civilians with car bombs, killing numerous innocent people — as terrorists. Chávez spoke the same language as the Colombian guerrillas. On October 25, 2002, he said in a speech that "representative democracy doesn't work for any Latin American government," because "all it's been good for is letting a bastard class take over and plunge the people into misery."

After interviewing several South American presidents and former presidents who confirmed they were gravely suspicious about Chávez's aiding violent groups in the region, I had little doubt that some kind of activity of this kind existed. The big question was whether Chávez was personally in charge, or whether his subordinates did this amid the managerial chaos of his administration. And the other big question was: If Chávez was exporting his revolution, why was the U.S. government not disclosing all the intelligence information it had on him?

At the end of the first Bush Administration, I posed this question during an interview in a Washington restaurant with a top Pentagon official who closely followed Colombia and the situation in Venezuela. He had just recited to me a long series of examples of alleged Venezuelan aid to the Colombian guerrillas. But when I took my pen out of my pocket to write down what he was saying, he cut me off, saying that everything he was telling me was off the record and couldn't be published. Why? I asked, perplexed. Wouldn't the Bush Administration want journalists to write about Chávez's alleged support of violent movements in Latin America? The official gave me a three-letter answer: "WMD" — weapons of mass destruction. I didn't understand. What did weapons of mass destruction, like those the government had never found in Iraq, have to do with Chávez's aid to Latin American rebels? "A lot," he answered, and explained that, after the international ridicule heaped on the United States for claiming that Saddam Hussein's regime had weapons of mass destruction, the CIA and other U.S. intelligence agencies were under strict orders to leak nothing that wasn't "100 percent" backed by documents, recordings, or other irrefutable evidence. "In Chávez's case, we've got intelligence corroborating about 95 percent of the information about his support for violent groups in other countries, but after Iraq we're not going public until we've got 150 percent corroboration. And since most of this information is eyewitness accounts from some defector and therefore hard to verify, we can't take that risk," the Pentagon official told me. The United States couldn't risk another intelligence fiasco like the one that had just taken place in Iraq.

Chávez, a highly unpredictable man

How would Chávez govern during the remainder of his term? Would he use the fresh political capital he gained from the 2004 referendum to destroy what little was left of democratic institutions and establish an absolutist dictatorship, thus protecting himself from future electoral setbacks if the price of oil declined? Or, conversely, would he conclude that he could continue to govern indefinitely while leaving spaces — albeit limited — for civil liberties?

Before I left Venezuela, after making several failed attempts through mutual acquaintances, I managed to set up an interview with the man who knew Chávez best: Luis Miquilena, his political mentor and the architect of his rise to power. The meeting was arranged at the home of Ignacio Arcaya, who until recently had been the Venezuelan ambassador in Washington and had been close to Miquilena for several years. Then 86, Miquilena walked with a slight limp, but he displayed a remarkable mental agility.

Miquilena had been Chávez's intellectual father, the man behind his first trip to Cuba, the campaign manager of his first electoral victory in 1998, and the all-powerful interior minister and president of Congress until he broke with Chávez and resigned in 2002. The two men first met shortly after the attempted coup in 1992, Miquilena said, when Chávez invited him for a visit in prison. At the time, Miquilena was proposing a constituent assembly to "re-found" the country, arguing that the party system itself was exhausted. Chávez, besides wanting to meet him personally, said he was interested in the project. The prison visit was set up through Pablo Medina, a leftist politician and mutual friend. "It was a pleasant meeting, quite cordial, entertaining. There was empathy. We managed to strike up a friendship," Miquilena recalls.

From that moment on, Miquilena, who was more than 40 years his elder, became Chávez's ideological mentor. A father-son relationship developed. After Chávez left prison he went to live in Miquilena's home, where he remained for five years until winning the presidential election in 1998. "We used to sit there and daydream, conversing about a decent nation, a humble nation, a nation without crooks that would combat the absolutely unjustifiable misery the country was suffering and continues to suffer," Miquilena recalled.

In 1994 Miquilena introduced his houseguest to the Cuban ambassador, who in turn invited Chávez to the island for the first time. "Chávez, Cuban ambassador Germán Sánchez, and I had lunch at my home, where we planned the trip to Cuba," Miquilena told me. The Cubans were eager that Chávez travel as soon as possible: Venezuelan president Caldera had just received Miami Cuban-exile leader Jorge Mas Canosa, and the Castro regime wanted to get back at Caldera by inviting Chávez to speak at the House of the Americas in Havana. During that lunch Miquilena, a frequent traveler to Havana, insisted to the ambassador that Chávez meet with Castro "because it seemed to me that going to Cuba and not seeing Fidel made no sense at all." The ambassador said he couldn't provide guarantees, and the invitation was solely for Chávez to give a speech. "After he told me they weren't sure, I said well, in that case, I'm not going. And Chávez went alone," Miquilena recalled.

To the surprise of both Chávez and Miquilena, Castro not only spoke with Chávez during the trip, but greeted him at the airport when he arrived. "Fidel was waiting for him at the airplane stairs and didn't leave him until he was placed on the return flight. He was with Fidel all night. What's more, they couldn't find a place to eat and went over to the Venezuelan Embassy in the middle of the night. The [Venezuelan] ambassador told me afterward that since his wife wasn't there and he had nothing to offer them, Fidel accompanied Chávez to one of those "protocol houses" — special residences reserved for foreign dignitaries and other government guests — where they dined at midnight. From that point on, Chávez became a sympathizer, a friend of Fidel's who shared his ideas."

Miquilena had retired from the government in mid-2002, frustrated by the fact that Chávez wouldn't follow his advice and tone down the incendiary nature of his speeches, which were increasingly turning labor unions, business people, the Church, and the military against him and creating more and more enemies for the government. Since then, and until I interviewed him two years later, Miquilena had kept a low profile, issuing a statement now and again respectfully asking his former disciple to respect the democratic rules, but rarely speaking to the press. For several months after his departure from government, he and Chávez had maintained sporadic communication, during which they had treated one another like old friends.

"How would you define Chávez?" I asked Miquilena. Is he a new Castro, a Pinochet disguised as a leftist, or what? Miquilena, recalling anecdotes from his nearly 10 years of daily contact with Chávez, described him as an intellectually limited man, impulsive, temperamental, surrounded by low-level lackeys, disorganized in all aspects of his life, unpunctual, financially inept, and attracted to luxury. Above all, Chávez was erratic, Miquilena said.

"He is one of the most unpredictable men I've ever met. Making calculations about him is truly difficult, because he's temperamental, emotional, erratic. And because since he isn't a man with much light in the attic, or a man with a defined ideology [...] it's like he was made for confrontation. He doesn't understand exercising power as the nation's arbiter, as a man who has to establish the rules of the game and manage conflicts from a democratic perspective. He's not prepared for that," Miquilena answered.

But hadn't he just told me that Chávez shared Castro's ideas? "Yes and no," he replied. After his first trip to Cuba in 1994 and the unexpected welcome from Castro, "Chávez said that Fidel's experience was interesting, that it had been successful. [He saw] Fidel's success as a personal success, because he had remained in power for so long. But at that time he was perfectly aware that [Cuba] was nothing like Venezuela, and that in today's world these things wouldn't fly," Miquilena said.

"And what changed later on? Did he become more radical with time?" I asked. Miquilena said the dynamics of events carried Chávez closer and closer to Castro, but more for reasons of temperament than ideology. Perhaps Chávez's narcissism had led him to an increasingly confrontational rhetoric — very similar to Castro's — because that was what would get him the most attention worldwide and allow him to project himself as a continental political leader. The more "anti-imperialist" his speeches were, the bigger the headlines, and the more Latin American leftists would take him seriously. Likewise, the more evident the political deterioration of Venezuela became, the more he needed an outside excuse to explain it, and nothing went over better in the region — especially with Bush in power — than blaming the United States for real and imaginary "aggressions." Finally, "from the beginning, Fidel had gotten into [Chávez's] head the idea that they were going to kill him," Miquilena said. That's why Chávez began to train with Castro's personal guard and to bring more and more Cubans into his security and intelligence organizations. When the petroleum strike began in 2002, Cuba sent technicians and engineers to help the government overcome the problem. And once his power was consolidated, Chávez had happily accepted the 17,000 Cuban doctors and teachers who would allow him to furnish medical attention and education to the country's most backward areas.

But Chávez never had a defined ideology or a long-range plan, because he was fundamentally a man who lacked discipline, Miquilena said. His style of governing was almost adolescent. He summoned his ministers after midnight to share a brilliant idea he had just had, he gave instructions right and left, everyone said yes, and no one ever followed up on his orders. Afterward, when things didn't work out, he would replace the ministers. It was no accident that, in five years of government, he had made those 80 Cabinet changes.

"He's surrounded by what people in the army call 'orderlies.' There's no chance that anyone near him would dare contradict him," Miquilena recalled. Arcaya, Chávez's former ambassador to Washington, who had been his minister of government and justice, had told me not long before that Chávez used to call him late at night, sometimes at 4 in the morning, with some request that he almost invariably forgot the next day. "I once told him: 'Hugo, the main cause behind the disorganization is you,'" Arcaya recalled. "He asked, 'Why do you say that?' Well, because you ask a minister to prepare a report on education, and then you ask that he fix you a sandwich, and then that he pop over to the United States to talk to the bank, and then that he come back and take your kids to a baseball game. And you can't do that. Because ministers are never going to tell you that it can't be done. They're going to say, 'Of course, Mr. President,' and then they're going to do nothing."

One night, when Arcaya was still a Cabinet minister, the president called him at 10 P.M. to request an urgent report about a problem that had arisen in a prison. "Bring it to me tomorrow at La Casona, 6 A.M.," Chávez instructed him. Arcaya started calling his subordinates and everyone who might know something about the subject, but at that late hour he couldn't find anyone. Finally, with a friend, he stayed up until 5 in the morning trying to put together the report as best he could. At 6 A.M. he showed up at La Casona with the report in hand. When he asked to see the president, his private secretary told him, "Impossible, he went to Margarita [Island] at midnight." And the president never did ask about the report. Upon his return from Margarita, he had some other issue in his head and had completely forgotten about the prison.

Although Chávez treated Miquilena much better than his other ministers, the powerful interior minister also had to endure the president's chaotic style. "He's the most absolutely unpunctual man you can imagine, he's late for everything. He doesn't keep a schedule at all, he doesn't preside over the Cabinet, he goes to the office whenever he feels like it," Miquilena recalled. Plus, he treated his staff very badly. "The actual treatment he gives his subordinates is despotic, humiliating. He humiliates them. In front of all us top officials, he once told a governor that he was full of crap, that he was good for nothing, that 'You will leave here immediately,' etc." Miquilena said. "Later on, he recognizes he made a mistake, he realizes he's made a mess of things [...] but in a little while, he does the same all over again."

As for managing the economy, Chávez operates in a completely arbitrary fashion, as if he were running his own ranch. He has no idea of finance. Absolutely no rules of control. Out of the blue, he would order, "Give such and such bank so many millions," Miquilena said. A few days before, Chávez had given a speech at the Bank for Women, where he had been presented with a plan he liked. He had said, "This is very good. You're doing a great job. Are there any ministers here? Anyone from the military high command? Oh, González, you're here. Good. Write it down there: let's give this bank 4 billion." The Venezuelan president had said this in a scene broadcast on national television. This happened every day, and in most cases the order would be quickly forgotten, the ex-interior minister said.

According to Miquilena, Chávez's fiery rhetoric was not only making more and more unnecessary enemies in the government, it was also undermining his credibility within his own party, because he was talking about a fictitious revolution that had nothing to do with what he was doing. "Chávez started to use a rhetoric that divided society between rich and the poor, between oligarchs and the people, and using a revolutionary language that in no way corresponded to what was going on in real life, nor has it happened yet, nor will it ever happen, in my view," Miquilena said. While Chávez was talking about a continental "Bolivarian Revolution" that would end the oligarchy, in fact he was following free market "neo-liberal" economic policies, awarding the most advantageous concession in history to multinational U.S. oil companies. "I would constantly suggest to him that with this rhetoric he was fooling those who believe they are revolutionaries, and that this would lead to bloodshed, because they would discover they had been lied to," he recalled. "So with these lies, we're striking fear in the heart of the economic sector, and we're conning the old leftists who still dream of revolution." Miquilena had grown tired of recommending to his boss that, with this kind of talk, the government wasn't gaining anything and was losing support on both sides.

"And how did Chávez react when you told him this?" I asked. He would react well, and often he would ask Miquilena and José Vicente Rangel — who in the first five years Chávez was in power had served successively as foreign minister, defense minister, and vice president — to fix things with anyone who had been affected. "For example, Chávez would violently attack a journalist in a speech, and I would tell him that this couldn't be done, that this wasn't the role of a head of state. He would agree with me, and I would call the journalist to tell him that everything was all right. But immediately afterward, he'd be on a rampage again, because he's unstoppable when he's in front of a microphone before 5,000," Miquilena said.

"On one occasion Chávez asked me to go talk to [television magnate] Gustavo Cisneros so that we could come to an agreement, because Cisneros had taken a very aggressive stance as a member of the opposition. And I invited him with great pleasure," he recalled. Miquilena invited along Isaías Rodríguez, who later became attorney general, and all three had a long lunch at which they came to an understanding that both sides would tone down their rhetoric in the interest of domestic tranquility. After the lunch came to an end, Miquilena was returning to his office and asked his driver to turn on the radio. To his shock, at that very moment Chávez was giving a speech attacking and insulting Cisneros. "He was making this speech while I was having a conversation proposed by him to make peace with Cisneros! That's who this character is. That defines the nature of a man who's unpredictable in every way you can think of," he said.

When Miquilena finally concluded he couldn't change Chávez's personality, he decided that only Fidel Castro would help him convince Chávez to get his act togeher. "Before breaking up for good with Chávez, I asked him to set up a meeting between Fidel, him, and myself so we could talk about the situation in Venezuela," he recalled. "I thought, Fidel is an intelligent man, who has to be aware that a clumsy, poorly managed Venezuela won't lead to anything but the failure of any project that might benefit him, and that it was more advantageous for him to have a friendly government here than an unfriendly one." The meeting took place in 2002 during the Nueva Esparta Summit in Margarita. The three of them spoke for two hours. Miquilena had openly expressed his fear that the Venezuelan government's aggressive rhetoric would lead only to chaos and a state of ungovernability. "To my satisfaction, Fidel pretty much agreed with me on the need for a more moderate approach. And [he] categorically said, word for word: 'A revolution is not in the cards for Venezuela.' Of course, Fidel knew what a revolution was, and Chávez didn't. For Fidel, a revolution is a social transfer of the means of production from one social class to another. But he knew that Chávez wasn't making a revolution, that he couldn't. It wasn't even in the cards for Venezuela to do so," he recalled.

Castro, in effect, was a realist, and more than anything valued keeping Chávez in power for the help he could provide Cuba. And how did Chávez react? I asked. "He said yes, that he agreed," Miquilena remembered. But, as so many times before, Chávez resumed his fiery rhetoric as soon as he returned to Caracas. And the position his interior minister had taken in Castro's presence couldn't have gone over too well. Soon after, Miquilena resigned.

Before our interview ended, I couldn't help but ask the burning question once more, the one I had been asking myself since I had arrived in Venezuela. Who was right — Petkoff, who said Chávez wasn't leading Venezuela to a dictatorship but rather through "a process of weakening of institutions in order to strengthen a strongman" — or Garrido, who said Chávez was following a careful plan toward securing absolute power, one he had calculated from the beginning would take 20 years from the time he became president? "I believe Garrido assumes Chávez is an ideologically structured man, someone educated to take this path. I would have to disagree with him on that. I believe that all Chávez has got in his head is a scramble of mush, and that he lets himself be carried away by what happens to him each day. He's a purely temperamental man [...] his guiding star is to remain in power [...] He hasn't got the discipline, or a clear theory about where he's going." After winning the referendum, Chávez would maintain certain democratic façades, Miquilena said. He would create "an authoritarian government, trying to perfume himself with certain democratic things, like maintaining a mock judicial system, a mock parliament, and mock elections," Miquilena predicted.

The man with two pedals

As many feared, Chávez became more radical after his electoral victory in 2004. By mid-2005, with oil at $60 a barrel — nearly eight times more than when he took office — and a demoralized, intimidated opposition, Chávez had accumulated powers that were unprecedented in the modern history of Venezuela. A few months after the referendum, his party won 22 out of 24 governorships across the country and around 280 of 335 mayoralties. Simultaneously, he arbitrarily expanded the Supreme Court from 20 to 32 magistrates, appointing people unconditionally loyal to him to all the recently created positions; he had a "content law" approved for the press that gave him the power to shut down opposition media at will, and he changed the *modus operandi* of Congress so that crucial laws could be approved by a simple majority, assuring him control over the legislative branch, where his supporters had a slight majority.

At the same time, he dedicated himself to buying arms around the world, restructuring the armed forces, and changing their uniforms to give them an "anti-imperialist" look, expanding the reserve corps from 90,000 to over 500,000. Among other things, he ordered 15 Russian Mi-17 and Mi-35 helicopters, as well as over 100,000 AK-103 rifles from Russia, 10 troop transport planes, and eight patrol boats from Spain, and 24 Super Tucano light attack jets from Brazil, and began negotiating to buy 50 Russian MiG-29 hunter bombers: all for a total of over $2 billion. For the Venezuelan opposition, most worrisome was the increase of reserves, given that they wouldn't answer directly to the defense minister but to the president himself. Many feared swelling the reserves would be nothing other than creating "popular militias" to keep an eye on the population, Cuban-style. By then Chávez and Castro had publicly announced that Cuba would increase the number of its doctors, teachers, and other "internationalists" in Venezuela from 17,000 to 30,000. And while Chávez raised the volume of his rhetoric against the United States — calling Secretary of State Rice "Condolence" and "illiterate" — and increased subsidized oil shipments to Cuba from 53,000 to 90,000 barrels a day, he was investing more and more petrodollars in expanding his influence across the region through projects like Telesur, a Chávez-funded television network co-sponsored by Cuba, Argentina, and Uruguay, and oil accords with the Caribbean countries that included a clause of support for the Bolivarian Alternative for America (ALBA in Spanish), the southern regional integration initiative he proposed.[xxv] "The Cuban and Venezuelan revolutions are already one, the Cuban and Venezuelan people are already one," Chávez declared on July 9, 2005, during an event in Caracas at which he decorated 96 Cuban advisors.[xxvi]

Intrigued by the course that Chávez's administration was taking, I phoned Petkoff to ask if — given recent events — he still believed that Venezuela wasn't embarking on a Cuban-style revolution. Nearly a year had passed since our last conversation in Caracas at the time of the referendum. Petkoff, one of the most brilliant minds in Venezuela, answered that although Chávez had undoubtedly increased his control over institutions, "his rhetoric isn't accompanied by what is normally associated with a revolutionary transformation, such as structural changes to the economy or institutions."[xxvii] Instead, there was "a strengthening of his personal power, for which he has increased control over institutions," Petkoff said.

Then had Venezuela become a totalitarian system, or a democracy with a strongman?" I asked. Petkoff said he didn't pay much attention to Chávez's revolutionary speeches. "He's driving with one foot on the pedal of authoritarianism, and the other foot on the pedal of democratic institutions. He presses one or the other depending on the situation," he answered. "After the referendum, obviously, he's been pushing harder on the authoritarian pedal."[xxviii]

Putting into perspective what Petkoff was saying and what Miquilena had told me in Caracas, I became more convinced than ever that Chávez was what I had always suspected: an intellectually rudimentary military man, but extremely astute, clinging to power, whose political success was due largely to the skyrocketing of oil prices under his watch. His messianic utterances had grown in direct proportion to the rise of oil prices. By mid-2005, when crude had reached a record $60 a barrel, the same man who had once campaigned as a moderate, whose first priority was fighting corruption, was presenting himself as Venezuela's savior after 500 years of oppression: "The polarization between rich and poor was created by capitalism and neo-liberalism, not by Chávez," he said in an interview with the Arab channel Al-Jazeera. "It was created by a system of slavery that has lasted for over five centuries. Five centuries of exploitation...This system created difficult conditions that led to a social explosion. In 1989 I was an army officer and saw that the country had exploded like a volcano. Then there were two military operations, in one of which I participated together with thousands of military and civilian comrades."[xxix]

The authoritarian pedal

By 2007 Chávez was pressing the totalitarian pedal at full speed. After sweeping the December, 2006, elections for a new six-year term with 63 percent of the vote, he proclaimed that the next six years would be dedicated to beginning to implement his "Socialism of the XXIst Century," as part of the "National Simón Bolívar Project of 2007–2021." In January 2007 the Chávez-run National Assembly gave the president full powers to rule by decree for 18 months, allowing him among other things to nationalize key sectors of the economy, turn the military into a "socialist" institution, and clamp down on independent media.

Shortly after the start of his second term, Chávez announced the "re-nationalization" of the country's main telecommunications company, CANTV, as well as the takeover of the electric utility in Caracas and heavy oil production facilities in the Orinoco River basin previously run by multinationals. In an April 12, 2007, speech to the military, Chávez declared Venezuela's armed forces to be "socialist," and said that "today every commander at every level is obliged to repeat, from the soul and raising the flag high, "Fatherland, Socialism, or Death."[xxx]

Chávez was emboldened by ever-climbing oil prices, which by now had already reached $70 a barrel, and — ironically — by continued U.S. oil purchases that had given Venezuela a nearly $28 billion trade surplus with Washington a year earlier. So in May he followed through on his vow not to renew the license of RCTV, the country's oldest private television network. That meant shutting down the only network with a national reach that was consistently critical of his regime. The decision set off student riots in Venezuela, and was condemned in the U.S., Chilean, and Brazilian congresses.

The Chávez government argued that not renewing a television license was well within a democratic government's right. But virtually all international press freedom groups agreed it was a blatant case of censorship. Five months earlier Chávez had openly said he would not renew RCTV's license because of its sympathetic coverage of the 2002 coup attempt, but he had failed to call for public bidding that would have allowed others to buy the network. Instead, he simply accused RCTV of promoting "the anti-values of capitalism," and replaced the network with a sixth government-run channel, called TVes.[xxxi] As a result, Chávez dominated virtually all major television networks. The only big one that remained openly critical to his regime — Globovision — was available only via cable and did not reach the whole country. And if it continued lashing out at the government it would be shut down as well, he warned. As he accumulated unprecedented powers, Chávez stepped up his attacks on what he now called "bourgeois democracy." In a June 2, 2007, televised speech, Chávez charged that "North American imperialism" was trying to impose on developing countries ideas such as "the division of powers, the alternation in power, representation as a basis of democracy. Big lies!"

Had Garrido, the former university professor and *El Universal* columnist, been right all along when he told me three years earlier that Chávez was embarked on a 20-year revolutionary project, and that whoever didn't want to see that was kidding himself? Perhaps the best answer to this question came from Manuel Caballero, one of Venezuela's best-known leftist intellectuals. When I asked him whether Chávez was showing his true colors and would end up a full-blown Marxist dictator, he said that Chávez's leftism should be taken with a grain of salt. After observing him for several years, Caballero said he concluded: "Chávez is neither a communist, nor a capitalist, nor a Muslim, nor a Christian. He's all of these things, as long as they help guarantee that he'll stay in power until 2021."[xxxii]

NOTES

[i] Instituto Nacional de Estadística, República Bolivariana de Venezuela, Reporte Estadístico, No. 2, 2004, p. 5.

[ii] Interview with Teodoro Petkoff, Caracas, Venezuela, August 10, 2004.

[iii] Alberto Garrido, *Documentos de la Revolución Bolivariana*, Ediciones del Autor, Mérida, 2002, p. 142.

[iv] Andrés Oppenheimer, "Venezuela's wealth turns bankrupt," The *Miami Herald*, March 6, 1989.

[v] Andrés Oppenheimer, "Venezuela suspends key rights," The *Miami Herald*, February 5, 1992.

[vi] Associated Press newswire by Bart Jones, August 3, 1998.

[vii] Andrés Oppenheimer and Tim Johnson, "The Man Who Would Be President," The *Miami Herald*, October 5, 1998.

[viii] Conindustria Industrial Chamber, "Lineamientos para el Desarrollo Productivo del País," p. 4, July 2003.

[ix] Economic Commission for Latin America and the Caribbean (ECLAC), Preliminary Overview of the Economies of Latin America and the Caribbean, 2004.

[x] Idem, p. 188, Graph A-22, December 2004.

[xi] Ricardo Hausman, "Venezuela needs and electoral solution soon," The *Miami Herald*, October 9, 2002.

[xii] Juan Tamayo, "Venezuela's rebellion a bizarre mix of events," The *Miami Herald*, April 16, 2002.

[xiii] Tim Johnson, "Leader's exit pleases U.S., method doesn't," The *Miami Herald*, April 13, 2002.

[xiv] "A Clear U.S. Policy in Venezuela," The *Miami Herald*, August 3, 2002.

[xv] Idem.

[xvi] Interview with Otto Reich, January 5, 2005.

[xvii] Idem.

[xviii] "No Encouragement given for Venezuela coup, White House insists," The *Miami Herald*, April 17, 2002.

[xix] Interview with Alfredo Peña, August 13, 2004, in Caracas.

[xx] Instituto Nacional de Estadística, Bolivarian Republic of Venezuela, Reporte Social, No. 2, 2004, p. 5.

[xxi] "Chávez needs only listen to his neighbors," The *Miami Herald*, December 10, 2000.

[xxii] "Neighbors say Chávez aids violent groups," The *Miami Herald*, December 5, 2000.

[xxiii] Linda Robinson, "Terror Close to Home," *U.S. News and World Report*, October 6, 2003.

[xxiv] Interview with Luis Miquilena in Caracas, Venezuela, on August 12, 2004.

[xxv] Gary Marx, "Venezuelan oil is boosting Cuban economy," *Chicago Tribune*, May 16, 2005.

[xxvi] Alejandra M. Hernández, "Chávez condecoró a asesores cubanos de Misión Robinson," *El Universal*, Caracas, July 9, 2005. Chávez's quote was also disseminated by the international agency Reuters on July 9, 2005.

[xxvii] Telephone interview with Teodoro Petkoff, July 7, 2005.

[xxviii] Idem.

[xxix] "U.S. bombing of Iraq 'horrendous terrorism,' Venezuela's Chávez tells Al-Jazeera," BBC Monitoring, December 6, 2004.

[xxx] Christopher Toothaker, "Chávez to Military: Socialism or Leave," The *Associated Press*, April 12, 2007.

[xxxi] Phil Gunson, "Protests bring subtle shift," The *Miami Herald*, June 9, 2007.

[xxxii] Interview with Manuel Caballero, Caracas, August 14, 2004.

CHAPTER 9

Mexico's Political Paralysis

Tall tale: "Like a locomotive that after taking off, starts gradually picking up speed, Mexico today is advancing faster and faster." (Internet portal of the Presidency of the Republic, message from President Vicente Fox, October 22, 2004).

M EXICO CITY — WHAT SURPRISED ME MOST ABOUT MEXICO'S July 2, 2006, elections — in addition to the unexpected victory of center-right candidate Felipe Calderón — was that the candidate of continuity, globalization, and closer ties with the United States was so popular with the young. The youth vote had been pivotal: of 13 million registered new voters, 12 million were ages 18 to 23. And many of them liked pro-business candidate Calderón. Contrary to the conventional wisdom that young people favor leftist candidates and radical change — a perception fed by daily images of campus rallies with students wearing Che Guevara T-shirts — an exit poll by the Mexico daily *Reforma* showed that 38 percent of voters from 18 to 29 years old had voted for pro-business Calderón, 34 percent for leftist former Mexico City mayor Andrés Manuel López Obrador, and the remainder for centrist candidates. It was older voters who went more heavily for the leftist candidate: among people 50 and older, López Obrador got 37 percent of the vote, Calderón 34 percent.

Was Mexico's youth shifting to the right? Or had the country's left fallen out of touch with the generation of Mexicans that had come of age since the 1994 free-trade agreement with the United States? Calderón, 43, was nine years younger than López Obrador. But Calderón — a church-going conservative who dressed in dark suits, wore glasses, and looked like a bookish lawyer — had appealed to the young mostly thanks to his down-to-earth, pragmatic message.

His campaign slogan had been *"más inversión, más empleos"* ("more investment, more jobs.") At his rallies he had called for a more globalized Mexico that would draw money from abroad, increase exports, and become more competitive in the world economy.

By contrast, López Obrador's campaign focused on the traditional issues of Mexico's left: the high levels of inequality, the excessive concentration of economic power, the need to launch massive programs to reduce poverty, and a foreign policy based on "national sovereignty" and "self-determination" to protect the country from undue U.S. influence. "Young people saw a more promising future under Calderón than under López Obrador," I was told by César Ortega, head of the polling firm Ipsos-Bimsa, which conducted a similar exit poll for the daily *El Universal.* "They felt more attracted by Calderón's pragmatic platform than by López Obrador's 19th-century heroic nationalism." Most pollsters say votes for Calderón were votes for continuity, and were cast by people who felt the country was going in the right direction. In addition to the young, Calderón won among women, city dwellers, people with the highest education levels, and those who said they were better off this year than last, the polls showed. López Obrador won among the elderly, people in rural areas, and the poorest of the poor. But Mexico had become a more urban country in recent years — more than 80 percent of its people live in cities. After several years of sluggish growth the economy was growing by more than 4 percent. And over the previous five years, Mexico's poverty had fallen from 53 percent to 47 percent of the population — not a huge decline, but one that could become meaningful if the downward trend continued.

Still, Calderón had won by the narrowest margin in recent history: he won by 0.58 percent of the vote over López Obrador, who immediately denounced the election as a fraud, pronounced himself as "legitimate president of Mexico," and even appointed a cabinet in a brief attempt to overturn the election. His leftist Party of the Democratic Revolution had for the first time become the second-largest bloc in the Mexican Congress, where it was a formidable political force. And few in Mexico dared to bet that López Obrador would not be back in 2012.

The Secret Letter

Not long before the 2006 election, López Obrador was so far ahead in the polls that he seemed like a sure winner. The conventional wisdom in Mexico was that only a well-planned government campaign to portray him as a Mexican version of Venezuela's Hugo Chávez could possibly undermine his popularity, and even that was unlikely to cause him to lose. And López Obrador, at the urging of his closest advisors, had taken steps to stave off any scare tactics from his political rivals.

On March 11, 2005, López Obrador had sent a confidential letter to the nation's hundred wealthiest businessmen. The letter, which had never been made public, began with "Dear Friend," and seemed to fully contradict his incendiary public appeals. It denounced attempts by his opponents to "stigmatize" him among businessmen "with negative, baseless descriptions." That was clearly a reference to allegations that López Obrador would become a radical populist president, like Chávez. In reality, López Obrador said in his letter, there was nothing to fear: his government would not by any means seek to break away from Mexico's macroeconomic policies.

"The solution to the problem isn't going back to the 1970s, when presidents Luis Echeverría and José López Portillo governed," the letter said. "Today we live in a more democratic country, with an economy and a society that won't withstand another state bankruptcy, under a Free Trade Agreement that contributes to the production of major industrial exports, on which a great many workers depend, in a global economy, which we must exploit to our benefit." That's why, he added, "as we evolve toward an alternative project, the country shouldn't put its stability at risk: macroeconomic equilibrium should be respected to avoid inflationary spikes that would damage public finances and society. There ought to be a responsible fiscal and monetary policy, one that begins by reducing current spending."

In other words, the business elite had nothing to worry about. If, for the first time in Mexico, power was shifted to the leftist candidate of the Democratic Revolutionary Party (PRD), there might be a minor change in tone — "development policies are needed," "a greater stimulus in the industrial construction area," and "new concessions to regional banks that can bring credit closer to productive activities," the letter said — but no revolution, no radical change. The country needed to emulate Chile, China, and India, the text stated, suggesting that if López Obrador should be compared to any other Latin American president it would be Chile's pro-globalization socialist, Ricardo Lagos.

Was the letter sincere? Or was it a cold, political move — much as Chávez had made in his first election — calculated to pick up support within the business sector and win centrist votes? Beyond a doubt, López Obrador needed to shift toward the center: his strategists read the polls and knew that Mexico was a much more conservative country than its intellectuals acknowledge. A national survey conducted by Ipsos-Bimsa not long before López Obrador wrote the letter found that "there are more Mexicans who identify with the right than with the left": 36 percent of Mexicans consider themselves "right-wing," 28 percent "centrists," and just 17 percent "leftists," while the rest don't situate themselves anywhere along the political spectrum.[i] López Obrador knew that to win he would have to beat the 24 percent support that the PRD had achieved in its heyday. Advised by congressman Manuel Camacho Solís — a former foreign minister and mayor of Mexico City who had been one step away from becoming a presidential candidate for the Institutional Revolutionary Party (PRI) before switching to the PRD — López Obrador had dedicated himself to neutralizing issues that might cause alarm about his candidacy among big business, the United States, and the international media. And he didn't do badly at it.

A few months after his private letter to the businessmen, his adviser Camacho traveled to Washington in June 2005 to meet with the top Latin America specialists in the Bush Administration.

During his meeting with Roger Noriega, then assistant secretary for Western Hemispheric affairs at the State Department, and Tom Shannon, then director for inter-American affairs on the White House National Security Council, he brought a message similar to the one in the letter: the United States would have nothing to fear from a López Obrador victory. "They looked very calm to me," Camacho told me a few days after the Washington meeting. Noriega and Shannon had expressed more concern over the crime wave along the Mexican border than over any possible ideological shifts in Mexico's leadership, he added.[ii] It wasn't the first time the Bush Administration had expressed itself in a similar fashion: in November 2004, during a visit to Mexico, Secretary of State Colin Powell had given tacit backing to López Obrador when asked what the reaction of the United States would be if the leftist won. "President Bush will welcome that Mexican leader as warmly as he would welcome any other Mexican leader,"[iii] Powell said. Then, before he formally launched his presidential campaign, López Obrador starting giving interviews, one after the other, to the *Miami Herald*, the *New York Times*, the *Financial Times*, to send the same reassuring message.

"My reference is General Cárdenas"

When I interviewed López Obrador in his Mexico City mayor's office a few days after Powell's remarks, he was smiling from ear to ear. It was the first time he had received a favorable word from the U.S. government. Sitting in his office, with congressman Camacho beside him, he presented himself as a model of political moderation, modern leftism with a touch of "new age" spirituality. But, from what he told me, his political inspiration derived from the most retrograde, populist Mexican nationalism.

López Obrador was a retiring but cordial man. His office had few personal touches and was in keeping with his austere image. I saw no photos with national or international leaders, the standard feature of politicians' offices, or souvenirs from trips. The night before, over dinner, two well-known Mexican intellectuals had commented that López Obrador was a politician totally out of touch with what was going on in the rest of the world, who had never traveled abroad, who didn't even have a passport. "False," he answered, shrugging, when I asked him. He had traveled abroad more than once, and had even met with economists from brokerage firms in New York and State Department officials in Washington.

Since I didn't know how much time he had for me — in the end, he wound up giving me more than an hour — I decided to get right to the point. "How would you define yourself politically?" I asked him. "In whose leftist framework do you stand: In Ricardo Lagos's, Lula's, or Chávez's?"

L.O.: I'm a humanist. They always ask me if I'm like Chávez, if I'm like Lula. Well, I'm Andrés Manuel. Every leader has his own history, his own circumstances. There are no carbon copies.

A.O.: Yes, but there are examples, there are models...

L.O.: Yes, but I believe we have to concentrate specifically on the Mexican process, our history, what has been the democratic movement in this country. I'd say I'm inspired by the best of our national history.

A.O.: Sorry, but you haven't really told me anything.

L.O.: I would tell you I'm not Chávez, but I'm not Lula either, or Felipe González, or Lagos. I have a lot of respect for all of them, just as I do for any head of state, any president from another country. And I would tell you that I respect them independently of their political stance, whether they're from the left, the center, or the right.

A.O.: In Mexico your critics say you're going to be another Chávez.

L.O.: That's just cheap politics. You can't take that seriously. That has to do with the advance of an alternative project and the failure of the policies that have been applied in this country in recent years. So how do they label others? How do they spread fear? Well, they talk about populism. I would tell you that from the conceptual point of view, they haven't any intellectual rigor. They don't even know what populism is. In our history, the history that belongs to Mexico, we've had popular politicians. There's the case of General [Lázaro] Cárdenas. What has happened here, for example, has been right-wing populism. I would tell you that populism is associated more with the right than with the left, or the center.

A.O.: Is Cárdenas a point of reference for you?

L.O. For me, yes. He's a reference. As is [José María] Morelos, who sought equality, as is [Benito] Juárez, one of the most important politicians not only in Mexico, but also in the entire world. To understand what has happened in Mexico, we'd have to see what has taken place since the Revolution [1910–1917] up until 1970. Mexico grew from 1934, from the beginning of General Cárdenas' administration, until 1970.

I thought about his answers. The fact that at this point in contemporary history his point of reference was General Cárdenas was troublesome. If the 20th century had taught us anything, it was that the countries that progressed — including the ones he mentioned: China, India, and Chile — had done so precisely by abandoning the state-controlled interventionist policies that had characterized Cárdenas's government. Strictly speaking, although Cárdenas had his virtues, such as a passion for indigenous rights, he had been an authoritarian president with economic policies that over time had ruined the country. Claiming a return to the original principles of the Mexican Revolution, his government, from 1934 to 1940, distributed much more than the country was producing or was able to produce. He nationalized the railroads and the oil industry, and carried out an agrarian reform that encouraged small land-holdings and communal property, two ownership models that turned out to be highly unproductive. Cárdenas's government triggered a rebellion among businesspeople in northern Mexico, who founded the National Action Party (PAN) in 1939 as a reaction to the populism he fostered.

According to the official history of the PAN, *La historia del Partido Acción Nacional, 1939-1940* [*The History of the National Action Party, 1939-1940*], the party was born in response to Cárdenas's authoritarianism, as well as his administration's corruption and disregard for basic values such as hard work, sacrifice, and perseverance. Cárdenas's policies had taken Mexico back to "the mirage of solutions from above, replacing technical solutions with rhetorical ones."[iv] PAN's founder, Manuel Gómez Morín, had worked with the post-revolutionary government, but was quickly disappointed, founding his new party in "open opposition to the total collectivization of the economy [...] and the inept and corrupt intervention of the Mexican State as owner and entrepreneur in a shattered economy."[v] Perhaps the growth of the PAN was too heavily skewed toward the perspective of northern Mexico's business elite, but didn't it also reflect a reaction to populist solutions that already sounded deceptive nearly a century ago and had failed in all the countries in which they were applied?

"A little more relative autonomy"

Once he finished speaking, I commented, "In every country I know where a candidate accused of populism has presented a radical scheme, all he has produced is a vicious cycle of capital flight, business shutdowns, more unemployment, and more poverty." By naming General Cárdenas as a political reference, wasn't he promising precisely that? López Obrador, perhaps feeling that he had wandered off the path into a swamp, brought the conversation back to the present.

"But I'm not proposing a radical scheme," he replied. "I think we have to maintain macroeconomic policies, adding only the variable of economic growth, as the economists say, or as the technocrats say. And that has not happened." Mexican economic policy "has been a dismal failure," he continued. Offering a quick recap of past decades, López Obrador recalled that from 1954 to 1970, starting with the presidency of Adolfo Ruiz Cortines, Mexico experienced a "stabilizing development" in which the economy grew nearly 7 percent annually. "What you're seeing in China is what we've already experienced in Mexico," he observed. "Of course, without income distribution and with problems of inequality, but with economic growth."

Then, starting in 1970, came the stage known as "shared development" under presidents Luis Echeverría and José López Portillo, with annual growth rates of 6 percent. "Sure, with macroeconomic imbalances, and with inflation, debt, and devaluations, but also with economic growth," he continued. "Afterward came the stage of the technocrats, starting in 1982, and the economy went completely stagnant," he said. "The technocrats came into power and said, 'Let's make structural changes.' From '82 to the present, however, annual economic growth has been 2 percent. Per capita growth has been zero. So, how can they justify that their model works? It's been 21 years without economic growth. Never in recent Mexican history have we suffered a recession, stagnation, like what we're experiencing now. Never, not even during the Revolution," López Obrador said.

The speech was politically attractive, but a little devious, I thought to myself. When the candidate said that the Mexican economy hadn't grown at all since the technocrats had come into power in 1982, he was beginning with the Miguel de la Madrid administration. And the only thing technocratic about De la Madrid was that he had had no choice but to try and heal the economic disaster inherited from López Portillo, who just before leaving office had devalued the peso, nationalized banks, and fixed the exchange rates. López Obrador was measuring average economic growth over two decades that included the consequences of the economic collapses of 1982, 1987, and 1995, all caused by the waste of PRI state-centered government. The reality showed the exact opposite: from 1995 to 2004, when the policies of economic openness backed by technocrats were applied, the average per capita income had grown 43 percent, from $6,780 to $9,666 per year.[vi] Didn't these figures prove the exact opposite of what López Obrador was saying? Obviously, it all depended on how you read the figures.

Supporters of López Obrador had already been mistaken once in the recent past, when they opposed the Free Trade Agreement with the United States and Canada (NAFTA). Before it came into effect in 1994, the old-guard Mexican left had opposed the treaty, describing it as a maneuver by the United States to colonize Mexico. But a decade later it was so evident that Mexico had come out ahead of the United States under the agreement that even López Obrador himself no longer spoke of disavowing it altogether. NAFTA had undoubtedly been a success for Mexico: its trade balance with the United States had gone from a deficit of $3.15 billion in 1994 to a surplus of $55.5 billion in 2004.[vii] What better proof could there be that López Obrador's party had been monumentally mistaken in putting its ideological prejudices before the country's economic interests?

"On the subject of development, countries that, like Mexico, have adjusted themselves more than necessary to the dictates of international financial organizations haven't done well," López Obrador continued. "Here the problem that we've had with those who run the economy is that they've gone above and beyond what international financial organizations asked them to do. They're very orthodox, like fundamentalists. The countries that have been able to move forward are those that have maintained a little more relative autonomy, without rejecting either macroeconomic policies or globalization policies. As is the case of Chile or Spain, not to mention the Asian countries, nearly all of them. They have higher rates of economic growth, more development, because they've also had more autonomy in the management of their policies," he said.

Once again, his economic conclusions seemed to clash with the reality I had seen during my trips to China, Chile, and other successful countries that — whether they followed the prescriptions of international financial organizations or not — had bet heavily on economic openness and globalization. Some countries, like China, had followed the economic openness formula on their own, without asking for conditioned loans from the International Monetary Fund. Others, like Chile, had shown greater independence on secondary themes, but as far as major structural reforms were concerned, pretty much followed the recommendations of financial organizations to the letter. But all right, I thought, it was obvious that López Obrador had a political line he probably believed in and, certainly, it was the one his followers wanted to hear. His strength wasn't the economy — and it had never been, even during his school days, as we shall see. Surmising that we had exhausted the subject, I decided to move on.

And what were his points of reference in terms of international policy? I asked him. Did he know Lula, Chávez, or Castro personally? What did he think of them? "I know Lula and I know Felipe [González]. I don't know Chávez. Or Fidel. I have never spoken to Chávez or Fidel. I have spoken to Lula and Felipe. And I have not met Lagos, or Tabaré Vázquez," he answered. And what was his opinion of the Venezuelan and Cuban processes? "I don't want to give an opinion. I believe that every country has its circumstances and its history. I'm not going to pass judgment on that," he replied.

From local politician to national leader

López Obrador's critics depicted him as an authoritarian man with a tortured past — his 15-year-old brother had died from a gunshot wound in 1968, while playing with a pistol they had both found in their father's shop[viii] — and a degree of paranoia that made him imagine conspiracies everywhere. Born in Tabasco in 1953, López Obrador had been a student activist and perpetual student at the National Autonomous University of Mexico (UNAM): it took him no less than 14 years to get a degree in political and social science. He graduated in 1987 at age 34.[ix] In the meantime, he had been a militant in the PRI, standing out as an enthusiastic political cadre in indigenous communities, where few non-indigenous members of the PRI were interested in spending much of their time. In 1987 he was named Tabasco delegate of the National Indigenist Institute (INI in Spanish) based in Nacajuca, about 20 miles from the state capital, Villahermosa. He rapidly became a key figure for the PRI statewide because of his influence among indigenous voters, and in 1982, at age 29, he was placed in charge of directing the PRI statewide. In 1988, following in the footsteps of Cuauhtémoc Cárdenas and other leftist PRI politicians who had left the PRI the year before, he ran for governor of Tabasco from the National Democratic Front, the coalition of parties that supported Cárdenas. After Carlos Salinas de Gortari's dubious electoral victory, López Obrador joined the recently founded PRD to try once again for the state governorship in 1994. In that race he faced the man who years later would become his main rival in the 2006 presidential elections, PRI candidate Roberto Madrazo. After one of the most scandalous elections in Mexico's recent history, Madrazo was named the winner and López Obrador went public denouncing — probably with good cause — a giant fraud.

The Tabasco fraud made López Obrador turn more radical. He organized a "caravan for democracy" to Mexico City that gave him enormous visibility nationwide. In 1996, ignoring requests for moderation from the PRD national leadership, López Obrador encouraged the blockade of more than 500 plants of state oil monopoly PEMEX in Tabasco, demanding the company contribute more money to the local economy. A blockade of the oil wells threatened to paralyze the country, and shortly thereafter the administration of PRI President Ernesto Zedillo capitulated, allotting greater resources to the state-owned company in Tabasco. The Tabasco movement made López Obrador into a national PRD leader. But at the same time, it began to sow doubts in political and business circles in the capital. Could moderation and common sense be expected from a political leader who took oil wells by force?

Many works, many debts

In 2000 López Obrador was elected head of the Mexico City government, the country's second-most prominent political post. From his first day on the job, he started making daily headlines in the national press thanks to his brilliant communications policy. He began holding a press conference every morning at 6, which not only allowed him to project an image of dynamism and a connection with the millions of workers and farmers who also get up at the crack of dawn, but enabled him as well to announce the day's political agenda to the national media. Every day, during the press conferences that were often broadcast live on several radio stations — where else would they get "fresh" political news at that hour? — López Obrador would make some statement that immediately became a focus of debate, "stealing the show" from the national government and putting it on the defensive. Often his announcements were nothing more than promises, but in contrast with the image of stagnation and somnolence of Fox's administration, they gave the impression of an efficient metropolitan government, constantly on the move.

Simultaneously, López Obrador undertook public works of great visual impact, like remodeling Reforma Boulevard — the second level of the Periférico (the ring highway) — and the economic revival of the city's Historic Downtown Area, carried out with the help of megamillionaire Carlos Slim, owner of Telmex. Other measures, like subsidies for senior citizens and aid to single mothers, had a great media impact that overshadowed criticism that they put the city deeply in debt. According to figures from Mexico City's Legislative Assembly, the city's debt grew from $2.6 billion at the start of López Obrador's administration in 2000 to nearly $4 billion by late 2004. It was a considerable amount, although, to be fair, not without precedent in the history of Mexico's capital city.[x]

An authoritarian man?

But López Obrador's critics also pointed out that his administration was marked by authoritarianism, corruption, paranoia, and irresponsibility. When his main collaborators, Gustavo Ponce and René Bejarano, were arrested for corruption — the former was videotaped betting heavily in a Las Vegas casino, the latter receiving briefcases stuffed with dollars from a businessman connected with the PRD — López Obrador, rather than demanding a thorough investigation of his aides and strict enforcement of the law, denounced the arrests as part of a plot by the Fox administration and the United States to discredit him. Much of the media fell into the trap: the Mexican press didn't necessarily believe him, but instead of digging deeper into PRD corruption, they concentrated on finding out whether his accusations had merit. Once again, López Obrador took over the agenda, spinning it to his advantage, and the issue of corruption faded into the background.

Later on, when it became clear López Obrador had weathered a political storm, Fox's administration attempted to put the brakes on his candidacy — without ever admitting it — through an attempt to impeach him for a relatively minor misdeed. It was a case of contempt of court, in which he was accused of disobeying a warrant for expropriation, but it could have kept him from running for office in 2006. López Obrador went on the offensive, accusing Fox and the PRI of conspiring to deny him his political rights, and he came out stronger than ever in his role as victim of a conspiracy hatched by the rich and powerful. Wrapped in that mantle and aided by his simple lifestyle and his reputation for high-profile public works, he became increasingly resistant to charges of corruption and economic irresponsibility. With his massive rallies, aided by a PRI-style patronage-driven use of public resources that allowed him to bus tens of thousands of people to attend his public appearances, he forced Fox to back off from his attempt to impeach him by implying that nationwide chaos could ensue. How could it be that the government would rigorously apply the law to López Obrador on minor charges and not apply it against the rich and powerful in much more serious cases, many Mexicans asked themselves, and not without cause. In April 2005 Fox decided to make the best of a bad situation: he fired his attorney general, General Rafael Macedo de la Concha, who had filed the charges, and the whole affair was shelved.

What made Fox backtrack after having gambled so much on the impeachment and political destruction of López Obrador? The most obvious reason was a cool calculation that national and international public opinion was tilting toward López Obrador, and it was best for the government to back off quickly, with less than a year to go before the elections, in hopes that the episode would be forgotten. But there were two additional, less well-known motives that were decisive in the government's decision, according to members of López Obrador's inner circle. First, the day before Fox's decision, Secretary of Defense Ricardo Clemente Vega had told the president that the Mexican Army would not move against López Obrador supporters if there were renewed mass protests, and that it was necessary to seek a political solution to the crisis. "The general was against repression," a top official in López Obrador's campaign told me. Second, on the same day, a member of the Supreme Court privately confided to two members of the Fox Cabinet that the case against López Obrador was filled with technical flaws, and that there was a strong possibility the court would declare a mistrial. In that context, Fox decided a retreat was the least costly alternative. Afterward Santiago Creel, then government secretary, denied both of these rumors. According to him, Fox made the decision exclusively because a judge had dismissed the case and there were serious doubts that the legal proceedings would be successful. "The protests didn't concern us. We were concerned about the political effect," Creel told me months later.[xi]

This political victory of López Obrador allowed him not only to shift attention from the video scandals of former collaborators Bejarano and Ponce, who in at least one case had claimed their boss was aware of their questionable activities, but several other accusations against his government as well. Among others, a Spanish investment firm, Eumex — the city's largest holder of bus-stop shelter concessions, with 2,500 *parabuses* laden with advertising — accused López Obrador of instigating ferocious harassment of its employees and executives, in the worst Cosa Nostra fashion, in order to take away the concessions Eumex had enjoyed since 1995.

López Obrador's adversaries in the PAN and the PRI said that the mayor's public works were a monument to populism: they were very showy, like the remodeling of Reforma Boulevard, but they had been carried out at the cost of mounting debt and the downgrading of basic services, something that would bring dire consequences to the city in the future. According to the PRI-run government of neighboring state of Mexico, Mexico City would be without drinking water as early as 2007 due to a lack of investment and maintenance of the supply network during López Obrador's administration. "López Obrador wasn't concerned about maintaining the water network, or educating the public to reduce their consumption,"[xii] said Benjamín Fournier, secretary of water and public works for the state of Mexico.

López Obrador showed no talent for building bridges to the opposition while he governed the city, his critics said. During his four-and-a-half years in office he never received any representatives of the PAN opposition in the municipal assembly, not even the parliamentary coordinator of the local Congress. Two PAN assembly members had to file and win a legal challenge to be able to enter a press conference and ask him questions. "Imagine that you're running the city and you haven't had a [meeting] with the most important opposition party in the city, which is the PAN," Creel pointed out to me. "Imagine that. It smacks of close-minded authority, one that doesn't listen, that won't see, that doesn't dialogue with whoever sits across the table. These are not democratic features that go with the country's democratic change and democratic transition."[xiii]

The problem with López Obrador: What he wouldn't do

What conclusion did I draw from López Obrador after talking to him and comparing what he said with what his critics claimed? The left-wing candidate had some positive attributes, including his personal austerity. He had always lived in small, unassuming homes, driving a modest Nissan Sentra. Unlike a great many in the Mexican political class, he led an orderly personal life. Before being widowed in 2003, he had remained close by his wife's side during her long terminal illness and had taken care of their three children. He didn't care for the high life, nor was he interested in money. His obsession was power. His habit of waking up at five in the morning said it all, setting him apart from the vast majority of Mexican politicians. His history of living in indigenous communities also distinguished him from many of his rivals, who claimed they were concerned about Mexico's Indians but had never demonstrated any commitment beyond words. López Obrador was a man who felt close to Native Mexican people, and not only during an election year.

However, what concerned me most about López Obrador was that economy wasn't his strong.suit. During his years as a university student he flunked seven classes, most of which had to do with numbers: economics twice, mathematics, and statistics.[xiv] This was no minor detail, since it was fully consistent with his political discourse, his instinctive rejection of everything — good and bad — that sounded "technocratic," and with the confusion he had shown during his answers regarding the fundamentals of economic success in China and Chile, as well as his dubious stewardship of public finances during his tenure in Mexico City.

If he became president, would he assign competitiveness, growth, and poverty the priority they deserved? Would he make the same structural economic changes as China, Chile, and other countries had to ensure long-term growth? Would he confront protectionist businessmen, corrupt labor unions, and pre-modern state universities to rouse Mexico from its lethargy? These were not idle questions: a great deal of López Obrador's support came from sectors that clung most tightly to pre-modern Mexico, including the gigantic National Autonomous University of Mexico (UNAM in Spanish), the largest state university with the biggest budget in the country, and one which, as we shall see in the following section, is a monument to educational backwardness. In other words, the most troublesome thing about a López Obrador victory wasn't what he might do, but what he might fail to do.

In the end, he caused his own undoing. The leftist candidate was leading in the polls before Election Day but lost significant ground in the final stretch of the campaign, when he launched a verbal attack on the Business Coordinating Council, the country's most powerful big-business association. That made him an easy target for Calderón's claims that a leftist government would bring about social confrontation, capital flight, factory closings, and fewer jobs. Many people got scared, and ended up voting for Calderón.

Vicente Fox and Mexican paralysis

Early in the 2006 electoral campaign there seemed no doubt that the country urgently needed reforms. Mexico had fallen asleep at the switch. In general terms, President Vicente Fox had done a decent job governing, but — whether because of a lack of courage, poor political management, or because his opponents systematically blocked all of his initiatives — the country had barely crept forward, whereas China, India, and other emerging powers were speeding ahead. By nearly all the worldwide indexes, Mexico had fallen behind during Fox's six-year reign. According to the Worldwide Economic Forum global competitiveness ranking, which takes into account each country's economic, technological, and institutional vigor, Mexico had fallen from 31st in 2000 to 48th in 2005. According to the Foreign Direct Investment Confidence Index compiled by multinational consulting firm AT Kearney, Mexico had plummeted from 5th place in 2001 to 22nd in 2004. According to the World Competitiveness Center I M D ranking, Mexico had tumbled from 14th in the world in 2000 to 56th in 2005. And according to the global business climate index of the Intelligence Unit of the *Economist*, Mexico had slipped from 31st in 2000 to 33rd in 2005.

What happened? Fox, the first opposition president after seven decades of iron-fisted PRI control, ran a minority government. His most important bills were systematically annihilated by the opposition, which held a majority in Congress. His reluctance to play hardball — for example, by putting corrupt PRI politicians from previous administrations behind bars — undermined his capacity to negotiate with the PRI bench in Congress from a position of strength. Likewise, his government had a dose of bad luck: his first three years in office coincided with the first U.S. economic deceleration in a decade, reducing Mexican manufacturing exports and paralyzing the country's economic growth. Finally, the attacks of September 11, 2001, were a devastating blow for Mexican hopes of expanding the free trade agreement with the United States and negotiating immigration reform. The Bush Administration — which just days before 9/11 had pronounced Mexico the "main bilateral relation" of the United States in the world — threw itself into the war on Islamic terrorism in Afghanistan and Iraq. Overnight, Mexico went from being Washington's main bilateral relation to a strategic irrelevancy.

The Fox administration argued that, despite those setbacks it had success on several fronts: poverty dropped by 4 percentage points during his first two years in office, according to the World Bank.[xv] Later but somewhat inconsistent data from the government itself suggested the reduction in poverty was even greater. Fox claimed that during his administration 7 million Mexicans were lifted out of extreme poverty, reducing that sector from 24 million to 17 million people. But the Technical Committee for the Measurement of Poverty, formed by academics handpicked by the Secretariat of Social Development, estimated the reduction in extreme poverty reduction as less, about 5.6 million people.[xvi]

Be that as it may, economic discipline, an increase in social spending — from 8.4 percent of the gross product to 9.8 percent, according to the World Bank — and the absence of economic crises, like those that rocked previous administrations, allowed Mexico to raise its living standards during Fox's first five years, although by much less than the expectations generated at the start of the so-called "government of change." Per-capita income increased from $8,900 annually in 2000 to $9,700.[xvii] Plus, that was achieved without corruption scandals comparable to those of PRI administrations and within a climate of democracy in which the government passed a law of transparency and public access to government information, allowing its people to see details of all government purchases for the first time.

In terms of foreign policy, Fox earned the distinction of changing Mexico's image as an unconditional ally of the Cuban dictatorship and — while continuing to oppose the U.S. trade embargo against Cuba — joining the modern democracies of Europe in defense of human rights as a governing principle for his country's international relations.

These were all signs of progress that in some cases were the work of the Fox administration, in others, of providence. Part of the poverty reduction came about thanks to a purely fortuitous factor: the flood of remittances from Mexicans working in the United States, which shot up from $6.5 billion per year in 2000 to $16.6 billion in 2004.[xviii] This was cash that went directly into the pockets of poor people and had an enormous impact in rescuing millions of Mexicans from misery, increasing internal consumption and stimulating the economy. Mexico was receiving nearly as much money from family remittances as from foreign investment. And it was hardly something Fox could point to as a great achievement of his administration.

Creel lacked a strong hand

The Fox government made several big mistakes right from the start. And his Secretary of Government Santiago Creel, who later tried unsuccessfully to win the ruling party's presidential nomination, was at center-stage for many — though not all — of them. Fox might have taken advantage of his own post-election surge of popularity and concentrated from the start on making Congress approve tax, labor, and energy reforms that by general consensus Mexico needed to compete with China, India, and Eastern Europe. Instead, the Mexican president wasted his first six months in office on the "pacification" of Chiapas and the search for a political agreement with local leader Sub-Commander Marcos and his Zapatista forces. Not only did the initiative go nowhere, as was foreseeable; it also meant squandering political capital on an issue that had not been a threat to national security for a long time and that had disappeared from the front pages years before.

Soon after, in mid-2002, the government suffered a major political defeat by canceling what it had presented as its main infrastructural project: a gigantic $2.3 billion airport to replace the nearly century-old Mexico City aerodrome. After nine months of protests and blocked roads by about 300 farmers supported by the PRD, who demanded greater compensation for their land before they would free several officials they had taken hostage, the government aborted construction of the new airport. To many Mexicans, Fox had showed signs of weakness, or at any rate had mismanaged the affair by not coming to an agreement with the farmers before trumpeting the project. Be that as it may, the signature initiative of Fox's administration had vanished, while in the meantime López Obrador began to inaugurate his flashy public works.

In December 2002 the government once again gave the impression of indecision when protestors from the leftist group El Barzón, some of them on horseback, burst into Congress demanding more resources for health and education, beating up whoever tried to stop them — legislators included — and causing property damage. The coordinator of the PAN bench at the time, Felipe Calderón, blamed the PRD for financing the violence, but the government folded its arms and took no action against those who caused the disturbance.

Perhaps one of Fox's greatest initial mistakes was his failure to jail any fat cats for corruption during the previous six-year administration, as his PRI predecessors Salinas de Gortari and Zedillo had done, so that they could take office with strong-handed measures. Likewise, he decided not to support the proposal of several Cabinet members, led by Foreign Minister Jorge Castañeda and National Security Adviser Adolfo Aguilar Zínser, to create a "Truth Commission" to clear up disappearances and other human rights violations committed by the state in the late 1960s. Although this was one of the "government of change" campaign promises, the idea was discarded at government secretary Creel's recommendation a few months into the new administration.

The First Lady's aspirations

One of Fox's continuing mistakes, as the years went by, was allowing his wife, Marta Sahagún, to stir the political waters and grab public attention by constantly hinting about her supposed intention to run for office in 2006. It was a political project that probably started out as a trial balloon for a later candidacy of greater importance — perhaps the mayoralty of Mexico City, or a seat in the Senate — but one that radically undermined Fox's promise of a "government of change" that would put an end to the tradition of PRI presidents' naming their successors by "finger-tapping" them and using state power to win elections.

Sahagún's ambitions weren't invented by the press, they were often encouraged by her own office. When in early 2004 I asked the First Lady's spokesman, David Monjaraz, whether journalistic speculation about Sahagún's candidacy had any basis, he answered, with a conspiratorial smile, that the polls showed enormous support for the First Lady. When I asked him for an official reaction, he said: "Marta is leaving all her options open. She hasn't said yes, but she hasn't said no."[xix] Months later, when I asked Sahagún herself on my television program whether she was considering running once her husband's six-year term had ended, she replied, "This isn't the right moment to determine whether I will run or not. I am under no obligation right now to do so. But what I'm absolutely sure of, is that at the proper time I'll have to act while keeping an eye on my responsibilities and my own conscience."[xx]

The leaders of the governing party saw the First Lady's aspirations as an element that disrupted the government's agenda. "She, like many others, has the right to seek candidacy if it's convenient to her career. But it's really madness to talk about candidates in the middle of an administration," the head of the PAN bench in the Senate at the time, Diego Fernández de Cevallos, told me. "I believe that, incredibly, we're missing out on a historic moment during this administration to achieve the great fiscal and judiciary changes that are so desperately needed to improve the living conditions of 100 million Mexicans." Instead of being a meritocracy, Mexico ran the risk of becoming a "maritocracy."[xxi] In July 2004 the First Lady's political meddling had become so frequent within the inner circle of government that Fox's private "super secretary," Alfonso Durazo, fled in dismay. Frustrated by what he saw as Sahagún's constant interference in government decisions, he wrote in his resignation letter that it was necessary "to put an end to the ever more widespread notion that presidential power is being exercised by a married couple."[xxii]

Why hadn't Fox, at the height of his popularity, taken a tougher stand against corruption and human rights abuses? "After the 2000 election, the PRI was dumbfounded, dazed, in bad shape," political analyst Denise Dresser concluded toward the end of the six-year administration. "That was the moment to promote divisions and use them in their favor. It was the perfect time to seduce with carrots and punish with big sticks. It was the right time to offer co-government to modernizers, and persecute the corrupt. It was the right time to offer immunity to potential allies and the full brunt of the law to all the rest [...] With that strategy, [the PRI] could have built majorities in Congress and dismantled the united front it later confronted there."[xxiii]

When I asked members of the Mexican Cabinet why Fox had been so cautious, so fearful of jeopardizing the peace even when harmony meant paralyzing the country, the answer was almost always the same: Secretary of Government Creel had convinced the president that he was about to obtain PRI support in Congress to approve tax, labor, and energy reforms that would give the Mexican economy a substantial boost. The economic future of the country should not be endangered, Creel argued. But the strategy was a disaster: five years later, after numerous announcements that the government was one step away from getting the votes it needed in Congress to approve certain reforms, Fox found himself empty-handed. Congress never approved the economic reforms proposed by the government, nor did it curtail its attacks, nor did the government keep its campaign promise to punish the abuses of previous administrations. Many believed the PRI had spent five years taking advantage of the secretary of the government's goodwill. "Creel lacked a strong hand," said Calderón, the former coordinator of the PAN bench in Congress who would later become energy secretary and a presidential hopeful, during his internal campaign against Creel in mid-2005. "Anyone could size him up."[xxiv]

The conciliatory negotiator

"Why didn't you put any fat cats from the PRI behind bars for corruption?" I asked Creel, not long after he abandoned the government to compete for his party's presidential nomination in 2006. He responded that he had other priorities, such as "a change toward peace, a change with political stability, a change that would allow the country to maintain economic stability. Could we have done a few things? Yes, but it would have put stability at risk."[xxv]

His answer seemed poor to me, unless Creel — who had been in charge of the government's chief intelligence agencies — knew something the rest of us didn't know about threats to Mexico's political stability in the early years of the administration. Was there a hidden threat? Was the PRI or PRD in any condition, after losing the 2000 elections, to disrupt public order? Seeing that his response hadn't convinced me, he insisted that the government had acted this way out of principle, to distinguish itself from the arbitrariness of the past. It was evident that Fox could have followed in the footsteps of Salinas de Gortari when — sidestepping several legal procedures — he imprisoned union leader Joaquín Hernández Galicia, alias "La Quina," in 1989, Creel explained, "but it was obvious that we weren't going to get anywhere this way." He added: "A lot of people wanted blood, they wanted a show, they wanted to see these fat cats behind bars in the very near future. We took measures that were not very spectacular, but in the end they did a lot to solidify our country."[xxvi]

Why wasn't a Truth Commission formed to clear up the crimes of the '60s and '70s, something that also would have given the government leverage to exert pressure on the PRI, which had been in power at the time of the human rights abuses? I asked Creel as a follow-up. Because, legally, it wouldn't have led to any trial against the guilty parties, the former secretary of government replied. In order to punish anyone, it would first have been necessary for the Supreme Court to revoke the statutes of limitations that made prosecution for some of the crimes impossible. It would have done little good to have a Truth Commission that fingered the guilty without being able to do anything about it, he said. Once again, "we chose the sad and boring path of institutionality, and today the Court has ruled that genocide in this country is not subject to the statute of limitations. That's President Fox's achievement and a success over the debate of all those who wanted a Truth Commission."[xxvii] Thanks to the Court's ruling, human rights abuses could now be prosecuted many years down the road, without time limitations, he said. And why had they invested all their political capital during the first few months of government on seeking an agreement in Chiapas, when the war had ended six years earlier? I asked. That was a mistake, Creel admitted. But it wasn't his idea, rather it was the responsibility of National Security Adviser Adolfo Aguilar Zinser, Foreign Minister Jorge Castañeda, and government spokesman Rodolfo "El Negro" Elizondo, who "were very much invested in the role that had been played by Zapatismo," he answered.[xxviii] However, as Castañeda told me later, Creel was never against the idea, "and it would have been inconceivable for Fox to make a decision like that, in domestic policy issues, against the wishes of his secretary of government and in favor of the foreign minister."[xxix]

The September blunder

Finally, I asked Creel if he hadn't been responsible for the administration's poor handling of U.S. relations following the attacks of 2001. Although it had never seemed objectionable to me that Mexico voted in the U.N. Security Council against Bush's decision to invade Iraq without evidence that Saddam Hussein was developing weapons of mass destruction, and although I did not fault Fox's later criticism of the U.S. military intervention in Iraq without U.N. approval, the Mexican government had acted clumsily in the days after the 9/11 attacks.

While Canada and Europe pledged their absolute solidarity with the United States, Mexico took considerable time before openly expressing its support. It didn't order Mexicans to lower the national flag to half-staff, not even in memory of the Mexicans who died in the Twin Towers of New York, nor did it carry out any symbolic gestures — like sending a team of nurses or volunteer firefighters — that would have scored propaganda points in the United States at no cost to political independence. After the attacks, Mexico was left paralyzed. For a country that depends on the United States for nearly 90 percent of its commerce, a country that was desperately seeking an immigration accord and that spent millions of dollars lobbying the U.S. Congress, it was a big mistake that would give additional ammunition to isolationists in Washington who opposed any measure of integration with Mexico. Fox sent a protocol message of support to Washington, but his administration got bogged down in an academic debate about the extent to which Mexico ought to support the United States. Foreign Minister Castañeda immediately declared following the attacks that Mexico should not haggle over its support to the United States, but Creel publicly contradicted him, maintaining that they couldn't give Washington unconditional support. According to several witnesses, Creel argued before Fox that if Mexico took a position that was too pro-U.S., PRI support for the tax reform the president so desperately wanted would be lost.

As Canada and Washington's European allies offered all kinds of aid to the United States, criticism began to rain down in Mexico, Washington's second-largest trade partner, for dragging its feet. The 11 Cabinet members closest to Fox during his first year of government held an emergency meeting at the president's offices to evaluate what they should do. As Castañeda recalls, "Someone proposed that once Fox came out onto the balcony to give the cry [of independence] on September 15, he could ask for a moment of silence for the Mexicans, Latin Americans, Chinese, and all the rest who died in the Twin Towers, and 'of course, for our American neighbors and business partners, who constituted most of the victims.' Even if there were catcalls, it was planned that the environmental sound on the television [microphones] would be turned off."[xxx] The proposal was approved. However, when Fox went out onto the balcony to give the cry, he didn't ask for the moment of silence. "We never knew why," Castañeda says. The former minister recalls suspecting that Creel was among those who may have dissuaded the president at the last moment, even though he admits he has no proof.

Simultaneously, the First Lady offered to make a symbolic gesture to keep her country's silence from becoming a public relations disaster. She suggested conducting a ceremony of solidarity with the victims of terrorism in the garden of the presidential home, Los Pinos, where she would donate blood for the wounded of the 9/11 attacks before photographers from international news agencies. The image of the First Lady giving blood would be more effective from a public relations standpoint than all the money Mexico had spent on lobbying in Washington. However, the Cabinet rejected Sahagún's idea. "I wanted to do it, but they wouldn't let me," she commented shortly afterward to a foreign visitor.[xxxi] Creel had blocked the idea, the First Lady said. The motive? Fear of antagonizing the PRI opposition in Congress.

"Lies!" Creel said to me when I asked him about both initiatives. "What happened was a statement I made about one nation not supporting another unconditionally. Period. That was my statement."[xxxii]

Another key figure in Fox's Cabinet, the head of the President's Office for Governmental Innovation, Ramón Muñoz, gave me a more self-critical and plausible explanation: the new Fox administration was concentrating solely on domestic policy at the time and lacked the international experience to give a quick, appropriate response. "More than an ideological reaction, it was shock derived from not being accustomed to handling this kind of contingency on an international scale. The machinery wasn't in place. There was no response capability," Muñoz said.[xxxiii]

Although the United States never officially admitted to any bad feelings with Mexico over the matter, relations deteriorated significantly. Years later, during an interview for this book, then-assistant secretary of state for the Western Hemisphere Otto Reich admitted for the first time that Bush was "deeply hurt" by Mexico and by Fox. "It was like a friend turning against you. It was that precise feeling. It wasn't exactly anger, rather it was disappointment," Reich recalled.[xxxiv]

"We weren't expecting Mexico to send troops to Afghanistan," Reich told me. Bush knew that Mexico had a tradition of non-intervention in armed conflicts, and that — regardless of his friend-ship with Fox — the Mexican president couldn't commit to military support without paying a very high political price. Besides, the Mexi-can army didn't have the equipment or experience in international operations needed to make more than a symbolic contribution to the Afghanistan invasion. However, Bush had expected a gesture of solidarity. "What surprised everyone [in the White House]," Reich said, "wasn't that Mexicans didn't offer troops, it was that they hadn't done anything else to express their pain over what had happened. Several days passed after September 11... and nothing. Meanwhile, Mexico got bogged down in an internal debate over what should be done. Can you imagine that? It's as if your neighbor's mother dies, and instead of expressing your condolences, you start getting into an argument over... well, the truth is that she was pretty noisy, and a lot of times she didn't say hello... It took them a long time to express their condolences. And after that, they didn't offer anything.

All the countries of the world that offered help were a lot farther away, and some had much less in terms of resources. Mexico didn't do anything. And I believe that was a tough blow to Bush." Four years later the Fox administration recovered part of Washington's trust when Mexico sent a convoy with military cooks and food to New Orleans for the victims of Hurricane Katrina. But key years had been lost, years that consumed nearly the entire Fox presidency and Bush's first term.

Creel's leading role before and after September 11 had led to permanent disagreements with the man who would later defeat him for the ruling PAN party presidential nomination in 2006, Calderón. During the entire Fox Administration, Calderón had tried — rarely with success — to convince the president not to delegate all negotiations with the opposition to Creel; that Fox take relations with key members of Congress into his own hands. But Calderón complained to me in an interview at the time that, even when he was leading the PAN legislative bloc in Congress, he was isolated from the president. "I was the one who talked to Fox the most, and I could only speak to him three times in one year, because Santiago (Creel) had told him he had everything under control," Calderón told me.[xxxv] At one point Calderón had advised Fox to act more like Colombian President Álvaro Uribe or Bill Clinton, both of whom personally contacted legislators from the opposition. "That never happened here. Four days before the budget vote, the PRI told Fox that there was going to be tax reform. I told him, 'They're laughing at us,' and I was right," Calderón commented. Even though many believed he had fallen from grace after his stint as energy secretary and his later departure from the government, Calderón never lost support within his party. On September 11, 2005, defying all predictions, Calderón won the first primary elections for the PAN candidacy against Creel. His campaign slogan, "A firm hand, passion for Mexico," and his sincere, upfront style had dealt a severe blow to the presidential aspirations of the former secretary of government, who had been Fox's first choice.

Fox's gamble for 2006

At the official residence of Los Pinos, the widespread view of Fox's inner circle a year before the election was that, even though López Obrador had a big lead in the polls, the foe for the governing party to beat in 2006 wasn't the leftist candidate, but the once-ruling Institutional Revolutionary Party, PRI. And even though Fox's party, the PAN, came in last on most polls in late 2005, officials were confident of a very good showing by mid-2006.

On what did the PANists base their optimism, when the polls showed great disappointment with the government? Ramon Muñoz, Fox's chief of staff and main strategist, told me that López Obrador had already reached the peak of his popularity after the failed impeachment attempt, and he was likely to go steadily downhill from there. López Obrador's advantage in the polls in late 2005 didn't mean much, Muñoz said: in November 1999 the candidate for the PRI, Francisco Labastida, had been 21 points ahead in the polls and went on to lose the election, Muñoz recalled. Unlike his two opponents, López Obrador didn't plan to carry out a primary in his party, which would rob him of several weeks of free publicity in the media. And after leaving the government of Mexico City, he would no longer have a powerful podium for his daily early-morning press conferences. Besides, he had powerful enemies inside his own party, starting with former PRD presidential candidate Cuauhtémoc Cárdenas. "My theory is that López Obrador has already reached his peak, and has no more room to grow. And his party is like a basket of crabs, where one crab tries to get out and the rest try to drag him down,"[xxxvi] Muñoz said. Even more importantly, the leftist candidate was a relatively convenient adversary for Fox's party: "He's a man who doesn't represent a modern vision. That can be his weakest point. He doesn't speak English, he has no idea about the rest of the world," Muñoz said.[xxxvii]

The PRI, on the other hand, was regarded by Los Pinos as a formidable adversary. "They're doing a better job than the PRD in their bid to return to power in 2006," Muñoz said. As a party, not being tied to the presidency allowed the PRI to present itself as an option for change, and control over the richest states in the country gave it a huge amount of money for the campaign. Although PRI candidate Roberto Madrazo was a bad candidate, the PRI had a well-oiled political machine, and in a scenario of absenteeism he might be the one to benefit the most.

But, according to Muñoz, Fox's party would do much better in the election than many expected, because, among other things, although his government wasn't popular, Fox was. "My calculations are that by July 2006 President Fox will be have popularity percentages between 65 and 70 points. I haven't the slightest doubt that President Fox's administration will end well," Muñoz said. When I showed my skepticism and asked him what made him think so, he answered, "Because of what we're going to do during the remainder of his administration. A government here, or anywhere, spends several years planting seeds, then has its harvest ready to deliver to citizens at the end. And we're going to close as high as possible in terms of public works, health, and social issues."

What did they have planned to ring out the six-year administration? I asked. Fox's administration focused its hopes on education and health. Its strategy was to come into the 2006 elections announcing that every school in the country already had available in the fifth and sixth grades *Enciclomedia*, a new educational system copied from British schools that allowed the children to follow along in their textbooks from an electronic blackboard. This was amazing technology, with which any student could go to the front of the class, touch an underlined word that interested him or her on the blackboard and — as on any computer — access an educational video. If the textbook talked about Mayan pyramids, for example, the child would touch the words "Mayan pyramids" on the blackboard and the entire class could watch a documentary two or three minutes long with music about the pyramids. "By August 2006 we'll have around 115,000 equipped classrooms, or 100 percent of fifth- and sixth-grade classrooms. If you ask me what I'm left with after this administration, I'd say, it's this," Muñoz told me.[xxxiv] The Fox administration also had planned to announce universal health coverage in late 2006, before the president passed the baton on December 1 of that year. In addition to local public works that all governments leave for the last minute so that they'll remain fresh in voters' minds, these were measures that could give the governing party a tailwind toward the end of the presidential race, or at least push it out of last place. And, what Muñoz did not mention, Fox's scare tactics — deriding López Obrador as a potential Chávez — would help tilt the 2006 election toward the government-backed candidate.

Calderón's surprising victory

Calderón's razor-thin win on election day 2006 was especially amazing because he was the contender who was least expected to reach the presidency. Calderón had not only won the ruling party's nomination despite Fox — the president had backed Secretary of Government Creel from the start — but was far from a charismatic, imposing presidential candidate. When Calderón first launched his bid for the ruling party's nomination, few took it seriously. When he participated in a panel on my television show, I was left with the impression that even he didn't take his chances too seriously: toward the end of the program, when he said that he would become Mexico's next president and undertake a series of reforms, he said it with a naughty smile, as if he were almost embarrassed by his ambition.

Despite his bookish, low-key appearance, Calderón was a formidable politician. The son of one of the PAN's founders, he had been learning party politics since his student days. Calderón was born in the state of Morelia and became president of the PAN's youth movement in his early 20s. He remained involved in his party's politics throughout his political career, until becoming the party's president in 1996 at age 33. When I talked to him at the time, he came across as a young man who was hard to imagine in blue jeans: He always wore white shirts, dark ties, and black suits, and his big eyeglasses made him look much older than his years.

A lawyer by training, he spoke no English and had little knowledge of the outside world — a reason why, in 1999, he left his job as party leader to spend a year with his family in the United States at Harvard University's Kennedy School of Government. Upon his return, Calderón was elected to Congress in the 2000 election, and served as leader of the PAN legislative bloc. In 2003 Fox appointed him head of the Banobras development bank, and a year later secretary of energy. Calderón, however, had never been a member of Fox's inner circle — unlike Calderón, the president had never been a PAN insider. Yet Calderón's long-time activism in the ruling party helped him strike the alliances he needed to win an upset victory for the party nomination, and force the Fox government to support his candidacy. And Fox had little choice but to throw his enthusi-astic support behind Calderón — the president's top priority was to prevent a victory by López Obrador, which would have most likely spawned a political vendetta from an incoming leftist government against Fox and his closest aides.

Despite the worldwide headlines his upset victory brought him in 2006, Calderón was far from beginning his six-year term as a strong president. On the contrary, he started as the weakest leader in Mexico's recent history. While former president Ernesto Zedillo had won the 1994 election with 50 percent of the vote, and Fox had won the 2000 election with 43 percent, Calderón was proclaimed the winner with only 36 percent — and with his better-known rival, López Obrador, claiming the election had been stolen. Even though López Obrador's complaints eventually faded from the front pages — as growing numbers of leftist supporters were dismayed by his refusal to accept the election results even after a recount and by his self-proclamation as "legitimate president" — Calderón was hardly anybody's hero. As pollster Francisco Abundis told me a day after the elections in Mexico City, "People didn't necessarily vote for Calderón, they voted against López Obrador. They did so because of a combination of fear and rejection." Worse, Calderón would have to rule with a 42 percent minority in Congress, and would need the support of the center-left PRI to pass critical reforms. The PRI had systematically blocked Fox's attempts to pass energy, labor, and fiscal measures that most economists agreed were critical to compete globally. It was far from clear after the election that the PRI would be any more willing to work with Calderón than it had been with Fox.

"Architecturally doomed to paralysis"

Would Mexico be able to recover the ground lost to China, India, and Eastern Europe? Months before the 2006 elections, I put this question to former PRI president Genaro Borrego, one of the leaders of the modernizing wing of the longtime dominant center-left party, who knew as few others did the inner workings of Mexican politics. Borrego was now a PRI senator, and he was pessimistic. Mexico had gone from the authoritarian governments of the PRI to a divided government, with a president who lacked a majority in Congress, and whose most important bills were routinely blocked by the opposition, he told me. Everything indicated that this would continue to be the case, no matter who won the election. The fact that Mexico had three major parties — PRI, PAN, and PRD — and had no provision for runoff elections, practically guaranteed that whoever won the presidency would take office with a minority of around one-third of the votes and an obstructionist majority in Congress. "We're architecturally doomed to paralysis," Borrego said.[xxxix]

When I asked Fox's former secretary of government Creel the same question, he agreed, pointing out that it was urgent to approve political reforms because "this system we have has no incentive for collaboration. If he can only hope that political goodwill and altruism will take us forward, that's going to lead us to failure."[xl] However, even though everyone agreed about the problem, the interests of those who saw themselves with the best likelihood of winning the next presidency would always end up blocking political reforms.

"Everyone agrees with the generalities and common issues, but the moment you go into details, they back out," said former foreign minister Castañeda, who after leaving government had started a legal case to be allowed to run as an independent presidential candidate outside the three major parties.[xli]

Mexico was, indeed, paralyzed by its political system. To overcome its stagnation, the country needed to change its Constitution to allow several key reforms: a runoff election to enable presidents to take office with a majority vote; creation of a prime ministership or Cabinet chief job approved by Congress, which would give the president a much stronger link to the legislature. That would make it easier to pass key laws, and would also allow the head of state to fire the prime minister in the event of a political crisis without upending the presidency; and the re-election of members of Congress, which would make legislators accountable to their constituents. Under the current system, in which deputies and senators must go home after one term, they have more incentives to remain on good terms with their party leaders — on whom they depend for their next job — than with the electorate. As a result, there's not much motivation to serve the people, and no incentive for legislators to vote their conscience instead of following party lines.

The Mexican Constitution stipulates only that there be a direct election for president, and leaves the details to the electoral code. From 1998 to 2002 three bills were introduced in Congress that would add a runoff to the electoral code. None received a majority vote. In 1998, when the PRI was in power, the bill was introduced by the PAN, while in 2001 and 2002, when Fox was in power, similar bills were introduced by the two opposition parties. In a nutshell, they're all in agreement on political reform, as long as it benefits them. As for the creation of a semi-presidential system, with a prime minister or head of government approved by Congress, from 2000 to 2003 alone at least seven bills were presented — nearly all of them by the PRD — to amend the Constitution and make this reform possible. No parties were opposed at the outset, but at the last moment the bills failed. And proposals to annul the ban on re-electing legislators, as stipulated in the Constitution, were floated for over four decades without going anywhere. In 2003 PRD senator Demetrio Sodi presented one of the legislative re-election bills that had received the most support. It was about to be approved on February 10, 2005. However, the attempt failed in the Senate, with 50 votes in favor, 51 against, and one abstention. Several PRI senators who had supported the bill in the beginning did an about-face at the last moment under pressure from the party leadership.[xlii]

"Mexico has everything it needs to take off, but it's condemned to mediocrity because of the selfishness of its political class," I told Muñoz, Fox's right-hand man, hoping to goad him into accepting or rejecting this premise. To my surprise, he was optimistic that whoever won in 2006 would manage to approve the reforms that the country needed to cut the political knot that kept the government's hands tied. According to Muñoz, pressure was mounting for political reform, and that pressure would rapidly increase as 2007 approached, when among other things, money would run out to pay retirement pensions due to a lack of consensus in Congress. "We've calculated that by 2007 or 2008 the issue [of pensions] is going to explode like a volcano, and there won't be enough money to pay the retirees," he told me. "That's going to make parties say: 'This doesn't work for anyone, not you, not me.' Besides, whoever is in power will have more political practice than this administration did when it started out. We've all accumulated more experience, and there will be better conditions to get it done," he added.

Muñoz was partly right: a few months after Calderón's December 1, 2006, victory, an alliance between the ruling PAN party and the PRI in Congress approved a social-security reform that had been languishing for years. It was the first major reform passed by Congress in years, and led to growing optimism that the new president would succeed where Fox had failed. Calderón, as a former congressional leader, had more experience than his predecessor in making deals, and enjoyed the process. As the new president had told me during the campaign, when he complained that Fox seldom saw him when he was heading the PAN bloc in Congress, Calderón spent much of his time massaging congressional egos. His early decisions helped him overcome his image as a politically weak incoming president. On inauguration day Calderón raised eyebrows when, contrary to speculation in the media that he would not be sworn in as scheduled because López Obrador's supporters had blocked the area surrounding the Congress, Calderón made his way to the building and took the oath of office. Then, after a few weeks in office, Calderón unleashed an all-out military crackdown on drug traffickers, which — despite criticism from several experts about its effectiveness — further helped cement his image as a leader.

Optimists claimed that Calderón had the potential to shake up Mexico and turn it into a vibrant emerging power. They pointed out that while Fox had started his presidency with enormous popularity, which he had lost along the way, Calderón had begun with low numbers that had risen steadily. After six months in office Calderón's popularity had doubled to 68 percent. His no-nonsense, results-oriented, cautious rhetoric and firm stance on crime were seen as a welcome change from Fox's often wavering governance. But the question remained whether, despite overcoming major obstacles to win the presidency, he would be able to break Mexico free of its political paralysis.

About a year after Calderón's election, I called Borrego, who by now had left the Senate and quit the PRI to support Calderón, whether anything had changed about Mexico's political architecture that could create room for optimism. Borrego noted that Congress had passed a law forcing itself to make major political reforms by mid-2008 to untangle the country's chronic legislative gridlock, although he was skeptical that it would lead to major change. The good news was that Calderón was more willing to work Congress than his predecessor, and that the PRI seemed to have learned that systematically blocking government-sponsored bills was not playing well with voters. "We are a little bit better than last time we talked, thanks to Calderón's negotiating skills in Congress and the PRI's negative experience with systematic legislative obstructionism. But the country's political architecture remains the same," Borrego said.

Ironically, while Mexicans were wondering whether Calderón would become a leader capable of propelling Mexico into growth rates similar to those of China or India, the future of Mexico depended not so much on whether the president would rise to the occasion, but on whether he would be allowed to govern — or whether the country would change the rules that kept it from ending its perpetual political impasse.

NOTES

[i] "Ideología y valores de los mexicanos," National face-to-face poll by Ipsos-Bimsa carried out from February 9-14, 2005.

[ii] Interview with Manuel Camacho, Mexico City, June 20, 2005.

[iii] "Mexico's leftist leader gets help from Colin Powell," The Miami Herald, November 14, 2004.

[iv] La historia del Partido Acción Nacional, 1939-1940, National Action Party, 1993, p. 6.

[v] Enrique Maza, Proceso, Mexico, June 5, 1995, p. 23.

[vi] "World Economic Outlook," International Monetary Fund, April 2005.

[vii] Secretariat of the Economy, with data from the Bank of Mexico, 2005.

[viii] Jorge Zepeda Patterson, Los suspirantes, Planeta, 2005, p. 12.

[ix] "De calificaciones y sustos varios," Enfoque (Reforma's supplement), April 15, 2005.

[x] "Crece la deuda $400 al año (per capita)," Reforma, February 22, 2005.

[xi] Interview with Santiago Creel, Mexico City, June 23, 2005.

[xii] Interview with Benjamín Fournier, in Miami, June 27, 2005.

[xiii] Interview with Santiago Creel, Mexico City, June 23, 2005.

[xiv] "De calificaciones y sustos varios," Enfoque (Reforma's supplement), April 15, 2005.

[xv] "Disminuye pobreza, persiste atraso," Reforma, July 29, 2004.

[xvi] "Infla presidente pobreza superada," Reforma, June 25, 2005.

[xvii] "World Economic Outlook Database," International Monetary Fund, April 2005.

[xviii] Bank of Mexico, Payment Balance, cited by Eduardo Sojo, De la alternancia al desarrollo, Fondo de Cultura Económica, 2005, p. 143, and the Inter-American Development Bank.

xix Andrés Oppenheimer, "México, ¿hacia una 'maritocracia'?" The *Miami Herald*, February 6, 2004.

xx Interview with Marta Sahagún, on *Oppenheimer Presenta*, May 24, 2004.

xxi Andrés Oppenheimer, "México, ¿hacia una 'maritocracia'?", The *Miami Herald*, Feruary 6, 2004.

xxii "Deja a Fox, culpa a Marta," *Reforma*, July 6, 2004.

xxiii Denise Dresser, "Autopsia adelantada," *Reforma*, July 4, 2005.

xxiv Interview with Felipe Calderón in Mexico City, June 21, 2005.

xxv Interview with Santiago Creel, in Mexico City, June 22, 2005.

xxvi Idem.

xxvii Idem.

xxviii Idem.

xxix Interview with Jorge Castañeda, Mexico City, June 23, 2005.

xxx Telephone interview with Jorge Castañeda, July 5, 2005.

xxxi Andrés Oppenheimer, *México en la frontera del caos*, Second edition, July 2002, Ediciones B, Mexico, p. 19.

xxxii Interview with Santiago Creel. Mexico City, June 23, 2005.

xxxiii Interview with Ramón Muñoz, head of the President's Office for Governmental Innovation, July 20, 2005.

xxxiv Interview with Otto Reich, August 3, 2004.

xxxv Interview with Felipe Calderón, Mexico City, June 21, 2005.

xxxvi Interview with Ramón Muñoz, head of the Presidential Office for Governmental Innovation, July 20, 2005.

xxxvii Idem.

xxxviii Idem.

xxxix Interview with Genaro Borrego, Mexico City, June 20, 2005.

xl Interview with Santiago Creel, Mexico City, June 23, 2005.

xli Interview with Jorge Castañeda, June 7, 2005.

xlii Jeffrey M. Weldon, "State Reform in Mexico", *Mexican Governance*, CSIS Press, 2005, p. 27

CHAPTER 10

Latin America in the New Century

Tall tale: "The next war... is going to be over natural resources, such as oil, gas and water." (Evo Morales, coca farmers' leader, legislator and future president of Bolivia, *Granma*, November 29, 2002).

BEIJING—NEW DELHI—WASHINGTON—MEXICO CITY—BUENOS AIRES — Latin America's old-guard left-wingers and right-wing nationalists share little common ground. But they agree that international politics in the 21st century will be driven by all-out competition over natural resources, and that the top priority for commodity-rich Latin American countries should be preventing foreign countries and multinational companies from taking control of those resources. That perspective makes for ringing political oratory and weighty academic treatises, but it doesn't reflect the economic realities of the new millennium. Unlike centuries past, when raw materials were the most important source of wealth for most countries, today the wealth of nations lies to a large extent in the production of ideas. Many Latin American leaders — and not just those from oil-rich Venezuela and Ecuador — are oblivious to the fact that we are living in the era of the knowledge economy.

Raw materials are no longer a guarantor of progress; moreover, in Latin America they often have been a curse. Look at any map: Venezuela, Ecuador, and Bolivia, countries with fabulous energy resources that historically have had some of the region's highest poverty levels. Conversely, some of the most prosperous countries in the world have had virtually no natural resources. Instead, they bet on education, science, and technology. The list of countries with the highest per-capita incomes is led by Luxembourg, with $54,000 per inhabitant, despite having a minuscule territory and no raw materials.[i] "In past centuries, when economic development was based on agriculture or mass industrial production, being bigger, richer in natural resources, or having more people was an advantage. Today it's a disadvantage," says Juan Enríquez Cabot, a former Harvard Business School professor and author of As the Future Catches You.

The Soviet Union, with perhaps the world's richest supplies of natural resources, collapsed. And neither South Africa, with its diamonds, nor Nigeria, Venezuela, and Mexico, with their oil, nor Brazil and Argentina, with their agricultural products, have managed to eradicate poverty. Most of those countries are poorer now than they were 20 years ago. Yet nations with few natural resources, like Luxembourg, Ireland, Liechtenstein, Singapore, Taiwan, and Israel are among those with the highest per-capita incomes in the world.

The case of Singapore is particularly striking. It was an impoverished British colony that did not even gain independence until 1965. It was so poor its leaders had implored neighboring Malaysia for annexation. Malaysia refused, believing that taking charge of Singapore would be bad for business. In August 1965, when Singapore became a nation, the Sydney Morning Star of Australia indicated that "there's nothing in the current situation that allows us to foresee a viable country in Singapore."[ii] In fact, Singapore quickly became one of the richest countries in the world. President Lee Kuan Yew, who had been a lawyer for communist labor unions, concentrated all his efforts on education. He made English the official language in 1978, and devoted his energy to attracting technology firms from around the world. By the end of the century per-capita income had risen to nearly that of Great Britain, its former colonial master — an achievement similar to Ireland's, once Britain's destitute neighbor, as we saw in Chapter 3.

Why does Holland produce more flowers than Colombia?

How can one explain why Holland exports more flowers than any Latin American country? As Michael Porter, a professor at Harvard, has written, the region should be the world's largest producer of flowers. It has cheap labor, plenty of land, a lot of sunshine, major water reserves, and a huge variety of flora. Instead, the biggest producer of flowers is Holland, a country with little sun, even less space, and one of the most expensive labor forces in the world. The explanation is quite simple: what matters today in the flower industry is genetic engineering, distribution capacity and marketing.[iii]

Similarly, how can one explain that, while Latin America has some of the world's biggest coffee-producing nations, it gets only a tiny fraction of coffee-industry income? Take the case of Starbucks, the largest coffee-shop chain in the world. It was born in the United States in the early 1970s, and today it comprises about 6,500 cafés in the United States plus another 1,500 in 31 countries. Coffee experts say that for every $3 cup of coffee sold in the United States, only 3 percent goes to Latin American coffee producers. When I cited this example in a speech in El Salvador, one of that country's biggest coffee producers approached me at the end to tell me that my figure was wrong — it was closer to 1 percent. What's valued in the new global economy is not the act of planting a seed, or owning the land where it's sown, but the creation of the seed in genetic laboratories, the processing, packaging, branding, marketing, and distribution. "In Latin America, if we continue to believe that our biodiversity is going to save us, we're going to have more and more problems. We still think that oil, mines, or seacoasts are the most important thing. The truth is that, in economic terms, it's easier to make mistakes when you're a big country with vast natural resources than when you're poor and isolated," Enríquez Cabot, who was raised in Mexico, said.

Indeed, most Latin American politicians and academics continue to spread the fiction that their countries have it made because they own oil, gas, water, or other natural resources. What they don't say, maybe because they don't realize it, is that the prices of raw materials — even after rising considerably over the past few years — plummeted over 80 percent in the 20th century and currently account for a small share of the world economy. In 1960, when a large number of today's Latin American presidents were politically educated, raw materials constituted 30 percent of the worldwide gross product; they represent just 4 percent today. The biggest share of the world's economy is in the service sector (68 percent) and the industrial sector (29 percent).[iv] Multinational retail, banking, or technology companies like Wal-Mart, Citigroup, or IBM have much higher incomes than those that produce food or most other raw materials. In 1955 half of the top 20 spots on the Fortune 500 list of America's biggest companies sold oil or steel. By 2007 only three of the top 20 U.S. corporations on the list sold oil or steel, while the majority were in the retail, banking, insurance, car-making, and health-care sectors. Unfortunately, in the early 21st century Latin America continues to live in the economy of the past. The enormous majority of its big companies remain in the basic-products business. The four largest — PEMEX, PDVSA, Petrobras and PEMEX Refinación — are oil companies. Of the region's 12 largest companies, only four sell products that aren't oil or minerals (Wal-Mart de México, Teléfonos de México, América Móvil, and General Motors de México).[v]

Today much of South America's energies in international trade negotiations focus on demanding that the United States and the European Union reduce their agricultural subsidies, which hurt Latin American exports. It is a legitimate and just cause, but in many cases distracts Latin American governments' attention from the need to produce and export higher value-added goods. At stake is, at most, expanding the region's slice of the 4 percent of worldwide trade accounted for by raw materials, instead becoming more competitive and entering the knowledge economy of the 21st century.

Nokia: From lumber to cell phones

Should Latin American countries abandon production of raw materials? Of course not. When I put that question to David de Ferranti, Latin America director of the World Bank, he shook his head, as if to say the issue had already been settled. "Agriculture, mining, and extraction of other raw materials are comparative-advantage sectors for Argentina, Brazil, Chile, and several other countries. They should take advantage of the opportunity to become more efficient producers of these raw materials and diversify from these industries into others with more sophisticated products. They should do what Finland did," he said.

Finland, one of the most developed nations in the world, was until not long ago chiefly a timber-exporting country. Then it started producing and exporting furniture. Later, it specialized in furniture design. Then it started to focus on technology design, which was much more profitable, and began designing all kinds of products, including cellular telephones. Then the Finns starting producing cellular telephones themselves. The evolution is exemplified by the story of Nokia, now one of the world's dominant cell-phone manufacturers. Nokia started in 1865 as a lumber company, founded by a mining engineer in southeast Finland. By the mid-20th century it was designing furniture and started to apply its creativity to all sorts of industrial designs. In 1967 it merged with a Finnish tire company and a cable company, creating a telecommunications conglomerate known today as the Nokia Corporation, with 51,000 employees and annual sales of $42 billion — which according to the World Bank amounts to five times Bolivia's gross national income and more than twice Costa Rica's.

Something similar happened with multinational Wipro Ltd. of India, which started out selling cooking oil and is today one of the world's largest software companies. Azim Premji — sometimes called the Bill Gates of India — became the richest man in his country and 38th on the list of the richest people in the world, according to *Forbes* magazine, by radically transforming his family business. He was studying engineering at Stanford University in the United States when his father died in 1966, and he had to go back home when he was 21 years old to take over the family business, Western India Vegetable Products Ltd. (Wipro). The company was valued at

$2 million and sold cooking oil to supermarkets. Premji immediately began to diversify, starting out by producing hand soaps. In 1977, taking advantage of the gap vacuum created by the expulsion of IBM from the country, he began manufacturing computers. The business prospered and shifted into software, where it developed a reputation as an innovative and creative company. Today Wipro has annual revenues of more than $3 billion. Of that, 85 percent comes from its software division and the rest from its computers, electric lamps, medical diagnosis equipment and — though it may seem sentimental — hand soaps and cooking oils. Its workforce has more than tripled since 2002 to 66,000. Its home office in Bangalore hires an average of 24 people each day.

Like Nokia and Wipro, hundreds of big businesses started out producing raw materials and then diversified into more profitable sectors. "The old debate as to whether it's good or bad to produce raw materials is a false dilemma," De Ferranti told me. "The valid question is how to take advantage of the industries one has, to use them as springboards to more modern sectors of the economy." To do that, the experience of China, Ireland, Poland, the Czech Republic, and several other countries shows that you need to invest more in education, science, and technology in order to have a population capable of producing sophisticated industrial goods, services, or manufacturing products in the knowledge economy.

Patents ranking

One revealing way to measure the progress of nations is by their patents for inventions in the world's largest markets. From 1977 to 2003, the U.S. Patent Office registered approximately 1.631 million patents from U.S. citizens or businesses, 537,900 from Japan, 210,000 from Germany, 1,600 from Brazil, 1,500 from Mexico, 830 from Argentina, 570 from Venezuela, 180 from Chile, 160 from Colombia, and 150 from Costa Rica.[vi] In 2003 the office registered about 36,800 patents from businesses or investors in Japan and 4,200 from South

Korea. By comparison, it registered 200 patents from Brazil, 130 from Mexico, 76 from Argentina, 30 from Venezuela, 16 from Chile, 14 from Colombia, and 5 from Ecuador — a pitiful percentage of the total. Among patent offices in Latin America the situation is similar: in Mexico only 4 percent of patents registered come from Mexican individuals or businesses; the remaining 96 percent are from multinational companies like Procter & Gamble, 3M, Kimberly-Clark, Pfizer, Hoechst, and Motorola.[vii]

The countries that register the most patents are, of course, the ones that invest the most in science and technology. In this category are the United States, which spends 36 percent of the worldwide total dedicated to research and development, the European Union, with 23 percent, and Japan, with 13 percent. By comparison, Latin American and Caribbean nations invested only 2.9 percent of the world R&D total in 2000, according to the UNESCO publication, *A World of Science.*

As for creating qualified workforces to manufacture high-value-added products, the situation of Latin American countries isn't much better. China graduates 350,000 engineers each year, India around 300,000. By comparison, Mexico produces 13,000 engineers and Argentina, 3,000, according to official figures. Of course China and India have much larger populations, and therefore they produce more engineers. But their sum total of engineering graduates is an important factor in the global economy. When time comes to choose which country to invest in, information technology companies and others that produce sophisticated products favor those with the greatest qualified labor force at the best price.

According to Mark Wall, now president of General Electric Plastics in China and formerly head of its operations in Brazil, China is currently the most dynamic place in the world for the manufacturing industry, not only because of its cheap labor, but because of its qualified labor.[viii] China offers an army of newly minted engineers, hungry for factory jobs and ready to work as many hours as necessary to improve the quality of their products. The ambiance is similar to that of

Silicon Valley, California, in the '90s; there is an enormous enthusiasm that translates into more and better professionals, increasing investment in manufacturing, and aggressive R&D into new products. General Electric recently opened a research center in Shanghai, with about 1,200 engineers and technicians. Motorola already owns 19 research centers in China, coming up with new products for domestic sales and for export. Motorola cell phones in China were designed there, customized for the Chinese market. And it wouldn't be surprising if before long Chinese cell phone–related technology were exported to the entire world. In Beijing people can use their cell phones on a moving subway without losing their connections, something I've never been able to do in the United States, where calls are constantly disconnected, even in the open. Motorola is developing many of these technologies in Chengdu, the capital of the Sichuan province in southwestern China, where foreign companies benefit from special tax breaks, the presence of some 40 universities, and more than one million engineers.

Orthodox economists and international financial institutions have been slow to recognize the importance of education in the development of nations. In the '90s they preached economic and political reforms, but failed to put the same emphasis on education. If anything has been clearly shown, it's that Latin American countries can slash public spending, lower inflation, pay off foreign debt, reduce corruption, and improve the quality of political institutions — as the IMF demands — and continue to be poor, as long as they fail to come up with more sophisticated products. "Mexicans, Brazilians, Argentines, Chileans, and Africans continue to restructure their economies time and again... yet they remain poor... and their future is growing darker... because they produce and export very little knowledge," Enríquez Cabot said.[ix]

The worst universities in the world?

A 2004 ranking of the world's best 200 universities conducted by London's *Times Higher Education Supplement* (*THES*) gave dismal marks to Latin American universities. The survey concluded that only one Latin American university belonged on the list — and it was nearly at the bottom, ranked 195. Are Latin American universities that bad? I asked myself when I read the ranking. Are Latin Americans being fed fairy tales when their governments tell them that their academics and scientists are acclaimed in the United States and Europe? Or is it just that the *THES* ranking is skewed in favor of universities from wealthy nations?

According to the ranking, the best universities in the world are in the United States, led by Harvard, the University of California at Berkeley, and the Massachusetts Institute of Technology. Of the 20 best universities, 11 are in the United States, followed by those in Europe, Australia, Japan, China, India, and Israel. The only Latin American university on the list is the National Autonomous University of Mexico (UNAM), a heavily-subsidized monster of 269,000 students that — save for a few exceptions, like the schools of medicine and engineering — is highly over-rated within Mexico.[x]

When I hosted a television program with several deans of Latin American universities, I asked them about Latin America's poor showing in this ranking, and most of them kicked up a fuss. It was untrue, unfair, slanderous, several said. If our universities were that bad, we wouldn't have so many graduates on the faculties of Harvard, Stanford, or the Sorbonne, they proclaimed. The *Times* poll was biased, they said, very likely based on the views of U.S. and European academicians, and on the numbers of scholarly works published in the main international academic reviews, which are all written in English. There Latin American universities are at a clear disadvantage. One of the few who sounded a discordant note was Jeffrey Puryear, an expert on Latin American education issues with the Inter-American Dialogue, a Washington think tank. "The general results of the ranking don't surprise me one bit," Puryear said. "Many Latin American universities are state-owned, and the governments haven't demanded much from them in terms of quality control. And when they try to demand quality, the universities resist, shielding themselves behind the principle of academic autonomy."

When I called the *Times Higher Education Supplement* to ask how the ranking was done, I was told it was on five criteria, including a poll among academicians from 88 countries, the number of citations in academic publications, and the ratio between professors and students at each institution. The weight assigned to academic citations in the total evaluation accounted for 20 percent of the total. There was also suitable geographic representation, according to the *THES*: Of the 1,300 academics interviewed, nearly 300 were from Latin America. If the poll had included more academicians from developing nations, the results would have been similar, they added. The University of Shanghai had carried out a ranking of the top 500 universities in the world and its selection of the top 200 had been fairly similar to that of the *THES*.

Indeed, Jiao Tong University of Shanghai, one of the oldest and most prominent in China, had published its index in 2004 with the goal of helping China's universities, and their students, decide where to send its brightest students. The Chinese rankings were based on the number of Nobel prizes at each university, research citations in academic publications, and the quality of education. And the study had concluded that of the 10 best universities in the world, eight were in the United States — led by Harvard and Stanford — and two in Great Britain. The Jiao Tong list had relatively few from outside the United States and Europe: nine in China, eight in South Korea, five in Hong Kong, five in Taiwan, four in South Africa, four in Brazil, one in Mexico, one in Chile, and one in Argentina. And the Latin Americans were far from the top: UNAM in Mexico and São Paulo University in Brazil were clustered with others tied at 153 to 201, while the University of Buenos Aires (UBA) was among 100 universities tied for positions 202 through 301, and the University of Chile, the State University of Campinas, and the Federal University of Rio de Janeiro appeared together with nearly 100 other universities between spots 302 and 403.[xi]

The truth is that both the *THES* and Jiao Tong rankings suggest that Latin American governments are living in denial. The UNAM, which receives $1.5 billion from the Mexican government every year,[xii] and UBA, which receives $165 million from the Argentine state per year,[xiii] are scandalous examples of the lack of accountability in each country. They both refuse to submit to accreditation examinations by their ministries of education, claiming they are too prestigious to be compared with other universities from their own countries. "The UNAM is an institution closed to outside evaluation," Reyes Tamez Guerra, Mexico's secretary of education, told me in an interview. "Practically all public universities in the country have agreed to undergo outside evaluation, except for the UNAM."[xiv] Argentine Minister of Education Daniel Filmus told me the same thing about the UBA: "When we started accrediting universities, the UBA decided not to accredit. It appealed [in court]. The argument is that its level is such that there's no one who can accredit it, and that it is an attack against university autonomy to have an organization outside the university accredit it. They filed a lawsuit against the Ministry of Education."[xv]

Professors without salaries, classrooms without computers

The UNAM of Mexico and UBA of Argentina are both sacred cows in their countries that few dare to criticize, even though they are monuments to inefficiency and underdevelopment. When the 2004 *Times Higher Education Supplement* ranking was published, Mexican newspapers published the news — taken from the university's own jubilant press releases — as if the evaluation had been excellent. *Reforma*, the most influential newspaper in Mexico, ran a front-page headline proclaiming: "UNAM is among the top two hundred."[xvi]

"The National Autonomous University of Mexico is one of the two hundred best in the world, and the only Latin American institution of higher education named in a study carried out by the supplement specializing in higher education by the London daily the *Times*," the article said. UNAM President Juan Ramón de la Fuente gave out glowing interviews, as if the school had won a major sports tournament. In a similar fashion, when the ranking of Shanghai University was announced, another Mexican newspaper, *La Jornada*, ran the headline: "The UNAM, best university of Latin America, worldwide study says."[xvii] The article mentioned prominently that "no private Mexican institutions of higher education appear in the international ranking," failing to point out that no private university was receiving UNAM's extraordinary state subsidies. In fact, the poor performance of the UNAM on both studies — despite the fact that the university received much more money from the state than dozens of universities from other countries that were ranked higher — and the absence of other Latin American universities in the ranking, should have triggered a national and regional debate. In France, when they heard that Shanghai University included only 22 French universities among the best in the world and that the first was ranked 65th on the list, there was a national outcry that prompted the European Union to start an exhaustive investigation on how to improve the standards of Europe's universities.

Latin American countries don't spend enough on education, and what they do spend often goes to the wrong things, including paying teachers who don't teach and subsidizing students who don't need subsidy so they can pursue degrees they'll never get in fields of study that their society doesn't need. The countries of Latin America invest less in education than those of Europe and Asia. Norway, Sweden, Denmark, Finland, and Israel, for example, channel about 7 percent of their annual gross national product into education. Former Soviet-bloc countries invest around 5 percent. By comparison, Mexico earmarks 4.4 percent; Chile, 4.2; Argentina, 4; Peru, 3.3; Colombia, 2.5; and Guatemala, 1.7 percent.[xviii] "And we not only spend less, we also spend it badly," I was told by Juan José Llach, a former minister of education in Argentina. According to Llach, nearly all educational spending in many countries of the region goes to paying salaries, and not even the salaries of the teaching staff, but of maintenance and administrative personnel. According to a World Bank study, 90 percent of public spending in Brazilian universities goes to pay the salaries of current and retired staff, whereas in Argentina, the figure is 80 percent.[xix] As a result, the Latin American university system suffers from "low quality," with overpopulated universities, deteriorating buildings, a lack of equipment, obsolete instruction materials, and insufficient training and dedication among professors. The study indicates that while in Great Britain 40 percent of university professors have Ph.D.s, in Brazil the figure is 30 percent, in Argentina and Chile 12 percent, in Venezuela 6 percent, in Mexico 3 percent, and in Colombia 2 percent.[xx]

Incredibly, nearly 40 percent of professors at the University of Buenos Aires are *ad honorem;* they work for free because the most prestigious university in Argentina can't afford to pay them. According to a teachers survey in UBA, 11,003 professors work for no pay in its 13 faculties; most are recent graduates who are designated as "auxiliary professors."[xxi]

Poor students subsidizing rich students

Perhaps the reason Norway and Sweden can spend 7 percent of their GNP on education is that they don't have people starving in the streets. But other countries that have dramatically raised their educational standards in recent decades didn't do so by redirecting state money from the poor. Instead, they made middle- and upper-class students pay for their studies, either before or after they graduate. Latin America, in fact, is one of the last regions in the world where education is subsidized even for those who can pay. It's an absurd system in which all of society — including the poor — subsidize a considerable number of affluent students. According to the World Bank, more than 30 percent of students at state universities in Mexico, Brazil, Colombia, Chile, Venezuela, and Argentina come from the wealthiest 20 percent of society.[xxii] "University education in Latin America continues to be highly elitist, and most students come from the wealthier social strata," the report states. In Brazil 70 percent of university students belong to the wealthiest 20 percent of society, while only 3 percent of students come from the poorest sectors. In Mexico 60 percent of the university population comes from the wealthiest 20 percent, and in Argentina, 32 percent. Another study, by UNESCO, calculates that 80 percent of Brazilian university students, 70 percent of Mexicans, and 60 percent of Argentines are from the wealthiest classes.[xxiii] How do you explain this? The authors of the study say the reason is simple: students from humble origins who went to public schools are so badly prepared for college that most drop out soon after they begin. This leads to a paradoxical situation in which the rich are overrepresented in free universities, meaning that the system "acts as a recipe to increase inequality," the World Bank concludes.

In recent years, European countries generally abandoned free university education and started charging those who could pay. Britain's state universities began charging their students in 1997. In Spain all students in public universities pay, except those who come from poor households or from families with more than three children. María Jesús San Segundo, education minister in socialist president José Luis Rodríguez Zapatero's government, told me in an interview that the number of university students that don't pay tuition in her country is "around 40 percent."[xxiv] Payments from the remaining 60 percent of middle- and upper-class students contribute to covering a fairly appreciable 15 percent of the university budget. The trend in Europe is toward paying for college. According to what the minister told me, nearly all European countries depend on student tuition payments for around 20 percent of their university budgets. In Germany, after a long legal battle, the Supreme Court authorized all universities to charge their students, something that some had already been doing.

In a few Latin American countries this subsidy to the rich has already been corrected to some extent: Chile, Colombia, Ecuador, Jamaica, and Costa Rica have systems under which students of means must pay tuition. But when the UNAM tried to introduce a similar system in Mexico in 1999 during President Ernesto Zedillo's administration, a student strike paralyzed the government and compelled authorities to back off. When Fox came into power, neither the government nor the university officials dared broach the subject again.

In Communist China, students pay

To my surprise, I found that even in Communist China university students pay for their studies, and thus help subsidize the education of the poorest people and contribute to increasing the resources of universities. This may help explain why China has some of the best universities in the world — the University of Beijing ranked 17 in the *THES* ranking of the world's 200 best universities — even though China spends just 2.1 percent of its gross national product on education. That's a lower percentage than nearly any Latin American country, according to figures from the United Nations Development Program.

All 1,552 Chinese universities have modernized, partly thanks to the tuition payments of their students, as Chinese officials explained to me. When I visited the Ministry of Education in Beijing and interviewed several of its officials, what surprised me most was that payments made by university students to their centers of learning are not at all symbolic. Since universal free education came to an end in 1996, fees have gradually increased. Zhu Muju, a top ministry official, told me that "in the beginning, we charged the equivalent of $25 per student, per year. But the figure has grown to $500 or $600 per year. It's a lot of money for the students, but tuition constitutes a considerable portion of university income."[xxv]

In fact, in 2003 Chinese universities were financed 65 percent by state funds and 35 percent by student tuition, according to official figures. But didn't this contradict a basic tenet of socialist philosophy? I asked. The official gave me a puzzled look and explained: "China is a country with enormous educational needs that the government cannot fulfill. We are not able to offer free education. I believe that the current system is good: it promotes the development of education and encourages students to take their studies more seriously and study harder." He continued: "Only the poorest students, most of them in rural zones, do not pay for their studies, and in many cases they receive additional subsidies in order to be able to study without having to work at the same time."

How ironic, I thought. While Latin America's old-guard left continued to defend free university education and Latin American universities had less and less money to buy computers or pay their professors, the mightiest Communist power on earth was demanding tuition from millions of students and managing to position its universities among the best in the world. Why did the old-guard left in Latin America continue to insist on free university education, even for the rich? Some did because they're dogmatic, others, out of ignorance and others, because they believe that, given the levels of corruption in Latin America, the system of charging the rich in order to give scholarships to the poor would never work. Accordingly, the educational bureaucracy would end up stealing a large portion of the money, and the poor would be left with neither free education nor scholarships. Theoretically, the argument has merit: but it crumbles under the fact that China has at least as much corruption as Latin America. Given the calamitous state of Latin American universities today, both rich and poor are losing out. Instead of rich schools for poor students, it's a system of poor schools for all.

Should a system of paid universities be instituted in countries like Argentina and Mexico? Probably this would be too hard a blow for the middle class, which in many countries has already been hit hard by recent economic crises. But intermediate alternatives would be of enormous help in increasing university budgets and providing scholarships for the needy. The most attractive option would be a mixed system, like that of Australia, where young people study for free but must pay once they graduate and find jobs with good salaries. Australian universities are 40 percent dependent on the state budget, 40 percent on tuition paid by graduates once they reached a certain pay scale, and the remaining 20 percent on the sale of services to the private sector. Such a system in Latin America would be much more generous to students than the Chinese or American systems, but it would still contribute to improving the quality and social equality of higher education in the region.

Nearly everyone gets in, few finish

Another intolerable feature of big Latin American universities, one abolished long ago in China and India, is unrestrained enrollment that creates a population of "perpetual students." In their quest for universal access to higher education, the big universities of Mexico, Brazil, and Argentina guarantee that almost no one will study well. In Argentina, only two out of every 10 students who enter state universities ever graduate.[xxvi] Hence, in a system with nearly 1.5 million students, taxpayers sustain hundreds of thousands who will never complete their degrees. In Mexico, with 1.8 million undergraduates, only a little over 30 percent of those who register each year end up with degrees.[xxvii] In Chile and Colombia, which limit how many students are allowed to enter universities, efficiency is somewhat higher: between three and four of every 10 students who enroll in state universities graduate.[xxviii]

All China's universities require a two-day entrance exam, which each year is taken by over 6 million students. It isn't easy. Only 60 percent of those who take it pass, according to the Ministry of Education. Competition for places in the best universities is intense. Not long before my visit to China, a corruption scandal had exploded after the revelation by the television program "Focus TV", on the

Chinese Central Television Network (CCTV), that three employees of the Beijing Aeronautics and Astronautics University had black-mailed several applicants, demanding the equivalent of $12,000 from each in exchange for admission. CCTV had recorded the telephone conversations, and the case had led to prison sentences. According to the official news agency Xinhua, this was not an isolated event. A few months before, officials from the Xi'an Music Conservatory in the northern province of Shaanxi had demanded bribes of $3,620 per applicant. The scandal came to light when some students refused to pay and notified the authorities. "Some critics claim these incidents expose the tip of the iceberg," the government newspaper *China Daily* reported.[xxix]

Although Chinese universities admit on the whole 60 percent of students who take the entrance exams, the best universities accept only 10 to 20 percent of applicants. In Mexico, on the other hand, the largest university in the country — the UNAM — admits 85 percent of students without entrance exams, according to Julio Rubio, assistant secretary for higher education in Mexico.[xxx] The UNAM confers an "automatic pass" to all high-school graduates within its scholastic network, so many students attend UNAM-associated high schools in order to avoid taking entrance exams. "That has affected the quality of the UNAM," Rubio told me in an interview. By comparison, some 428 public and private universities in Mexico require entrance exams.

In Argentina the situation is similar. When I asked Filmus, the education minister, why the UBA has no entrance exam, he told me that in countries with high social inequality, like Argentina, an exam of that kind would be unfair. Young people leave high school ill-prepared, and subjecting them to entrance exams would be the equivalent of rewarding those who went to private schools. That's why there's a basic entrance course: if students pass six subjects, they are admitted to the university, he explained. The entrance course is a filter: 50 percent of students do not pass all six subjects, and therefore cannot enroll. "In practice, the candidate has six entrance exams, or none, depending on how you look at it," he concluded.[xxxi] Maybe, but most experts on education policy agree that it would be more efficient for the state to channel those resources into elementary and middle schools to avert overcrowding in the universities, given that 80 percent of post-secondary students never graduate.

India's educational meritocracy

When I visited New Delhi, India, in early 2007, one of the issues in the front pages of the *Times* of India and other national newspapers was a debate over entrance exams at Indian kindergartens. My first reaction was to make sure that I had read it right. Entrance tests at kindergarten? Indeed. India's Supreme Court had just ruled that would-be kindergarteners should not be interviewed or tested over the next academic year pending a ruling on the issue. Kindergartens had been interviewing four-year-olds and their parents and often subjecting children to tests. Some of the tests required the four-year-olds to read three-letter words; others gave the children sets of numbers from 1 to 100 and asked them to identify the higher numbers — things the court decided amounted to excessive pressure on children too early in life. But I didn't find many Indians willing to bet that the court would be scrupulously obeyed by private kindergartens, or that the ban would be maintained after the temporary prohibition expired at the end of the year. In India's educational meritocracy, where schools compete over their students' national board scores, thousands of private kindergartens were likely to circumvent the law and administer the tests in a less conspicuous way, I was told.

The matter of the pre-kindergarten tests made me shake my head in disbelief: while Indian children faced entrance exams to get into kindergarten, Latin America students were not even required to pass such exams to enter the region's top universities. The most striking example of India's educational meritocracy was the Indian Institutes of Technology, the jewel in the crown of the country's higher education system. India's seven IITs, which are spread throughout the country and together have about 30,000 students, apply a series of tests so rigorous that only one of every 130 applicants is admitted. By comparison, at Harvard, about 1 out of 10 applicants gets in.

There were big similarities and big differences in what India and most Latin American countries have done in terms of educating their populations. In both places, the primary and secondary education systems are disasters. But India, unlike most Latin America countries, decided in the 1950s that it needed to invest heavily in technology education, and in 1952 — at the suggestion of a government-convened commission on education — decided to create the IITs. India's Prime Minister Jawaharlal Nehru created seven institutes, and linked them to the best technology universities in the world: while the New Delhi Institute of Technology had many professors from Britain's Imperial College, the IIT of Karpur had professors from M.I.T. and other U.S. universities, and the IIT of Mumbai had academics from the former Soviet Union. "Faculty from these countries came here and taught here. A lot of faculty was imported," Prof. Surendra Prasad, the director of the IIT of New Delhi, told me in an interview at his office.

At first, Nehru was heavily criticized for spending a fortune on elite technology institutes in a country where the majority of the population was illiterate. Even now, fewer than 10 of every 100 Indian children finish high school. But Nehru stuck to the plan, believing India would never emerge from poverty unless it had a world-class technological elite. Over the years, Nehru's stubbornness paid off: IIT graduates would start some of India's most successful information technology companies — including the 72,000-employee giant Infosys — that soon became the most dynamic sector of the country's economy. With highly-educated Indian engineers offering computer software solutions at a fraction of the cost of their counterparts in the United States and Europe, India became a world information technology center, much as China became a manufacturing powerhouse.

Architecturally, the IIT of New Delhi is — like many things in India — deceptive. When I got to the front entrance, I couldn't help asking myself whether this was really one of the world's top educational institutions. The main entrance looked more like a semi-abandoned rural Third World high school than the academic incubator for some the world's most innovative technological advances. The front gate was surrounded by a dirt ground — there had been grass at one point, but it had long dried out — and the sign with the name of the school at one side of the gate was simply painted on the wall. The IIT buildings dated from 1961, and looked pretty grim: the corridors were dark, and on the day I visited there was little heating despite the cold of the New Delhi winter. Still, the differences between the IIT and its Latin American counterparts were amazing.

"Education is very, very competitive here," IIT director Prasad told me. The race to get into an IIT starts in primary school, when Indian children are subjected to the first standardized tests. In high school, students have to pass several more standardized tests, and once they graduate, a national board examination. Then the IITs have their own entrance exam, which only students who have scored well on the national board exam can take. When talking about the IITs' ultra-competitive admissions system, it's hard for Indian academics not to tell stories — real or imagined — about well-known Indians whose children could not get in, and went to Harvard or M.I.T. instead.

But is the IITs meritocracy fair? Doesn't the system create an unfair advantage for middle- and upper-middle-class students, who have studied in private schools and have the necessary academic background? IIT director Prasad said nearly 50 percent of the IIT students come from the upper classes, but that — through affirmative action programs enacted by Parliament — 50 percent are from deprived backgrounds. Didn't the IITs create a huge drain on India's resources? Yes, but the IITs were already generating 30 percent of their budget from research grants, consulting fees, and student tuition, which amounts to about $150 a year. And the IITs have proven immensely profitable for India as a nation: they not only produce a world-class information technology workforce, but a growing technological innovation capability. In 2004 India elevated the status of its government office in charge of technology to Cabinet rank — the Ministry of Science and Technology — and the new agency was working with the IITs and private-sector investors in the development of, among other things, a $200 laptop computer for Third World classrooms and a new drug for psoriasis. By 2007, India exported $23 billion a year in information technology goods and services, and government officials expected the figure to soar to $60 billion a year by 2009. While many skeptics in India wonder whether the information technology sector will be able to provide enough jobs to make a serious dent on poverty, the industry is booming. "The rate of growth of information technology exports is of 45 percent a year," M.N. Vidyashankar, secretary of information technology of Karnataka State, home of the software industry mecca of Bangalore, told me in an interview. "Everybody wants to get into the information technology sector. The salary of a just-graduated information technology engineer is three times higher than that of a just-graduated medical doctor. Some doctors are getting into the information technology sector because they make much more."

Vidyashankar's home state of Karnataka and its capital Bangalore, which accounts for much of India's information technology boom, is in itself a metaphor of India's rise in the 21st-century knowledge economy. Unlike mineral-rich states such as Bihar or Uttar Pradesh, which were among India's wealthiest a century ago, the southwestern Indian state of Karnataka has few natural resources and had traditionally been one of the country's poorest states. But, thanks to what Vidyashankar described as "enlightened rulers" who had bet heavily on education during the British colonial era, Karnataka now has a technological and scientific elite. Today it is the fourth-richest of India's 35 states, while Bihar and Uttar Pradesh have sunk almost to the bottom, Vidyashanka said. "We are reaping the benefits now of those kings who spread a culture of knowledge," he told me. "Everybody wants to come here now: two months ago the prime minister of Japan came to Bangalore first, and then went on to New Delhi."

A boom in foreign students

China and India are creating an increasingly competitive scientific-technical elite. They are accomplishing that not only by pursuing rigorous academic curricula and creating scientific and technological universities, but by sending large numbers of students to the best academic institutions of the United States and Europe. China and India are not alone: an avalanche of students from South Korea, Japan, Singapore, and other Asian countries has descended on U.S. and European universities. In the meantime, the number of Latin American students abroad remains stagnant, and in some cases is declining.

Most of the 565,000 foreign students in U.S. colleges are from Asia, which has about 327,000 students in the United States, five times more than the 65,000 Latin Americans. The country with the most post-secondary students in the United States is India, with 77,000, followed by China, with 63,000, and South Korea, with 58,000. Mexico has just 14,000 university students in the United States, Brazil 7,000, and Colombia 6,800. And the gap seems to widen: while the number of Asian students in U.S. colleges grew by nearly 1 percent in 2006, the number of Latin Americans declined by 2 percent. By that year even Communist-ruled Vietnam had more students in U.S. universities than either Argentina or Peru.[xxxii]

Contrary to what I believed, the flood of Asian students isn't a result of government scholarships from their countries of origin. When I asked the experts at the Institute of International Education (IIE), the non-governmental group that compiles the foreign student figures, to explain the extraordinary increase in students from India and China, they answered that it is largely because of the culture of investment in education among Asian families. Allan E. Goodman, president of IIE, told me, "Globalization is creating a very large middle class in India and China of people who really value education. People there are willing to make a major financial sacrifice to invest in their children's education." According to Goodman, only 2.5 percent of foreign university students in the United States have scholarships from their governments or universities, and Asian students are no exception.[xxxiii]

None of this is good news for Latin America. It means that Asians are creating a more globalized political and business class than Latin America is, giving them greater advantages in the world of business, science, and technology. If the consensus among academicians worldwide is that the United States and Europe have the best universities, as both the London and Shanghai rankings indicate, one doesn't have to be a futurologist to suspect that — in the era of the knowledge economy — their graduates will be better prepared and have stronger personal and cultural connections with the world's leading industrial and post-industrial economies.

Too many psychologists, not enough engineers

Incredible as it may seem, Mexico's UNAM graduates 15 times more psychologists than petroleum engineers. In a country where petroleum continues to be a major industry, the UNAM produces around 620 undergraduate degrees in psychology, 70 in sociology, and only 40 in petroleum engineering each year.[xxxiv] Mexico is far from exceptional. At the University of Buenos Aires (UBA), in Argentina, 2,400 lawyers and 1,300 psychologists graduate each year, compared with only 240 engineers and 173 students with degrees in agriculture and livestock sciences. The state is producing five times more psychologists than engineers.[xxxv] If we examine the student body in general — not just graduates — the data are even more astonishing: in 2004 UNAM had 6,485 students in philosophy and literature and only 343 in computer sciences. Eighty percent of 269,000 students in the UNAM were pursuing careers in social sciences, the humanities, arts, and medicine, while only 20 percent were studying engineering, physics, or mathematics.[xxxvi] The disconnect between educational programs and labor-market demands make the great universities produce legions of professionals who seem destined for unemployment. A study by the National Association of Universities and Institutes of Higher Education (ANUIES) warns that if Mexico does nothing to correct its over-production of university graduates without employment potential, it will soon find itself with 1.5 million jobless graduates. "This could generate an unprecedented social problem," the study says.

In Argentina, 40 percent of the 152,000 students at the UBA are enrolled in social sciences, psychology, and philosophy, while only 3 percent are studying computer sciences, physics, or mathematics. UBA has 27,000 psychology students and 6,000 who study engineering.[xxxvii] "In Argentina, up until the year 2003, only three textile engineers were graduating each year," education Minister Filmus told me, horrified. In the largest universities of Brazil, 52 percent of students are enrolled in social sciences and humanities, while only 17 percent study engineering, physics, and mathematics, according to the Ministry of Education.

Latin America's oversupply of attorneys is reflected at the highest levels of government, and could be one of the reasons for the region's scant attention to engineering, science, and technology education. Chinese president Hu Jintao is a hydraulic engineer, and all eight members of China's ruling Politburo are engineers, Indian president Abdul Kalam is a space scientist, and his prime minister Dr. Manmohan Singh a science-obsessed economist. But most Latin American presidents — among them, the leaders of Argentina, Colombia, Cuba, Peru, and Mexico — are lawyers. "Instead of investing so much in training more lawyers, Latin American governments should invest in the creation of intermediate schools and technical institutes," says Eduardo Gamarra, director of the Latin American & Caribbean Center at Florida International University in Miami. "Latin American economies are going towards industries with greater technological requirements in order to produce exports of higher value-added. They need more technicians and fewer law and political science graduates."

The UNAM: Model of inefficiency

The president of the UNAM, Juan Ramón de la Fuente, went off on a tangent when I asked him in an interview if it didn't seem absurd that his university produced so many philosophers and so few engineers. "The first thing I'd like to make clear," he replied, "is that the UNAM carries out 50 percent of all the research done in Mexico. For many years now, the UNAM has been the driving force behind the development of scientific research, which in Mexico is accomplished fundamentally through public universities."

That shouldn't be surprising, I thought, since the Mexican government gives the university $1.5 billion a year and UNAM soaks up 30 percent of the national budget for higher education, which is supposed to be shared among all 99 public universities. De la Fuente continued: "The problem is fundamentally due to the fact that there has been no state policy in Mexico with a mid- and long-term vision that would have allowed us, as in some Pacific Rim countries, to develop in ways that would have been much more fruitful," he said.

"Aren't you just passing the buck to the government?" I asked him, after several attempts to interrupt him. "Shouldn't the university complement the revenue it receives from the state with other sources of financing? Because if you look at the statistics of the number of scientists and engineers per million inhabitants, Mexico is doing lousy: Finland has 5,000 scientists and engineers per million inhabitants; Argentina, 713; Chile, 370; and Mexico, only 225. That is to say, fewer than anyone."

"The immense majority of them were educated by the UNAM," De la Fuente replied. Then, he again passed the buck to the government. "What's missing in Mexico is a state policy bringing together universities, the private sector, and the state itself, which cannot avoid its responsibility. Because no single institution, I insist, no matter what its commitment — like that of the UNAM to science — can be the sole catalyst for the country's development. What you need is a mid- and long-range vision, because investment in science is not instantly profitable. We're always pressed by immediate needs."

Hmmm. Perhaps De la Fuente didn't have the necessary government backing to carry out deep reforms, or perhaps he didn't have the intellectual courage to do so, or perhaps he wasn't even aware of the need for them, but in any case the president of the UNAM was — like most of his colleagues — handing off his responsibilities. The UNAM received $1.5 billion per year to teach 260,000 students, while Harvard collected $2.6 billion to teach just 20,000 students. Why should Harvard have so much greater resources? Because while the UNAM spends much of its energy imploring the state for more money, Harvard brings in generous donations from alumni, charges students who can pay, and signs million-dollar research contracts with the private sector and the state that favor one and all.

The UNAM, like most major state universities in Latin America, is inefficient no matter how you look at it. Tens of thousands of students spend seven or more years in its classrooms, driving up the cost of teaching enormously. The former mayor of Mexico City and defeated presidential candidate López Obrador, for example, spent 14 years as a UNAM student.[xxxviii] The university's refusal to submit to external evaluation, as most other Mexican universities do, is scandalous. According to Ministry of Education officials, this was a result of the 1999 students' strike. "At the end of the strike, one of the agreements was that the UNAM break away form the [accreditation institute] CENEVAL, arguing that it's a pro–free market group linked to private business," Assistant Secretary of Education Rubio explained. In 2005 two-thirds of the public and private universities in Mexico, including the Technological Institute of Monterrey and the University of Valle de México, had agreed to be evaluated by CENEVAL. Even within the UNAM, the rejection of external evaluation caused so much uproar in certain sectors that some of the more prestigious faculties in the university — like engineering — rebelled, and asked to undergo external evaluation. Others, like medicine, were forced to do so because the government issued a requirement that students from this department be educated in accredited schools, to ensure that no under-trained doctors would graduate. But in the 2005 ranking of Mexican universities with faculties accredited by the independent organization authorized by the Secretariat of Education, the UNAM was at the bottom. While 100 percent of undergraduate degrees at the Technological University of Tlaxcala were accredited, that was true of only 22 percent of UNAM's degrees in the same category.[xxxix] Conclusion? "The UNAM ranks very high in research, but this doesn't reflect on its academic programs," Rubio told me. "Since the 1999 conflict, the UNAM has deteriorated a lot in terms of image and quality."[xl]

English in China

At this moment more children are studying English in China than in the United States. Indeed, China has launched a massive program of English instruction in every school nationwide, teaching around 250 million children — several times more than the total number of students in elementary and middle schools in the United States. While in China intensive English studies start in third grade, in nearly all countries of Latin America, including Mexico, compulsory English instruction does not begin until seventh grade. This fact is impressive. How does one explain that China, a country on the other side of the planet with a written language completely different from ours, is requiring English at all public schools starting four years earlier than Mexico, a country that shares a border, an alphabet, and a free-trade agreement with the United States, which also happens to buy 90 percent of its exports?

The commitment to English instruction in China was a political decision made by the government. It began timidly with the first stirrings of the country's economic opening in 1978, then accelerated after 1999, when English was made mandatory in all schools. Before traveling to China, I had interviewed Chen Lin, chairman of the Ministry of Education committee in charge of the English instruction program, by telephone. He had assured me with pride — and in perfect English — that "China already is the world's largest English-speaking country."[xli] According to Chen, English teaching in his country took off with the decision to join the World Trade Organization in 1999, and got a huge push when China was picked to host the 2008 Olympics. "We started a movement called 'Beijing Speaks English,' under which all citizens of Beijing need to be able to speak at least one foreign language by the time the tourists arrive in 2008," Chen told me. "And people are participating enthusiastically, because they know if you speak English it's easier to find a good job." Among other things, the number of mandatory hours of foreign-language instruction was raised and a language exam for all students wishing to attend universities was introduced. "In some northeastern states, Russian or Japanese is studied, but 96 percent of students sign up for English classes," Chen told me.

I must say that on my visits to Beijing and Shanghai, I didn't find many Chinese who could speak English. Most salespeople in the stores didn't understand a single word I said to them. They didn't even understand numbers in English, when I would ask the price of a product. Taxi drivers were even worse. Like nearly all tourists, I had to ask hotel concierges, or some acquaintance, to write down the address where I was going so that the taxi driver would read it and take me without difficulty. Was this vast official English-teaching program imaginary, or were there millions of people learning the language whom I never ran into? When I told officials that I hadn't found many English-speaking Chinese in the streets, they claimed this would change over the next five to 10 years, as the new generation that has started to learn English joins the workforce.

Zhu Muju, director of textbook development at the Ministry of Education, told me that although the obligatory English-teaching guidelines were announced in 1999, they're just starting to be applied nationwide. In the beginning, there weren't enough teachers trained in English instruction, above all in rural schools, to accompany long-distance classes by television. Only recently, in 2005, were 90 percent of China's schools covered, Zhu said. How many English classes will students attend each week? I asked her. "The schools must provide four courses per week starting in third grade; two are classes of one hour each, and two are 25 minutes long," she said.[xlii] "Moreover, the plan demands that schools have activities in English, including debates, games, singing, and acting classes." As I left the interview, one of Zhu's assistants told me, "In three or four years there will be far fewer cases of foreign tourists unable to find someone in the street who can give them directions in English. It will be enough for them to find any child to communicate, at least on a basic level."

In Beijing alone, 1,000 private English schools

But perhaps the most impressive fact involving English instruction in China was the number of children studying the language on their own time. Beijing alone has an estimated 1,000 schools dedicated to English. Around 30 of them are huge; their advertising in the media and on billboards describes their courses as a passport to modernity.

Out of curiosity, I asked to interview the director of China's largest private English-teaching institute, the New Oriental School. The school's home office is in a three-story building that takes up an entire city block in the heart of Beijing. I was received by Zhou Changgang, vice president of the school, a 42-year-old with an Australian master's degree in communications who formerly worked as an Asia correspondent with the BBC. He said that in the mid- '90s he brought up the idea of creating a private English and mathematics institute with a financial backer, a former schoolmate from Yu Minhong high school. His friend immediately saw a business opportunity and provided the money for the first school. Ten years later, the institute had schools in 11 cities and was opening up in another four. How many students do you have now? I asked Zhou. When he answered, I almost fell over backward: "In 2004 we had around 600,000. About half are students who need to reinforce their English in order to pass exams in school; the other half are adults who want to study in order to improve their curriculum," he answered. "By 2007, we calculate we'll have one million English students."[xliii]

For growing numbers of Chinese, studying English is considered an investment in the future, Zhou said. "When I graduated in the 1980s, someone with a university degree could find a good job without any trouble. That's no longer the case. Today you need more knowledge. A diploma is not enough: you need a second diploma, or a third, or studies abroad," he said. This trend began 15 years ago, when China opened up to the world. "Due to economic reforms, state businesses started closing their doors. And in their place came foreign companies, which are far more demanding. That's why Chinese parents spend more than those in most other countries on their children's education. Most Chinese families save their entire lives to provide their children with the best possible education." The New Oriental School, which charges around $100 per student for its short courses, was making a fortune: it reported an annual income of $70 million. Zhou said he expected that number to rise substantially with the introduction of new courses, among them one that teaches techniques for handling job interviews.

India's thriving private schools

Like China, India has a thriving industry of private schools. But in India they are often full-fledged elementary schools, which although they offer English as a marquee attraction are a response to the sweeping failure of Indian public education in general. According to New Delhi's Center for Civil Society, a non-governmental group, the public school system is so bad even the poor are sending their children to low-budget private schools, which also ensures them an English-language education. More than 20 million children in big cities and 18.5 million in rural areas, most of them from poor families, are attending these private schools to circumvent the public school system and make sure to learn English, the language of the country's elite. Combined, low-budget private schools — often huts with dirt floors — get 40 million of India's 140 million children aged 6 to 14 who are receiving a formal education, for tuition fees of up to $2 a month, the Center says.

"It's a completely new phenomenon," Raj Cherubal, a senior education expert with the Center, told me at his office. "The conditions in the government school system are pretty pathetic." It's a system where 25 percent of the teachers don't show up, and 50 percent of those who do show up don't teach, Cherubal added. India has the highest teacher absentee levels in government schools after Uganda, yet teachers face no system of accountability. Much as in many Latin American countries, teachers have life-long tenure. Once hired, they can't be fired, and they have powerful unions to protect their jobs. Still, some things have changed in recent years. "In the past, you either went to an elite private school or a bad government school. Now the poor are sending their children to low-budget private schools. It's the poor people's rebellion against bad government education," Cherubal said.

A Center study of primary and high schools in the slums of North Shahdara, one of the poorest areas of New Delhi, found that of 265 schools in the area, 175 were private low-budget schools without any links to the government. Visiting classrooms unannounced, researchers found that only 38 percent of government teachers were teaching, compared with around 70 percent of teachers in private schools. The study, titled "Private Schools Serving the Poor," tested 3,500 children in mathematics, Hindi, and English, and found that on average children in low-budget private schools tested 246 percent higher than government-school children in English, 83 percent higher in Hindi, and 72 percent higher in math.

English teaching is a big part of the appeal of India's low-budget private schools. In most slums in major Indian cities, one can find dozens of these schools. Most have Western names, such as "St. Mary's" or "St. Anthony's." They often have three small rooms, with about 30 children per class. Many are registered with the government school system so that their students can take standardized tests at the end of the year in public schools. They study throughout the year in their private schools, where teachers guarantee their attendance and a heavy emphasis on English instruction, and show up at the district public schools once a year — at testing time. "Most poor people want English education because they see the benefit of it in a market economy," Cherubal told me. "While most low-budget private schools are in English, most government schools are in local languages." Not surprisingly, many Indians say — only half-jokingly — that the three fastest growing industries in India are low-budget private schools, private security guards, and bottled water. As Parth J. Shah, the Center for Civil Society's president, told me, "Like in many other parts of the world, there is a big debate on education in India. But the poor are not waiting — they are voting with their feet."

Steps taken by Chile, Mexico, Brazil, and Argentina

Granted, large numbers of middle- and upper-middle-class Latin Americans study English in private elementary or high schools, or in after-school English-language private institutes. But, while there are several small-scale English programs for the poor, mostly run by private foundations, I have seen no massive effort to teach English or other foreign languages to Latin America's poor, at least not in the scale I saw in China or India.

In early 2004, Chile announced that to hasten its integration into the global economy it was adopting English as a second official language. Chile, which became the first Latin American country to do this, was preparing to host a meeting of education ministers from the Asia-Pacific Economic Cooperation Forum (APEC) that April. As organizers of the meeting, the Chileans decided that English instruction should be on top of the agenda. Chile already suspected that Latin America was lagging in this area and that Asians were far ahead. A preparatory study for the conference on English instruction had confirmed Chilean suspicions. The results, announced at the meeting, were startling: Singapore, Thailand, and Malaysia were teaching English in every school starting in the first grade, while China and South Korea were starting in third grade, and most Latin American countries in seventh grade. But that wasn't all. While Singapore began with eight hours per week of English and China with four hours, in Chile and Mexico they started not only years later but with only two hours per week. The differences were abysmal. English instruction alone didn't explain the economic progress of Asian countries, but it was yet another element in the formula that had allowed them to integrate themselves into the global economy, grow rapidly and reduce poverty.

When Chile announced it was adopting English as a second language in 2004, the news went almost unnoticed in the rest of the region. In Chile, as in most neighboring countries, only 2 percent of the population could read and hold a basic conversation in English, according to official studies. But the government of the Chilean Socialist Party had made English teaching into a political cause. "English opens the door to starting up an export business, and it opens the door to digital alphabetization," said Education Minister Sergio Bitar. "English definitely opens the door to the world."[xliv] Starting in 2004, besides making English instruction obligatory from fifth grade on, Chile provided free English textbooks to all students in fifth and sixth grades, establishing as a goal for 2010 that all eighth-graders be required to pass the Key English Test (KET) — an international exam for English comprehension and reading as a second language. It also started offering tax breaks to companies that provided English courses for their employees, in order to help the country become more receptive to international tourism and compete with Asians in luring customer-service call centers to Chile. CORFO, the Chilean Development Corporation, spent $700,000 in 2004 to test 17,000 people on English proficiency and create a database of bilingual or

nearly bilingual individuals. Around 12,000 passed the exam and were listed. "We have their names and telephone numbers in a databank that is available to any company wishing to establish itself in Chile," Bitar explained.

In Mexico, although its proximity to the United States might seem to ensure access to a huge supply of potential English instructors, the Fox Administration concluded it couldn't follow Chile's example because it didn't have enough English teachers for all fifth-graders. While Mexico has the same overall literacy rate as Chile — 96 percent of children in both countries have completed primary school — the government believed such areas as malnutrition and infant mortality were more deserving of resources than English classes. So it opted for long-distance English learning, through the Enciclomedia electronic blackboard program, in all fifth- and sixth-grade classrooms. "The idea is that there be no school in the country, no matter how rural or indigenous, that is left unequipped by 2006," said Secretary of Education Reyes Tamez.[xlv] For the main Latin American business partner of the United States, and China's main competitor for the U.S. market, individualized English instruction continues to be a distant goal.

In Argentina, compulsory English teaching in most provinces begins in seventh grade, Education Minister Filmus told me. But after the economic debacle of 2001, the idea of devoting time and money to a second language was eclipsed by other priorities: 511,000 young people out of a total student population of 8.2 million were dropping out, most of them in the three years following primary school. The governments that took over after the crisis concluded that students left school because of extreme poverty, and that the educational priority from then on was to prevent school dropouts.

For South American countries, English isn't the only foreign-language need. Many education officials in the region say Portuguese instruction is just as important, considering that Portuguese-speaking Brazil accounts for more than half of South America's economic output. At the end of the '90s, during the Mercosur boom, ambitious Portuguese instruction programs were launched, as were Spanish lessons in Brazil. In Argentina, then-minister of education Susana B. Decibe proclaimed that by the year 2000 most schools would be teaching Portuguese. "For a long time, our countries have turned their backs on each other. But now we are undergoing a very interesting process of cultural integration," Decibe had told me in a 1998 interview. But the Brazilian devaluation a year later dealt a hard blow to Mercosur and South American integration, and the whole plan was largely abandoned. Years later, another Argentine minister of education, Andrés Delich, told me all that remained of the national Portuguese instruction campaign were school programs in the northern province of Misiones, bordering Brazil, which accounted for 5 percent of school enrollment in Argentina.

In Brazil, Congress in 1998 started debating a plan to teach Spanish in all schools, which evolved into a bill in 2000. Several southern states, such as Rio Grande do Sul, Paraná, and São Paulo, had already begun giving Spanish lessons, and Congress's plan was to extend those programs nationwide over the next 10 years — if and when the 27 states found a way to hire the 75,000 Spanish teachers they needed. Congress approved the bill in 2005 and ordered the Ministry of Education to make optional Spanish courses available in all elementary schools across the country, from fifth to eighth grade, over a five-year period.

Wasn't it an extravagance, teaching a second language in countries that still hadn't managed to eradicate illiteracy? "I believe Chileans are capable of walking and chewing gum at the same time," Minister of Education Bitar told me. "You can study Spanish, science, and English at the same time." That's probably true. Anyone who has traveled to Sweden, Holland, or Denmark knows that people are perfectly capable of speaking two, three, even four languages if they start learning them from childhood. In several poorer countries, the same thing is happening. I have found people living in the most precarious conditions on the Caribbean island of Curaçao, or among poor populations of Nicaragua and Honduras, who are perfectly bilingual. If the Chinese — with a totally different system of writing — are starting to learn English in elementary school, there's no reason why millions of Latin Americans who grew up watching Hollywood movies, singing American rock tunes, and exploring Internet sites in English can't do the same.

Why do Asians study more?

Perhaps of all the people I met in China, the one who impressed me most was Xue Shang Jie, a 10-year-old boy I met during a visit to the private Boya School in Beijing. After interviewing the school's director, I asked if I could enter a classroom and watch. We walked through the corridor, where I peeked into several classrooms while classes were under way. I picked one of them. It was around six in the afternoon, and a dozen children were sitting at their desks in the first row. In the rear of the classroom sat several men and women, evidently grandparents, who were reading or doing crossword puzzles to kill time.

When the school director opened the door and introduced me as a visitor from the United States, there was general surprise, giggles, and welcoming gestures from the teacher. I sat down, watched the class, and soon one child in particular caught my eye. He was in the front row, he wore enormous glasses, he expressed himself in English admirably, and he brimmed with good humor. I wasn't surprised when, at the end of the lesson, I was told that Xue was the best student in his class and was taking private English and math classes after hours to improve his grades even further, in order to be able to compete in the international student Olympics.

What do you want to be when you grow up? I asked Xue later, when we were chatting in the hallway. "A singer, maybe," the boy told me, shrugging and laughing, while his schoolmates celebrated his answer and joked about his future in show business. I asked him what his parents did for a living. Because of his mastery of English, I guessed he was the son of diplomats who had lived abroad, or that he came from a family of means that had hired tutors for years. But I was wrong. Xue told me his father was an army officer and his mother was an office worker. From the description he offered of his family, and from what the school director and the Chinese assistant who accompanied me confirmed later, Xue's family was middle, or lower-middle class.

What's a typical day like for you? I then asked. He told me he woke up at seven, got to school by eight, and took classes until three or four in the afternoon, depending on the day of the week. Afterward, he did homework until six, when his father came to pick him up. So, can you watch television the rest of the day? I asked him. "I can only watch 30 minutes of television every day," he answered, continuing to smile. "When I get home, I play the piano and do chores. That's until seven-thirty at night. Then, I can watch television for half and hour and I go to bed at nine." But that's not all: one afternoon a week, after school and on Sunday afternoons he took private English classes at the Boya School. On Saturday afternoons, for two hours, he took math and Chinese classes at the same private institute. And do you like studying so much? I asked him, intrigued. "Yes," he answered me, grinning from ear to ear. "It's very interesting. And if I study hard, my father gives me a toy."[xlvi]

The case of South Korea

This single-minded dedication to learning isn't just a Chinese or Indian phenomenon, but pan-Asian. Just as in China and India, children in South Korea, Singapore, and several other countries in the region study nearly twice as many hours per day as students in the United States or Latin America. In South Korea the average amount of study per day for elementary students is 10 hours, twice as much as in Mexico, Brazil, or Argentina. Jae-Ho Lee, a 14-year-old Korean, has an almost military daily routine: he leaves home at seven in the morning, arrives at school half an hour before class to review his lessons from the previous day, and returns home at four in the afternoon. Afterward, he takes private lessons in English and mathematics, not because he's lagging behind in these subjects, but to maintain his high scores. "I want to continue to be among the top of my class, because my future depends on it," the boy told the Brazilian magazine *Veja*, which ran a cover story on the education phenomenon in South Korea.[xlvii]

According to South Korea's Ministry of Education, 80 percent of children study at least 10 hours per day, and 83 percent take additional classes in math or science. The education revolution has driven the percentage of post-secondary students from 7 percent of the university-age population in 1960 to 82 percent today. By comparison, most Latin American countries have 20 percent of their young people studying in universities, and in many cases, even less. While 30 percent of Korean university graduates have degrees in engineering, in Latin America the comparable number is 15 percent.[xlviii]

In South Korea, for years now the immense majority of schools have had electronic blackboards — like the kind Mexico recently adopted — on which professors show videos to illustrate their lessons. Plus, they have computer rooms connected to wide-band Internet, and professors who earn salaries equivalent to $6,000 per month, six times more than their equivalents in Latin America. "It's a career that confers a lot of status," the *Veja* article indicates. A poll at the National University of Seoul revealed that for Korean women, male teachers are seen as "the best catch in marriage," because they have good salaries, stable jobs, and long vacations, and they like children. Teachers also benefit from excellent working conditions, which include four hours a day — paid, of course — to prepare classes and greet their students. Education in Korea is taken so seriously that even kindergarten teachers need university degrees. In general terms, economists believe the Korean investment in education has paid off, and then some. Thanks to the avalanche in international investment attracted by its supply of skilled labor, Korea went from a per-capita income equivalent to half of Brazil's in 1960 to average earnings that are three times higher than Brazil's today.[xlvix]

Why do young people in Asia study more? The most common answer I heard in China is that this is no recent phenomenon, but the continuation of a historic tradition that dates from the teachings of the philosopher Confucius, who was spreading values such as commitment to work and study in the 5th century B.C. Confucius said, "If your objective is to advance one year, sow wheat. If your objective is to advance 10 years, sow trees. If your objective is to advance 100 years, educate your children." Academic fever had been quashed during the Chinese Cultural Revolution, but staged a comeback starting with the economic reforms in the 1980s, when — as Zhou, the vice president of the New Oriental School in Beijing pointed out — newly privatized businesses began to demand a workforce with superior levels of education.

That said, in China there's yet another key motive that explains the academic fever, one that isn't quite so exportable to other countries: the One Child Policy. Since the 1970s, as a population control measure couples are permitted to have only one child apiece, and those that have more must pay punitive taxes for their second child. This means that each boy or girl — and there are more boys than girls, since male babies are preferred — is the exclusive focus of attention for both parents, all four grandparents, and, in some cases, eight great-grandparents. "We are a country of little emperors and empresses," a tourist guide told me in Beijing. This translates into intense pressure on young people from parents and grandparents. "The whole family saves so that the child can study in the best universities and get a good job," Zhou explained to me. "We have a saying here: only child, only hope, only future." That helps explain why so many families send their children to private English classes after school, or save their entire lives to send their children to universities in the United States.

A further factor common to several Asian cultures is that young children need to learn more, and sooner: while most Western languages have alphabets of 26 or 27 letters, some East Asian languages have about 22,000 characters, although you need about 2,500 to acquire basic knowledge of the language. Asian children must start learning the characters of their language long before entering the first grade. Kindergarten is an intensive writing class. "When children enter first grade, they should already be familiar with about 2,000 characters," Chen Quan, a teacher in Beijing, told me. Learning is so hard that parents and grandparents spend weekends teaching their children and grandchildren to draw these characters, so that by the time they enter elementary school they already have a study discipline far greater than that of American or Latin American children. Therefore, Asians take it for granted that they should study ten hours a day. Watching television, playing soccer, and partying are not among the first priorities of hundreds of millions of Asian youths.

A culture of evaluation

There's a growing consensus among international education experts — which has yet to find broad acceptance in Latin America — that the best way to improve academic achievement isn't simply by investing more money in schools, or increasing study time, or reducing the number of students per classroom; it's by creating a culture of evaluation that compels students to do better and better. If money were the answer, China and South Korea, whose governments spend far less than other countries on education, should be among the most backward in the world. Nor is it just a question of hours in the classroom or group size, since countries like Norway and Austria that differ greatly in those terms achieve similar results on standardized tests. However, there is one common factor: most countries whose students do well in comparative studies also compile rigorous rankings of students, professors, and schools. They encourage an atmosphere of competitiveness, where the educational system must constantly justify itself to the government and to parents.

Zhu Muju, the high-ranking official from the Ministry of Education whom I interviewed in Beijing, told me that teachers in

376 | SAVING THE AMERICAS

China post the grades students receive in their classes on blackboards for everyone to see. "Chinese students do very well on exams, because they're accustomed from an early age to being evaluated, from first to last in the class. That makes them very competitive and prompts them to improve their grades, so they can move up on the list," Zhu said. "We in the government do not encourage this practice of rankings," but it was clear that they weren't discouraging it, either. The same thing goes for university rankings, she added: they encourage universities to improve themselves and enable the state to evaluate its investment in education.

According to Jeffrey Puryear, the education expert at Inter-American Dialogue in Washington, countries that are falling behind should introduce three basic features, aside from greater parental participation: more demanding standards from primary school onward, student evaluations, and a system of accountability among teachers and school principals. "Educational institutions must be accountable to someone, perhaps parents or society in general. They can't be allowed to do just anything, or avoid the consequences of their performance," Puryear said. "In the Latin American educational system there are practically no consequences. There can be good or bad professors, but that doesn't matter, since there's no difference in how they're treated. A teacher doesn't lose his job because of poor performance, or earn more for good performance." In several Asian countries, just as in New Zealand, Australia, and Holland, educational reforms have been carried out to promote accountability and the evaluation of students and schools, with excellent results, he added. "In Latin America quantity is still considered a priority, not quality. And that's a serious problem."[1]

Even though many Latin American education ministers agree that countries that adopt a quality culture improve their educational systems, most still believe such reforms are appropriate only in developed countries. Filmus, Argentina's minister of education, told me, "Our problem with rankings is that they often end up defending neither the capacity nor the quality, but the socio-economic level."

In Argentina, social inequalities force young people to attend elementary and secondary schools of dramatically different quality and arrive at university with very different levels of preparation. "If a boy didn't go to kindergarten but went to a horrible elementary school and then a middle school where no one studied, he'll be at a disadvantage compared with someone who went to a very good kindergarten, then a very good, private, bilingual school... So the question is, how to even out the playing field," he said. The answer, he said, isn't grueling university entrance exams that punish the underprivileged, but providing additional courses in high school and entrance courses in the university that allow them to get up to speed.

Still, the minister agreed his country would benefit from a stronger culture of evaluation. "Here in Argentina we're behind in that sense. Over the past 30 years there hasn't been a culture of excellence, or effort, or hard work. You've got a culture that's much more linked to what Argentineans refer to as 'zafe,' which means passing the grade no matter how, rather than doing it based on effort, hard work, and research. The question is how to introduce a culture of quality," he said. Argentine officials have decided the best way was to begin with the evaluation and accreditation of university studies. But, just as in Mexico, they were running into a wall at the nation's largest university.

China, India, and Latin America

A news item I read while visiting China in 2005 reported that without much fanfare, and with the low profile that characterizes some of their most notable achievements, China had exported its first automobile to Europe. It was a five-door SUV similar to the Jeep Cherokee and manufactured by Jiangling Motors Group, and it arrived at the Belgian port of Antwerp as part of a first shipment of 200 vehicles to be sold at around $22,000 each. A few days later the first shipment of 150 Honda automobiles made in China under the name Jazz arrived in Europe.[li] Over the next year, Chinese car exports — which until then had been confined to Asian countries — skyrocketed from 173,000 units in 2005 to 340,000 in 2006, and were projected to reach 700,000 in 2007. Nearly all Chinese vehicles for export come from Guangzhou, the industrial center that has become emblematic of globalization. Its airport terminals were built by a U.S. company, the bridges that carry passengers to their airplanes were manufactured by a Dutch company, its control tower is operated by a firm from Singapore, many of its operations are carried out by robots designed and supervised by Chinese engineers. In all likelihood Chinese automakers will soon seek to dominate the biggest markets in the world, just as the Japanese and South Koreans have in recent decades.

During my 2007 trip to India, hardly a day went by without headlines suggesting a country poised for tremendous growth, with unprecedented opportunities to create prosperity and reduce poverty. One story reported that IBM, already with 53,000 employees in India, would open a new software center in the western city of Pune to serve international and U.S. insurance and health-care companies, as part of a $6 billion investment in the country over the next three years. Other information technology giants such as Accenture and Capgemini were expanding their operations in India, as were homegrown companies such as Infosys, Tata Consultancy Services, Wipro, and I-flex. Other stories said that India was rapidly moving on from tech support and back-office data processing for foreign companies to much more sophisticated — and better compensated — functions. In addition to call centers and routine data work, Indian companies were starting to export knowledge services, in which workers contribute analysis, judgments, and decision-making. Soon, not only will U.S. accounting firms send client tax returns to be processed in India, but — according to a Forrester Research study — U.S. law firms will outsource 25,000 legal jobs to India by 2010 and 30,000 by 2015. Many of India's 500 law schools, which produce about 20,000 lawyers a year, are already stepping up training in

U.S. law, information technology (IT) regulatory issues, and cross-border business transactions, to allow India to draft many of the world's IT-related contracts in coming years. And that's only the beginning. Another headline reported the successful launch of the Polar Satellite Launch Vehicle (PSLV), which put four satellites into orbit to provide data for cartography, urban and rural infrastructure development, and land information — a world market estimated at $400 million. India's space agency, Isro, announced it hoped to launch its first unmanned mission to the moon in 2008.

What does all of that mean for Latin America? That China, India, and several Eastern European countries are leapfrogging ahead and moving at an amazing rate from exporting cheap toys or low-cost services to selling sophisticated products around the world. And Latin American countries run the risk of being left increasingly behind if they remain as raw-material extraction economies happily celebrating the recent rise in commodity prices, or hoping their proximity to the U.S. market will guarantee an easy prosperity, instead of shifting into production of higher value-added goods and services and wresting preferential trade access to the world's leading economic blocs. As former Brazilian President Cardoso said in the first pages of this book, the challenge for Latin American nations will become far greater in the next few years, when Asian countries inaugurate the largest free-trade agreement in the world, formed by China and the ASEAN countries — perhaps including even India. By integrating chains of production and taking advantage of cheap, qualified labor, the Asian bloc will become a formidable competitor in the struggle to gain market share in the United States and Europe, now the largest trade blocs.

China's exports of SUVs, India's satellite-launching rockets, or Poland's car manufacturing centers, far from scaring Latin American countries, should inspire them to get moving. The train of progress rolls on, and those who don't climb aboard will be left behind. As Ireland has shown, countries can rise from poverty almost overnight. And there are already many examples across Latin America of industries that can compete and produce goods of higher added value. The Brazilian aircraft giant Embraer has become the world's largest manufacturer of commercial jets of up to 120 seats, and the 4th largest aircraft maker in the world, selling planes to such airlines as JetBlue in the United States, Air Canada, Hong Kong Express Airways, Saudi Arabian Airlines, and EgyptAir Express. By early 2007 Embraer had an order backlog of $15 billion, including contracts with the U.S. Department of Defense for reconnaissance craft with a potential value of $7 billion over the next 20 years. In Mexico, the Cemex concrete giant, with operations in 50 countries, became the world's largest building-material supplier in mid-2007. Mexico's Grupo Modelo sells its Corona Extra in 150 countries, and has turned it into the best-selling imported beer in the United States. Costa Rica's exports of microprocessors made by Intel represent a growing part of the country's total exports, and Intel was setting up small but potentially important research centers in Guadalajara, Mexico, and Córdoba, Argentina, taking advantage of the region's shared time zones with the United States. Chile, which used to depend on copper for the bulk of its export income, has become a leading world supplier of fresh fruits, salmon, and wines, and its companies are increasingly in charge of the processing, marketing, and delivery of their products abroad.

But for now, these and other similar cases are exceptions to the rule. The biggest Latin American corporations — Mexico's Pemex, Venezuela's PDVSA, and Brazil's Petrobras — continue to sell oil or other raw materials, with little value-added. Many countries in the region have yet to break out of their peripheral blindness and realize that while they are blinkered by ideology and obsessed with the past, rapidly-growing Asian and Eastern European countries are driven by pragmatism and committed to the future. As Ireland proved, there are no innate or cultural reasons why Latin American countries can't turn around almost overnight, and become economic and social success stories. As Chile has shown, by strengthening their institutions and the rule of law — whether it's through internal consensus or thanks to supranational agreements — and by taking a page from the growing trade, academic, and scientific competitiveness of other developing countries around the world, Latin American countries can raise standards of living and dramatically reduce poverty in very little time.

Can that be done at a time when Chávez's petrodollar diplomacy is fueling populist anger throughout the region? Of course it can. While the media tend to focus on Chávez's Jurassic brand of socialism, a new — and promising — phenomenon is happening in Latin America: the emergence of leftist or left-of-center governments that pursue ambitious social programs without engaging in irresponsible economic policies, leaving behind the region's traditional curse of boom and bust, and guaranteeing long-term stability. Chile is no longer the sole exception to the rule: in recent years, we have seen responsible left or center-left governments in Brazil, Peru, and Uruguay, among others. By its sheer economic weight, Brazil is likely to set an example of sound economic management with socially-conscious programs. If Mexico's left learned anything from its lower support among the young, urban sectors of the population in the 2006 election, it will offer a more pro-investment ticket in 2012. These countries may already have a critical mass that will prevent Latin America from becoming the region plagued by internal conflicts, government ineffectiveness, and "an increasing risk of the rise of charismatic, self-styled populist leaders," as envisioned by the CIA-linked National Intelligence Council in its report on the world in the year 2020 cited in the opening pages of this book. The recent success of China, India, and other Asian countries in reducing poverty and the rise of a new brand of modern leftist governments in Latin America will leave their mark on future leaders in the region, and could sway the region toward a new — more prosperous — future.

NOTES

[i] UNDP, Human Development Report, 2003, p. 278.

[ii] Juan Enríquez Cabot, *As the Future Catches You*, Crown Business, 2000, p. 51.

[iii] Juan Rendon, "Behold the indigenous Brain," *Loft*, June 2005, p. 59.

[iv] World Bank, "World Development Indicators," 2004.

[v] "Ranking 2005 de las 500 mayores empresas de América Latina," *América Economía*, July 15, 2005.

[vi] Juan Rendón, "Behold the Indigenous Brain," *Loft*, June 2005, p. 59.

[vii] Idem, pp. 64-66.

[viii] Ted Fishman, *China Inc.*, Scribner Publishers, p. 217.

[ix] Juan Enríquez Cabot, *As the Future Catches You*, Crown Business, 2000.

[x] In its 2006 edition, the worldwide *THES* ranking was led by Harvard, Cambridge, and Oxford, while Yale and M.I.T tied for fourth place. Mexico's UNAM had climbed up to 74th place, but remained the only Latin American university in the ranking's top 200 places.

[xi] "Academic Ranking of World Universities, 2004," Shanghai Jiao Tong University, 2004.

[xii] UNAM, *Agenda Estadística 2004*, p. 24.

[xiii] Estadísticas Universitarias, Yearbook 99-03, Ministry of Education, p. 148.

[xiv] Interview of Reyes Tamez Guerra, Secretary of Education, in Mexico City, June 21, 2005.

[xv] Interview with Minister of Education Daniel Filmus. Buenos Aires, April 20, 2005.

[xvi] *Reforma*, November 12, 2004.

[xvii] *La Jornada*, March 1, 2004.

[xviii] UNDP, Human Development Report, 2003, p. 295.

[xix] Lauritz Hom and Kristian Thorn, "Higher Education in Latin America: A regional overview," World Bank.

[xx] Idem.

[xxi] "En la UBA, hay más de 11.000 docentes que no cobran sueldo," *La Nación*, May 23, 2005.

[xxii] Lauritz Hom and Kristian Thorn, "Higher Education in Latin America: A regional overview," p. 12, World Bank.

[xxiii] "Relevamiento de la Unesco: En Argentina, los pobres están muy lejos de la Universidad," *La Nación*, July 14, 2005.

[xxiv] Interview with the Minister of Education of Spain, María Jesús San Segundo, July 18, 2005, in Miami.

[xxv] Interview with Zhu Muju, Director of Textbook Development at the Chinese Ministry of Education, Beijing, February 2, 2005.

xxvi "Universidad: Entran diez, pero ocho no se reciben," *Clarín*, April 10, 2005.

xxvii ANUIES, *Anuario Estadístico 2003*.

xxviii "Universidad: Entran diez, pero ocho no se reciben," *Clarín*, April 10, 2005.

xxix "Stopping university admission abuse," *China Daily*, August 19, 2004.

xxx Interview with Julio Rubio, Assistant Secretary of Higher Education in Mexico, Mexico City, June 22, 2005.

xxxi Interview with Minister of Education Daniel Filmus, Buenos Aires, April 20, 2005.

xxxii Open Doors 2006, Institute of International Education, Washington D.C.

xxxiii "More Latin Americans should study in U.S.", "The Oppenheimer Report," The *Miami Herald*, December 7, 2004.

xxxiv UNAM, *Agenda Estadística 2004*, pp. 81-84.

xxxv University Statistics, 1999-2003 Yearbook, Ministry of Education, 2004, Argentina, p. 53.

xxxvi UNAM, *Agenda Estadística 2004*, p. 56.

xxxvii University Statistics, 1999-2003 Yearbook, Ministry of Education, 2004, p. 31.

xxxviii "De calificaciones y sustos varios," *Enfoque* (*Reforma's* supplement), April 15, 2005.

xxxix Assistant Secretariat of Higher Education, Integrated Institutional Strengthening Program, 2005.

xl Interview with Julio Rubio, Mexico City, June 22, 2005.

xli Chen Lin, Chairman of the Committee of the English Studies Program, Ministry of Education of China. Telephone interview from Santiago, Chile, April 29, 2004.

xlii Interview with Zhu Muju, Director of Textbook Development at the Chinese Ministry of Education, Beijing, February 2, 2005.

xliii Interview with Zhou Ghenggang, Vice President of the New Oriental School, Beijing, February 1, 2005.

xliv Interview with the Minister of Education of Chile, Sergio Bitar, April 10, 2004.

xlv Telephone interview with Mexican Secretary of Education Reyes Tamez, April 22, 2004.

xlvi Interview with Xue Snag Jie in Beijing, Feburary 1, 2005.

xlvii *Veja*, No. 1892, February 16, 2005, p. 62.

xlviii Idem.

xlix UNDP, Human Development Report, 2003, pp. 278-279.

l Interview of Jeffrey Puryear by Mariza Carvajal, published by Inter-American Dialogue in October, 2004.

li "First Chinese cars arrive in Western Europe," *China Daily*, July 6, 2005.

Afterword for the North American Edition

—

As this edition went to print, the 2008 presidential campaign season was starting at full swing in the United States. While Latin America was unlikely to become a major campaign issue, the November 4, 2008, vote would nevertheless offer an opportunity to begin to redress the broken relationship between Washington and much of the region. Much of Latin America's hostility toward the United States during the Bush Administration — reflected in a 2005 Zogby International poll of Latin American opinion-makers that found only 12 percent had a positive image of the United States — was linked to the U.S. war in Iraq, which exposed latent animosities in a region with a long history of U.S. military interventions. A new U.S. administration, with a new foreign policy that sought to distance itself from Bush's "pre-emptive strikes" doctrine and offered greater multilateralism in approaching world problems, would begin to restore a general sense of common purpose and collective opportunity in the region.

What should the United States do about Venezuela's narcissist-Leninist leader, and his "anti-imperialist revolution?" First, in addition to withholding approval from any undemocratic moves against Chávez, it should stop subsidizing Venezuela by buying $37 billion a year in its oil. As long as America persists in its dependence to foreign oil — imports soared from 35 percent of U.S. oil consumption in 1973 to 60 percent in 2006 — Chávez's megalomania will continue to be funded by the United States. Second, Washington should bypass Venezuela and inaugurate a positive agenda for the rest of Latin America, deepening the 1994 free trade deal with Mexico, strengthening the 2007 deal with Brazil to jointly develop sugarcane-based ethanol throughout Latin America, and launching a new Alliance for Progress-style plan for the region that not only focuses on free trade, but on development aid for the poor contingent on responsible economic policies. For instance, Washington should use more of its $1.5 billion annual economic aid to the region to offer low-interest loans to family businesses in poor areas, as well as technical assistance to help the poor get property titles to their homes, transforming them into credit-worthy individuals. And it could start programs to encourage use of the $45 billion in annual family remittances to Latin America for small businesses in general. Either way, the United States should start lending more to the poor, and not just to the rich.

In Chapter 5 we mentioned several concrete things the United States could do, including exploring a hemispheric health cooperation plan that could allow some of the projected 100 million Americans who will retire over the next 30 years to use their medical insurance in low-cost U.S.-certified hospitals and nursing homes in the region, much as German and Swedish retirees do in Spain; promoting student exchanges to get more American youths to choose Latin American destinations; or launching educational English-language programs run by established U.S. universities through the Internet for Latin American students and professionals. A new U.S. administration could also write a fresh chapter in U.S.-Latin American relations by removing a sore point in bilateral ties: the $7 billion fence along the U.S.-Mexican border that was authorized by a law signed by President Bush, which by some estimates could end up costing up to $37 billion once electronic surveillance is included. Granted, many Americans — prodded by xenophobic cable television fear-mongers — believe a border fence could help stop the flow of undocumented migrants. But that fantasy could be quickly debunked, and the money redirected to useful goals, if new leadership in Washington insisted on presenting hard facts to the U.S. public — for example, that nearly 50 percent of undocumented migrants from Latin America enter the United States legally through airports and overstay their visas, and that the proposed 700-mile border fence along a 2,000-mile border will only force migrants to cross through unprotected areas. In today's increasingly isolationist, anti-immigrant climate, the battle will be tough, but it can be won by just getting the facts out.

I ended the Spanish-language edition of this book by saying that if the preceding pages had helped enable even a small number of Latin Americans to see what other countries were doing to reduce poverty and to persuade them into rejecting the siren songs of populist leaders who are curtailing fundamental freedoms in the name of totalitarian utopias, I would consider myself satisfied. By the same token, I would like to finish these pages stating that if this book moved even a small number of Americans to consider that a rising tide lifts all boats, and that the best way to solve illegal immigration, drug trafficking, transnational crime, and environmental degradation in the United States — as well as to increase U.S. exports — is by forging greater economic and cultural ties with our neighbors, the effort will have been worthwhile. The odds are formidable, but we will always be neighbors, and — as Octavio Paz once told me — geography is the mother of history.

Andrés Oppenheimer

Saving the Americas, de Andrés Oppenheimer
se terminó de imprimir en septiembre de 2007 en
Gráficas Monte Albán, S.A. de C.V.
Fracc. Agro Industrial La Cruz
El Marqués, Querétaro
México